D1490936

THE
EASTERN
EUROPE
COLLECTION

AUSTRIA-HUNGARY
BASED ON THE WORK OF
PAUL LOUIS LEGER

William E. Lingelbach

ARNO PRESS & THE NEW YORK TIMES
New York · 1971

Reprint Edition 1971 by Arno Press Inc.

Reprinted by permission of
Crowell Collier Educational Corporation

Reprinted from a copy in
The Harvard University Library

LC# 70-135846

ISBN 0-405-02788-5

The Eastern Europe Collection

ISBN for complete set: 0-405-02730-3

Manufactured in the United States of America

THE
HISTORY
OF NATIONS

AUSTRIA-HUNGARY

A HUSSITE PRIEST ADMINISTERS THE HOLY COMMUNION UNDER BOTH FORMS TO THE FIRST PROTESTANT CONGREGATION IN BOHEMIA

Painting by Vaclav Brozik

THE HISTORY OF NATIONS
HENRY CABOT LODGE, Ph.D., LL.D., EDITOR-IN-CHIEF

AUSTRIA-HUNGARY

Based on the work of

PAUL LOUIS LEGER

College de France

by

WM. E. LINGELBACH, Ph.D.

Assistant Professor of European History

University of Pennsylvania

Volume XVII

Illustrated

John D. Morris and Company
Philadelphia

THE HISTORY OF NATIONS

EDITOR-IN-CHIEF

HENRY CABOT LODGE, Ph. D., LL. D.

Associate Editors and Authors

ARCHIBALD HENRY SAYCE, LL. D.,
Professor of Assyriology, Oxford University

CHRISTOPHER JOHNSTON, M. D., Ph. D.,
Associate Professor of Oriental History and Archaeology, Johns Hopkins University

C. W. C. OMAN, LL. D.,
Professor of History, Oxford University

THEODOR MOMMSEN,
Late Professor of Ancient History, University of Berlin

ARTHUR C. HOWLAND, Ph. D.,
Department of History, University of Pennsylvania

CHARLES MERIVALE, LL. D.,
Late Dean of Ely, formerly Lecturer in History, Cambridge University

J. HIGGINSON CABOT, Ph. D.,
Department of History, Wellesley College

SIR WILLIAM W. HUNTER, F. R. S.,
Late Director-General of Statistics in India

GEORGE M. DUTCHER, Ph. D.,
Professor of History, Wesleyan University

SIR ROBERT K. DOUGLAS,
Professor of Chinese, King's College, London

JEREMIAH WHIPPLE JENKS, Ph. D., LL. D.,
Professor of Political Economy and Politics, Cornell University

KANICHI ASAKAWA, Ph. D.,
Instructor in the History of Japanese Civilization, Yale University

WILFRED HAROLD MUNRO, Ph. D.,
Professor of European History, Brown University

G. MERCER ADAM,
Historian and Editor

FRED MORROW FLING, Ph. D.,
Professor of European History, University of Nebraska

FRANÇOIS AUGUSTE MARIE MIGNET,
Late Member of the French Academy

JAMES WESTFALL THOMPSON, Ph. D.,
Department of History, University of Chicago

SAMUEL RAWSON GARDINER, LL. D.,
Professor of Modern History, King's College, London

R. W. JOYCE, LL. D.,
Commissioner for the Publication of the Ancient Laws of Ireland

ASSOCIATE EDITORS AND AUTHORS

AUTHOR'S PREFACE

HISTORIES of Austria have hitherto occupied themselves more with the international relations of the House of Hapsburg than with the destiny of the peoples under its rule. The title of German Emperor [1] has caused them to overlook the less high-sounding but much more real titles of King of Bohemia and of Hungary. The history of Austria has been found in Switzerland, in Italy, and in the Low Countries; in fact everywhere except among those countries upon which the power of Austria has always rested. It is my intention in the present work to ignore this traditional point of view; the story of the Hapsburgs in their relations with countries not essentially a part of Austria is therefore omitted. Especial attention is, on the other hand, directed to the three groups which to-day form the basis of the Austro-Hungarian monarchy—the hereditary provinces, the Kingdom of Hungary and the Kingdom of Bohemia. I have endeavored to bring out clearly the relative importance of the part played by each of these three groups; I have studied the divergent tendencies of the large racial groups, the Slav, the Magyar, and the German, which in the Middle Ages, divided between them the mountain forelands of the Alps and the valleys of the Upper Elbe and of the Danube. I have left to the historians of Germany, Belgium and Italy, everything that does not properly fall within the limits of the Austrian state, and, thus rigorously circumscribed, my task, which has involved fifteen years of study and travel, gains much in interest and unity.

PAUL LOUIS LEGER

[1] The French reads, "*le titre de l'empereur allemand*," though the title the author has in mind is manifestly that of emperor of the Holy Roman Empire.

EDITOR'S PREFACE

THE present history of Austria-Hungary is based on the fourth edition of "*L'Histoire de l'Autriche-Hongrie,*" by Professor Leger, which appeared in 1895. In translating and adapting this work I have had to deal very freely with the original, often recasting and re-writing entire sections. In the interests of historical accuracy and fairness I have also, where possible, avoided the strong Slavophil tone of M. Leger's work. With his main thesis, that the countries under the Hapsburg rule have at no time constituted a nation in the true sense of the word, I thoroughly agree. Austria-Hungary, since its dual organization was effected in 1867, quite as much as was Austria under the absolutist régime, is a political system rather than a nation. This fact makes imperative a method of treatment that involves, as Professor Freeman has pointed out, a good deal of going backward and forward in telling the story of the lands that have at different times come under the dominion of the Austrian princes; the story of each land by itself and the story of them all in relation to the common power; but it is the only way to arrive at a just appreciation of their history. "There is no subject," says the same authority in 1889, "on which ordinary readers stand more in need of a clear setting forth of facts than on that which M. Leger has taken in hand. The facts in themselves need some thought, and some clearness of thought, to grasp them, and the difficulty is heightened by popular confusions both of thought and of language. Much mischief has been done by one small fashion of modern speech. . . . The 'interests' of England or France mean the interests of the English or French people. A 'friend' of England or France would mean a friend of the English or French people. But when we hear, as we have heard of a 'friend of Turkey,' does that mean a friend of the people of the land marked 'Turkey' on the map, or a friend of their foreign oppressor the Turk? Do the 'interests of Turkey' mean the interests of the Turk, or the exactly opposite interests of the nations which the Turk holds in bondage? So with

'Austria.' One has heard of the 'interests of Austria,' the 'policy of Austria'; I have seen the words 'Austrian national honor'; I have come across people who believed that 'Austria' was one land inhabited by 'Austrians' and that 'Austrians' spoke the 'Austrian' language. All such phrases are misapplied. It is to be presumed that in all of them 'Austria' means something more than the true Austria, the archduchy; what is commonly meant by them is the whole dominions of the sovereign of Austria. People fancy that the inhabitants of those dominions have a common being, a common interest like that of the people of England, France or Italy.

"Now it is hardly needful to stop to prove that there is no such thing as an Austrian language, that a whole crowd of languages are spoken within the dominions of the sovereign of Austria—German, Magyar, Italian, Ruman, and the various dialects of the great Slavonic majority. Each of these is the language of a nation, the whole or part of which is under the rule of an Austrian prince; but there is no Austrian language, no Austrian nation; therefore there can be no such thing as 'Austrian national honor.' Nor can there be an 'Austrian policy' in the same sense in which there is an English or a French policy, that is, a policy in which the English or French government carries out the will of the English or French nation. Nor can there be a common 'Austrian interest' for all the dominions of the sovereign of Austria; for the interests of the German and the Magyar on the one hand, of the Slav and the Ruman on the other, are always different, and often opposed. In truth, such phrases as 'Austrian interests,' 'Austrian policy' and the like, do not mean the interests or policy of any nation at all. They simply mean the interests and policy of a particular ruling family, which may often be the same as the interests and wishes of particular parts of their dominions, but which can never represent any common interest or common wish on the part of the whole.

"It leads to confusion thus to personify 'Austria' in the way now so common, just as it leads to yet worse confusion so to personify 'Turkey.' Our fathers avoided such confusions. They spoke of 'the Turk' 'the Grand Turk,' 'the Grand Seignior,' names which accurately distinguished the foreign oppressor from the lands and nation which he holds in bondage. So they spoke of 'the House of Austria,' a form which accurately distinguished the ruling family from the various kingdoms, duchies, counties, etc., over which the head of that house holds rule. We must ever remember that the dominions of the House of Austria are simply a collection of kingdoms, duchies, etc., brought together by various accidental causes, but which really have nothing in common, no common speech, no common feeling, no common interest. In one case only, that of the Magyars in Hungary, does the House of Austria rule over a whole nation; the other kingdoms, duchies, etc., are only parts of nations, having no tie to one another, but having the closest ties to other parts of the several nations which lie close to them, but which are under other governments. The only bond among them all is that a series of marriages, wars, treaties, and so forth, have given them a common sovereign. The same person is King of Hungary, Archduke of Austria, Count of Tyrol, Lord of Trieste and a hundred other things. That is all.

" The growth and the abiding dominion of the House of Austria is one of the most remarkable phenomena in European history. Powers of the same kind have arisen twice before; but in both cases they were very short-lived, while the power of the House of Austria has lasted for several centuries. The power of the House of Anjou in the twelfth century, the power of the House of Burgundy in the fifteenth century, were powers of exactly the same kind. They too were collections of scraps, with no natural connection, brought together by the accidents of warfare, marriage or diplomacy. Now why is it that both those powers broke in pieces almost at once, after the reigns of two princes in each case, while the power of the House of Austria has lasted so long? Two causes suggest themselves. One is the long connection between the House of Austria and the Holy Roman Empire and the Kingdom of Germany. So many Austrian princes were elected emperors as to make the Austrian House seem great and imperial in itself. I believe that this cause has done a great deal towards the result; but I believe that another cause has done yet more. This is that, though the Austrian power is not a national power, there is, as has been already noticed, a nation within it. While it contains only scraps of other nations, it contains the whole of the Magyar nation. It thus gets something of the strength of a national power. The possession of Hungary has more than once saved the Austrian power from altogether breaking in pieces. And it is certain that, at this moment, the policy of the House of Austria, so far as it is anything more than the mere policy of a family, is the policy of the Kingdom of Hungary."

These remarks by Professor Freeman are found in the preface to an English translation of the first edition of Leger's history of Austria-Hungary by Mrs. Berbeck Hill. To this work I am indebted for considerable assistance, sometimes availing myself freely of Mrs. Hill's rendering of the original.

In the difficult matter of the spelling of geographical and proper names I have not followed Leger's attempt to give the form used by the people themselves, since that would have introduced too many unintelligible Slav and Magyar forms. I have, instead, followed the usage of the standard English histories and geographies; the result is that where the word has not been anglicized the German form has, as a rule, been used, as against the Magyar or Czech.

In writing the history of Austria-Hungary for the last twelve years I have sought to give an impartial account of the exciting conflicts that mark the political side of Austrian history during this period. In this, as in the survey of the country's economic and social development and of its international relations, I have throughout allowed the facts to tell their own story, endeavoring to secure the proper emphasis by selection and arrangement rather than by comment of my own.

Wm. E. Lingelbach

University of Pennsylvania

CONTENTS

PART I

ORIGIN AND FORMATION OF THE STATES THAT CONSTITUTE
THE AUSTRO-HUNGARIAN MONARCHY. FROM
PRIMITIVE TIMES TO 1272

PART II

BOHEMIA AND HUNGARY UNDER ELECTIVE KINGS. 1310-1526

PART III

THE ACQUISITION OF BOHEMIA AND HUNGARY, AND THE UNI-
FICATION OF THE MONARCHY UNDER THE
EMPERORS. 1493-1740

PART IV

THE STRUGGLE FOR THE UNITY OF THE MONARCHY. 1740-1792

PART V

AUSTRIA DURING THE REVOLUTIONARY AND NAPOLEONIC
ERAS. 1792-1815

PART VI

THE PERIOD OF REACTION AND THE AWAKENING OF THE
NATIONALITIES. 1815-1848

PART VII

REVOLUTION AND REACTION. 1848-1867

PART VIII

AUSTRIA-HUNGARY. 1867-1906

LIST OF ILLUSTRATIONS

PART I

ORIGIN AND FORMATION OF THE STATES
THAT CONSTITUTE THE AUSTRO-HUN-
GARIAN MONARCHY. FROM PRIMITIVE
TIMES TO 1272

HISTORY OF
AUSTRIA-HUNGARY

Chapter I

THE MONARCHY: ITS CHARACTER AND COMPONENT PARTS

THE Austro-Hungarian monarchy, notwithstanding the ancient traditions of the house of Austria, is one of the youngest of the European states. In its present form it dates back only to 1867, the year immediately following Austria's ill-fated war with Prussia, through which she was separated from Germany, and forced thenceforward to seek her destiny among the peoples and lands of the Danube valley. Among these the Hungarians in particular have had a strong national development of their own, and, with the Bohemians, from the time of their first union with Austria have always been more or less separate and distinct, enjoying rights and privileges respected, in principle at least, by all the rulers of the house of Hapsburg.

The history of the Austro-Hungarian state is, therefore, not the history of a united, homogeneous people. One tie only is common to all; it is, and has been for centuries, the house of Hapsburg. But even the story of the house of Hapsburg cannot more than furnish a thread for a history of this remarkable Austro-Hungarian state. Nations have an existence independent of that of princely families, however illustrious these may have been.

The kingdoms of Hungary and Bohemia, in offering their crown to Ferdinand I. of Austria, early in the sixteenth century (1526), did not understand that they were subordinating their individuality to a factitious conglomeration of foreign states. After having had a free and glorious past, under their own national monarchs, they sought, in a purely personal union with Austria, the strength necessary to resist the Ottoman invasions. They did not contemplate losing their identity either in an Austrian monarchy or in the Holy Roman Empire. Ferdinand I. brought with him only the hereditary states, that is, Upper and Lower Austria,

Styria, Carinthia, Carniola, Gorica, Gradiska, a part of Istria and the Tyrol, whose total population of Germans and Slavs even to-day numbers only about seven million inhabitants, not a sixth of the total population of the Austro-Hungarian monarchy. Nor could this group, either because of its importance, the brilliancy of its history, or the superiority of its civilization, claim a right to absorb or assimilate the two kingdoms of Bohemia and Hungary. On receiving the crowns of St. Vacslav and of St. Stephen, the Emperor Ferdinand bound himself to respect the rights and privileges which pertained thereto, having given a similar pledge in regard to Croatia, previously annexed to the crown of Hungary. Thus it was that, by a series of mutual agreements, freely consented to, Bohemia, Hungary, and the group of hereditary Austrian provinces passed under the rule of the same sovereign. Nor should the fact be overlooked that at that time several of the provinces that make up the monarchy of to-day still belonged to neighboring states; Galicia, for example, was a part of the kingdom of Poland, from which it was not detached until 1773, and Dalmatia was still subject to the republic of Venice. Lombardy and Venetia, later held by Austria for more than half a century, were lost as a consequence of the wars of 1859 and 1866.

It will readily appear, therefore, that Austria-Hungary is essentially a state based upon historic rights, rights which have not been set aside either by conquest or by the suppression of unsuccessful revolts.

Nor is there in the history of this complex state that steady growth of a great race, as in France or in Germany; that influence of geographic unity, so strong a factor in national development, as in the case of Italy; nor the permanent unity of interests and aspirations which is seen in the case of the republic of Switzerland. Austria-Hungary does not have natural frontiers; those physical boundaries determined beforehand by seas, mountain ranges, and rivers have been largely ignored in the territorial expansion of the Austrian state. The middle basin of the Danube, with its mountainous surroundings of the Dinaric system, forms a large, well-knit geographic unit which, from the standpoint of geography, might well be expected to serve as the seat of a united, homogeneous people. But the Austro-Hungarian monarchy has pushed out beyond this natural base in nearly every direction. "From the hydrographic standpoint," says Reclus, " the Danube and its tributaries indeed unite in one basin the mountains of Austria and the plains of Hungary, but a considerable part of the monarchy is found outside of these Danubian regions, in the basin of the Elbe, of the Vistula, of the Dnieper, and of the Adige."

As to the mountain chains, they seldom coincide with the boundaries of the monarchy. The great chain of the Carpathians which bounds it on the northeast does not enclose Bukowina, Galicia, and Silesia, which are entirely exposed on the north to attack from Germany or Russia. Bohemia is almost encircled by a series of lesser mountains, forming a geographic unit by itself, and is part of the basin of the Elbe. Toward the southwest the Austrian frontier is better defined by the Alps, the Adriatic, and the parallel courses of the Save and the Drave, but even here Istria lies outside.

Without geographic unity, Austria-Hungary presents, at the same time, the greatest confusion and anarchy from the ethnographic standpoint. This region, so poorly defined by physical features, belongs in no sense to one race, strong in its solidarity and obedience to the same traditions, and prepared for any sacrifice in order to work out its common future. The races of the monarchy are many, but four among them, representing the four great ethnic groups of Europe, have contributed most largely to its history. They are, first, the Germans of the hereditary provinces; second, the Slavs, divided into groups according as they inhabit Bohemia, Galicia, or the provinces of the southeast; third, the Magyars, of Turanian extraction, in Hungary, and fourth, the Latins, Rumanians, in Transylvania, and Italians, in the southern Tyrol and on the shores of the Adriatic.

The relative numerical strength of the different nationalities of Austria-Hungary has varied considerably from time to time. According to the census reports of 1900 the total population of forty-five and a half million was distributed among the different nationalities as follows:

GERMAN		11,306,795
MAGYAR		8,751,877
LATIN		
Rumanians . . .	3,030,442	
Italians	727,102	
		3,757,544

SLAVIC

Poles	. . .	4,252,483
Ruthenians	. .	3,811,017
Slovenes	. . .	1,192,780
Servians and Croa-tians	. . .	3,442,129
Czechs and Slovaks		7,975,038

20,673,447

GYPSIES AND OTHER NATIONALITIES   915,604 . .

TOTAL POPULATION . .   45,405,267

These incongruous elements have not assimilated with time. They have conserved their languages and their traditions, and they live side by side without amalgamating. The life of the Austro-Hungarian state rests upon the carefully poised equilibrium of the ethnic groups that compose it, and this equilibrium, always more or less unstable, must be preserved or the state will fall to pieces.

Much too considerable a rôle is generally attributed to the Germans. This arises from a number of causes, among others the political dominance of the German element, especially in the eighteenth and early nineteenth centuries, and from a lack of knowledge, not only of their numerical inferiority, but also of the fact that they are geographically scattered. Austria, considered as a German state, does not exist. The number of Germans is only a little over nine million, though the total is increased by including two million Jews scattered throughout the monarchy, whose mother tongue is German, and who exert no inconsiderable influence on the economic conditions of the provinces in which they live. But the eleven million are far from forming a compact group. The only provinces of the Austro-Hungarian state that are entirely German are the two Austrias and the duchy of Salzburg. To this compact mass are joined the Germans of Styria, Carinthia, and the Tyrol, who live among the Slavs and Italians of their respective provinces. The group formed by these five provinces comprises, at the most, five and a half million Germans, and this group is the only one that can be considered as forming a legitimate part of the greater Germany of the pan-Germans. Supposing that they should one day enter into this greater Germany because of the principle of nationality, this very principle will not permit the absorption of the Italians of the Tyrol, or the Slavs of the Adriatic. Almost thirty leagues would still separate the Germans from Triest, which they look upon as their great seaport on the Adriatic.

As for the Germans of Bohemia, they constitute scarcely two-fifths of the present population of the kingdom. They stretch along the frontiers of Bavaria and Saxony and do not form a geographic group. In Moravia a group of about five hundred thousand Germans occupies the north of the province, the remainder of whose population is largely Slavic. Even if it is admitted that the German population of Bohemia and of Moravia approximates three million, it must be remembered that this figure is of slight importance in comparison with the great Czech population, which numbers nearly six million. Nevertheless the Germans lay claim to Bohemia on the basis of nationality, as in the case of Alsace, and also on the basis of a pretended historic right derived from the Holy Roman Empire. Besides, Bohemia, they say, penetrates to the heart of Germany, it intercepts the natural boundary, is a thorn in the German flesh, and must be removed.

In all other parts of the monarchy the Germans form insignificant groups, colonies without special political rights, except in the case of the Saxons of Transylvania, who, because of custom and because of their scientific and industrial superiority, enjoy special privileges and advantages. Taken together, therefore, the numerical strength of the Germans makes a very respectable showing, but its importance is singularly diminished by the fact that the different parts which compose it are scattered among Slavic, Magyar, and Rumanian populations.

The other race which, with the German, is in political control in Austria-Hungary, is the Hungarian, or Magyar. It occupies all of the kingdom of Hungary, but not exclusively, for Slavs, Germans, and Rumanians share it with them. Indeed, only about fifty per cent. of the population are Hungarians proper, or Magyars, though over eighty per cent. of the entire population now speak the Hungarian language, and this proportion is steadily increasing. The Magyars owe their strength to their central position on the Danube, to the size and homogeneity of their group, and to certain peculiar political and military qualities which explain why they have been able to subordinate and Magyarize the less united populations of the great Hungarian plain.

The Slavic race occupies the north and south of the monarchy.

The Czechs inhabit the larger part of Bohemia, or the upper Elbe basin, Moravia, and Silesia; the Slovaks, northern Hungary; the Poles, the northwest of Galicia; the Ruthenians, the remainder, a part of Bukowina, and some districts in the northeast of Hungary.

The Slavs of the north are separated from the Slavs of the south by the Germans, the Magyars, and the Rumanians. This geographic separation, added to the dislike of the race for a strong government, is frequently given as the reason that, in spite of their numerical superiority, they have never been able to dominate the Germans and Magyars, or even to enforce a recognition of their

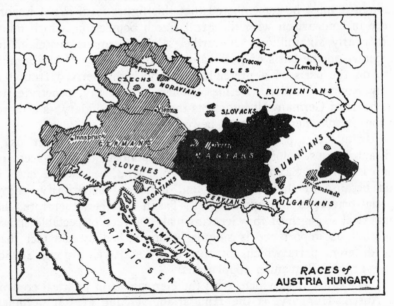

RACES of
AUSTRIA HUNGARY

claim to equal political rights with these in the monarchy. The Slavs of the south fall into two groups: the Serbo-Croatians, occupying the region from Croatia eastward, and including the provinces of Bosnia and Herzegovina; and the Slovenes, who inhabit Carinthia, Carniola, a part of Istria, and Styria.

The Rumanians are located in the southeast of Hungary, in Transylvania, and in Bukowina. The Italians form a compact group in the southern Tyrol, and have colonies in the principal cities of Istria and the Dalmatian coast.

The vitality as well as the diversity of these different elements appears in the number of languages possessing a distinct literature.

It is not a mere matter of dialects or local idioms, as is the case in Germany or in Italy, but of forms of speech fixed in literature, used by the church, consecrated by usage in political assemblies, and made familiar every day in the press. Austria is a veritable Tower of Babel. It publishes German, Hungarian, Polish, Ruthenian, Czech, Slovak, Serbo-Croatian, Slovene, Rumanian, and Italian newspapers. And these newspapers are in languages, as a rule, unintelligible to all except those immediately concerned, and very frequently represent diametrically opposite tendencies. Certain groups even go so far as to seek their center of gravity outside of the monarchy altogether. The Germans look to a greater Germany, the Poles to a regenerated Poland, the Italians toward Italy, the Slavs of the south toward their kindred in Turkey, the Rumanians toward their kindred in Rumania. Only the Czechs and the Magyars find the aspirations of their nationality within the empire.

In conformity with the heterogeneous character of the people, the emperor of Austria, in the protocols of the chancellery, assumes the following titles: emperor of Austria, king of Hungary and of Bohemia, of Dalmatia, Croatia and Slavonia, of Galicia and Lodomeria, king of Illyria, grand duke of Austria, of Bukowina, of Styria, Carniola, of Carinthia, grand prince of Silesia, margrave of Moravia, count of Hapsburg and the Tyrol. Of all these titles those which most represent real sovereign power are those of Bohemia and Hungary. And yet the history of the two kingdoms of St. Vacslav and St. Stephen, and the ethnographic make-up of the territories brought together under the Hapsburg rule, have been almost entirely neglected by the historians of the old school.

Chapter II

PRIMITIVE TIMES, THE ROMAN OCCUPATION AND THE GERMAN INVASIONS. 365 B.C.-565 A.D.

LITTLE is known of the people who occupied the Austro-Hungarian lands before the Christian era. Their history practically begins with the Roman conquest, and even on this period the knowledge that has been transmitted is generally vague and inexact. The Romans, like the Greeks, regarded the barbarian peoples with prejudiced eyes; they cared little about their early history, paid no attention to the native language, of which they generally remained ignorant, and accepted all kinds of fantastic legends. There is no doubt, however, that the Austro-Hungarian territory was inhabited during the stone age. Cut flints found in Upper and Lower Austria, Bohemia, Moravia, Hungary, and Galicia establish the fact without question. Articles in bronze are numerous; and, as utensils in iron are also found, there is every reason to believe that these different strata reveal an uninterrupted succession of inhabitants and civilization in primitive times. On the other hand, it is difficult to determine the race which inhabited these regions during this period. Were they Finns, Iberians, or Aryans? No one knows.

If we disregard the Greek legends about Illyria and the Adriatic coast, it would seem as if the first race which occupied the soil of present-day Austria was that of the Celts. After having pushed onward to the extreme west of Europe, in the wake of the great primeval migration, the Celtic wave swept back toward the center and east. According to a tradition, the Celts spread out over the territory between the Rhine and the Vistula and, under their chief, Sigovesius, occupied the ranges of the Alps and the basin of the Danube during the fourth century B.C. We know definitely that in the year 335 B.C. Alexander the Great received Celtic deputies, on the lower Danube, offering peace and friendship. The Celts established themselves under different names in the various districts. The Boii occupied Bohemia, to which they gave their name; the Taurisci established themselves in the region of Salzburg, Styria, and Carinthia, the Scordisci in Croatia and Slavonia, the Ambrones toward the mouth of the Vistula. The famous bronze boars found in Bohemia are regarded as relics of this Celtic civilization.

The tribes on the shores of the Adriatic known as Illyrians did not blend with the Celts. The piracies of these maritime populations brought them into conflict with the Romans, and, under Agron, their king, and later his widow, Teuts, they were conquered and obliged to pay tribute. Aquileia was built in 180 B.C., Istria became a Roman province, and the city of Triest rose to hold the conquered people in check. In the year 168 B.C. Genthius, king of the Illyrians, having allied himself with Perseus of Macedonia, was conquered and his territory made tributary to Rome. The persistency of classic culture and the use of the Italian language upon the Dalmatian coast to-day go back to this first Roman conquest.

Once masters of the Adriatic coast, the Romans penetrated little by little into the interior, and soon found themselves in touch with the Taurisci and the Rhaeti, who lived isolated among the mountains of the Tyrol. In the year 115 B.C. the Consul Marius Aemilius Scaurus attacked and overthrew the Taurisci, but as he pushed farther north he came in contact with the Germans. About this time the Cimbri descended toward the south, and defeated the Romans, who tried to check them at Noreia in Carinthia. But ten years later the barbarians suffered defeat before the walls of Aix, in 102 B.C., and at Vercelli in 101 B.C. From this time forward the Alps, Bohemia, and the basin of the Danube continued to be threatened by the German tribes. The Suevi, the Marcomanni, and the Hermunduri incessantly attacked the Celts, and these, thus hemmed in by the Teutons and the Romans, instead of uniting in order to ward off the danger, divided and weakened themselves by internal dissensions.

While the Marcomanni were pushing into the country of the Boii, the Dacians, a people inhabiting the region of the lower Danube, established a powerful state extending over eastern Hungary, the banate of Temesvar, Wallachia, Moldavia, Bukowina, and Transylvania. The nationality of the Dacians is still a matter of dispute, but they are known to have been a warlike, though agricultural, people, skilled in working in metal, and enthusiastic believers in the immortality of the soul. About the middle of the first century before Christ they were ruled by Berebistas, an ambitious monarch, eager for conquests and ready to profit by the discords among his neighbors. The Celts afforded him excellent opportunities; a conflict having broken out between the Scordisci and the Boii, the former sought the aid of Berebistas, and through him defeated the Boii. They were forced to leave their country, which was for a long time known as *Deserta Boiorum*. Gradually, however, the Marcomanni and the Quadi settled the deserted regions.

Under Octavius the peoples of the Adriatic were brought more completely than ever under Roman rule. Sisca, on the Save, received a Roman garrison and was united to Aquileia by a military road, later becoming one of the great military posts of the Romans, and a basis for their actions against the Pannonians who occupied the lands between the Save, the Danube, and the Alps. Shortly after this the Dalmatians were also conquered. Then followed the attack upon the Alpine tribes, and after a hard struggle the Rhaeti and the Vindelici were conquered and made subjects of the empire in 13 B.C. To these new provinces Noricum was added without a struggle and the Danube became the frontier of the Roman empire.

Behind this frontier Rome organized the conquered territory, gave to it her laws and her language, and became in time the instrument of its conversion to Christianity. Pannonia was placed under a *legatus consularis,* Noricum under a procurator, and the present Carniola became the meeting point of the frontiers of Italy, Pannonia, and Noricum. Strong garrisons of from 60,000 to 70,000 men secured the submission of the natives. Among the fortified towns was one called Vindobona, the Vienna of to-day, which was held by a legion and, toward the end of the empire, by a squadron of the Danube fleet. As early at 51 A.D. the Save and the Danube were guarded by a fleet, which was largely increased under Vespasian and put under the supreme command of an officer at Vindobona. Three main roads started from Aquileia, intersecting the provinces, and at Laibach a great number of secondary roads met. Military boundary stones can still be seen in many places at distances reckoned from Aquileia, Milan, Sirmium, Bregenz, and Augsburg.

The immediate neighbors of the Romans to the east, after the occupation of Pannonia, were the Marcomanni. At first the relations with them were friendly. Maroboduus, the son of a prince of the Marcomanni, was even sent to the court of Augustus to be educated. But after the conquest of Noricum and Rhaetia these friendly relations gave way to distrust. Maroboduus, eager to extend his power, occupied Bohemia, Moravia, and a large part of Germany, and fortified his capital, which became a refuge for all who conspired against Rome. A Roman army led by Tiberius brought him to terms but was forced to retrace its steps because of a revolt of Pannonia and Dalmatia. Indeed, it was the Germans themselves, under Hermann, who, in 17 A.D., finally destroyed the power of Maroboduus. Two years later Maroboduus found a refuge from the invading Goths, at Ravenna, which Tiberius appointed as his place of residence. Some time afterward a number of wandering races that had settled in the basin of the Theiss, on the ruins of the kingdom of Dacia, were united under a king, Decebalus, who obtained Roman architects and artisans, built fortifications, and worked the rich mines of Transylvania. As his power grew he defied the Romans, destroyed two armies sent against him by Domitian, and obliged him to conclude a shameful peace in 90 A.D., by which Rome bound herself to pay tribute to the barbarian, and undertook to furnish him with the workmen of whom he should have need.

Terms such as these Trajan, Domitian's successor, was not likely to fulfill. He refused to pay the tribute, threw two bridges over the Danube (not far from the present town of Orsova), crossed the river, and beat Decebalus on the plains of Temesvar. He then pushed on into Transylvania, where he forced Decebalus to fight a second time under the walls of his capital, Sarmizege-thusa. The Dacian king was obliged to make peace and to give up the conquered territory, which included his own capital, in 101 A.D. Three years afterward he tried to renew the war; once more vanquished, he slew himself, and Dacia became a Roman province. The colonists whom Trajan left on the lower Danube are believed to be the forefathers of the Rumanian nation of to-day.

The conquest of Trajan marks the highest point reached by the Roman power in the Danube valley. From the beginning of the second century onward, the German races, who had been for a time kept back by fear of the Romans, again invaded the country, and in the second half of the century the waves of this vast flood, which was by and by to inundate the whole empire, began to break over the frontiers. About the year 165 of our era the barbarians invaded Noricum, Pannonia, Rhaetia, and penetrated as far as Aquileia. In the year 170 A.D. the legate Vindex sustained a defeat which cost him no less than 20,000 men. In 175 A.D., however, Marcus Aurelius succeeded in stemming the invading torrent, and was even able to conclude an advantageous peace. But two years later the Marcomanni and Quadi revolted, and Marcus Aurelius died at Sirmium, or, some say, Vindobona, leading an expedition against them. His son Commodus allowed the Vandals to settle on the banks of the upper Danube, in the lands which now form Bavaria and Upper Austria, and for some years it seemed as if the main current of invasion were going to turn back upon the upper Danube and the Main. But the prestige of Rome had suffered greatly and the time had come when emperors were made and unmade by armies. Rhaetia and Noricum were again attacked by the Marcomanni, and part of Dacia was occupied by the Goths, while the Gepidæ and the Burgundians took possession of the northern parts of Transylvania and Hungary. By 274 A.D. Rome was obliged to abandon the whole of Dacia to the invaders, and, the Goths becoming masters of the entire province, they founded a double kingdom on the shores of the lower Danube and the Black Sea. That of the West Goths (Visigoths) included Transylvania, Wallachia, Moldavia, and Bessarabia; that of the East Goths (Ostrogoths) lay between the Dniester and the Dnieper, on lands which now form part of Russia. It then seemed as if the German race were destined to control in these lands which now belong to the Slavs.

From the first century onward fervent adherents of Christianity were found on the shores of the Adriatic and along the Save and the Danube. According to tradition, St. Mark evangelized Aquileia, and consecrated as its first bishop St. Hermagoras, whose name is still popular among the Slovenes. The apostle St. Luke is said to have preached in Dalmatia, and Andronicus, one of the seventy disciples of Christ, is regarded as the first bishop of Sirmium. However that may be, at the beginning of the fourth century Christian communities and an organized clergy were to be found in all the large towns of Rhaetia, Noricum, Pannonia, and Dalmatia. Under Diocletian these communities were especially remarkable for the fervor of their faith and the constancy of their martyrs. By the edict of Milan Constantine guaranteed the free exercise of their religion to the Christians, and the church was able to organize itself openly. In the course of the fourth century Aquileia and Sirmium became the seats of archbishops, to whom the neighboring bishops were subject. At Sirmium, in 380 A.D., and at Aquileia, in 381 A.D., were held councils in which the doctrines of Arius, which had made great progress in Pannonia, were condemned.

During the reign of Constantine bands of Sarmatians led by their king, Rausimond, came from the borders of the Sea of Azov, settled themselves on the banks of the lower Danube, and repeatedly ravaged the Roman provinces from 319 to 322 A.D. The emperor repulsed them. Later on the Sarmatians sought help from Rome, and Constantine helped them to repulse the Goths. Later still we find a band of Jazyges, chased by the Sarmatians, crossing the Danube and settling themselves as guests and colonists in Thrace and Macedonia. From this time the slow but steady infiltration of these barbarians continued, until the great invasion of the Slavs, Avars, and Hungarians. Under Constantius, in 356 A.D., the Alemanni, Quadi, and Sarmatians ravaged Rhaetia and Pannonia, but were repulsed with heavy loss.

In 364 A.D. Valentinian, a Pannonian, was chosen emperor. He divided the empire with his brother Valens, himself keeping the three prefectures of the West, with Milan and Sirmium as his capitals, while Valens took the East and resided at Constantinople. Both had great difficulty in keeping back the Goths. Valentinian repelled their attack upon Pannonia, but Sirmium was hard pressed, and before his death, in 375 A. D., the Western emperor was in a treaty with them.

Thanks to the great strength of her organization and to the influence of Christianity and civilization, Rome had hitherto been able to restrain and absorb the races which pressed her on so many sides. But to these was now added a new element, hitherto unknown in Europe, endowed with formidable energy, well disciplined, and more to be dreaded than all other barbarians. The Huns had long lived on the great plains between the Don and the Caspian. In the year of Valentinian's death they attacked their neighbors, the Ostrogoths, crossed the Dniester into the kingdom of the Visigoths, and forced them back upon the Danube. After

the destruction of the two kingdoms of the Goths the Huns occupied the whole of the country between the Dnieper and the Danube; they next crossed the latter stream and took possession of a
part of Pannonia. Their invasions had driven away the various
races whom they had met on the road, but in the perpetual changes
of this epoch they had no time to form new states. Thence they
pushed on to the attack of Italy. On the death of Theodosius,
in 395 A.D., the empire was finally divided between his sons Honorius and Arcadius. The two rival divisions quarreled, and the
Huns made use of these quarrels to offer their services to the one
who paid them best. The Emperor Theodosius II. was obliged
to give them an annual tribute of 350, afterward increased to 700,
pounds of gold.

In the year 437 A.D. the command of the Huns fell to Attila,
or Etzel, whom the Middle Ages called, in their terror, the Scourge
of God. He united his people more closely, and led them on terrible ravaging expeditions against Pannonia, Moesia, Thrace, and
Macedonia, before invading Italy and Gaul. In 447 A. D. the empire abandoned Sirmium to him, and undertook to pay him a heavy
tribute. His two expeditions into Italy and Gaul are well known.
He returned to die in his camp between the Danube and the Theiss.
The Hungarians, who belong to the same family of nations as
the Huns, regard Attila as one of their most renowned heroes.
Some of their historians praise him enthusiastically. To this day
the " Attila " is the national dress of the Magyar nobleman.

The empire of Attila did not outlive him; his sons were unable to defend it against the Germans, and the Huns were forced
back to the shores of the Black Sea. The Ostrogoths remained
masters of Pannonia; the Visigoths and the Gepidæ of the basin
of the Theiss and of Transylvania. But Italy, and Rome itself,
was the goal of these German invaders, and before them the Roman
empire was soon to disappear: the Ostrogoths of Pannonia pressed
on into Moesia, and, in 476 A.D., Odoacer destroyed the empire
of the West.

Theodoric took possession of Italy in 493 and extended his
rule over Dalmatia, Noricum, and Rhaetia. The Germans who
were settled in the latter province recognized his authority; but
for them the country would have contained nothing but ruins. In
the following century Justinian avenged the Western empire, and
reconquered these provinces, together with Italy. A new people,

the Lombards, had lent him aid in these expeditions, and were settled by him in Pannonia and Noricum, which they had to defend against the Gepidæ. Their king, Alboin, sought allies in this struggle among the Avars, a people akin to the Huns, and with their help drove out the Gepidæ in 565 A.D. Soon after, the emigration of the Lombards into Italy left these Avars sole masters of the Danubian territory. With this emigration of the Lombards into Italy the ceaseless wanderings of the German races over the Danubian lands come to an end. Like successive tidal waves they had passed over the region, destroying all traces of Roman culture and civilization, but at no time remaining long enough to establish an empire of their own. One or two fertile districts only, the Tyrol with its valleys and mountains, Salzburg, and Upper Austria, tempted some to remain behind in the forward movement upon Rome. The Avars might have been able to found something more lasting; but as the Germans retired they were followed by a new migration, which was to have a great permanent effect upon the countries of the Elbe and the Danube, that of the Slavs.

Chapter III

THE SLAVS. 450-650

NOTWITHSTANDING the extensive historical research of the present century, the origin of the Slav races is still wrapped in mystery. Whole series of conjectures, based on philological inductions, have been made. One fact only is certain; it is that the Slavs, when they first appear in history, are not a conquering race, broken up into separate tribes. They occupied the immense plains which stretch behind the Carpathians, the Vistula, and the Dnieper; and they long remained unknown. They had no Cæsar like the Gauls, no Tacitus like the Germans, to relate their history or write their annals. All we can say is that gradually as the Germans advanced southward and westward, the Slavs occupied the lands they abandoned, pushing forward even into the country between the Elbe and the Oder.

At an unknown date, but doubtless toward the middle of the fifth century, a branch of the Slavs, the Czechs, left Galicia proper and penetrated into the mountain quadrilateral now known as Bohemia. History finds but little that is true among the legends that are told of this migration. But they are cherished by the Czech nation, and play so great a part in the struggle for existence which even to-day it is carrying on, that they must be given more than a passing notice. According to these traditions there were three brothers, Cech, Lech, and Rous. Lech, at the head of the Slav tribe, quitted the home of his race, reached Bohemia, and there gave his name to a new land. From the next brother, Cech, tradition derives the name of the race, though why no one has yet been able to explain. Curiously enough, the Latin chroniclers of the Middle Ages were altogether ignorant of this name, and persisted in calling the people who bore it Bohemians, because they occupied the land once held by the Boii.

The Slavs of Moravia, no doubt, soon followed in the track of their kinsfolk; then came those Slavs who had hitherto remained behind the Carpathians, but who now gradually invaded, first Upper Hungary and Lower Austria, and then Wallachia, Moldavia, and Transylvania, where they blended with the few remaining Dacians and Roman colonists, and formed the first elements of the Rumanian nation. Although the history of these Slav migrations remains obscure, they seem to have had a distinct character of their own which distinguishes them from the German migrations.

The Germans had invaded countries which had been occupied by the Romans and ruled over peoples whom they found there; the Slavs, on the other hand, took possession of the lands which the Germans had abandoned. They had no need to do so by force of arms; their invasion was entirely peaceful. But they were not long allowed to remain in tranquil possession of the lands they had so easily gained; they were obliged to defend them against the most pitiless enemies. The Avars first conquered the Slav tribe of the Dudlebes in Galicia; then, led by their chagán, the terrible Bajan, a new Attila, they crossed the Carpathians and conquered the Slavs of Moravia and Bohemia. During these invasions the Slavs had to suffer from the Avars what the Germans had previously had to bear from the Huns. The plains of Hungary, lying between the Danube and the Theiss, became the seat of the Avar power, and large fortified camps, called hrings, protected the invaders against attack. The Slavs had to pay them tribute, furnish them with soldiers, and at times submit to being transplanted from one district to another.

It was thus that Pannonia and Noricum were peopled by Slav colonists, who became the ancestors of the Slovenes. These Avarized Slavs, if one may so call them, came down as far as Friuli, where their descendants are to be found to this day, speaking a language which still bears traces of some Altaic influence. Those who were settled in the valley of the Ems and of the Mur became known as Carinthian Slavs.

Sure of the obedience and help of the Slavs, Bajan next ventured to attack the Eastern empire, conquered Sirmia, in 584 A.D., and made it the base of operations against Byzantium, and, later on, against Dalmatia and Istria. In 599 he reached Constantinople and might have taken it had not a pestilence broken out in his army. This second Attila died in 603. Quarrels broke out among his heirs. The Slavs who had been conquered demanded their freedom, and prepared for revolt, and it was at this moment that a mysterious person, known as Samo the Merchant, first appeared.

He is said by Fredegar to have been a Frank, who had come to trade among the Slavs. A later writer, an anonymous historian of the conversion of the Bavarians and Carinthians, calls him a Carinthian Slav; but his nationality is left uncertain by all authentic documents. But whatever his nationality was, Slav, Frank, or Roman, he made common cause with the people, who offered him their leadership; his rule spread over all the tribes of the Wends and Slavs, and, says Fredegar, " for five and twenty years he governed them happily. In his reign the Wends fought several battles against the Huns, and owing to his prudence and courage were always victorious. Samo had twelve wives chosen from the nation of the Wends, and had twenty-two sons and fifteen daughters." Gradually Samo became so dangerous a neighbor to the Franks that there could not fail to be a collision. " In the year 630 the Slavs," writes Fredegar, " slew a number of Frankish merchants in the kingdom of Samo, and stripped them of their goods. Thus began the quarrel between Dagobert and Samo. Dagobert sent Sicarius to this king to ask for justice. Samo did not wish to see Sicarius, and would not allow him to enter his presence, but Sicarius managed to get to him disguised in the dress of a Slav, and delivered the message he bore from Dagobert. Samo, however, would repair none of the wrongs committed, saying only that he intended to have the matter tried so that justice might be done both in these matters and in others that had arisen. The enraged envoy had recourse to threats, and declared that Samo and his people owed submission to the king of the Franks. Samo replied angrily, ' The land we dwell in is Dagobert's and we are his men, but only so long as he lives in friendliness with us.' Sicarius answered, ' It is not possible for the Christian servants of God to be the friends of dogs,' on which Samo replied, ' If you are the servants of God, we are the dogs of God; and because you continually go against His will, we have received permission from Him to rend you with our teeth,' and ordered Sicarius to be driven from his presence." Dagobert declared war on Samo, and made an alliance with the Lombards. He attacked the Czechs, while the Lombards made war on the Slovenes. Samo collected his forces at Wogastiburg, on the western frontier of Bohemia, and there fought a three days' battle, in which, as Fredegar himself confesses, the Franks were cut to pieces. They returned to their own country, leaving behind them in their flight even their tents and baggage.

This success increased the fame of Samo, and a prince of the Slavs of the Elbe district placed himself and his tribe under his protection. But Samo died in 658, and then his power crumbled to pieces; the Slav chiefs would recognize no central power, and anarchy once more reigned among them. Modern Slav historians are inclined to exaggerate the importance of this mysterious personage, Samo; they wish to see in him the first representative of that Slav unity which they are able only to guess at in the past or dream of for the future. But Samo possessed true political genius and a talent for organization, which appear to have been foreign to the race in the earlier ages of its history, and which would seem to prove that he was not a Slav. He might have played the same part in the history of the Slavs of the Danube as Rurik in that of primitive Russia.

The conquests of Samo had not, however, completely destroyed the power of the Avars. Shut in by him on the West, they had turned with all the more vigor against the Eastern empire, and attacked Constantinople. Heraclius, however, threatened on one side by the Avars, on the other by the Moslems, determined to repeople the desert countries of the Adriatic and the Save by settling in them new races who would have to defend the lands occupied by them, and who would doubtless become converts to the Christian faith.

Which race should be chosen? Naturally he turned to that which had been subdued and shamefully ill-treated by the Avars; and two Slav peoples, the Croats and the Servians, became the instruments of the imperial policy. They had settled themselves north of the Carpathian Mountains, where they were continually menaced by the Germans and the Mongols. Proposals were first made to the Croats, and one tribe answered to the appeal; Heraclius sent them to attack Dalmatia. The Avars, taken by surprise, were everywhere forced to retreat, and a war, lasting a few years, ended in the destruction of a large part of the Avar population and the enslavement of the rest. Heraclius then turned to the Servians, and induced one of the chiefs of that nation to bring half the tribes from the north of the Danube to settle in parts of Thessalonica. Discontented, however, with his lot, this chief returned home; but the prospect of a struggle with the Avars made him

wiser and less exacting. He implored pardon, and appealed to the
kindness of the emperor, who granted him the deserted districts
of upper Moesia, lower Dacia, and Dardania.

Thus were established on the ruins of the Avar race two new
nations, who founded flourishing states, which, in spite of various
vicissitudes, have lasted to our day. We have no certain informa-
tion of the date of this migration, but it appears to have taken
place about the year 635 or 638. In their own tongue these two
races were called Serbi and Hervati. The land they occupied was
roughly marked out by the Adriatic, on the west, and by the three
rivers, the Drin to the south, the Save to the north, and the Morava
to the east. The frontier between the Servians and the Croats
was uncertain and fluctuating, and their language was similar;
the differences which exist between them at the present day have
been produced largely by historical events. To the one race Christianity came from Rome, to the other from Byzantium; Latin
became the language of the church of the former, while that of
the latter remained faithful to the Slav idiom. This history of
the two peoples reflects the struggle between the two ecclesiastical
capitals.

There had remained in Dalmatia a Roman element which the
Avars had not completely destroyed. This now receded before
the new colonists, taking refuge in the islands and towns on the
coasts. When the Croats freed themselves from the nominal suzerainty of Byzantium, these islands and towns still continued in
their allegiance to it. And down to the present day the old Roman
tradition, kept alive by Italian influence, survives in the region.

The emperor and the Pope lost no time in converting the
new colonists to Christianity, and were able to do so with greater
ease than might have been expected. In the space of about five
and twenty years the Croats had become Christians, and Spalato
was their first metropolis. The Croats of the Save cannot have
been converted so early as those of Dalmatia; they were still occupied with their struggles against the Franks and Avars, and when
they accepted Christianity it came to them from the distant church
of Aquileia.

The series of Slav migrations into the lands now forming the
Austro-Hungarian state closes with the arrival of the Croats and
Servians. These migrations were distinguished, as we have already
remarked, by their peaceable character. The Slavs did not rush

down on the cultivated lands, attracted by the riches of soil, by the thirst for conquest, or the mildness of the climate. Their advances were made peaceably, and they usually took possession of those districts which had been abandoned by their inhabitants. Descending from their home on the farther side of the Carpathians, from the valleys of the Danube and the Vistula, they took the place of the Marcomanni in Bohemia, of the Heruli and Gepidæ in Moravia. Sometimes, like the Slovenes, who peopled Carinthia and Carniola, they allowed themselves to be enrolled in the armies of their conquerors; sometimes, like the Servians and the Croats, they simply occupied lands which had been offered to them. Nowhere do we find among them the spirit of pillage, the love of conquest; nowhere, except in the case of Samo, do we find any idea of a powerful organization founded either on the unity of race or on religious ideas. At the time we have now reached, that is to say, about the middle of the seventh century, they possessed almost the whole of the present Austria-Hungary—the valley of the Elbe, the central valley of the Danube, and the shore of the Adriatic. These lands they defended against the Avars and the Germans, until the arrival from the steppes of the Ural of the Magyar, who introduced an entirely new and unexpected element into these regions.

As we have just seen, the valleys of the Dnieper and the Vistula seem to have been the cradle of the Slavic race. The name which we now give to the Slavs was not originally borne by the whole race; it belonged only to the northern tribes living in the Russia of to-day, toward the Valdai plateau. Those Slavs who lived near the Carpathians were called Serbs. The importance of this name will strike us if we recall the frequent mention of the Sorabes in German history; it is still borne by the Servians of Turkey, and by their distant kinsmen in Saxon and Prussian Lusatia. The dialects spoken at Bautzen and at Belgrade are so different that two Slavs from these two towns, brought suddenly face to face, would be unable to understand each other, and yet both call themselves Serbi. History has more or less incorrectly preserved the names of a large number of Slav tribes which it is unnecessary here to enumerate. On the other hand, it must not be forgotten that the Germans, in the Latin chronicles, give to the Slavs the name of Wends.

The constitution of the family among the Slavs, if we may

judge from written testimony and, in cases even, from the examples still to be seen, was entirely patriarchal. The family lived in common around its chief or elder (*staresphina*). The men cultivated the ground, the women were occupied with domestic work. The elder represented all tribal interests, offered sacrifices to the gods, and apportioned to each his share of labor. The members of the tribe all bore the same name, which was taken from that of its

EUROPE
END OF THE VIITH CENTURY ◄—   Roman Empire ▦

founder. This name always ended in *ici*, pronounced *itsi*, a termination which still plays a great part in the geographical names; for example, the descendants of Lobek were called Lobkovici, whence Lobkowitz, the name of a family well known in Bohemian history. Family names sometimes became those of villages they inhabited. When a family grew too large it sent out colonies, which in their turn took the name of their leaders, and founded new communities. The union of a certain number of families constituted a tribe. Frequently the tribe took its name from some feature of the land it inhabited; thus the Poles were the dwellers of the plain (*pole*); the Rietchanes were dwellers by the stream (*rieka*); the Drevlianes the inhabitants of the forest (*drevo*, wood). Occasionally it was taken from some pursuit practiced by the tribe, as the Roudnici, the miners. The common interests of the tribes were discussed in meetings of the heads of the families. The chief filled all the most important offices; he was priest, judge, and leader of the armies. Among the Slavs the love of liberty seems to have been stronger than any wish for law or order. Procopius says, " They are not governed by a single man, but live as a democracy." They are without government and hate one another," said the Emperor Maurice. The well-known saying of Tacitus may be applied to them, " I love rather a dangerous freedom than a peaceful slavery." How many troubles have come upon Poland from the custom of the *liberum veto,* that is, the necessity that every decision of the diet should be taken on a unanimous vote, one single opposing voice paralyzing all legislation! Traces of this custom are to be found in other Slavonic peoples.

Each tribe had a fortified enclosure, which was used as a place of shelter, or as a basis of attack in time of war. This was called *grad* (the strong), and this word is still to be found in that of some German towns, which were at first Slavonic and were then gradually Germanized, as the town of Gratz in Styria. The names of towns, rivers, and tribes, and of the features of the ground were almost identical in all Slavonic lands, however widely separated from one another.

Gradually tribes were united, sometimes as a means of self-defense, sometimes as the result of war, which resulted in the submission of the conquered. Thus nations were formed; thus the Czechs took possession of the whole of Bohemia; thus the Russians of Novgorod came at last to give their name to an immense empire. With the birth of nations came that of monarchy, which ended by becoming the monopoly of a ruling family, and national dynasties were founded. But to the Slavs the idea of equality was too dear to allow monarchical institutions to develop easily. The members of the royal family obtained appanages on which they maintained the greatest independence, and hence the internal wars of which the history of the early Slavonic monarchies is so full. The idea of the right of primogeniture had not yet appeared.

As we have already stated, the first Slavs were not conquerors, but rather cultivators of the soil. The very nature of the vast plains on which they dwelt directed their efforts and led them to cultivate corn and raise cattle. They seem to have had little taste for life among mountains; to have early learned the use of agricultural tools, such as the plow and spade; to have kept bees, and to have known how to make beer and hydromel.

The comparative study of the Slav dialects enables us to guess what degree of perfection the domestic arts had reached. The words common to all or most of the dialects are sufficient to show that the Slavs not only cultivated the ground, but that they knew how to practice, no doubt in clumsy fashion, some industries which are unknown to savage peoples. They were acquainted with iron and the commoner tools which are made of it; with gold, silver, copper, and utensils wrought out of these metals; they knew how to weave vestments of linen, and even glass was to be found among them. It is possible that some among them were acquainted with a rude kind of writing. "They read and calculated with strokes and notches," says an ancient witness.

They knew how to make war, though they cared little for fighting. We have already learned that they built fortified enclosures to defend their frontiers. They knew how to use the sword, the lance, the bow, the helmet, and the shield. Among them conquering tribes were rare, and the old historians speak of their peaceful habits. They tell us that they were kind, industrious, hospitable, chaste, and passionately fond of music and song. Their women were held in respect, and were chosen sometimes to lead the family, the tribe, and even the nation. Polygamy was met with occasionally, but it was the exception. They had laws, tribunals, and trials by ordeal; at the same time private revenge, such as exists to-day in Corsica and Montenegro, appears to have had, among the early Slavs, all the force of an institution sanctioned by custom.

They had a religious system of their own considerably developed, though it does not seem to have been of a kind to produce fanaticism. It readily made way for Christianity, directly the new faith came to them by means of friendly apostles and not through conquering missionaries. Among the Slavs of the Elbe and of Russia paganism developed into a complicated system, but it would take us long to learn all the gods of their pantheon, and we find hardly any trace of these divinities among the Slavs of Bohemia,

CREMATING THE BODY OF A SLAV CHIEFTAIN WITH HIS WAR-HORSE AND SLAVES

Painting by Henry von Siemiradzki

Moravia, and Carniola. Nowhere would it seem that they worshiped deified men or recognized a blind power in fate.

"The religion of the ancient Slavs," says Jireck, "was a true worship of nature. According to them the world was peopled with superior beings, who were good (*bozi*) or bad (*biesi*). The bozi were the more powerful, and the biesi could only act by their permission. Health, happiness, and victory were all the work of the bozi; sickness, wretchedness, defeat, were due to the biesi. In the winter time, however, the biesi got the upper hand. Sacrifices and vows were offered to the gods to propitiate them. These beings formed a vast society like that of human beings; they were all the sons of one greater than them all. The highest god was the god of heaven, Svarog; the sun and fire were his sons, and together bore the father's name and were called Svarozici. Among the other gods the more important were Veles, god of flocks, and Vesna, called also Siva or Lada, the goddess of spring and of fruitfulness. Among the biesi we must mention Morana, the goddess of winter and of death; Tras, the demon of terror, and Stribog, the demon of the tempest; and among the inferior beings should be mentioned the Vilas, nymphs, and the Vjedi, who dwelt in the air, and the Jezdibaby, sorcerers, who dwelt on the earth. The eclipses of the sun and moon were supposed to be the work of the Vjedi.

"A belief in vampires was common to all the Slavs. They believed the soul to be immortal; after having quitted the body it flew from tree to tree until the body had been burned, and then it went to the Home of Shadows, which the Slavs called Nav, and which they pictured to themselves as a region of green fields and groves. In Nav everyone occupied a position similar to that which he had held during his life; if he died before the other members of his family, he found himself alone and deserted. Hence arose the custom of wives causing themselves to be burned on the funeral pyres of their husbands. There were also indications of a belief in a place of sojourn with the biesi, as well as of a home with the gods."

None of the Slav tribes, except those of the Elbe, had temples or priests. The head of the family or of the tribe, the prince, offered the sacrifices to the gods, which consisted in the burning of animals, especially oxen. The sacrificial fire was lighted on mountain tops, or other high places. Forests were the usual places of worship; in them images of the gods were raised, and objects of sacrifice were placed under the trees. The great festivals of the year were that of the winter solstice, when vast sacrifices were offered to the gods of earth and water; that of the renewal, when Morana (winter) was burned under the form of a manikin, and Vesna (spring) was carried in triumph; and that of the summer solstice, when sacrifices were offered to the sun and to fire. Besides these there were frequent festivals during the summer in honor of the sun and fire, and in commemoration of the dead.

Chapter IV

MORAVIA AND THE SLAV APOSTLES
658-903

THE long series of migrations which took place on the soil of the future state of Austria-Hungary does not close with the settlement of the Slavs in these regions. Two other elements, the Magyars and the Germans from the upper Danube, invade the land a few centuries later, and between them occupy both banks of the Austrian Danube. But the annals of the Czechs, Moravians, and their Slav relations, during the two centuries which passed between the death of Samo, in the seventh century, and the Hungarian invasion in the ninth, contain a number of interesting episodes generally but little known, but well worth noting.

On the death of Samo the Slav empire, which he had so quickly succeeded in founding, broke into three portions: Bohemia, within well-defined geographic boundaries; Moravia, including, besides the province of that name, the regions of the middle Danube; and the country inhabited by the Carinthian Slavs, Carinthia, Carniola, the north of Styria, and some parts of Lower Austria.

The history of these various nations during the second half of the seventh and the first half of the eighth centuries is very obscure. The account of the rise of Bohemia in the Latin and Czech chronicles is fabulous, and only owes what reality it possesses to that religious faith in it which patriotism and poetry have inspired. It is a curious fact that Bohemian legends know nothing of Samo, who played so great a part in the annals of the country. The first prince mentioned by them is a certain Krok, who is said to have reigned in the second half of the seventh century. Krok had three daughters, who are still dear to popular memory. One of these, Libusa, on the death of her father, was chosen to rule his lands. Notwithstanding that wisdom with which tradition endows her, she felt herself too weak to govern a turbulent people alone, and chose for her husband the laborer Premysl of Stadice. Tradition still points out the field where this Cincinnatus of the Slavs received the invitation to leave his plow, and where at the beginning of the last century a monument was raised to him. Premysl became the founder of a royal dynasty which ruled over Bohemia down to the year 1306. The chroniclers praise his wisdom and that of his wife, Libusa, and to her they attribute the founding of Prague, on the right bank of the Moldau. The German annals supply us with a few facts. In the year 791 the Czechs allied themselves with Charles the Great against the Avars; about the year 806 the Franks invaded Bohemia with three armies, and forced the inhabitants to pay tribute; in 845 fourteen Bohemian nobles were baptized at Regensburg. But Bohemian history really begins with the reign of Borivoj, who was baptized toward the end of the ninth century. Christianity had made very little progress for three centuries, largely, it is supposed, because the Czechs had had many a struggle with the Germans, and would be little inclined to receive kindly the Gospel which came to them through the hands of German apostles; for, because of the alliance between Charles the Great and the Pope, Christianity meant nothing but conquest and slavery to the Slavs. The sword roused hatred against the cross. The example, also, of the Saxons, and of the Slavs of the Elbe, was not likely to encourage the Czechs to embrace the new religion. When, however, it came to them from Moravia, through the Slav missionaries, without any suspicion of conquest, it was easily able to obtain over them the salutary influence it had already gained over the races of the west and south.

Less fortunate than Bohemia, her neighbor, Moravia has not even a legendary history. Her name appears for the first time at the beginning of the ninth century, under its Slav form, Morava (German *March, Moehren*). The first prince whose name is known was Moimir, who ruled at the beginning of the ninth century; like the Czech, Premysl, he gave his name to a dynasty. During his reign Christianity made considerable progress in Moravia, and the oldest Christian church of which there is any record among the Moravians was consecrated at Nitra by the Archbishop of Salzburg. But in Moravia also it was not until Christianity possessed a national clergy that the new religion made rapid progress. The people, as we have already said, distrusted the German preachers, and, knowing no Latin, could neither understand the German sermons nor the Roman liturgy. As late as 852 the council of Mainz pointed out Moravia as a land still knowing little of Christianity: *rudis adhuc christianitatis.* Moimir tried to withstand the Germans, but was not successful; and in 846 Louis the German invaded his country, deposed him, and made his nephew, Rostislav, whom the chroniclers call Rastiz, ruler in his stead.

The new prince determined to secure both the political and moral freedom of his country. He fortified his frontiers and then declared war against the emperor. He was victorious, and when once peace was secured he undertook the systematic conversion of his people. Thus came about one of the great episodes in the history of the Slavs and their church, the mission of the Apostles Cyril and Methodius.

The Slavs of the Danubian valley had already come into contact with both the great centers of Christianity, Rome and Constantinople, between which the great schism had not as yet taken place. But Rome with all her zeal could only send to the Slavs foreign missionaries, who were either ignorant or distrusted by the people; Constantinople, on the contrary, was surrounded by Slav Christians, who already possessed a native clergy. Rostislav, therefore, sent to the Emperor Michael III., writing: " Our people have renounced paganism and have accepted the Christian faith; but we have no master who can preach to us the Christian truths in our tongue. Send us one." At that time there were living at Constantinople the two brothers Constantine, two priests already celebrated for their knowledge and the success of their mission work. In the church they were known by the names of Cyril and Methodius. Were they Greeks or Slavs? No one knows. They were born in Thessalonica, a city of many languages, and their father held there an important office in the state. They had studied science and languages and had distinguished themselves among the most learned men of the court of Byzantium. The one had become a monk, the other a priest, and their reputation had been increased by their missions to the Arabs and the Khazars. Their success as missionaries was considered miraculous, and languages of all kinds were familiar to them. Cyril had been named the Philosopher; Methodius had refused an archbishopric offered him by the emperor and the patriarch; everything seemed to point them out for the post. They accepted the honorable office as apostles to the Moravians; and Cyril undertook, before setting out on his mission, to create for the Slav tongue that alphabet which it had never yet possessed, and to which his name is still attached (the Cyrillic alphabet). He also translated the New Testament into Slav and carried his translation with him into the country. The two brothers reached Moravia at the end of the year 863, or the beginning of 864, and were received with great honor by Rostislav. They soon gathered round them the young men destined for the priesthood, to whom they taught the new alphabet, while they continued their translations of the sacred books and the liturgy. " Then," says a Slav legend, " according to the word of the prophet, the ears of the deaf heard, and the tongue of the dumb was unloosed."

The names of the new apostles and the news of their success soon reached the ears of the Pope. He summoned them to Rome, and they responded to his call. As they crossed lower Pannonia they visited the Slav Prince Kocel, who confided to their care a certain number of young ecclesiastics. At Rome they were received with the highest honors; Pope Adrian II. made them bishops and consecrated as priests, deacons, or subdeacons several of the disciples they had brought with them, besides authorizing them to celebrate the liturgy in the Slav tongue, and approving their translation of the Scriptures. Cyril died in Rome in February, 869, and was buried there. Methodius returned alone to his work, the Pope having assigned to him, as his diocese, all the Slav countries, and given him a letter to Rostislav and his princely neighbors, Svatopluk and Kocel. He approved of the use of the Slav liturgy, but recommended that the Gospels should be read in Latin, as a sign of the unity of the church. On his return from Rome Methodius again spent some time at the court of Kocel in Pannonia.

When Methodius once more reached Moravia Rostislav was no longer there to receive him. After having struggled successfully for some time against the Germans, he had been betrayed by his nephew and vassal, Svatopluk, into the hands of Karloman, duke of Carinthia and son of Louis the German, who put out his eyes and shut him up in a monastery. Svatopluk believed himself sure of the succession as the price of his treachery, but a very different reward fell to his lot, as Karloman, trusting but little in his fidelity to the Germans, threw him also into captivity. Later he was released by Karloman, who hoped he would aid him against the revolt of the Moravians. Instead, Svatopluk joined them and successfully attacked the Germans. The independence of Moravia was secured, and, by the Treaty of Forcheim, in 874, it was recognized.

The German bishops had not seen without envy the success of Cyril and Methodius and the favors bestowed on them by the Pope. The extent of their jurisdiction and the value of their tithes had been considerably lessened by the creation of the new Slav diocese. They looked upon Methodius as a usurper, and as such cited him before them and imprisoned him in a convent, where they kept him for two years. From this time the life of Methodius was one long struggle against the German clergy. They constantly intrigued against him, and endeavored to withdraw from him the favor of the Pontiff. He nevertheless persisted in his work, and about 874 baptized the prince of Bohemia, Borivoj, and by this means introduced the Slav liturgy into Bohemia. Accusations against him continually reached the Pope; now he was accused of heresy, now he was denounced for his use of the Slav liturgy; and he was but ill-supported by Svatopluk. He was obliged to go to Rome to defend himself, but came out victorious from the trial, Pope John VIII. recognizing his orthodoxy, and once more confirming the privileges granted him. It would take us too long to relate here how the enemies of Methodius substituted false documents for those which had been drawn up by the Pope himself. Methodius was again obliged to appeal to the Pontiff, who sanctioned his action in a letter which was publicly read to the assembled people. He passed the last years of his troubled life in completing his translation of the sacred books, and died in 885. On his death his disciples had no protection from the persecutions of their enemies, and were forced to seek refuge among the Bulgarians, by whom they were eagerly welcomed.

The departure of the disciples of Methodius completely disorganized the Slav church. The German bishops of the neighboring dioceses drew up and sent to the Pope, John IX., in 900, a *factum* in which they claimed for themselves jurisdiction over the country of the Moravians, "a country," said they, "which has been subject to our kings and our people both as regards Christian worship and the payment of tribute." "With their will or against their will," adds this evangelical *factum,* "they shall be subject to us": *sive velint sive nolint, regno nostro subacti erunt.* These controversies, which were so little animated by the spirit of that religion which was their object, were put an end to in a most unexpected and bloody fashion by the invasion of the Magyars. Moravia was thrown into a state of anarchy, and the Slav liturgy perished. But few traces of it can be discovered in the history of those lands which gave it birth. Proscribed in Moravia, it flourished for a time in Bulgaria; thence it passed to the Servians, Russians, and the Croats, and then gradually disappeared.

At the present time throughout the empire of Austria Latin is the language of the Catholic Church. The Slav liturgy is used only by about three millions of Uniate Ruthenians in Galicia, three millions of Servians and Rumanians, and about eighty thousand Catholics on the shores of the Adriatic. Though they returned more or less willingly to the use of the Latin liturgy, the Slavs of the Western rite have by no means forgotten the great apostles of their race; their millennium was celebrated in 1863 with imposing solemnity, and they are still considered the representatives of that literary and religious unity of the Slavs which is the dream of many. Cyril and Methodius deserve a far higher place in religious history than has hitherto been assigned to them. Their knowledge, their zeal for the Gospel, their indomitable perseverance, have nothing to fear from comparison with the apostles of Germany.

But we must return to Svatopluk and his ephemeral empire. The Treaty of Forcheim secured the independence of Moravia and thenceforward peace reigned between Svatopluk and Louis the German. Complete master in his country, strong in the power of his army and of his Slav-speaking clergy, Svatopluk might have put himself forward as the representative and defender of the Slavs against the Germans. But he did not appreciate the possibilities of such action. Instead, he showed a marked sympathy for the Germans and invited them to his court. While helping to spread the Slav liturgy in his provinces, he himself made use of the Roman liturgy, and thus opened the door to the pretensions of the German clergy. He began his reign with a crime, he ended it with blunders; he possessed great talents, but his character was not equal to them, and his policy appears to have been fortunate rather than able. At one time he was the most powerful monarch of the Slavs; Rome was in treaty with him, Bohemia gravitated toward Moravia, and Moravia held in check the ambitions of the empire. The emperor himself, Charles the Fat, came to the Ostmark to try to put an end to the struggle between Svatopluk and Arnulf of Pannonia, and there received, in 884, a visit from Svatopluk, who promised to respect the lands of the empire. In 888 Svatopluk concluded a treaty of friendship and alliance with Arnulf, which was renewed in 891. At this time the kingdom of Svatopluk was a powerful state; it included, besides the Moravia of to-day, Austrian Silesia, the subject country of Bohemia, the Slav tribes on the Elbe and the Vistula as far as the neighborhood of Magdeburg, part of western Galicia, the country of the Slovaks, and lower Pannonia.

But two such ambitious men as Svatopluk and Arnulf could not trust each other; their friendship was based only on·mutual fear; and as soon as Arnulf believed that he had secured sufficiently strong allies he once more attacked Svatopluk. He entered into an alliance with Braclav, a Slovene prince, sought the aid of the king of the Bulgarians, and, what was of far graver importance, summoned to his help the Magyars, who had just settled on the lower Danube. Swabians, Bavarians, Franks, Magyars, and Slovenes moved simultaneously upon Moravia. Overwhelmed by numbers, Svatopluk made no attempt at resistance: he shut up his troops in fortresses, and abandoned the open country to the enemy, who ravaged it for four weeks. Then hostilities ceased; but no durable peace could exist between the two adversaries. War again began in the following year, when death freed Arnulf from Svatopluk. The populace, which loves to surround its great men with legendary glory, would not believe that Svatopluk had died like any ordinary mortal. From the tenth century onward a marvelous story has been told of him. One night the great Moravian chief left his camp unobserved, mounted his faithful steed, and gained the wooded sides of Mount Zobor, near Nitra, where was a well-known hermitage. Here he slew his horse, buried his sword in the earth, presented himself before the hermits of the mountain, became a monk, and lived long without making known his rank, which he only revealed at the moment of death. Through many vicissitudes his name remained popular in Moravia, and to this day the people make use of a proverb, " Seek for Svatopluk," when they wish to imply, " Seek for justice." Historians have criticised this prince severely, but we must not forget that almost all we know of him has reached us through his enemies. " He was a vessel of treachery," say the annals of Fulda; " he overturned the countries with his greed, and thirsted for human blood." " He was a man of great genius and great cleverness," writes Regino. " He was valiant and strong and dreaded by his neighbors," says Constantine Porphyrogenitus. Modern Slavonic writers give him a high place in the history of the race, and look upon him as a successor of Samo, and the second great leader in the cause of Slavic unity in the West.

At his death he left three sons. The eldest, Moimir II., he chose as his heir, and assigned appanages to each of the others. On his deathbed he begged them to live at peace with one another, but his advice was not followed. The Moravian kingdom was far from forming a homogeneous whole. Bohemia refused to remain a vassal state; the Magyars invaded Moravian Pannonia, and forced Moimir into an alliance with them. Arnulf fomented the discord between Moimir II. and Svatopluk II.; and, in the year 900, the Bavarians, together with the Czechs, invaded Moravia. In 903 the name of Moimir disappears. Cosmas of Prague shows us Moravia at the mercy of Germans, Czechs, and Hungarians; then history is silent, towns and castles crumble, churches are overthrown, the people scattered. "A mournful silence reigns over the universal desolation," says the Czech historian Palacky, "and we know not when or how this work of horror was accomplished." The brief duration of the Moravian kingdom has been justly compared to that of the mounds of sand which are raised by the breath of the tempest, and by the tempest dispersed. This monarchy of a day has not even left ruins behind it; we hardly know the site of the capital of Svatopluk, that marvelous city of Velehrad (*ineffabilis munitio*), where Methodius baptized the prince of Bohemia. The poetry of the people alone remains, bewailing the memory of a vanished world:

"Hard by the broad Danube, hard by the foaming waves of the Morava, . . . bleeds the wounded heart of the Slavs. O land of our noble fathers! theater echoing to our ancient struggles! thou liest entombed in thy vast expanse; the arrow of misfortune has pierced thy breast. Thy time has gone by; thy glory sleeps an internal sleep. Thy sons find only the shadow of their fathers' glory.

"The sword of Moimir slumbers; beneath ruins the helmet of Svatopluk lies buried. Only once in a long while from this bosom of forgetfulness a memory flies to heaven in song.

"Nitra, dear Nitra! great Nitra! where are the times of thy prosperity? Nitra, dear Nitra! thou mother of the Slavs, when I think of thee, I needs must weep. Formerly thou wast the mother of the whole Danube, the Vistula, and the Morava. Thou wast the throne of Svatopluk, when his powerful hand ruled; thou wast the holy city of Methodius, when he taught our fathers the word of God. Now is thy glory veiled in shadow. Thus do times change! thus the world passes!"

The Slovenes, or Slavs of Carinthia and Carniola, were of little importance during these early times. After the death of Samo they separated from the Czechs, and were able to organize a state. Borut, their first prince whose name is known, sought the aid of Pepin the Short against the Avars in 748, and obtained it at the price of almost complete submission to the Frankish monarch. His successor, Karat, was obliged to renew this vassalage. Chotimir, who was a cousin of Borut, was brought up in Bavaria, and was a Christian; he was a fervent apostle of the Gospel among the Slovenes. With the help of Virgil, bishop of Salzburg, he worked hard at the conversion of his people, which was effected solely through the German clergy, and its first result was the complete Germanizing of the Slavs of Salzburg and the Tyrol. The history of these Slavs belongs in the main to that of the Ostmark and the empire.

One thing only deserves to be recorded here, and that is the curious mode in which the Carinthians installed their princes. The ceremony took place near the town of Klagenfurt. A peasant mounted on a rock awaited the coming of the new prince, who advanced, clothed in rustic garments. The peasant asked, "Who is this who approaches?" The people answered, "It is the prince of this land." The peasant then asked, "Is he a good judge? is he the friend of truth?" and, on receiving a reply in the affirmative, the peasant yielded his place to the newcomer, who mounted the rock and, brandishing his sword, swore to defend the country of the Slovenes. This custom lasted down to the fifteenth century. The people who had imagined it deserved a more brilliant destiny.

The historic individuality of the Croats is much more clearly marked than that of the Slovenes. We have already seen how, on their arrival in their new country, they adopted Christianity without difficulty. The Germans could invoke no pretense of conversion to justify their attempts at conquest among the Croats, but it was sufficient reason for German ambition that the Croats bordered on the empire. In 796 Charles the Great crushed the Avars by taking their fortified camp, and after 822 even their name disappears from the chronicles. Thus master of the country between the

Danube and the Theiss, Charles the Great's dominions included the numerous and still independent Croats. The margrave of Friuli was appointed to attack their coast, and the Croats of Dalmatia and Slavonia passed from the yoke of Byzantium to that of the empire. But they did not willingly accept the Frankish rule. Their chief, Ljudevit (823), revolted against the foreign yoke, but was defeated and forced to fly to Servia, where he was assassinated. We cannot undertake to relate the tangled history of the Croats of Dalmatia and the Save districts. Toward the end of the ninth century they were finally united, and the great zhupan Mutimir (892-900) proclaimed himself chief of the Croats by the grace of God, organizing his court on the model of the other European courts.

In Croatia, as in Moravia, Western influences banished the Slav liturgy, and the Croats found themselves more and more separated from the Servians, while the introduction of the Latin language prepared the way for the Venetians. These gradually took possession of the whole coast of the Adriatic, and their doges adopted the title of dukes of Dalmatia. For the rest of the land the over-lordship of Byzantium was gradually renounced by Drzislav (970-1001). One of his successors, Peter Kresimir, called the Great, recovered the Dalmatian cities and the Isles, and took the title of king of Dalmatia; conquered from the Bulgarians the district of Sirmia which they had captured, and from the Servians part of Bosnia; he also seized part of Carniola, Styria, and Istria.

During his reign a council was held at Spalato to combat the Slav liturgy, which still enjoyed the popular favor in spite of all the anathemas hurled against it, and Kresimir supported Pope Nicholas II. in his measures for driving the national tongue out of the church. It took refuge in a few isles of the Adriatic, where it has lasted down to our time.

King Svinimir, or Zvonimir (1075), is known best from his relations with Pope Gregory VII. That Pontiff, who was carrying on an energetic struggle with the empire, aimed at directly attaching to the Holy See those secondary states which were dependents neither of Germany nor Byzantium. He sent Cardinal Gebizon to Croatia, bearing royal insignia to Zvonimir. Zvonimir was consecrated in the basilica of St. Peter, in Spalato (1076), in the name of the Pope, and received from the hands of his envoy the royal diadem, sword, and scepter. In return for this honor he promised to remain faithful and obedient to the Holy See, to cause tithes to be paid, to oblige the clergy to live decent lives, and to prevent all marriages forbidden by the laws of the church, and all traffic in slaves. He also undertook to pay two hundred ducats yearly to the Pope. The chronicles of Croatia look upon the reign of Zvonimir as the climax of the national power: " Under good King Zvonimir the country lived in joy, the cities were full of gold and of silver. The poor man had no fear that the rich would do him wrong; the servant dreaded no wrongdoing from his master. The king defended them, and they had nought to fear but the anger of God." Zvonimir died without children, and the nobles of Croatia and Dalmatia elected one of his relations, Stephen II., who reigned but a short time. He was the last king of the line of the Derzislavic, and on his death the Croats, after long discussion, offered their crown to Ladislas, king of Hungary, who accepted it.

The organization of the kingdom of Croatia and its institutions deserve a passing mention. The Croats were grouped together in families in the same way as the other Slav races. A certain number of families made up a zhupa, at the head of which was a zhupan. In early times one among the zhupans was recognized as the head of the nation, with the title of the great zhupan; he had no absolute authority, but took counsel with his colleagues. These zhupans, who are named in the Latin texts *zuppani,* were called by foreigners *duces, comites,* and *principes.*

Around the great zhupan, or king, gathered a nobility of the counts and barons. The powers of the great zhupan do not seem to have differed from those exercised later on by the kings; this supreme authority, moreover, was hereditary. At the same time we find that when there was no lawful heir, the people exercised the right of election: it was thus that the ban Zvonimir was elected *concordi totius cleri et populi electione.* Legislative, administrative, and judicial functions were exercised by the king with the aid of a national assembly. The capital was Belgrade.

After the king, the most important officers of the state were the bans. At first there was but one ban, who was a kind of lieutenant general; but later on there were seven of them, each known by the name of the province he governed. To this day the royal lieutenant of Croatia is called the ban. All grave questions of legislation, of peace and war, and of election to the throne were treated in the diets, whose organization is but ill-defined. The towns on the Dalamatian coast had preserved municipal institutions of Roman origin, which were independent of the rest of the kingdom.

At the head of the church was the archbishop of Spalato, which was the metropolis of the rest of the kingdom. Byzantine orthodoxy made but little progress in Croatia, and we have already seen with what distrust the Roman clergy and the Holy See treated the Slav liturgy, even though it was Catholic. The court of Rome remained all-powerful in Croatia; the church was rich, and the monasteries, especially those of the Benedictines, very numerous. The Latin language, owing to the influence of Rome, became the official language of politics, literature, and religion. At the same time there remain some manuscripts which prove that the national tongue was occasionally used in legal proceedings.

Chapter V

THE FOUNDING OF THE MAGYAR STATE
892-1038

THE Hungarian nation appears in history under two names, that of Magyar, used by themselves, and that of Hungarian, used by foreigners. The first time we hear of them they are spoken of as living by the chase near the Volga River and the Ural Mountains. Nomadic tribes wandering over the immense plains of eastern Russia, they gradually made their way westward, and settled near the shores of the Black Sea. There seven tribes are said to have given command to a young leader named Arpad, who became the founder of a dynasty. The wealth of Europe seems to have attracted them, as Italy had formerly attracted the Germans, and the imprudence of the Western monarchs opened a way for them to the very heart of its fertile lands. First the Eastern emperor implored their help against the Bulgarians, and then Arnulf sought their aid against Svatopluk.

The region of the Danube into which they came had been ravaged and occupied by their ancestors or kinsmen for more than two centuries. The Huns of Attila had encamped there, and they had been followed by the Avars, who had settled there from the end of the sixth century down to the time when Charles the Great destroyed their great hring between the Danube and the Theiss in 796.

The first attack of the Magyars, which was directed against Moravia in 892, was unsuccessful. Two years later, however, they returned, determined this time to settle in whatever part of the land they might be able to conquer. Few examples of a migration so vast are to be found in the history of barbarian invasions. Two hundred and sixteen thousand men bearing arms, which implies a total population of almost a million, are the numbers mentioned in the national traditions, where it is said that this multitude took nearly three years to cross the Carpathians.

The nation was led with so exact and wise a discipline as to call forth the admiration of an illustrious Byzantine critic. " Their

41

vigorous bodies," says Sayous, "used to the privations of the desert, felt neither heat nor cold, neither hunger nor thirst. Accustomed to all manner of hardships, no task seemed impossible to them. Every kind of weapon, sword, bow, or lance, was alike to them, for they knew how to fight both on foot and on horseback; but, horsemen rather than foot soldiers, they preferred to fight on their small and agile steeds, which never felt fatigue, and the arrow was their favorite weapon. When arrayed for battle they were divided into bodies of one thousand men each, who were equally prepared to form one compact mass or to pour down upon the enemy in flying squadrons from every side at once. A cloud of arrows was the prelude to a furious onslaught which bore all before it, and often a pretended flight finished the complete rout of their enemies when they were madly confident of victory."

The legends of the Magyars tell us the names of some of the small Slav princes who were the first to give way before this terrible invasion. But they tell us nothing of the manner in which the Moravian kingdom was conquered. By the end of the tenth century we find the ruin of that power completed, and the rule of the Magyars established in the whole of the district along whose center runs the Danube, and whose north and east are bounded by the Carpathian Mountains.

The invasion had the gravest consequences for the history of these lands. "It was not a mere immigration of a Finnish race, destined to disappear as the Huns and Avars had already disappeared, or to become absorbed like the Bulgarians among the conquered race. The intellectual qualities of the Magyars, the finest of the Altaic races, their physical strength, their immense numbers, their keen patriotism, guaranteed them against destruction or absorption, slow or rapid."

The advent of this people and their settlement upon the ruins of Moravia was a mortal blow to the Slavs. The Czech historian Palacky says, "The invasion of the Hungarians was the greatest misfortune that ever befell our race. From Holstein to the Peloponnesus the Slav tribes extended; they were but loosely united and their customs differed, but they were all vigorous and ready for civilization. In the center of this vast region a nucleus had been formed by the efforts of Svatopluk, about which a great Slav civilization might have developed. But the hopes of the Slavs were ruthlessly destroyed by the appearance of the Magyars."

THE MAGYAR STATE

The lands on which they had settled did not suffice for the new conquerors. The Magyar hordes brought with them nomadic and warlike instincts which time and the influence of the Christian religion alone could transform and prepare for civilization. They invaded the Venetian country; but the city of the lagoons beat them back, as it had already beaten back the Huns. In 907 Arpad died, and, according to tradition, his remains lie at the foot of the rock of Buda, where he had located his capital or camp. Under his son Zoltan the invasions continued; the Germans suffered a terrible defeat at Presburg in 907; then again in 910, near Augsburg; but

SOUTHEASTERN EUROPE Eastern Empire ▦
CIRCA 910 A.D.

they repulsed the Magyars before Wels, where, if we are to believe their account, eighty-six Magyars alone escaped. An old German poem proudly celebrates this victory: " They fought a terrible fight. Many a Hungarian lost his life; the Bavarians avenged their women and children. So many Hungarians were killed that no one could tell the number nor count the dead. They fled night and day till they reached the Leitha. Yet were they not weary of the fight."

In 924 it was again Italy that they attacked, and even Provence and Champagne saw the terrible horsemen within their borders. At last, however, their progress was definitely stopped by the

battle of Augsburg, in 955. Thenceforward the Magyars were
forced to fall back, and to content themselves with those lands
which they had secured in the valley of the Danube. King Geiza
(972-997) was the first pacific ruler of pagan Hungary.

Thus a new military state appeared which was destined to play
an important part in the history of these lands. Within the limits
of the Magyar kingdom, in almost every part, was a large Slav
population, whose language and laws were to exercise a lasting
influence on the Hungarians. On the southeast they touched on
the Romance element, which, from the time of the Roman colonies
of Trajan, had continued to develop there. Numerous marriages
with these neighbors gradually modified the primitive type of the
Magyars; they have long since lost the high cheek bones and slant-
ing eyes of the Mongols, and, improved by the intermixture of
races, they have become one of the most beautiful, perhaps the
most beautiful, race in Europe.

Few traces of the religion of the pagan Magyars are left to-
day, and it is difficult to make out their system of mythology from
the popular superstitions. They seem to have recognized a supreme
god, Isten, the father of men, and below him a number of secondary deities, such as the demon Ordog, and Mano, the evil
spirit. Below these again are the *tünder*, fairies and apparitions
who influence the destiny of man in various ways. Sayous says:
" Somewhere among the mountains of Transylvania lies the palace
of the king of the *tünder*, where he dwells with his queen and many
beautiful maidens; this palace is built of silver and copper, and is
guarded by a golden lion; it is reflected in a shining lake and surrounded by great forests, where the song of birds fills the air with
delightful melody. A tradition of the comitat of Houth tells
how, in a spot which is now deserted and covered with stones, with
here and there the stump of an old tree, there formerly lived fairies
who, at break of day, combed their golden locks over the country
in such fashion that every one was rich; but a miser seized one of
the fairies, intending to cut off all of her hair, whereupon they all
took flight, and the land was filled with desolation, and poverty
took the place of plenty. In the town of Deva the good fairy used
to appear every seven years; while other fairies built walls for men
and made them rich with their treasures, till human ingratitude continually disappointed them and forced them to quit the place. Besides the fairies of the earth there were also those of the air and

of the water. One of the most poetical and most original fancies
of the Magyar imagination was Delibab, the fairy of the south,
the personification of the mirage, who was the daughter of the
plain, the sister of the sea, the beloved of the wind. Lakes and
rivers were peopled by mysterious spirits. The elements were the
objects of worship. And further, " Alone among all created things
the human soul preserved an indestructible and immortal existence;
it could return to earth, especially if it had been the soul of an
illustrious warrior. The soul passed beneath the vault of death
on horseback, and crossed a bridge which led to happiness in another world—a warrior's happiness, as the funeral ceremonies had
been those of a warrior."

Power was divided between the priests and the prince. The
priests offered songs and prayers, and even human sacrifices, upon
altars in the woods. A nomadic race, such as were the Magyars
before their conversion to Christianity, could have but a very imperfect form of government. It was military rather than political.
The power of the highest chief had no limits but those imposed by
the right of self-government possessed by each tribe. He was
chosen by the voice of the people, and it would seem that the choice
had become hereditary in the family of Arpad, though without the
right of primogeniture being recognized either by custom or
law. This election was confirmed by the supreme judicial power,
and by the general assembly of the chiefs, assisted by many of the
freemen.

All the members of a family, and even of a tribe, looked upon
each other as brothers; they were all free and all noble. Here we
find the origin of that numerous class of *petite noblesse* which has
always been the strength of Hungary. " The headship of the families and tribes was partly hereditary, partly elective. The land assigned to the tribe or family by the duke or by the national assembly was the property of all, even when the various branches of the
family had divided it into portions. On these they might build the
huts which gradually became houses, and pasture their cattle until
it was brought under cultivation, but still it remained the property
of the tribe. The chief had no peculiar domain. It was not until
later, when Hungary had become an agricultural country, that
properties were well defined, and that the chiefs became proprietors
of part of the land and feudal lords of the rest. In early times the
ducal tribe, the one which was under the immediate authority of the

prince, settled in the center of the country near Pesth and Stuhlweissenburg."

Naturally the old Magyars had but little taste for town life; they left the towns to their old inhabitants, or else peopled them with colonists from foreign countries. Their nomadic life afforded but small opportunity for intellectual or artistic culture; the Magyar archæologists can find few ruins belonging to this pagan time, and not a verse has reached us of the rhapsodies sung by the bards in the honor of their heroes, or at the great festivals and marriages. All we know is that music played a large part on these solemn occasions. The weird melodies of the gypsies may perhaps have preserved some faint echoes of those early songs.

Geiza I., referred to above as the first pacific king of pagan Hungary, had married as his second wife a sister of the duke of Poland, Mieczyslaw. She had been converted to Christianity, and, like Clotilde of France, this princess knew how to use her influence in favor of her religion. She persuaded her husband to receive the missionaries who came to preach the Gospel in the country of the Magyars, and Pilgrim, archbishop of Lorch, undertook the systematic conversion of the nation. He sent priests from his diocese into Hungary, and in 974 he announced five thousand conversions to the Pope. Foreigners, who, up to this time, had practiced their religion secretly, began to profess it openly, had their children publicly baptized, and built churches. Geiza himself consented to be baptized, but long afterward he continued to mix pagan ceremonies with the Christian rites. The great Czech apostle, St. Adalbert, bishop of Prague, continued the work begun by Pilgrim. About 994 he went to Gran, where the duke of Hungary then dwelt, and solemnly baptized the son of Geiza, to whom he gave the name of Stephen. Henceforth the court of the duke became the resort of knights from all the neighboring countries, but especially from Germany, and these knights, entering into intimate relations with the native nobility, drew Hungary and the empire into still closer union. Prince Stephen, heir-presumptive to the throne, married the Princess Gisella, daughter of the duke of Bavaria, while one of the daughters of Geiza became the wife of the Polish Duke Boleslav, and another married Urseolus, doge of Venice. Through these alliances Hungary obtained for itself a recognized place among European states, and the work begun so well by Geiza was completed by Stephen, to whom was reserved the honor of establishing the position of his kingdom in Europe and of completing its conversion. When this prince came to the throne in 997, the countries surrounding Hungary were all ruled by celebrated princes. Otto III. governed Germany; Boleslav III., Bohemia; Boleslav the Brave, Poland; Vladimir the Great, Russia; and Basil II., Byzantium. In order to maintain the existence of Hungary among these flourishing states it was needful that it should attain the same degree of civilization, and this was the work of Stephen, honored by the Hungarians as the second founder of their nation.

In the very beginning of his reign Stephen had to struggle against the revolts of a pagan chief, Koppany, who saw in the introduction of Christianity danger to the native institutions. He overcame him beneath the walls of Veszprim, and, once freed from this formidable enemy, Stephen gave all his thoughts to the spread of Christianity among his people. His zeal was remarkable. " Hungary became Catholic," says the Magyar historian, Verboczy, " not through apostolic teaching, nor through the invitation of the Holy See, but through the laws of King Stephen." He was not always content to use persuasion alone to lead his subjects to the new faith; he hesitated not to use threats also. He sent an ambassador to Rome to treat directly with Pope Sylvester, who graciously received the homage offered for the kingdom, and by a letter, dated March 27, 1000, announced that he took the people of Hungary under the protection of the church.

On August 15, in the year 1000, the king was crowned at Gran with the crown sent to him by the Pontiff. The coronation of Stephen secured the continuance of power to the dynasty of Arpad. He still, however, met with some resistance, especially in Transylvania, where the native prince, Giulay, refused to sanction the Christian religion. Stephen marched against him, defeated him, and granted Transylvania to a voiévode of the race of Arpad. He reconquered part of Moravia from Bohemia, and dared even to attack Germany on the side of Bavaria, but being attacked in his turn, was obliged to make peace.

Under this great king Hungary became an independent kingdom between the two empires of the East and West, and was probably enabled to preserve its independence by that equilibrium which was now established between these two ambitious rivals. The state was completely united, and was not divided into appanages. The king was supreme, but he had a council of the old and wise men continually at hand to advise him, " For," said Stephen, in the directions which he wrote for his son Emerich, " it is right that each should busy himself with that which suits him best, the young with fighting, the old with counsel." He himself calls this institution *regalis senatus, regale concilium, primatum conventus, commune concilium.* Hungarian historians see in it the first elements of the national diet; rough beginnings, doubtless, and as little subject to fixed rules as had formerly been the meetings of the tribes in the plain.

Ecclesiastically the kingdom was divided into ten bishoprics, all subject to the archbishop of Gran. Stephen also founded several abbeys, which were granted to the Benedictines, who opened schools, while churches were built by Italian and Byzantine architects.

Politically the nation was divided into comitats. The germ of this division had existed already among the Slavs, who had to make way for the Magyars, and the name, like most of the political terms used in Hungary, was borrowed from the Slav language. The name zhupan became in the Magyar ispan, a word which plays so prominent a part in the history of the nation. Each comitat possessed a camp (*var*), and these camps formed together a complete system of defense. The comitat was governed by a count (ispan), who exercised civil and military authority in the name of the king; he was aided by a general, *major exercitus,* by a castellan, or governor, and by centurions and decurions.

When Stephen began to reign property was of two kinds, the property of the state and the property of the tribe. Stephen maintained the property of the state, but put an end to all tribal rights; he declared that each citizen had the right to keep and to bequeath to his children the possessions he had acquired, or which he had received from the king. But we must not look upon these royal gifts as hereditary fiefs. The aristocracy was formed of those who held high offices, and was divided into two classes. The first included the counts, bishops, the leaders of the army, and perhaps the descendants of the chiefs of the old Magyar tribes. The second was composed more especially of warriors. After these two classes came the soldiers of the fortified towns and the citizens. Quite early we find a large number of Germans among the inhabitants of certain towns; they were known by the name of hospites. The towns exercised municipal self-government under the control

of the ispan and the bishop. The mass of the peopl? did not possess land. The artisans were the connecting link between the nobles
and the serfs. Stephen did not suppress slavery, but he improved
the condition of the slaves.

The king was supreme judge, and under some circumstances
he administered justice in person. Bishops and abbots, civil and
military dignitaries, could only be summoned to appear in the
king's court, presided over either by the sovereign himself or by
the count palatine. This court acted also as a court of appeal
against all judgments delivered by the counts of towns, bishoprics,
or abbeys. Oral witness was admitted, as well as trial by single
combat. The penal code was very severe. The right of sanctuary was refused to all who conspired against the king or country,
and he who sowed discord among the people was condemned to
lose his tongue. A false witness had his arm cut off; murderers
had to pay a heavy fine; at the same time the murderer of a slave
was only obliged to pay the value of the slave to his master. The
murder of a wife was punished according to the rank of the murderer; a count paid to the family of his wife fifty young oxen, a warrior only ten. Human life was tolerably cheap. The loss of a
limb cost more; it could only be atoned for by the loss of the same
limb, thus putting in practice the old Bible precept, "an eye for
an eye, a tooth for a tooth." Rape was punished by the payment
of ten or five oxen, according to the rank of the criminal. The
thief who could not restore the value of the thing stolen was sold as
a slave. Thus did this imperfect legislation combine Mosaic principles with the customs of barbarians.

The revenue of the king was made up of the contributions of
the artisans and the lower classes, the taxes on towns, the produce of mines and salt works, a monopoly of the coinage, and
some portion of all fines. Besides this, subjects were bound to
maintain the royal household as the king traveled from place to
place. Every man had to serve as a soldier; the warriors of the
nation were summoned by a bloody sword sent from comitat to
comitat; and the castles were the meeting-places of the nobles. The
laws of Stephen are contained in fifty-six articles, divided into
two books. His ideas on all matters of government are also to be
found in the counsels which he wrote, or caused to be written,
for his son Emerich, and which have more than one claim to our
interest.

Chapter VI

HUNGARY UNDER THE SUCCESSORS OF
ST. STEPHEN. 1038-1301

THE son for whom the great king had written his maxims died before his father, in 1031, and is honored as a saint by the church. The last years of King Stephen were harassed by rivalries and plots. He died in 1038, thirty-eight years after his coronation to the very day, and was buried at Stuhl-weissenburg. Stephen had chosen as his successor his nephew, Peter, the son of the Doge Urseolus. This prince, a stranger in Hungary, made himself unpopular by his insolence and by the brutal way in which he behaved toward the widow of his predecessor; the Hungarians rose against him, and elected in his stead Samuel Ala, the chief of one of the tribes. Peter thereupon fled to Germany, and implored help from Henry III., promising to pay tribute to that prince if he would replace him on his throne. The German diet declared war against Hungary; the imperial army penetrated as far as Gran, and Samuel Ala was obliged to purchase peace on humiliating conditions. More fortunate in a second campaign, he repulsed the Germans, but his tyranny, which proved as great as that of Peter, provoked a fresh insurrection. Peter again sought his old allies, and on the occasion of a solemn festival he did homage to the emperor for the kingdom of Hungary and received investiture of it. This act of humiliation, however, was of no avail; a popular assembly at Csanad pronounced him dethroned, and, in 1046, proclaimed in his stead Andrew, son of Vladislav the Bald.

The beginning of Andrew's reign was marked by a violent reaction among the pagans against Christians and foreigners, but Andrew succeeded in maintaining his position, had himself consecrated, and was able at last to forbid, on pain of death, all exercise of the rites of paganism. He was attacked by the emperor, but with the help of his brother Bela successfully resisted him, and concluded an honorable peace. Soon afterward, however, in 1061, he was dethroned by Bela, and died fighting on the banks of the Theiss. Bela also had to suppress a new rising of the pagans against Christianity. He endeavored, by wise economic measures, to remedy the disastrous condition into which Hungary had fallen as the result of these perpetual struggles, but he died from an accident in 1063. According to an Asiatic custom which still prevails in Turkey, he was succeeded by his nephew Koloman. This prince was only twelve years of age, and the emperor, Henry IV., tried to take advantage of his youth. He was reproached for this, and Pope Gregory VII., who was then struggling against the emperor, encouraged the opposition. " The kingdom of Hungary," he said, " owes obedience to none but the church."

Ladislas the Holy succeeded in 1077, and made himself equally independent of emperor and Pope. He withstood successfully all Koloman's attempts to recover the crown which had been torn from him, and managed to keep on good terms with the court of Rome, which consented to canonize both King Stephen and his son Emerich. He was not less fortunate in his struggles against the Cumans and Petcheneguens, who continued to invade Hungary. He overcame them on the banks of the Temes, and then offered them a permanent settlement in the country on condition that they become Christians. They accepted his offer, and colonized a portion of the valley of the Theiss, being bound, in return for the land they received, to furnish bowmen to the royal army. On the death, moreover, of the Croat king, Stephen II., in 1090, Ladislas obliged that country to accept as their new king the Magyar prince Almos, son of Geiza I., and thus prepared the way for the union of the two crowns which was soon after to be effected.

Like St. Stephen, Ladislas was the law-giver of his country. In a great assembly of prelates, nobles, and citizens, held at Szabolcz in 1092, he promulgated laws of which the most important treat of religious matters. They authorize the marriage of priests, notwithstanding the decisions of Gregory VII. on ecclesiastical celibacy, and they carefully regulate the collection of tithes. They contain penal measures against the last adherents of paganism; anyone who offers sacrifices near a tree or spring is condemned to forfeit an ox; the Jew who works on Sunday, the Mussulman convert who returns to Mohammedanism, are both to be punished. Other laws of St. Ladislas concern the administration of justice, enact penalties for theft, and regulate the protection of property. They are extremely severe; the theft of a goose is punished by the loss of an eye, and all acts of violence are suppressed with Draconian rigor. The church has shown her gratitude to the monarch who gave her so many proofs of his attachment and submission by placing him among the number of her saints.

The dying Ladislas chose his nephew Koloman as his successor. This young prince, destined at first for the church, was very learned for those times, and was called by his contemporaries the Scholar. Shortly after his accession the Crusaders marched through Hungary. The excesses committed by these bands of enthusiastic but undisciplined men were but little likely to inspire the Magyars with respect for their cause. Koloman, after having allowed the first portions of the army to march through his lands, was obliged to arm his subjects against the plunderers who were ravaging his country. When Godfrey of Bouillon reached the frontier he demanded an interview with Koloman, in which the latter, in order to secure good order and the peace of the land, fixed the route of the Crusaders and demanded hostages. By these means all the annoyance and disorder which had arisen from the first armies was successfully avoided.

The most important act of this reign was the annexation of Croatia. In 1090 St. Ladislas had been elected to the throne of Croatia, and he, on his death, left the government of it to his nephew Almos, who very soon made himself unpopular. Koloman drove him out of Croatia, and had himself proclaimed king. He next set about the conquest of Dalmatia from the Venetians, seized the principal towns, and granted them full power of self-government. Then, in 1102, he had himself crowned at Belgrade king of Croatia and Dalmatia. From this time the position of Croatia, as regards Hungary, was very much the same as the position of Hungary in regard to Austria in later times. The destinies of the two kingdoms of St. Stephen and Zvonimir were united, but Croatia maintained a more or less definite individuality, and the ban or viceroy of Croatia was the representative of the autonomy of a Slav state associated with a Magyar state, a condition of things which has remained down to the present day. At this time the Croats freely chose as their king one who undertook to respect their laws. They preserved the right of administering their internal affairs, of electing their own bishops and zhupans, and of granting the rights of citizenship to whomsoever they would; they kept their own coinage, army, and taxes. The relations between the two kingdoms are still partly regulated by this old agreement, and the Croats proudly quote this maxim of public law: *regnum regno non præscribit leges.*

Koloman continued the legislative work of Stephen and Ladislas, and improved the penal laws of his predecessor, making them more merciful. He was sufficiently liberal and enlightened to do away with all trial for sorcery, " inasmuch as there are no sorcerers." He increased the number of the law courts, restrained judicial combats, and established a rigorous distinction between ecclesiastical and lay discipline, and no longer allowed the celibacy of the clergy.

The end of Koloman's reign was disturbed by revolts and conspiracies caused by his brother Almos, who had been deprived by him of the government of Croatia. After pardoning him several times, Koloman yielded to the barbarous spirit of the age, and caused the eyes of his brother, and of his little nephew of five years of age, to be put out; but this is the only act of barbarity that history records of this enlightened sovereign, who enlarged the kingdom till its boundary touched the sea, and finally secured its position in civilized Europe. Among the kings who occupied the throne of Hungary during the twelfth century, none can be compared with Koloman and St. Ladislas.

Stephen II., the son of Koloman, succeeded at the age of thirteen, and died in 1131, after an uneventful reign. As his successor he had appointed that son of Almos whom Koloman had blinded, and who reigned under the title of Bela II. the Blind. Bela revenged himself cruelly on all whom he suspected of having caused his misfortunes, and it is related that in one single day at the diet of Arad, in 1132, he ordered sixty-eight of his enemies to be slain. Geiza II., the son of Bela, succeeded him, in 1141, at the age of ten. Comparatively speaking, his reign was a happy one; and it was marked by an event of considerable importance in the internal history of Hungary—the arrival of Saxon colonists in northern Hungary and Transylvania. Faithful to the teaching of St. Stephen, Geiza settled them in the comitat of Zips at the foot of the Carpathians, and in the valley of Maros, on the left bank of the lower Theiss. The Germans were easily able to reclaim the forests which clothed the sides of the Tatra, and founded there four and twenty towns, which had the right of electing their own priests and magistrates according to statutes written in their own language. Their obligations to the king were light: they had to furnish him with a certain number of troops, and to recognize his supreme authority in judicial matters. The Saxons of Transylvania enjoyed complete autonomy. Sole proprietors of the soil, they could prevent the settlement on it of Magyars or Szeklers, and their national assemblies had an exclusive right to make the laws.

The reign of Stephen III., son of Geiza II., was disturbed by the rivalry of his two uncles, and unsuccessful attempts to bring Hungary under the Eastern empire. His brother, Bela III., owing to his Byzantine education, was at first received with distrust, but his ability and moderation gained him the confidence and love of his people. It was he who married Margaret of France, the daughter of Philip Augustus, and compiled a most interesting statement of the revenues of his kingdom.

The reigns of these three princes were signalized by wars against the Russians of Galicia and against Venice. Bela had, however, obliged one part of Galicia to do homage to him, and on this were founded the claims of Hungary to Galicia, claims to which Andrew II. hoped to give color by taking the title of king of Galicia and Lodomeria, and which were revived by Austria at the time of the first partition of Poland.

Meantime the republic of Venice, seeing the rule of Hungary definitely established on the shores of the Adriatic, took alarm at so formidable a neighbor. The Doge Falieri asked for the alliance and help of Constantinople, whose power was also threatened by the growth of Hungary. In the war which followed the town of Belgrade, where Koloman had had himself crowned, was entirely destroyed, and Zara, on the Adriatic, left in possession of the Venetians. The rest of Dalmatia remained in the hands of Bela III.; he treated the province well, and confided its defense to the family of the Frangipani, henceforward well known in history.

The relations of Hungary with the two empires of the East and West spread the renown of her power through the whole of Europe. In 1147 King Louis VII. and the Emperor Conrad crossed Hungary on their crusade, and Louis VII. speaks highly in his letters to Suger of the warm welcome which he received, though the German chronicler, Otto of Freising, draws a picture of the country which is not very flattering, and represents the Magyars as little more than well-disciplined savages: " One might well reproach fortune, or stand amazed at the long-suffering of God, when one sees so fair a country in the possession of such monsters." The connection with France was strengthened by the marriage of Bela with the Princess Margaret. Hungarian students began to find their way to Paris. When Frederick Barbarossa crossed the country at the head of the third Crusade, in 1189, he was received with great magnificence, fêtes were held in his honor, and Constance, the daughter of Bela, was affianced to the duke of Suabia. The relations of Hungary with Byzantium were less friendly. On several occasions Constantinople endeavored to bring the country under her control; but with the help of Vladislav, king of Bohemia, the Hungarians were able to maintain their independence.

The period following the death of Bela III. is marked by the rivalry between his two sons, Emerich, who ruled from 1196 to 1204, and Andrew, king from 1205 to 1235. The latter became very unpopular because of the infamous favorites brought to the court by his wife, Gertrude of Meran. Indignant at the scandalous life of the court, the people rose against the queen and slew her while her husband was absent in Galicia, which he was vainly trying to bring under his scepter. He soon married again, and in 1217 set out on a Crusade, from which he returned because of ill-health, without having reached the Holy Lands.

On his return he found Hungary in the greatest disorder. The royal authority had been much diminished since the days of Koloman, a feudal oligarchy had grown up, and the clergy had possessed themselves of secular estates. The hereditary right of the family of Arpad to the crown was still contested, nor was the law of primogeniture accepted within the family itself. We have already seen formidable rivals disputing the throne in several of the reigns. The support of the great territorial lords, lay and ecclesiastical, had become of great importance to the sovereign, and to obtain it he had gradually deprived himself of his domains to divide them among a powerful and greedy minority of his subjects. The smaller landholders were neglected, and diets met less frequently. The great dignitaries of the church, enriched by the royal bounty, had become a state within the state and relied upon the Pope to resist the royal commands. The Holy See, faithful to the traditions of Gregory VII., endeavored to exercise within the kingdom an authority equal, if not superior, to that of the king. The state of

the whole kingdom called for prompt remedies; but far from daring
to carry out energetic measures, Andrew yielded continually to the
current which had swept before it each one of his predecessors, and,
in 1219, he issued an edict making all gifts and honors granted by
previous kings irrevocable and hereditary. The result of such a
measure would have been to create a complete oligarchy, on which
thenceforth both king and populace would have been dependent.

But the edict gave rise to much discontent. A diet was summoned in 1222, and a law enacted known as the Golden Bull—the
Magna Charta of Hungary. In it Andrew II., calling himself
hereditary king of Hungary, Dalmatia, Croatia, Servia, Galicia,
and Lodomeria, solemnly enumerates the privileges of the people,
or rather of the small landowners. He promised to hold a solemn
diet each year in the town of Stuhlweissenburg; to imprison no
noble until he had been regularly tried and sentenced; to raise no
tax on the lands of either noble or priest; to summon no noble to
accompany the king, at his own expense, beyond the frontiers of
the kingdom; to allow no suit which involved the loss of life or
property to be tried by the palatine without the knowledge of the
king; to indemnify the families of those nobles who lost any relations
in the wars; to admit no guests or colonists on the soil of Hungary
to any dignity whatsoever without the consent of the diet; no
longer to make hereditary the grants of comitats or offices; to
allow tithes to be paid in kind and not in money; and to grant land
to no foreigner. The Golden Bull contained thirty-one articles,
of which these are the chief, while the last ordained that seven
copies should be made of it, and sent to the king, to the Pope, to the
Knights Hospitalers, to the Temple, to the chapter house at Gran,
to the chapter house at Kalosca, and to the palatine, who was to see
that the charter was observed by the kings and the nobles. If the
king should attempt to violate it, " the bishops and nobles of the
kingdom have the right to remonstrate, and to resist the sovereign,
sine nota alicujus infidelitatis," i. e., without by so doing laying
themselves open to the charge of high treason. This last article
was to play an important part in the history of Hungary, for to it
are due many of those rebellions which give so revolutionary a
character to the history of a country otherwise so conservative.

The constitution of Andrew II. is far from fulfilling the ideal
of modern times. It was, nevertheless, a great advantage then and
maintained the unity of Hungary by preventing hereditary succes-

sion to office and the consequent division of the country into a number of principalities. It secured to the nation—that is to say to the nobles—the right of criticising the administration, and it obliged the king to respect the national rights by placing all his actions under the control of the palatine, who thus became a sort of prime minister.

Soon after the promulgation of the Golden Bull a special charter was granted to the Saxons of Transylvania, securing their privileges. Their political and religious autonomy was confirmed; they were to be subject to no authority except a court chosen by the king. In return they were to furnish him with five hundred armed men in case of a defensive war, and one hundred for foreign expeditions. The Golden Bull was again solemnly confirmed in 1231, when some new clauses were added to it, which enacted that the bishops were to be present at the yearly diet at Stuhlweissenburg; that if the palatine ruled badly, the states were to choose one more worthy; and also that no Jew or Mussulman was to receive government employment.

The reign of Andrew II. has become memorable in the history of Hungary owing to the Golden Bull; apart from that it was not fortunate. Like King John of England, his name is associated with a legislative document of the highest importance, but, like him, he has left behind a reputation for feebleness and want of character. His son, Bela IV., began his reign in 1235, under the best auspices. He withstood his enemies both from within and without, among them the Emperor Frederick II., who had put forward a claim to tribute from Hungary. Unfortunately he soon had to deal with a more pitiless enemy than the Germans. The Tatar Khan, the Mongol Batou, followed by a formidable army, forced his way through the defiles of the Carpathians and invaded the valley of the Theiss.

The Mongols belonged to the same race as the Magyars, but the Magyars had become Christian and European. These pagan Mongols attacked Europe with a fanaticism which can be compared only with that of the Saracens; but while the Mussulmans founded new states, and had in fact attained to a high degree of civilization, the Mongols were nothing but destroyers.

The alarm of their approach was great throughout the land. The bloody sword was sent from town to town, from castle to castle. The Cumans, who formed the vanguard of national resistance, were unable to withstand their onslaught, and Waizen fell. In the general terror the Cumans were accused of treason, and their chief and the leading men among them were put to death, which so angered the tribe that they passed over to the side of the Mongols. The royal army came up with the forces of Batou on the banks of the Sajo, a tributary of the Theiss, and there suffered a terrible defeat, in which, according to some historians, a hundred thousand, according to others sixty thousand, men perished. *" Fere extinguitur militia regni Hungariæ,"* writes the emperor Frederick. Hungary as far as the Danube was at the mercy of the barbarians; Pesth was taken; Varad yielded after a heroic resistance; Csanad was destroyed. The Mongols pushed forward as far as Croatia, where the Croats put a stop to their further progress by the victory of Grobnik in 1241. After many adventures, Bela found refuge in Austria, where Duke Frederick, to whose care he had confided his family and treasures, took shameful advantage of his misfortunes. In exchange for the hospitality which he granted, he obliged Bela to give up to him the three Hungarian comitats which lay nearest to the Austrian states. At last Christendom was aroused. King Vacslav of Bohemia called upon the princes to come to the aid of Hungary, and the Pope ordered a crusade to be preached. With the usual disinterestedness of German sovereigns, the emperor offered to save Hungary on condition that he should receive her homage. Meantime, winter came on, and the frozen rivers became the allies of the invaders. The Mongols crossed the Danube and took Gran. Bela fled to Dalmatia, closely followed by the barbarians; but they did not succeed in seizing him, and the Slavs of Dalmatia and the Italian colonists finally repulsed them in furious conflicts. Beaten back, they next penetrated as far as Ragusa, and would have gone still farther had they not received orders to retrace their steps. The Asiatic hordes returned to Asia, the most horrible cruelty marking the last days of their ephemeral conquest.

Slowly Hungary recovered from the ruin they had caused; colonists from Germany filled up the gaps in the population, and towns were rebuilt, surrounded by stronger fortifications, and adorned with finer buildings. But from this time forward Hungary had an enemey even more formidable in the house of Austria. We have already seen how the unknightly Frederick had taken advantage of the misery of Hungary to get possession of three of her comitats. As soon as he was free from the Mongols Bela set to work to reconquer them. He marched against Frederick and defeated him on the banks of the Leitha, in 1246, Frederick perishing in the fight. With this prince the house of Babenberg came to an end. Bohemia and Hungary both laid claim to the inheritance, and though Bela was unable to prevent the king of Bohemia from gaining possession of Austria, he succeeded in establishing his own son Stephen in Styria. War broke out between the two kingdoms, and ended in favor of Bohemia. But Premysl Otokar II. proved a generous foe; he would not, according to his own expression, "enfeeble the great kingdom of Hungary, only to open again the road to the two kingdoms to the Tatars." Later on he married the daughter of the king of Hungary.

But there was soon to appear upon the scene a third combatant, who knew how to turn to his own advantage the rivalry of the two kingdoms; this was Rudolf of Hapsburg. Rudolf drew Ladislas IV. into an alliance, and at the battle of Marchfield, where Premysl Otokar fell, 56,000 Hungarians and Cumans fought by the side of Austria. Thus Hungary, while she ruined Bohemia, founded the power of Austria, which was so soon to be turned against herself. In his letters written at this time Rudolf shows the greatest tenderness for the Hungarians: "My beloved sons, bone of my bone, and flesh of my flesh"; a dozen years later, as emperor, he claimed the right to dispose of the crown of Hungary as its suzerain.

The last years of King Bela IV. had been disturbed by the revolts of his son Stephen. In fact this prince was the real king, and it was to him that the envoys of the duke of Anjou applied when they came to negotiate the marriages which were to secure Hungary to the Angevin house. His young son, Ladislas, succeeded him in 1272, a foolish and dissipated prince, who earned the hatred of his people by his avowed partiality for the Cumans. This wandering and half-pagan race were still looked upon as almost foreigners by the rest of the nation. Ladislas determined to convert them to Christianity and to a settled mode of life, and assigned to them that district between the Danube and the Theiss which is called to this day Greater and Lesser Cumania. Ladislas, who betrayed a partiality for their women that was unworthy of his position, was assassinated by the Cumans in 1290. He left no son, but he had adopted the grandson of Andrew II., and this prince was crowned under the name of Andrew III. Andrew energetically resisted the claims of the Hapsburgs and of the Holy See, repulsed the invasion of Albert of Austria, and laid siege to Vienna. The court of Rome, which was favorable to the Neapolitan princes of the house of Anjou, would never recognize Andrew III., and during his reign Charles Robert of Anjou forced his way into Croatia, and had himself crowned at Agram by the Papal legate. The death of Andrew, in 1301, put an end to these rivalries. He was the last prince of the house of Arpad.

Hungary is still grateful to these monarchs of the transition period who laid down the lines along which the Magyar race was to develop. On various occasions they had tried to extend their rule over the neighboring countries, but the titles of king of Servia, of Bosnia, of Galicia and Lodomeria, and of Bulgaria, had never represented any real authority, and at most recall a momentary occupation or an ephemeral protection. The only important acquisition of the dynasty of Arpad was the annexation of Croatia, which gave Hungary a seaboard. We have already described how Croatia preserved her autonomy. Transylvania also, at the other extremity of the kingdom, had her own peculiar constitution. The Transylvanian diet was divided into three nations, the Hungarians, the Szeklers, and the Saxons. The old inhabitants of the country, the Wallachians, who had been conquered by the Magyars or by the Saxon colonists, were only peasants and counted for nothing. The Szeklers, who were all freemen and noble, formed a special body of horsemen to whom was intrusted the defense of the frontier, and in return for this service they were exempted from taxation.

We have seen how the constitution of Andrew II. had placed obstacles in the way of the increase of power among the oligarchical aristocracy and territorial lords, and had aimed at preventing the partition of the kingdom. The lesser nobles were always on the watch to maintain their own privileges and to prevent encroachments on the part of the great lords. About this time we first see a distinction growing up between magnates and simple deputies. The assemblies of the comitats became periodical, and formed the best guarantee of public liberty. The citizen class was without political influence, and was largely composed of foreigners, Jews, Germans, and Italians. Considerable privileges were accorded to the Jews, who were so ill-treated in other parts of Europe. During this period also vines began to be cultivated and wine of good quality produced.

The Hungarian nobles gradually imitated the nobles of the rest of Europe, introducing into the country knightly manners and usages. They began to take an hereditary name from their estates, and to use coats-of-arms, and trials by combat became the fashion.

Those arts which are the most delicate expression of civilization had made much less progress in Hungary than elsewhere. The Gothic style of architecture, however, penetrated into the country, and French architects were employed at this time. A Frenchman, Villard de Hannecourt, built the Gothic church at Kassa, and Mathias of Arras the cathedral at Prague. The clergy distinguished themselves rather by their courage in battle or their ardor in fighting heresy than by their learning. In 1279 the synod of Buda, alarmed doubtless at the progress of the Patarine heresy, placed a limit on the knowledge which monks were to be allowed to acquire, and forbade them to study in foreign schools. The most important school in the kingdom was the *studium generale* at Veszprim, which conferred no degrees, but which endowed scholarships at the University of Paris for its best students. Latin was universally known and studied among the upper classes, but at the same time books were so rare that a complete copy of the Bible cost half of a village. The Magyar tongue tended to give way before Latin, which was the medium of the church and of the government; it was, however, still used, though very few fragments have come down to us from these primitive times: only a funeral oration and a legend of St. Margaret.

Chapter VII

BOHEMIA AND THE PREMYSLIDES
894-1278

BORIVOJ was the first Christian prince of Bohemia. He built the first Bohemian church, and dedicated it to St. Clement. His son Spytihnev (894-912) put an end to the connection of Bohemia with Moravia, and went to Regensburg to ask for the protection of Germany, in the vain belief that by so doing he made the independence of his kingdom more secure. Bohemia was attached to the bishopric of Ratisbon, and the Latin liturgy replaced the Slav liturgy, of which but few traces now remain in the country.

At this period Bohemia was far from being a united kingdom. It consisted of a number of small states, with the principality of Prague as the chief, which were often at war with one another. These dissensions proved most favorable to the ambition of Germany. In 928 Henry the Fowler, in alliance with Arnulf of Bavaria, entered Bohemia and obliged St. Vacslav, the prince, to pay him an annual tribute of 500 pieces of gold and 120 oxen. It was St. Vacslav who founded the cathedral of St. Vit, at Prague, and legends have surrounded his name with a halo of tender memories. Like Robert the Pious and St. Louis, he has become the typical example of a devout and charitable prince. During his life, as well as after his death, he was believed to work miracles. When engaged in single combat against a prince of the Czechs an angel from heaven bore him company and terrified his adversary by the wondrous sight. When they took his body from Boleslava to Prague the car which bore it crossed by itself a river over which there was no bridge. On arriving before the court of justice it stopped suddenly and could not be moved; it was discovered that an innocent man was unjustly imprisoned in the building, and as soon as he was set at liberty the car went on. The name of Vacslav, under its Latin form of Venceslas, or the German form Wenzel, became popular throughout Europe, and Bohemians still sing the old canticle of the Middle Ages: *"Svaty Vacslave, vevodo české zemé."* "St. Vacslav, voïévode of the land of the Czechs, our prince! pray for us to God and the Holy Spirit, kyrie eleison." His portrait long adorned the standards and the coins of Bohemia.

His brother and successor, Boleslav, who, it is said, assassinated him for patriotic reasons, tried to rid Bohemia of the suzerainty of the German emperor, but as a result of defeat in a war lasting from 936 to 950 he was obliged to submit to the Emperor Otto and pay the tribute. Afterward he became the firm ally of Otto, and sent a thousand Czechs to help him against the Magyars. He himself took possession of part of Moravia and the land of the Slovaks, while his conquests on the banks of the Vistula brought him into close neighborhood to the Poles. His daughter, Dubravka, married the Polish prince, Mieczyslaw, and converted him to Christianity, thus bringing Poland into the bosom of the church in 966.

Boleslav II. (967-999) continued his father's conquests toward the east, and took possession of Galicia, but that province was recovered later on by the Russian prince, Vladimir the Great in 981. At this period the power of Bohemia was considerable, and Boleslav was able to interfere as arbiter in the conflicts which took place between the German margraves and the duke of Poland. He obtained permission from the emperor and the bishop of Ratisbon to found a see at Prague, subject to the archbishop of Mainz; the bishop to be chosen by the prince and the people, but to receive investiture from the emperor. The first bishop was a Saxon priest called Thietmar, and his successor was the celebrated Czech saint, Vojtech, better known under the name of St. Adalbert, one of the great figures in the religious history of the Middle Ages.

After having organized the church of Bohemia, St. Adalbert was invited into Hungary by Geiza I., whose son, the future king St. Stephen, he baptized. Later on he gave up his bishopric, and after being for a time the confessor of Otto III., he traveled into Poland, whose king, Boleslav the Brave, sent him to convert the heathen on the shores of the Baltic. In these distant lands he was murdered by the Prussians in 997. Boleslav the Brave caused him to be buried in the church at Gnesen, whither, three years later, the Emperor Otto came to worship at his grave. The Poles ascribe to him the first of their religious songs, the most ancient monument of their language, the hymn to the Virgin beginning *"Boga rodzica."* Prince Boleslav II. successfully defended his country against the attacks of the Germans and Poles, notwithstanding the fact that Bohemia was distracted in his reign by civil wars. In his time monasteries were first founded, schools arose around the churches, and Latin civilization spread more and more throughout the land.

Under the successors of Boleslav II. Bohemia fell into a state of deplorable anarchy, and became alternately the tool of Germany and Poland. A powerful sovereign, Boleslav the Brave, reigned at this time in Poland, and he obliged Bohemia to accept as her ruler a Polish prince named Vladivoj, who, however, afterward recognized the suzerainty of the empire and acknowledged himself its vassal. Boleslav the Brave tried to conquer Bohemia for himself, but he did not succeed, Bretislav (1037-1055) finally establishing the independence of Bohemia and introducing an era of renewed vigor. He also took advantage of the fact that Poland had been left without a ruler. After the death of Boleslav the Brave he conquered Silesia and Lesser Poland, and took Cracow by assault. He next entered Greater Poland and pushed on to Gnesen, took possession of the remains of the national apostle, St. Adalbert, and bore them off to Prague. But he was ordered by the emperor to give up his conquests, and of all the territory he had seized he retained only a part of Silesia with the episcopal see of Vratislav, or Breslau.

Bretislav had five sons, and, fearful of the disputes which might arise among them, he ordained that henceforward succession to the throne should be determined by primogeniture, while younger sons were to receive dependent appanages, a settlement known as the seniorate. This wise arrangement was, however, but little respected. His successor, Spytihnev II., maintained his place with difficulty till his death, in 1061, when he was succeeded by Vratislav II., who became the first king of Bohemia (1061-1092). He divided Moravia between his two brothers, giving to the one Olmütz, and to the other Brünn. He also founded a bishopric at Olmütz. The beginning of his reign was marked by an incident which reveals the hostility of the Czechs to the German favorites who held high civil and ecclesiastical offices, and through princely marriages and the ecclesiastical organization drew Bohemia closer to Germany. When in 1069 Vratislav wished to nominate as bishop of Prague a German named Lanzon, the nobles and military chiefs who were assembled round his camp near Nachod demanded the bishopric for the Prince Jaromir, who, in the end, succeeded in obtaining it, though, according to custom, he was obliged to go to Mainz to receive investiture from the archbishop.

Vratislav lent the aid of his troops to the Emperor Henry IV. in his struggles against the Saxons, and in return for this he obtained possession of Lusatia, a Slav district, which was thus united to Bohemia. Later on he again helped the emperor in his expeditions against Italy, three hundred Czech warriors taking part in the siege of Rome, and as a reward for this service the emperor granted him the title of king in 1086. He also gave up the tribute hitherto paid to the empire by Bohemia in exchange for a loan of four thousand marks of silver. Henceforward Bohemia was only bound to furnish to the emperor three hundred armed knights, well equipped, for expeditions into Italy. On June 15, 1086, Vratislav and his wife Svatova were solemnly crowned at Prague, in the cathedral of St. Vit, by the Archbishop Egilbert. Thus was constituted that kingdom of Bohemia which, with the kingdom of Hungary, was one day to form a principal part of the Austrian empire. In order to understand the struggles of modern politics it is needful to recall the double origin of the two kingdoms, the one founded by the Holy See, the other by the empire. Hence arose those retrospective claims on Bohemia which Germany has since put forward. The title of king bestowed on Vratislav was, however, purely personal, and was not transmitted to his successors.

The reigns of the immediate successors of Vratislav offer but few points of interest. Bretislav II. (1092-1111) abolished the wise law which had established primogeniture in the family of the Premyslides. He even asked the Emperor Henry IV. to grant the investiture to his brother Borivoi, and by so doing recognized the imperial right to treat Bohemia as a fief of the empire, threw her provinces into their old state of anarchy, and strengthened the claims which Germany was continually advancing over Bohemia. Hence arose a long series of conflicts between the princes of Prague, Olmütz, and Brünn, conflicts in which the empire took occasion more than once to interfere, selling its protection to one or the other of the combatants. Indeed, during this period Germany, Bohemia, Moravia, and Poland were perpetually at war with one another, and the emperor claimed the right to dispose of Bohemia as a fief. More than once these pretensions met with energetic resistance. Thus Prince Sobeslav I. did not hesitate to declare war against

Lothair, who had claimed the right of giving Bohemia to whom he pleased, and had bestowed it on Prince Otto of Olmütz. Sobeslav refused to appear before the tribunal before which he was cited by the emperor, and replied in these proud words: "My hope is in the mercy of God and in the help of St. Vacslav and St. Vojtech, who will not see this country delivered into the hands of foreigners." The Bohemians rallied round the standard of St. Vacslav, and the emperor, vanquished at Chlumec, was obliged to renounce his claims and to recognize Sobeslav as prince of Bohemia in 1126. He even conferred on him the title of high cupbearer of the empire.

During the reign of Sobeslav, in consequence of the increase in the number of the various branches of the Premyslide family, Bohemia and Moravia were broken up into a large number of appanages, which led to internal conflicts and revolts that had to be suppressed by the prince by force of arms. He endeavored to secure the crown for his son, and to this end had him elected by the diet of Sadsko. But immediately after his death the zhupans offered the throne to his nephew, Vladislav II. (1140-1173), whom they believed they could direct as they wished. Vladislav II. did not fulfill their hopes, and the Moravian princes and the great nobles entered into an alliance against him, raised an army, and obliged him to ask for help from the emperor. He defeated them, forced them to retreat to Moravia, and took from them the principalities of Znaim, Brünn, and Olmütz.

During his reign a Papal legate, Cardinal Guido, was sent to Bohemia to supervise the organization of the Catholic Church; celibacy was imposed upon the clergy, and the legate reconciled Vladislav with the Moravian princes, obtaining for them the restitution of their estates. Vladislav was the first Czech prince who went on the Crusades. He left the government in the hands of his brother Diepolt, in 1147, and with many Czechs followed the Emperor Conrad to Jerusalem. After his return he was soon at war with Frederick Barbarossa. Frederick had seized Silesia, which was a Bohemian fief, and in consequence of this act the prince of Bohemia refused the three hundred armed men for the expedition against Rome that Bohemia was bound by old treaties to furnish. In 1156 Silesia was restored to Bohemia, and finally Frederick granted Vladislav the title of king for himself and his successors. In return the new king, with a large force, joined the emperor in the expedition he was about to undertake against Milan. He was obliged, however, to raise the troops at his own expense, as the diet refused to admit his right to levy an army for so distant and useless an expedition.

Later on Vladislav went to the aid of the king of Hungary, Stephen III., whose two daughters his sons had married. Again the diet refused to grant him an army, but he set out with volunteers and fought with some success against the Eastern emperor. These victories, which spread his fame abroad in foreign lands, did not, however, prevent the revolt of the princes at home, and the Emperor Frederick, with but little gratitude for old services, favored their attempts. In 1173 Vladislav, weary of power, abdicated and retired to a convent. Several rivals contended for supreme power, and all were cited to appear before the tribunal of Barbarossa at Nuremberg. The emperor claimed the right of deciding the succession and, at the same time, suppressed the title of king which he had previously granted to Vladislav. Again Bohemia fell into anarchy. The emperor interfered continually in its affairs, and inglorious struggles mark the period. Only on the accession of Premysl Otokar I., in 1197, did the country again breathe freely.

This time of anarchy proved fatal to Bohemia. The quarrels among the princes increased the power of the nobles, who believed they had the right to decide the election to the throne, while they also made the interference of the empire in the internal affairs of the nation increasingly easy. The great lords oppressed the people and exacted from them heavy taxes and enforced labor. To escape from these exactions the small proprietors found themselves obliged to seek the protection of the more powerful lords, and this enabled the nobles to form bodies of vassals dependent on themselves. Magnates who had supported the prince at the time of his election claimed a right to be repaid for such support by gifts of land. In this way an hereditary nobility was gradually created, whose power no longer depended on the office they held in the household or army of the prince, but on the possession of large estates. The owners of these large estates claimed all the rights of sovereigns, the administration of justice, the levying of troops, and the power of leading them to battle under standards of their own. This hereditary great nobility begins to take form toward the end of the twelfth century. It was naturally much more independent of the

prince than an aristocracy of officials, and its assemblies were real
diets in which the acts of the prince were discussed and controlled.
As early as the twelfth century it was a generally established,
though unwritten, principle that the prince had no right, except in
the case of invasion, to summon the national army without the consent of the diet; and that laws could only be passed with its help. It
was only under extraordinary circumstances that the king might
levy taxes, as he possessed large estates which amply sufficed for his
own requirements. As was the case throughout Europe, the church
had acquired considerable influence. Papal legates frequently visited the country. There were six cathedral chapters in Bohemia
and nine Benedictine monasteries, besides many convents. Almost
all the peasants were serfs of the soil, some privileges and a certain
amount of freedom being granted, however, to those who had
cleared the ground of forests. There was but little commerce,
and what there was had fallen mainly into the hands of Jews and
foreigners, especially Germans. Ever since the time of Vratislav
there had been a German colony in Prague, and this colony, with a
special court of its own, obtained many of the more important positions in the state and the church, owing to the close relations with
the empire, the Czech princes usually marrying German princesses,
who used their influence in favor of their countrymen. We often
find the heir to the throne bearing two names, one Slav, the other
German, as for example Vladislav-Heinrich, and the policy of such
monarchs, who were half Slav and half German, was as a rule
dynastic rather than national.

On the death of the Emperor Henry IV., in 1197, Philip of
Suabia was elected emperor, but his rights were disputed by Otto
of Brunswick. Premysl took the side of Philip, and obtained important advantages for his country in exchange for his services.
The emperor agreed to interfere no more in the internal affairs of
Bohemia, but simply to confirm her own choice of a prince; he
restored the royal title, and renounced all right to the investiture
of the bishop of Prague. Premysl had himself solemnly crowned,
and, in 1204, Innocent III., by a special bull, confirmed the royal
title granted to the princes of Bohemia.

The friendship of the emperor and the new king lasted but
a short time. It was soon disturbed by a war which ended in a
treaty, followed by the betrothal of the emperor's daughter, Cunegunda, to the heir of the king of Bohemia. Later on Premysl lent

his aid to Frederick II., to insure his election to the empire, and again obtained payment for his services by important concessions from the emperor. The kings of Bohemia were no longer to be obliged to furnish three hundred men for expeditions to Rome, this tribute being replaced by the payment of three hundred marks in gold; they were no longer to be required to attend the diets of the empire, unless they were held in towns near their frontiers, such as Bamburg, Nuremberg, or Merseburg. Besides this Frederick gave Premysl several towns in Meissen, and when Premysl caused his son Vacslav to be elected and proclaimed by the national diet, this election was immediately recognized by the emperor. The succession to the throne by the law of primogeniture in the direct line thus became finally the law of the kingdom. Premysl more than once used his power with an energy which had never been shown by any of his predecessors; on the death of Vladislav, margrave of Moravia, he assigned that province as an appanage to his two younger sons, and in his own lifetime he had his son Vacslav crowned king of Bohemia. At this coronation was omitted for the first time the ceremony of showing to the new prince the sandals and wallet of the laborer Premysl, the founder of the dynasty; no doubt the Bohemians were ashamed of this old national custom, and did not care to make use of it before the foreign princes. But the populace saw in this omission an irritating sign of the increasing ascendency of the foreigner in their land. The number of Germans in the capital was growing rapidly, while in the provinces they had colonized certain towns, and had even begun to found whole villages on the northwest frontier of Bohemia.

Vacslav, called the One-eyed, peacefully succeeded his father in 1230. His education had been entirely German, and his reign proved a golden age for the Germans. They obtained leave to fortify the towns they dwelt in, and at this time the native nobility began to build for themselves strong castles, to which they usually gave German names, such as Steinberg and Lichtenburg. The knightly orders, such as the Hospitalers and Templars, also established " commanderies " in the country, while the Dominicans and Begging Friars multiplied greatly. Luxury increased, and knightly habits and customs became the fashion. King Vacslav was one of the most brilliant sovereigns in Europe; he invited minnesingers to his court, and himself composed love songs after the fashion of the day.

His reign, however, was not peaceful. The growing enmity of the house of the Premyslides and the house of Austria led to continual wars between them, in which Bavaria and Hungary took the side of Bohemia. In the end Frederick of Austria was obliged to give up to Vacslav some of his lands to the north of the Danube, and the Austrian Princess Gertrude, the heiress of the duke of Austria, was affianced to Vladislav, the heir-apparent of Bohemia. This marriage prepared the way for the annexation of Austria and Styria to the crown of Bohemia.

A more serious event was the invasion of Moravia by the Tatars, or Mongols. We have already seen how these dreaded hordes rushed in upon Europe. One of them at this time invaded Silesia, and the whole of Christendom took fright. Pope Gregory IX. caused a crusade to be preached against them, but the quarrels then going on between the Holy See and the empire made any united effort impossible, and the threatened lands were obliged to depend upon themselves for their defense. King Vacslav manfully withstood the storm, and assembled under his banner 40,000 foot soldiers and 6000 horsemen. The enemy had already penetrated into Moravia, where they pillaged, ravaged, and burned towns, castles, and monasteries. The inhabitants fled to the woods. The fortified towns of Olmütz and Brünn alone resisted the invaders, who overthrew everything in their course. The Czechs met the Tatars beneath the walls of Olmütz, where they were victorious, and the Tatars, either in consequence of the terror inspired by this defeat, or as the result of that capricious restlessness which has always distinguished Asiatic invaders, suddenly turned aside and threw themselves upon Hungary.

With the removal of the common danger the alliance with the house of Austria came to an end. Frederick even wished to give up the marriage proposed between the Princess Gertrude and Prince Vladislav, and war alone induced him to keep his word. The young prince received Moravia as a marriage gift from his father, a province in the hands of the king since the year 1239; and soon afterward, on the death of Frederick, the last of the Babenbergs, he obtained possession of Austria and Styria. But young Vladislav died the following year, and the emperor hastened to place a lieutenant of his own over these two provinces. Vacslav dared not interfere at that time, as his own throne was menaced by dangerous conspiracies. The greater part of the nobles had been irritated by his amours, his excessive prodigality, and his favorites. The malcontents insisted that Premysl Otokar, the son of Vacslav, should share the government with his father. War broke out between the father and son, and Vacslav put down the insurrection only with assistance from the German princes. Premysl Otokar, however, was invited, in 1251, by the states of Austria, to become their ruler, and in spite of the opposition of Bela, king of Hungary, who disputed the possession of Styria, he was able to retain the larger part of his new territory. Vacslav the One-eyed, who had rendered his son no assistance whatever in these difficult circumstances, died in 1253. It was in the reign of this knightly prince that Bohemia adopted the arms which she bears to this day, a crowned lion with two tails, *argent,* on a field of *gules.*

On his accession to the throne of Bohemia, Premysl Otokar II. was one of the most powerful monarchs of Europe, Bohemia, Moravia, Upper Lusatia, and Upper and Lower Austria being united under his rule. The character of the new king was equal to the character of his high position. He had apparently done wrong in taking up arms against his father, but the conduct of Vacslav and the interests of the kingdom had justified his rebellion. Just, hard-working, and valiant in war, he was both a wise ruler and an able leader. National historians accuse him of having, like his father and his uncle, encouraged foreign manners and customs too much, and consequently of having helped to increase the influence of the Germans in Bohemia. The rhymed chronicle of Dalemil exclaims, " How sad to think that so noble a king should not have remained true to his native tongue! What glory he would have acquired, and what riches! He could have destroyed all his enemies." Premysl Otokar's first care was the royal domain, which had been impoverished and dismembered by the carelessness of his father and by civil war. He obliged all estates held illegally to be given up to him, and built fortresses on his lands, which he placed in the hands of burgraves, whose business it was to maintain order and public security and to check all risings of the nobles. He increased the number of German colonies in Bohemia and Moravia, and created a certain number of royal towns, which paid taxes directly to the king and had the right of self-government, subject only to the royal control.

Owing to these measures the riches both of the kingdom and

of the royal domain increased considerably during the reign of
Premysl Otokar II.; but at the same time the increasing number
of foreigners and the introduction of a new system of law prepared
the way for numerous disputes in the future. No prince had ever
ascended the throne under such favorable circumstances. Frederick
II. had just died in Italy, and the long interregnum in the empire,
during which the electors offered the crown to the highest bidder,
had begun. Otokar was either the relative or the friend of almost
all his more powerful neighbors. In Bavaria alone he had enemies,
who envied him the possession of Upper Austria, while the king of
Hungary, supported by the princes of Cracow and Galicia, was the
only neighbor he needed to fear. Pope Innocent IV. was favorable
to him, and in the beginning of his reign invited him to undertake
a crusade against the pagan Prussians on the shores of the Baltic,
whom the Teutonic knights had not yet been able either to conquer
or convert. Such an enterprise had almost a national interest for
Bohemia, for it was in these distant lands that the great apostle of
the Czechs, St. Vojtech, had been martyred. Under the command
of Premysl Otokar and the margraves of Brandenburg and Meissen, 60,000 men marched northward and crossing the frozen rivers
made their way into the country of the pagans, burned the sacred
trees and the images of their gods, and defeated the Prussians, of
whom a large number were baptized. Otokar founded the city of
Königsberg in the conquered land. Thus, by a strange freak of
fortune, a king of Bohemia founded in a pagan land the town
where in later times the sovereigns of German Prussia were to
be crowned.

These exploits spread the fame of Premysl Otokar throughout
Europe, and in 1256 the archbishop of Cologne came to Prague to
offer him the imperial crown. He refused it, and the electors then
bestowed it on Richard of Cornwall, brother of the king of England, a prince who possessed but little power, and not an inch of
land in Germany. Premysl Otokar, however, was far from taking
no interest in the affairs of the neighboring lands. Soon after this
we find him interfering in favor of the archbishop of Salzburg, his
relative, whom the princes of Bavaria wished to deprive of his see.
This act of interference brought him into conflict with Hungary,
as Styria took advantage of it to free herself from the suzerainty
of Hungary, and Otokar settled one of his lieutenants at Gratz.
The struggle between Bohemia and Hungary began to take for-

midable proportions, for we find Bela IV. and his allies set on foot an army of 140,000 men, a considerable number for those times, while Otokar marched against them, aided by the margraves of Brandenburg and Meissen and the princes of Silesia and Carniola.

The two adversaries met in the plains of Austria, on the two banks of the Morava, or March, near its juncture with the Danube. Neither army dared cross the stream to begin the attack. According to the knightly custom of the time Otokar sent a messenger to the king of Hungary to demand either that he should cross the river or that he should allow the army of the Czechs to cross, in order that the battle should begin in proper form. Bela chose to cross himself, and Otokar withdrew his troops in order to leave him a clear field. The battle took place near the village of Cressennbrünn. The heavy Bohemian cavalry, clad in armor, repulsed the impetuous attack of the Hungarians, the Cumans fled, and Prince Stephen, heir-presumptive to the crown of Hungary, was seriously wounded. Soon the rout of the Hungarians became general; 18,000 men were slain, and it is said that 14,000 were drowned in the Morava. The Czechs pursued the enemy as far as Presburg. Bela sued for peace, abandoning all claims on Styria, and shortly after Richard of Cornwall granted the investiture of this Austrian province to Premysl Otokar.

This success increased the fame of Otokar. The Tatars named him the Iron King, because of the heavily armed knights whom he led to war; the Christian princes called him the Golden King, because of the magnificence of his court. But this mighty monarch had no heir. He therefore obtained permission from the Pope to divorce his wife, Margaret of Austria, widow of the last of the Babenbergs, whom he had married for ambition, and sought the hand of the Princess Cunegunda, daughter of the Russian prince, Michael Vsevolodovitch, who had taken refuge in Hungary at the time of the Tatar invasion. She was the granddaughter of Bela, and this marriage strengthened the alliance which had been concluded between the two kingdoms. It was celebrated with great pomp on the plain of Morava, which had so lately been the scene of the struggle between their armies.

Soon after this a successful expedition against Bavaria, undertaken on behalf of the archbishop of Salzburg, enabled Bohemia to acquire some new territories, among others, Eger, where Wallenstein was assassinated in later times. Otokar was now more

powerful than any of the German princes, and, finding himself in
a position to dictate to them, he resolved to free his country from
the spiritual suzerainty of the archbishopric of Mainz and to create
an archbishopric at Olmütz; but he was not able to carry out his
intention. In 1269 Ulric, duke of Carinthia and Carniola, dying
without children, left his lands to the king of Bohemia, who took
possession of them in 1269 in spite of the resistance offered by
the patriarch of Aquileia, Philip, and the king of Hungary, Stephen
V. The kingdom of Bohemia now extended from the Riesenge-
birge to the Adriatic. War broke out once more between Bohemia
and Hungary, during which the Magyars ravaged Austria and carried off 16,000 persons into captivity. Otokar, in return, invaded
Hungary, captured Presburg and Nitra, crossed the Danube, and
defied the Hungarians on the banks of the Leitha. Want of provisions and an unexpected attack by Duke Henry of Bavaria obliged
him, however, to make peace. Again in 1271 the archbishop of
Cologne came in the name of several of the German princes to offer
him the imperial crown, and again Otokar deemed it prudent to refuse. No doubt the crown of St. Vacslav, though it might be less
brilliant, appeared to him far more secure than that of the empire.

This was, however, a fatal mistake for Bohemia and her king,
as Rudolf of Hapsburg was elected in his stead, and Rudolf soon
found it impossible to maintain his position with dignity while so
powerful a rival as the king of Bohemia remained. The election
had taken place without Otokar's consent, and in defiance of his
rights as an elector, and no sooner did he hear of the accession of the
new sovereign than he hastily concluded a peace with Hungary,
against which country he had again taken up arms in consequence
of the assassination of his father-in-law, Bela. He protested against
the election of his rival, and appealed to the Pope, Gregory X. But
in 1274 the Sovereign Pontiff recognized the new emperor. Rudolf
prepared for the struggle with his formidable adversary, calling
to his aid both the power of the law and of arms. He persuaded
the assembly of princes, in a meeting held at Nuremberg, to decide
that all fiefs of the empire which had become vacant since the excommunication of Frederick II. ought to belong to the king of the
Romans, and that every vassal who should not receive investiture
in the space of a year and a day should forfeit his fiefs. This was
to demand from Otokar all that he had inherited from the houses
of Carinthia and Austria. The Count Palatine Ludwig cited

Otokar to appear before the tribunal of the empire, on the ground
that he had not done homage for his dominions in the appointed
time. Besides this Rudolf excited the subjects of Otokar in Austria, Carinthia, and Styria to revolt, invited the archbishop of Salzburg and the bishop of Passau to assist the rebels, and entered into
a secret understanding with some of those nobles in Bohemia who
could not forgive the king for having deprived them of the crown-
lands which they had unjustly appropriated. He also entered into
an alliance with Frederick, burgrave of Nuremberg, Menhardt, the
count of Tyrol, and Ludwig of Bavaria. All the enemies of Otokar
rallied round the emperor, but the king of Bohemia believed himself sufficiently powerful to hold his own against them. He subdued the revolts in Austria and Styria, and even invaded the domains of the church in Salzburg.

On May 15, 1275, Otokar was placed under the ban of the
empire, and all his lands and offices declared forfeited within a
year if he did not submit. At the expiration of that time a German
army assembled at Nuremberg for the invasion of Bohemia, while
the count of Tyrol prepared to attack Carinthia and Styria. The
duke of Bavaria, who had at first taken the side of Otokar, also
abandoned him, and the Hungarians, gained over by Rudolf, undertook to march against Austria and Moravia. Success crowned
the efforts of the allies. Carinthia and Styria fell into the hands of
Meinhardt of Tyrol, while Rudolf, throwing himself suddenly upon
Austria, captured Vienna. This town had been devoted to Otokar,
but yielded before the threat of Rudolf to tear up all the vines
which had been planted round the city.

Otokar had concentrated his army on the frontiers of Bavaria,
on which side he expected the enemy. Surprised by these unfore-
seen attacks, he now made a forced march on Austria, but at this
critical moment the family of the Vitkovici, one of the most powerful in his kingdom, whose chief was Zavisa of Falkenstein, abandoned the cause of their king, and set to work to ravage the royal
domain. It seemed impossible to withstand so many enemies
at once; the army of Otokar was reduced to 20,000 men, while the
forces of his adversary were far more considerable. The king
of Bohemia found himself forced to sue for peace, and to gain it he
was obliged to sacrifice to Rudolf those countries which, together
with the kingdoms of Hungary and Bohemia, were in time to form
the larger part of the Austrian empire, namely, Carinthia, Carniola,

Austria, and Styria, together with the territory of Eger. His only son, Vacslav, was to marry the daughter of Rudolf, and Hartmann, the son of Rudolf, the daughter of Otokar. The first of the Hapsburgs thus entered upon that policy of marriages which was one day to establish the fortunes of his house. Not content with having despoiled and humiliated the king of Bohemia, he secured for his heirs the inheritance of the crown of St. Vacslav, in case of the extinction of the house of Premyslides. Rudolf gave his daughter Lower Austria and forty thousand golden ducats as dowry, and a like sum to the daughter of Otokar. The king of Hungary was a third party to the treaty, and Bohemia was forced to restore all the lands she had taken from him in the last war.

By the terms of this treaty Otokar recognized Rudolf as the emperor, and accepted from his hands investiture for the kingdom of Bohemia and the landgraviate of Moravia. As it was understood by the king of Bohemia, this clause neither interfered with the independence of the realm nor with its internal government. Rudolf, however, insisted on regarding Bohemia as an integral part of the empire, and claimed the right to interfere in those disputes which arose between Otokar and the Bohemian nobles who had deserted, his cause; in a word, he meant to reduce Bohemia to a state of complete vassalage. Otokar resisted, and long negotiations were entered into by the two kings, but they came to nothing. Two such rivals could not be reconciled, and it was inevitable that one of them should be forced to submit to the other. Otokar had but a small army of 30,000 men with which to fight the empire, and no other allies than the princes of Silesia. Nevertheless, he began a fresh campaign, and during the summer of 1278 he made his way into Lower Austria by the Morava and reached Marchegg, close to the glorious battlefield of Cressennbrünn, on the right bank of the stream. Rudolf, who had established his seat of government at Vienna, marched to meet him, and soon forced him to retreat. On August 26, 1278, a battle took place which was one of the most terrible of the Middle Ages, and one of the most important in its results.

Rudolf had secured the alliance of the king of Hungary, and the battle began with a furious attack on the flanks of the Bohemian army by the Cuman horsemen on their swift steeds. The two kings themselves more than once took part in the fight, and the fortunes of the day remained for some time doubtful, but suddenly the rear

RUDOLF VON HAPSBURG VIEWS THE DEAD BODY OF OTOKAR, SLAIN ON
THE MARCHEGG, 1278
Painting by A. Zick

guard of the Bohemian army, at the moment of their advance, took to flight, and the day was lost. Otokar rushed into the midst of his enemies and gave himself up as prisoner, but he was slain by two Austrian knights, and his body, stripped of its armor, was shamefully outraged. Rudolf, who arrived too late to save his life, caused his remains to be gathered together and carried to Vienna, where they were clothed in the royal purple and exposed for four and twenty days. The court of Rome, which was one of the many allies of Rudolf, had placed the king of Bohemia under an interdict, and his body was, in consequence, refused Christian burial. But Bohemia took no heed of the interdict. Both the church and the nation mourned for the sovereign who, notwithstanding his faults, had gained so much glory for his kingdom. There were some who regretted him even in Germany. " Virtue and honor," says Henry of Heimburg, " weep for the king of Bohemia; his hand was liberal; he was the rampart of Christendom against the pagans; he was a lion of courage, an eagle of goodness."

Rudolf did not lay down his arms on the death of the king of Bohemia, but, at the head of his victorious army, he made his way into Moravia. The towns here were mostly inhabited by German colonists, by whom he was gladly welcomed, but he allowed the country districts to be horribly ravaged, and treated the whole land as conquered territory and a fief of the empire. To some of the towns he granted important privileges, making Brünn one of the free cities of the empire. The nobles submitted, and Cunegunda, the widow of Otokar, threw herself and her son on the mercy of the conqueror. In Bohemia, meanwhile, the greatest confusion prevailed. Those nobles who had been faithless to Otokar, and whom he had banished from the kingdom, returned and prepared to offer the crown to Rudolf, while the patriots who wished to maintain the independence of their country made ready to defend it. Young Vacslav, the heir of Otokar, was only seven years of age. Two princes were eager to become his guardians—Henry of Breslau and Otto of Brandenburg; the latter was nephew of the late king, and was able to furnish some troops for the defense of Bohemia. Meantime Rudolf had invaded Bohemia, but he did not feel himself sufficiently strong to complete its conquest. He therefore determined to conclude a treaty that would leave him complete freedom of action in the future. Accordingly an agreement was entered into by which he was allowed to keep Moravia in his

power for five years, during which time the government of Bohemia was to be left in the hands of Otto of Brandenburg. The
old arrangements regarding marriages between the Hapsburgs and
the Premyslides were renewed, and it was decided that Vacslav
should marry the Princess Guta, who was the daughter of Rudolf,
and the emperor's son, Rudolf, Aneska, the daughter of Otokar.
The oldest of these children who were thus sacrificed to the ambition of their father was not ten years of age. But Rudolf was not
satisfied with a simple promise; he insisted that these unions should
receive the sanction of the church, and the double marriage was
celebrated on the same day in the town of Iglau in Moravia.
After the ceremony the children returned to the care of their parents, that their education, which had scarcely been begun, might
be completed. The queen-mother of Bohemia and the new regent
established themselves at Prague, and Rudolf returned to Austria,
after having confided the temporary government of Moravia to the
bishop of Olmütz, who had formerly been one of the devoted adherents of Otokar, and was now the no less zealous supporter of
his successful adversary.

It was no spirit of self-sacrifice which led the margrave of
Brandenburg to undertake the guardianship of his young cousin.
No sooner was he settled at Prague than he set himself indus-
triously to work to plunder the country which he had been appointed to rule. At last the Czech nobles grew tired of the insolence of Otto, and becoming indignant at the insults inflicted on the
heir of the king, obliged Otto to quit Bohemia and return to his
own country. But he carried off the young prince with him and
left the government in the hands of Eberhardt, bishop of Brandenburg. The latter suppressed the insurrection with the help not
only of the Germans already settled in Bohemia, but of adventurers
of all kinds who had come out of Saxony prepared to take possession of the country as their prey, and Bohemia became the scene of
furious struggles, in which the sentiment of nationality so long
dead among the nobles was again thoroughly aroused by the new
invasion of the Germans. At last Rudolf interfered. In the
month of September, 1280, he entered Bohemia, and brought about
a truce by which the nobles and the representatives of the towns
agreed to maintain the regency of Otto of Brandenburg, provided
that he would not leave the government in the hands of foreigners
during his frequent absences from the country; that he would send

all the foreign troops back into Brandenburg; oblige all Germans who were not settled in the land to leave it within three days on pain of death; and that, on the payment of fifteen thousand marks of gold, he would bring back the young Prince Vacslav to his capital. But notwithstanding this agreement Otto managed to keep Vacslav in his power for three years longer, and finally agreed to give him up to his people only on condition of their paying an additional ransom of twenty thousand marks of gold, or, should they fail to produce the sum required, the surrender of a certain number of the most important strongholds in the kingdom.

At last, in 1283, after a delay of five years, Vacslav returned from his captivity and ascended the throne. Rudolf, true to his engagements, gave up Moravia to him, and later on interfered to prevent the payment of the twenty thousand marks which the margrave of Brandenburg tried to extort. The Bohemians had looked forward with impatience to the accession of a prince who symbolized to them the reawakening of the spirit of nationality and the new life which animated the kingdom. But Vacslav was too young to govern alone, and his mother, Cunegunda, came with him to Prague. During her exile in Moravia she had married Zavisa of Falkenstein, a Czech nobleman, who was an elegant cavalier and a poet of some talent. He had won the love of the royal widow by his brilliant qualities, and obtained great influence over Vacslav. This influence continued even after the death of Cunegunda, and enabled him to enrich himself at the expense of the state, while he encouraged Vacslav in his love of pleasure. When the young Queen Guta was sent to Prague, Rudolf insisted on the removal of Zavisa from the court, and he was forced to retire to his estates on the confines of Bohemia and Moravia. Still powerful and still ambitious, he married the sister of Ladislas, king of Hungary, and was accused of endeavoring to make his lands an independent principality. Such a subject was too formidable not to be an object of fear to the king. Vacslav invited him to visit Prague, and then threw him into prison. He amused himself during his captivity by the composition of songs in the Bohemian tongue, which continued popular for a long time, but which have now entirely disappeared. The friends of the prisoner rose in arms, and help was sent to them by the king of Hungary, while Rudolf also interfered by sending troops to his son-in-law. The rebels held out for some time, and it was necessary to besiege them one by one in their castles. Rudolf gave Vacslav a piece of advice which was rather politic than Christian, when he suggested that he should take his prisoner Zavisa on all his expeditions, and summon each burgrave to surrender, telling him that, in case of refusal, the head of Zavisa would be cut off. This advice was followed, and several of the rebels submitted in consequence. At last the king arrived before the castle of Hluboka, not far from Budweiss, which was commanded by Vitek, the brother of Zavisa. The dreadful summons was proclaimed, but Vitek did not believe the threat and would not yield, whereupon the head of his brother was cut off before his eyes in front of the castle ditch. The tragic end of Zavisa, his brilliant qualities and his poetic talents secured for his name great popularity, which has been revived in the present century through newly awakened interest in the national literature.

At the time of the execution of Zavisa, Vacslav was only nineteen, and this act of severity so frightened the rebels that the royal authority was thenceforward recognized throughout the land. The young king increased the revenues of the crown, and worked on a large scale the silver mines of Bohemia, which were then extremely rich, especially that of Kutna Hora, " the mountain of mines." He kept up a luxurious court, which enriched the town of Prague, and made it a favorite abode of foreigners. It became in his day the seat of several renowned schools. At the same time a series of fortunate events placed the crown of Poland on the head of Vacslav, making him one of the most powerful monarchs of Christendom.

For some time past the custom of creating appanages had seriously weakened Poland. It was now more or less equally divided among all the princes who were descended from the dynasty of the Piasts; the one who ruled Lesser Poland, and whose seat of government was at Cracow, being the overlord. His power, however, had become almost nominal, for the right of primogeniture was but little respected, and Mazovia, Silesia, and Greater Poland had each in turn endeavored to get possession of his territories. Even the lesser principalities themselves began to split up, and in Silesia alone we hear of no less than ten princes. A party in Cracow was formed, which offered the province of Lesser Poland to the king of Bohemia. Vacslav accepted the offer, proceeded to Cracow, and took possession of that town and of the duchy of Sandomir.

But the troubles of Poland continued, and a few years later the nobles of Greater Poland also offered their province to Vacslav. He caused himself to be crowned at Gnesen, obliged the princes of Mazovia to recognize his suzerainty, and thus united the kingdom of the Piasts to that of the Premyslides. This union, which might have proved so very advantageous for the two countries, was unfortunately of very short duration, and did not last beyond the life of Vacslav. The time had not yet come for the Slav peoples to understand the duties which their common origin imposed upon them and the need there was for common action against the Germans. Only a short time before Premysl Otokar had invited the Poles to help him in his struggles against the insatiable ambition of the Germans, and had received but little assistance. In years to come the two crowns of Bohemia and Poland were once more to be united on the same head; but the two countries were unable to form a permanent state.

In 1301, the house of Arpad having become extinct, the crown of Hungary was also offered to Vacslav, but fearing to accept it for himself because the Pope had already chosen Robert of Anjou, he induced the Magyars to crown his young son. This election the Pope and Emperor Albert refused to acknowledge. The latter called upon Vacslav to renounce the crown and demanded the cession of Meissen and Eger, and the payment of the arrears of the tenths due the empire from the mines of Kutna Hora. To enforce his claims he invaded Bohemia, but was unsuccessful. Vacslav in turn prepared to invade Austria, but died before he could carry out his project.

His successor, Vacslav V., concluded an unfavorable peace, surrendering Meissen and Eger, the emperor agreeing not to meddle in the relations between Bohemia, Hungary, and Poland. The new ruler was, moreover, a frivolous, debauched prince, with little care for his prerogative. He gave away his claim to Hungary and Poland, though in the latter case he relented and tried to reassert his rights. But on his march to Poland he was treacherously assassinated at Olmütz. Vacslav left no son, and with him the dynasty of the Premyslides, who had reigned over Bohemia since mythical times, became extinct in 1306. The race of Arpad in Hungaria, as we have seen, died out in 1301. There is something curious in this coincidence.

The death of the last of the Premyslides marks an important

date in the history of Bohemia. Up to this time, notwithstanding
frequent periods of anarchy, the country had recognized the hereditary authority of a national dynasty. But after the death of Vacslav without heirs, we rarely find it governed by a national king.
The foreign elements which had settled within it continued to increase in numbers and power. Before turning to this new period
it will be worth while to look back for a brief survey of Bohemia's
relations with the empire, and of her internal condition and the
development of her civilization.

The neighborhood of Germany has always been dangerous for
non-German nations, and Bohemia has felt this more than most
countries. Since the time when Charles the Great, with the help of
the Pope, restored the empire of the West, the emperor had looked
upon himself as the temporal head of Christendom. Those lands
which the emperor did not attempt to conquer were regarded as
owing that privilege directly to the imperial generosity. At times
it was necessary to purchase the privilege by payment of tribute,
and thus, according to the somewhat doubtful testimony of Ein-
hard, Bohemia paid tribute to Charles the Great. In a document
of the year 817 Louis the Pious represents Bohemia, and also the
country of the Avars, and of the Slavs to the west of Bavaria,
as all forming part of the empire. At the end of the ninth century,
as we have already seen, Bohemia was paying to the emperor a
tribute of 120 oxen and 500 marks of silver. In 895 the two
princes, Spytihnev and Vratislav, tired of the authority of Svatopluk, did homage for their states to the emperor. In 928 Prince
Vacslav I. renewed the engagement to pay the tribute of oxen and
silver.

In 1081 this was changed into an agreement which bound
Bohemia to furnish 300 knights to accompany the emperor to Rome
for his coronation. On the other hand, we do not hear of the
princes of Bohemia doing homage or claiming investiture at the
accession of each German sovereign, and the payment of tribute
proves nothing more than that there was an international treaty between them. Vassals did not pay tribute. Louis the Child and
Henry the Fowler paid tribute to Hungary, but they were not the
vassals of Hungary; Poland at one time paid tribute to Bohemia in
the same way, but she was not her vassal. The emperor never exercised any right of sovereignty over Bohemia; he never levied
troops, he exercised no judicial authority, nor could he bind Bo-

THE PREMYSLIDES

hemia by the treaties which he entered into with the court of Rome. The interference of the empire in the disputes of the princes of Bohemia was exactly the same in character as the interference of the Czechs themselves in the affairs of Poland and Hungary. The Emperor Lothar failed in his attempts to impose a prince on Bohemia in 1126. At the beginning of the twelfth century a Bohemian prince received the honorary title of cupbearer as a reward for services rendered to the empire. Later on Otokar I. and Vacslav I. took part in the election of the emperor, but this title of elector was a purely personal one, and involved no sort of obligation on the part of Bohemia itself. As time went on the German emperors took advantage of the rivalries and quarrels of the Bohemian princes, and tried more than once to get possession of certain portions of Bohemia, such as the bishopric of Prague and the margravate of Moravia, but after each attempt the unity of the kingdom was quickly restored. When once the Pope had given his sanction to the adoption of the royal title, any special connection between the prince of Bohemia and the emperor resting on the imperial grant must have disappeared. After the election of Rudolf, Premysl Otokar II. was called upon to do homage for Bohemia and Moravia, and we have seen to what a struggle this claim gave rise. Albert I., in his treaty with Vacslav, renounced this claim, but we shall soon see how it was revived during the time of anarchy which followed the tragic death of the last of the Premyslides. Thus the claim of the empire was never clearly defined. The power and individual pretensions of each sovereign differed, and history can only state the facts without being able to lay down any definite rule.

The crown of Bohemia was elective before it became hereditary, and the prince was assisted by a diet which was at first composed of the chiefs of tribes, heads of families, and the representatives of the free cities. Later on the earlier Premyslides convoked diets, in which we find the princes of the royal family, the higher clergy, twelve judges chosen by the sovereign, and the representatives of the nobles. The powers of this diet were mainly judicial and deliberative; but it elected the prince, who could only be chosen from the ruling family; called out the national militia, and in exceptional cases levied taxes. It also elected the bishop of Prague. But its powers were never very clearly defined, and the prince often governed without its aid. From the end of the twelfth century the power of the diets increased, and we often find them refusing their permission to the sovereign to levy troops and extraordinary taxes. The diet was also the highest court of justice. The earliest authentic documents dealing with the relations between the prince and the diet bear the date 1310. The nobility was at first formed of the chiefs of the tribes, and later on of officials chosen by the prince, but the whole order of nobility was gradually modified by the feudal ideas which prevailed in Germany.

The territory of the kingdom of Bohemia during this period repeatedly extended beyond the present limits of Bohemia and Moravia, but the outlying districts, most of which were occupied by inhabitants not belonging to the Czech race, were soon lost. Their loss would have been of but slight importance if the Czechs had been a strong and united nation within the quadrilateral formed by the mountains of Bohemia and Moravia. Unfortunately this was not the case. They allowed themselves to be not only weakened externally, but also internally, by the constant infiltration of a German element, which, from many points of view, was far more dangerous than serious defeats in the field. The time came when Bohemia had to struggle not only against enemies from without, but also with enemies from within. The Czechs had found Bohemia deserted and they had occupied only the center of the country; the Germans had gradually taken possession of the mountainous districts and the frontiers, which had at first remained uncultivated and uninhabited. The Christian princes of Bohemia, unhappily, sought their wives among the Germans, and these foreign princesses brought to the court a large number of their countrymen, while a great many German priests and monks found their way into the churches and monasteries. German merchants, who settled in the *vicus Teutonicorum* in Prague, ended by getting possession of an entire district of the town. From the twelfth century onward whole towns and villages of Germans were to be found along the frontiers, where the soil had been lately reclaimed, and many royal and baronial towns which were built by the king, nobles, and abbots were occupied by German settlers. The celebrated poets of Germany, Ulric of Turlin, Wolfram of Eschenbach, and Henry of Freiburg, now appeared at the Bohemian court, and renowned soldiers peopled their estates with Germans. The mines of Kutna Hora and of the German Ford also attracted many foreigners.

The Slav agriculturists gladly left all trade and industry in the hands of foreigners: in Poland the Jews, and in Bohemia the Germans, acquired their monopoly. Some far-seeing patriots became alarmed at the growth of German influence. The Czech chronicle of Dalemil, compiled probably in the fourteenth century, expresses, sometimes in very outspoken fashion, the grief and anger of a Slav who sees his native tongue and his fatherland threatened. The following words are put into the mouth of the Princess Libusa: " If a foreigner comes to rule you, your nation will not last. A wise man does not consult foreigners. A foreigner will employ the people of his own tongue and will seek to do you evil. He will divide your inheritance among his own people. Look well that you trust not your fortune to the stranger, O Bohemian chief! There, where but one language is spoken, there glory is to be found." But these warnings of the unknown patriot were to remain without any echo till the days when the Hussites unfurled the standard alike of religious reform and of national unity.

Bohemia had been Christianized by Moravia and Germany, but in consequence of the destruction of the archbishopric of the Moravians she had been placed under the jurisdiction of Ratisbon, and remained so until the creation of the episcopal see of Prague, which was attached to the archbishopric of Mainz. The Pope, when he made Bohemia into a bishopric, insisted that the Roman liturgy alone should be employed. At first the bishop was usually elected by the diet and the prince together; after the middle of the twelfth century, however, he was chosen by the chapter, whose choice was ratified by the prince.

Notwithstanding the Papal decrees, the Slav liturgy continued to find some adherents. Nevertheless the Latin soon supplanted the native tongue as the language of the church, and in this way helped not a little to clear the way for the progress of German influence. Most of the foreign orders flourished in Bohemia, and the only schools in the country belonged to them. In the thirteenth century the most celebrated school was the *Studium Generale* established in the castle at Prague, where grammar and logic were taught by eminent masters. The clergy possessed considerable influence, and Bohemia remained faithful to Catholic unity down to the fourteenth century, the first heresies making their appearance in the beginning of that century.

Though the literature of that time was but little developed, it had produced some works of interest. The Latin tongue, so dear to the priests, had not entirely put an end to national culture. Cosmos, dean of the chapter of Prague, wrote a chronicle of Bohemia at the beginning of the eleventh century, which now, in spite of the pseudo-classical style of the author, is extremely valuable. We find religious hymns, sacred texts, and lyric and heroic poems in the language of the Czechs—some describing the life of the nation and of great poetic value—others, imitations of Christian or romantic legends of the Middle Ages, such as the legends of St. Catherine, St. Dorothy, and Alexander the Great.

Neither were the fine arts neglected. The church interested itself in their development and employed them for religious purposes. At the end of the eleventh century Bozetech, abbot of the Slav monastery of Sazava, is spoken of as a clever painter and a skillful carver in wood and stone. The chronicle relates how the bishop of Prague, jealous of his powers, imposed upon him a singular penance; he ordered him to carve a Christ in wood of the size of life, and to bear it to Rome on his shoulders. The two styles of art, the Byzantine and the Italian, may be said to have met in Bohemia, but the triumph of the Roman church carried with it that of Italian art. A large number of churches were built in the twelfth and thirteenth centuries, among them the Roman basilica of St. Vit at Prague. Altogether about 150 churches in the Roman style are known to exist in Bohemia. Gothic art made its appearance there in the thirteenth century, and reached its highest point of delicacy in the fourteenth.

We have already seen how Prague became the seat of a brilliant and knightly court under the last Premyslides. The coronation of Vacslav II., in 1297, was one of the most brilliant ceremonies of the Middle Ages. " It was," says a German chronicle, " such a festival as had never been celebrated, either by a king of Assyria, or by Solomon himself." The numbers of strangers who flocked to it was so vast, that, according to contemporary accounts, food had to be found for nineteen thousand horses. There came to it not less than twenty-eight princes, lay and ecclesiastic; the archbishops of Mainz and Magdeburg, the bishops of Prague, Olmütz, Cracow, Basel. and Constance; the Archduke Albert of Austria, with a suite of seven thousand knights; the princes of Saxony, Brandenburg, and Meissen. The town of Prague was not large enough to hold the crowd of visitors, and a vast palace of wood, decorated with valuable tapestry, was built on the neighboring plain, and there the guests of high rank were entertained magnificently. In the public squares the fountains flowed with wine. The coronation took place in the cathedral of St. Vit. The royal crown was worth two thousand marks of silver; the sword and buckler, three thousand; the mantle, four thousand; and no one dared to say what was the worth of the girdle, the rings, and the royal cap.

Chapter VIII

EARLY HISTORY OF THE AUSTRIAN GROUP
—THE HOUSE OF BABENBERG. 973-1246

AUSTRIA, as is well known, is but another form of the German Oesterreich, the kingdom of the East. This celebrated historical name appears for the first time in 996, in a document signed by the Emperor Otto III., *in regione vulgari nomine Osterrichi.* The land to which it is there applied was created a *march,* or border province, after the destruction of the Avar empire, and was governed by two margraves or counts of the frontier. The two margravates included Friuli, properly so called, lower Pannonia to the south of the Drave, Carinthia, Istria, and the interior of Dalmatia, the seacoast having been ceded to the Eastern emperor, and lower Pannonia to the north of the Drave, upper Pannonia, and the Ostmark, properly so called, respectively. The Ostmark included the Traungau to the east of the Enns, which was completely German, and the Grunzvittigau. The ecclesiastical government of these lands was divided between the bishops of Salzburg and Aquileia. The bishopric of Salzburg had been founded in 710 by St. Emeran of Poitiers; that of Aquileia presumed to date its foundation from the time of the apostle St. Mark. The population was principally composed of Germans and Slavs, but except in Dalmatia these Slavs gradually lost their individuality and could not be distinguished from the rest of the inhabitants. The early history of these countries lacks that unity which dynastic and national interest gives to Hungary and Bohemia. They form but a portion of the German empire, and have no strongly marked life of their own.

The march, with its varying frontier, had not even geographical unity. In 876 it was enlarged by the addition of Bavaria; in 890 it lost Pannonia, which was given to Bracislav, the Croat prince, in return for his help against the Magyars; and in 937 it was destroyed and absorbed by the Magyars, who extended their frontier to the River Ems. After the battle of Lechfeld, or Augsburg, in 955, Germany and Italy being exposed to Hungarian invasions, the march was reconstituted and granted to the Margrave Burkhard, the brother-in-law of Henry of Bavaria. Leopold of Babenberg succeeded him in 973, and with him begins the dynasty of Babenberg, which ruled the country during the time of the Premyslides and the house of Arpad.

The Babenbergs derived their name from the castle of Babenberg, built by Henry, margrave of Nordgau, in honor of his wife, Baba, sister of Henry the Fowler. It reappears in the name of the town of Bamberg, which now forms part of the kingdom of Bavaria. Leopold, on whom the chroniclers bestow the title of the Illustrious, was already count of the Donaugau, the district in which lies the town of Ratisbon, and of the Traungau, while his father, Berthold, was count of the Nordgau, the land lying north of Ratisbon. In his time the town of Mölk, on the Danube above Vienna, was captured from the Magyars, and it is said Leopold there founded a monastery for twelve secular priests. He perished at Würzburg, struck by an arrow aimed at his nephew, Henry of Schweinfurt, to avenge the blinding of one of the knights of that town. His eldest son, Henry I. (994-1018), received investiture for the margravate from Otto III. Though not of right an hereditary office, the margravate soon became so, and remained in the family of the Babenbergs; the march was so important a part of the empire that no doubt the emperor was glad to make the defense of this exposed district the especial interest of one family. The other sons of Leopold were equally well provided for. Ernest obtained the duchy of Suabia, and Poppo the bishopric which had been recently founded at Bamberg, and afterward that of Triest. The emperor also granted a large number of hereditary domains along the shores of the Danube to the Margrave Henry. The conversion of the Magyars to Christianity had softened the manners of this conquering race, and made Henry's task of protecting Germany comparatively easy, but Adalbert (1018-1056) had a hard struggle against them, and owes his name of the Victorious to the successes he gained. He extended the march of Austria as far as the banks of the Leitha. He also helped the emperor considerably against Hungary, and received in return fresh grants of estates within the march for himself and his heirs.

The Ostmark was almost doubled in size under the rule of Adalbert, who chose the town of Tulln, on the Danube, between

Vienna and Mölk, as his place of residence. His son, Ernest the Valiant (1056-1075), gave a fresh proof of the loyalty of the Babenbergs to the emperor and empire by his death in battle against the Saxons at Unstrut. But Leopold the Handsome (1075-1096) proved faithless to the traditions of the family, and took the side of Gregory VII. against the Emperor Henry IV. in the quarrel about investitures. He was defeated by the imperial forces and reduced to submission, but soon after took up the cause of the anti-king, Hermann of Luxemburg. Henry IV. thereupon granted investiture for the march of Austria to Vratislav, duke of Bohemia, but Vratislav was never able to gain possession of the land, and in spite of the disloyalty of Leopold the Handsome, his son, Leopold III., succeeded him in the government of the march. This prince, who proudly styled himself margrave of Austria by the grace of God, entered into an alliance with the king of the Romans, Henry V., who had revolted against his father. Henry V. rewarded him for his valuable assistance by giving him his sister Agnes in marriage. She was the widow of Frederick of Suabia, so that the marriage allied the house of Austria with the future dynasty of the Hohenstaufen. Agnes had eighteen children, of whom two, Leopold and Henry, succeeded their father. One of these eighteen children was the celebrated annalist, Otto of Freisingen, bishop of the town of that name. By their marriage the daughters of Leopold allied the house of Babenberg with the ruling families of Thuringia and Montferrat, with the Piasts of Poland and the Premyslides of Bohemia. When the Salic dynasty became extinct in the person of Henry V., Leopold III. was proposed as emperor, together with Frederick of Suabia and Lothar of Saxony: a strong proof of the importance which had been acquired by the march of Austria and the family which governed it. Leopold retired in favor of Frederick, but the princes chose Lothar of Saxony.

Leopold was very generous toward the church. He founded new monasteries and enriched those which already existed. He gave Klosterneuburg to the Benedictines, and Heiligenkreuz to the Cistercians; he also richly endowed Kremmünster and St. Florian. On his death, the Emperor Lothar granted investiture to one of his younger sons, Leopold IV., 1136-1141. In 1138 the brother-in-law of Leopold, Conrad of Hohenstaufen, duke of Franconia, was made emperor. It was now that the struggle began between the house of Hohenstaufen and the great house of Welf, whose representative was Henry the Proud, duke of Saxony and Bavaria. Henry was defeated in the unequal strife, and was placed under the ban of the empire, while the duchy of Saxony was awarded to Albert the Bear, count of Brandenburg, and the duchy of Bavaria fell to the share of Leopold IV., in 1138. Henry the Proud died in the following year, leaving behind him a son under age, who was known later on as Henry the Lion. His uncle, Welf, would not submit to the forfeiture by his house of their old dominions, and marched against Leopold to reconquer Bavaria, but he was defeated by Conrad at the battle of Weinsberg in 1140. Leopold died shortly after this victory, and was succeeded both in the duchy of Bavaria and in the margravate of Austria by his brother, Henry II. This prince was surnamed Iasomirgott, from his favorite motto, *Iach sam mir Gott helfe*—so God be my aid. He was the first hereditary duke of Austria.

Henry II., Iasomirgott (1141-1177), endeavored to strengthen himself in Bavaria by marrying Gertrude, widow of Henry the Proud, and forcing her to obtain from her son, Henry the Lion, a renunciation of all his rights in favor of her new husband. But after the death of his mother Henry declared his renunciation null and void, and in 1156 the diet of the empire declared that Bavaria should be restored to Henry the Lion. It was owing to the wise council of his relation, Otto of Freisingen, that Henry Iasomirgott finally gave up Bavaria, which now became a separate duchy, an imperial edict, dated September 21, 1156, declaring the new duchy hereditary even in the female line. Henry II. was one of the founders of medieval Vienna. In Rome's imperial days Vindobona had been an important and a favorite municipium, but it had declined since then. Henry II. now constructed a fortress there, and, in order to civilize the surrounding country, sent for Scotch monks, of whom there were many at this time in Germany.

In 1177 Leopold V., called the Virtuous, succeeded Henry Iasomirgott. In his reign the duchy of Austria gained Styria, an important addition to its territory. Its duke, Otokar, dying without heirs, willed it to Leopold, and in 1192 Styria, which was inhabited by Germans and Slovenes, became a permanent part of Austria.

Leopold V. was the first of the Austrian princes whose name was known in Western Europe. He joined the third Crusade, and thus came in contact with most of the Catholic kings of the time. He

first visited the Holy Land in 1182; on his return thither in 1191 he
met Philip Augustus and Richard Cœur de Lion, and at the siege
of Acre quarreled with the turbulent king of England. In 1192
he returned to his own land. Shortly after, Richard Cœur de Lion
was over taken by a storm between Venice and Aquileia, and determined to cross Europe *incognito* in order to regain England.
Leopold heard of his presence in his territories, and was not slow

SOUTHEASTERN EUROPE
DURING THE CRUSADES
1095 -1270

to revenge himself on his detested rival. He had him made a prisoner and confined in the castle of Dürrenstein, near Krems on the
Danube, and before selling his prisoner to the emperor for twenty
thousand marks, extracted from him a promise of a marriage between the houses of Babenberg and Plantagenet.

The successor of Leopold V. was Frederick I. Like his father
he was an ardent Crusader, and only returned from Palestine to
die. During his absence his brother Leopold, surnamed the Proud,

who had been made duke of Styria by his father, was intrusted with the regency in Austria. He succeeded Frederick, in 1198, and played an important part in the affairs of Germany, attaching himself to the cause of Philip of Hohenstaufen. Later he left Austria to take part in a crusade in Spain against the Moors, and in 1217 he again took the cross, set out for Palestine, accompanied by Andrew II., king of Hungary, and distinguished himself in the expedition against Damietta.

The Emperor Frederick II. took every possible means of assuring the fidelity of so powerful a vassal and so valiant a knight. On the death of the archbishop of Cologne, he appointed him *Reichsverweser*, or vicar of the empire, and he gave his daughter in marriage to Leopold's son Henry. This alliance with the imperial house, and the important position in Christendom which Leopold had acquired, enabled him to play the part of mediator in the quarrels which arose between Frederick and the Pope, Honorius III. With this end in view he journeyed into Italy in 1229, where he died in the following year, after having successfully accomplished his mission.

At home Leopold endeavored to develop the commerce and trade of his country. He made Vienna the staple town, and lent a sum of thirty thousand marks of silver to the city to enable it to increase its trade. He adorned it with many new buildings, among them the Neue Burg. He strengthened the defenses of the frontiers, founded new monasteries, and granted municipal rights to Enns, Krems, and Vienna. But while busy with the interests of the state, Leopold did not forget those of his private domains, which he increased by the acquisition of various allodial estates within his duchy. Besides these he purchased lands in Carniola from Bishop Gerald of Freisingen, and paved the way to the future annexation of Carniola to Austria. The revenue of the state in his time rose to about sixty thousand marks of silver.

Leopold the Proud was succeeded by his son, Frederick the Fighter (1230-1246). The short reign of this prince was one continued struggle against his neighbors. With the Emperor Frederick II. he fought against Hungary and against Bohemia, and then he turned against Frederick to assist the Lombard cities, in support of the emperor's rival, Henry of Thuringia, who had married his sister Margaret. His aim seemed to be complete independence, and it was not long before he was placed under the ban of the empire, and Bohemia, Bavaria, Brandenburg, and Hungary all took up arms against him. The celebrated chancellor, Peter de Vinea, was called upon to write a violent pamphlet against him, in which he was represented as a treacherous member of the empire and a monster of iniquity who had forfeited the imperial clemency. The lands of the upper Enns as far as Linz fell into the hands of Otto of Bavaria, while Vienna was declared an imperial city, and a lieutenant was sent by the emperor to govern the conquered Austrian territory. But the Fighter defended himself with vigor, and in the end reconquered part of his land, and became reconciled with the emperor in 1240. Frederick annulled the privileges recently given to Vienna, and at the diet of Verona, in 1245, confirmed the powers which had been granted to the dukes of Austria in 1156. Thus the very revolts of Austria against the empire turned to her advantage, while the misfortunes which now burst over her neighbors were of equal benefit to her.

The Mongols had invaded Hungary, and King Bela applied for help to Austria, offering in exchange for her assistance to pledge to Frederick the Fighter three of his comitats. Frederick, who was as little generous toward Bela as his predecessor had been toward Richard Cœur de Lion, demanded their entire surrender, and then declared war against Hungary. He died on June 15, 1246, on the banks of the Leitha, slain, according to some, by the Hungarians; according to others, by one of his own followers. He was hated even by many of his own subjects. "A hard man," one of the chronicles calls him; "cruel in his judgment, brave in fight, greedy, and rapacious. He had filled with terror both his friends and his neighbors. No man loved him; all feared him." Ulric of Lichtenstein, the knightly poet of Styria, is more tender of his memory: "He is dead . . . he has left great woe behind him in Styria and in Austria. . . . Many are now poor who were rich. . . . His soul must be in heaven, for he was kind to the brave." With him the dynasty of Babenberg came to an end. Their remains lie in the church of the little town of Mölk, which has long since been eclipsed by the splendor of Vienna.

The immediate authority of the princes of the empire over the lands which had been intrusted to them had been greatly increased by the right of inheritance, conferred in the first instance upon the margraves, and afterward upon the dukes, while the quarrels with the Popes had helped to weaken the authority of the

HOUSE OF BABENBERG 95

emperors. Gradually corporations, lay and ecclesiastical, monasteries, towns, and citizens were freed from their dependence on the emperors, and placed under the authority of the princes. This authority is called by German historians *Landeshoheit, i. e.,* lordship over a particular district. We find this spirit of " particularism " especially strong in southern Germany. Thus as early as 1184 Otokar, duke of Styria, called himself *Landesherr,* lord of the land; and the annexation of Styria to Austria must have strengthened the feeling of local independence.

With the development of the *Landeshoheit* the old nobility declined, and its place was filled by an official nobility, composed of the followers of the prince who bore office about his person; and very soon the difference between these two classes disappeared, as both became equally dependent on the prince. In this matter again Styria set the example to Austria, the dukes of Austria having promised the *ministeriales* of Styria that they would observe those privileges which had been granted to them by their earlier princes.

As regards municipal law, also, Styria was ahead of Austria. As early as 1212 the towns of Enns obtained from the emperor a municipal code, or *stadtrecht,* the text of which is preserved to this day among its archives. According to this code, the lord of the land is the archduke, and for him is reserved the punishment of certain crimes; his will is law. Under him judicial authority is exercised by a town judge, assisted by an inferior magistrate (*nachrichter*) and by police (*schergen*), who are paid officials. The stadtrecht is mainly a code of criminal law founded on the principal of *wehrgeld;* in all cases of pecuniary compensation a third of the fine is allotted to the judge. Trials by ordeal are allowed. The law of inheritance permits the wife or child to inherit, or the nearest relations, if they reside on the land of the duchy; if not, they are only to have half. The foreigner who dies in the land is allowed to leave his property to whomsoever he likes; if he dies without a will, for a year and a day it is held in trust for his heirs; if no one then claims it, it is to become the property of the duke. A municipal council is formed by six of the highest burgesses, whose business it is to control the markets and to watch over the interests of the town. The legal maxim of England, " A man's house is his castle," is well known; the stadrecht maintains the inviolability of the household in almost the same words: " We will that for each citizen his house shall be a fortress (*pro muni-*

tione) for himself, his family, and whomsoever may enter his door." Every violation of the hearth is punished by a fine of five marks or the loss of a hand. The citizens are to have the right of keeping horses, both for their business and amusement.

Leopold VI. took this code as his model for the one he granted to Vienna in 1221, wherein, indeed, he carried its principals even farther. Thus to the laws concerning the inviolability of the household it is added that no one shall enter a house with a bow or a quiver; that no one shall walk about the town with a poignard at his girdle, under penalty of the payment of a talent and the forfeiture of the weapon; that he who shall conceal a weapon in his boot shall pay ten talents or lose his hand. The chief citizens of each district of the town are ordered to exercise supervision over all business transactions exceeding the amount of two talents. A striking analogy is to be found between the municipal laws of Babenberg and those of the Flemish and Picard towns, Ghent, Bruges, Ypres, Arras, Furnes, and Laon. This is explained by the large trade which the Flemings carried on in the Danubian countries, especially in Hungary. Flemish merchants resided in Vienna, and as early as 1208 we find them in possession of certain privileges.

The laws concerning the Jews deserve special notice, as they are singularly liberal for the time. From 1200 onward they have their synagogues in Vienna. The coining of money is intrusted to them, with the title of " counts of the chamber." Some of the laws show remarkable tolerance, especially if we consider the prejudices of the Middle Ages; for example, if a stolen article is found in the house of a Jew it is enough for him to swear that he has purchased it, and he has only to restore it for what he gave for it. The laws of Hungary, Poland, Bohemia, and Thuringia concerning Jews were all copied from those of Austria.

Under the protection of peaceful laws the trade and industry of Austria developed rapidly. The situation of the country was especially fortunate as regards commerce, placed as she was on the frontiers of Germany, Bohemia, and Hungary, and with the Danube as her river. A rhymed chronicler enthusiastically celebrates her splendor and prosperity: " This land has everything in abundance—cattle and wine, corn and other fruits, all that is needed for the food of man—game and fish and excellent bread. The Danube, with her clear waters, adorns the landscape, and brings day and night without pause all that is needed to the towns and the villages."

Commercial relations between Styria and Italy were established at an early date. To increase them Leopold built a bridge of stone over the Save, at the spot called to this day Steinbrück. But trade in those days was far from being free. For example, the town of Gratz had the rights of a staple town; all foreign goods had to be brought there to be weighed on the town scales, and could only be carried by the town wagons. The rules of the staple in some other towns contained still more irksome regulations. All goods sent through the town of Bruck, on the River Mur, had to be exposed in the public square and put up at auction, and only that portion which had found no purchaser among the citizens was allowed to leave the place.

Enns was the great commercial city on the way from Ratisbon to Vienna. It was the great warehouse of the Augsburg merchants, who went to buy furs at the fair of Kiev, and carried western wares into Russia. Along the same road were Medlich, St. Pölten, Tulln, Stein, and Mauthausen. Along it traveled the merchants of Burgundy, Lorraine, Cologne, and Maëstricht; the woven stuffs of the east, the furs of Hungary, the silks of Venice, found their way by it to the north and west. Purchase and sale were carried on partly by money, partly by barter. The money of the Babenbergs was coined at Venice and Neustadt; few of these coins remain. For those times the riches of Austria were great, and manners improved in consequence of this prosperity. The monasteries furnished a large number of chroniclers, and schools were opened by the monks. The theater seems to have been unknown; we meet with but one mention of an Easter mystery, *Osterspiel;* this was at the monastery of St. Florian. Poetry, however, was cultivated with ardor at the court of the Babenbergs, and, according to tradition, Leopold VI. was a poet and Frederick the Fighter wrote love songs. Three of the most celebrated of the minnesingers, Reinar von Hagenau, Walter von der Vogelweide, and Reinar von Zweter, passed part of their lives there. Walter called Austria his second fatherland. It was there, he said, that he had learned to sing and to relate stories. Several times he celebrates the names of Leopold VI. and Frederick the Fighter. Tannhaüser praised Frederick II. during his life and mourned for him after his death. " With him," he says, " all joy is dead." Another poet, Nidhart of Reuenthal, the Bavarian, also dwelt for some time in Austria, and his poems very pleasantly describe the dances and rustic games of the country.

But the minnesingers did not flourish in Austria only. We find them also in Styria, where lived Rudolf van Stadek, and where may still be seen the castle of Ulric von Lichtenstein, on the banks of the Mur. He was cupbearer to Duke Frederick. This singer of the most tender sentiments and most refined gallantry never knew how to read or write. At the famous poetical tournament at the Wartburg, at the court of Thuringia, where the seven greatest singers then living rivaled one another in singing the praises of their masters, it was to the sun itself, says the legend, that Henry of Oftedingen compared the duke of Austria.

Chapter IX

THE AUSTRIAN GROUP UNDER THE FIRST HAPSBURGS. 1273-1493

HISTORIANS have given the name of "the Austrian Interregnum" to the period which elapsed between the death of the last of the Babenbergs and the accession of the first prince of the house of Hapsburg. We have already seen, in the history of Bohemia, how the inheritance of the last Babenberg was for a time united to Bohemia; thirty years elapsed after the death of Frederick the Fighter before it fell into the hands of the family which now holds possession of it. The origin of this family has been a constant puzzle to the fertile imaginations of genealogists. Some among them trace it back to the Merovingians, others to the Carlovingians, others again, to Ethico, duke of Alamannia, who is supposed to have been the common stock from which sprang the houses of Hapsburg, Lorraine, and Baden. What is quite certain is that the house of Hapsburg is of Alamannic origin. The first domains held by it were in Alsace, Switzerland, and Suabia. It took its name from the castle of Hapsburg, which was built in the year 1027 by Werner, bishop of Strasburg, on the heights of Windisch, near the River Aar, in what is now the canton Aargau.

The first mention of the castle of Hapsburg, *Habichtsburg,* the castle of vultures, the ruins of which still remain, occurs in a document of the year 1099. The immediate successors of Werner increased the family possessions and influence through fortunate marriages and gifts, and especially by acting as advocates and stewards for neighboring abbeys and cities. But it was not till the succession of Rudolf of Hapsburg, first, in 1240, to the scattered family estates on the upper Rhine, and then, in 1273, to the imperial dignity, that the Hapsburgs take their place among the princely families of Europe. Rudolf was born in 1218, was early instructed in the exercise and use of arms and knightly practices, and became one of the most redoubtable warriors of his day. Ac-

tive, aggressive, warlike, and yet prudent, he soon won for himself a wide reputation for prowess and wisdom, and before his
death the Hapsburg possessions not only had been increased enor-
mously, but their political center of gravity shifted from the Rhine
to the middle Danube. It is to Rudolf that the Austrian state
owes its origin, and the extensive nature of his acquisition affords
ample justification for the exclamation of the bishop of Basel,
" Sit fast, good Lord, or Rudolf will have Thy throne."

Rudolf's acquisition of the Austrian lands in his great victory
on the March Field in 1278 over Otokar has been narrated in connection with the history of Bohemia. Upper and Lower Austria,
Styria, Carinthia, and Carniola, and rights of investiture in Bohemia and Moravia were added to the hereditary estates, and the
basis for the modern Austria was laid. It is true that Rudolf experienced great difficulty in transferring the Austrian territories
to his family, but in the end the Hapsburg sway was acknowledged by all. In 1282, after obtaining the sanction of the electors,
he solemnly invested his two sons, Albert and Rudolf, with Austria,
Styria, and Carniola; and a few years later, in 1286, he assigned
Carinthia to Menhardt of Tyrol, to reward him for the help he had
received from him in his war against Premysl Otokar. But the
states of Austria and Styria were but little satisfied with their new
master; they disliked the Suabian counselors whom Albert brought
with him, and before long a revolution broke out in Austria. The
town of Vienna, which, during the struggle with Otokar, Rudolf
had made into a fief directly dependent upon himself, revolted, and
was only subdued by force of arms. Nor was he more fortunate in
regard to the imperial dignity. For notwithstanding his signal
service to the empire and his earnest efforts to secure the election
for his only surviving son, Albert, the electors persistently refused
to comply with his wishes. Rudolf died on July 15, 1291, in his
seventy-third year, and his body was interred at Spire with those of
former emperors. He was a remarkable man and a ruler well
worthy of the illustrious house which for so many generations has
continued in unbroken descent as rulers in Austria. His personal appearance was most unusual. Over six feet in height, he was tall
and slender, with a small head, pale face, and large aquiline nose.
His face when in repose was grave and serious, but in conversation
at once became animated, reflecting the enthusiasm and energy of
his thoughts and feelings. He dressed very simply, and his man-

CAPTURE OF FREDERICK THE HANDSOME OF AUSTRIA AT THE BATTLE OF MÜHLDORF
Painting by H. Knackfuss

ners were pleasing and chivalrous. Of his reign his contemporary tells us that in spite of great wars "his very name spread fear and terror among the licentious barons, and joy among the people; as the light sprung from darkness, so arose peace and tranquillity from war and desolation. The peasant resumed the plow, which he had neglected; the merchant, whom the fear of plunder had confined to his dwelling, now traversed the country with confidence and security; and robbers and banditti, who had roved fearlessly in the face of day, now hid in coverts and wastes."

Rudolf's son and successor, Albert I., did not obtain the imperial crown till 1298, and in Austria his reign was disturbed by troubles with the town of Vienna and also with the archbishop of Salzburg. He did succeed in getting the crown of Bohemia for his son, but he was unable to retain it. Two centuries were to elapse before the house of Hapsburg was to gain possession of the kingdom of St. Vacslav. In 1308 Albert died at the hands of an assassin in Switzerland. His son, Frederick the Handsome, vainly tried to obtain the imperial crown; together with that of Bohemia it passed to the house of Luxemburg. Out of this grew a long war, which ended in the battle of Mühldorf and the defeat of Frederick in 1322. Nevertheless Frederick concluded a treaty with his rival which secured to them a joint jurisdiction. Frederick took the title of king of the Romans, but he had hardly any of the power attached to the name. He died in 1330. His two brothers, Albert the Wise and Otto the Gay, threatened to renew the war with the emperor, but a common danger from the king of Bohemia, who had married his second son, Henry, to the celebrated Margaret Maultasche, or Margaret of the pouch-mouth, daughter of the duke of Tyrol and Carinthia, and who hoped by this union to regain the duchies for Bohemia, again united the emperor and the Austrian princes. By the Treaty of Hagenau, in 1330, it was arranged that on the death of Duke Henry, who had no male heirs, Carinthia should become the property of Austria, and the Tyrol that of the emperor. Henry died in 1335, whereupon the emperor, Louis of Bavaria, declared that Margaret Maultasche had forfeited all rights of inheritance, and proceeded to assign the two provinces to the Austrian princes, with the exception of some portion of the Tyrol, which devolved on the house of Wittelsbach. Carinthia alone, however, obeyed the emperor; the Tyrolese nobles declared for Margaret, and with the help of her father-in-law, John of Bo-

hemia, she was able to keep possession of this part of her inheritance. Thus early did the Tyrolese display that loyalty for
which they afterward became so famous.

Carinthia also did not long remain in the undisputed possession of Austria. Margaret was soon divorced from her youthful
husband, and shortly after married the son of the Emperor Louis
of Bavaria, who hoped to be able to invest his son, not only with
the Tyrol, but also with Carinthia. During the whole of this time
Bohemia and Austria were in a perpetual state of oscillation and
unstabie equilibrium. When, however, Charles IV. of Bohemia
was chosen emperor, he consented to leave Carinthia in the possession of Austria. Albert did homage for it, and rejoiced all the
more at the restoration of peace with the empire because just then
his unsuccessful struggle with Zürich and Glarus claimed all his
attention.

This prince not only increased the territories of Austria, but
his home policy was also extremely able, and his good government
earned for him the surname of the Wise. He gave Vienna a
new municipal code, also one to Klagenfurt, the capital of Carinthia, and put an end to trial by combat in the latter country. He
died in 1358, at the age of sixty-nine. "He was," says a contemporary, "a man beloved of God, honored in many lands, and a
generous father to many kings and princes."

According to the wish of their father, the four sons of Albert
reigned after him; but the eldest, Rudolf IV., exercised executive
authority in the name of the others. This prince was called by four
surnames—the Silent, the Magnificent, the Learned, and the
Founder. "Each one," says Krones, "characterized one of his
qualities. He always preserved the greatest secrecy about his plans.
He surrounded himself by a magnificent court, and loved high-
sounding titles, not from childish vanity, but because he knew how
much importance the world attaches to such things. He was in all
things the rival of his father-in-law, Charles IV., but more especially in that which concerned foundations in favor of the church,
and of science and art; he was learned in the knowledge of history,
a knowledge rare among his contemporaries. We are even told that
he had a secret method of writing, which was no doubt the art of
writing in cipher." He was only nineteen when he came to the
throne, but he had already married one of the daughters of the
Emperor Charles IV. Notwithstanding this family alliance,

Charles had not given Austria such a place in the Golden Bull as seemed likely to secure either her territorial importance or a proper position for her princes. They had not been admitted into the electoral college of the empire, and yet their scattered possessions stretched from the banks of the Leitha to the Rhine; three dukes of Austria had filled the highest place in the empire, and yet they were excluded from its council, and were thrown into the shade by their old rival, the house of Luxemburg. These grievances were enhanced by their feeling of envy toward Bohemia, which had attained great prosperity under Charles IV. It was at this time that in order to increase the importance of his house, Rudolf or his officers of state had recourse to a measure which was often employed in that age by princes, religious bodies, and even by the Holy See. It was pretended that there were in existence a whole series of charters which had been granted to the house of Austria by various kings and emperors, and which secured to their princes a position entirely independent of both empire and emperor. According to these documents, and more especially the one called the *privilegium majus*, the duke of Austria owed no kind of service to the empire, which was, however, bound to protect him; only in case of an expedition against Hungary was he bound to furnish troops, and then only twelve knights; he was to appear at the diets with the title of archduke, and was to have the first place among the electors; the prince might dispose of the state as he wished without even consulting the emperor; he need not go outside his dominions to seek investiture, but was to receive it on his own land, and on horseback; no fief in his lands could be held by the emperor. All these privileges were secured, not only to the dominions of Austria at that time, but to all lands they might become possessed of in the future. Rudolf pretended that these documents had just come to light, and demanded their confirmation from Charles IV., who refused it. Nevertheless, on the strength of these lying charters, he took the title of palatine archduke, and used the royal insignia without waiting to ask the leave of Charles.

Charles IV., who could not fail to be irritated by these pretensions, in his turn revived the claims which he had inherited from Premysl Otokar II., to the lands of Austria, Styria, Carinthia, and Carniola. These claims, however, were simply theoretical, and no attempt was made to enforce them, and the mediation of Louis the Great, king of Hungary, finally led to a treaty, in 1364, between the two princes, which satisfied the ambition of the Hapsburgs. By this treaty the houses of Hapsburg in Austria and of Luxemburg in Bohemia each guaranteed the inheritance of their lands to the other, in case of the extinction of either of the two families, and the estates of Bohemia and Austria ratified this agreement. A similar compact was concluded between Austria and Hungary, and thus the boundaries of the future Austrian state were for the first time marked out.

Rudolf himself gained little by these long and intricate negotiations, the Tyrol being all he added to his territory. Margaret Maultasche had married her son Meinhard to the daughter of Albert the Wise, at the same time declaring that, in default of male heirs to her son, the Tyrol should once more become the possession of Austria, and it did so in 1363. This was a most important event to Austria. It united Austria with the old possessions of the Hapsburgs in Switzerland and Germany, and opened the way into Italy. Rudolf persuaded Margaret Maultasche to take up her residence in Vienna, in order to secure himself against any possible caprice on the part of that restless and dissolute princess. Her memory still survives among the Tyrolese. A woman of insatiable lust and boldness, she is one of the strange creatures of the Middle Ages, and plays a conspicuous part in the national legends. The Tyrolese peasant still believes that, on the nights following the fasts of the four seasons, the phantom of the *böse gret*, the wicked and voluptuous princess, may be seen among the ruins of the old castle of Neuhaus.

The reign of Rudolf IV., though so full of events, was but short. He endeavored to rival his father-in-law, Charles IV., in everything, and loved to say that in his own lands he would be pope, emperor, bishop, and dean. His home government was as able as his foreign policy. Though he had falsified charters, he never falsified the coinage, a financial expedient which was but too much in fashion in the Middle Ages. He imposed a tax on wine and beer, and encouraged trade and manufactures. On April 7, 1356, he laid the foundations of the cathedral of St. Stephen at Vienna, one of the noblest monuments of Gothic art in Europe. Charles IV. had founded the University of Prague; Rudolf instituted the University of Vienna on the model of that of Paris, and endowed it with large estates and numerous privileges. This university was divided into four nations, the Austrian, Rhenish, Hungarian, and Saxon, and from the first had teachers of renown, such as the theologians Henry of Langenstein and Henry of Aoyta.

Rudolf died in 1365 at Milan, whither he had gone to marry his young brother, Leopold, to the sister of Barnabo Visconti. He had reigned for seven years—one of the shortest reigns of his dynasty, but also one of the most important.

He left no childern. His two brothers, Albert with the Plaited Hair (*á la tresse*), and Leopold III., called the Pious, succeeded him. Their tempers were so different that they could not reign together, and, breaking through all the traditions of their family, they divided the hereditary estates in 1379. Albert kept Austria, and left Styria, Carinthia, the Tyrol, and the old possessions of the Hapsburgs in Suabia and Alsace to Leopold. The Emperor Charles IV. was only too glad to ratify a division which could not fail to weaken a formidable power. " We have long labored," he said, " to humiliate the house of Austria, and, behold, now it humbles itself! "

The reign of the first prince of the Albertine branch presents no feature of importance. In that of his son, Albert IV., 1395-1404, William, the eldest son of Leopold III., laid claim to the administration of all the Hapsburg domains, notwithstanding the agreement between their fathers, and after a long struggle a new compact was entered into by the cousins by which Albert kept Austria and even Carniola, recognizing William as co-regent. Under Albert IV. the sect of the Vaudois made considerable progress in Austria, in spite of the strong measures he took against them. He was a man of great piety, and liked to spend much of his time among the monks of Marbach. Some of his contemporaries give him the name of the Patient. In 1400 he undertook a dangerous pilgrimage to Palestine, the fame of which was much noised abroad, and earned for him the fanciful title of *Mirabilia Mundi*. He took the part of Vacslav IV., king of Bohemia, in his struggles against his enemies, and in return for his help received from that prince a ratification of the treaty of succession entered into by Bohemia and Austria in the time of Rudolf. He was equally successful in his dealings with Hungary, from whose king he obtained a similar convention. He died in 1404 on an expedition against Moravia to punish certain Moravian lords who had ravaged Austrian territory.

His son, Albert V., was only seven years old at the time of his father's death; during his minority the princes of the Leopoldine branch were his guardians. Their brutal government provoked serious discontent in Austria, and the nobles proclaimed the prince of age when he was only fourteen. Albert V. was a wise administrator. Moreover, his marriage with Elizabeth, daughter of the Emperor Sigismund, king of Bohemia and Hungary, in 1422, secured to him the possession of Moravia, which was the dowry of that princess, and the probable succession to the thrones of both those kingdoms. In 1437, after the pacification of Bohemia, Sigismund assembled the estates of Bohemia and Hungary and proposed Duke Albert as his successor, and he was accepted by the Hungarians and by the Catholics of Bohemia. On the death of his father-in-law he was chosen emperor under the name of Albert II., and thus, in 1438, united the three crowns which had been so much coveted by his family. Thenceforth the dynasty of the Hapsburgs was to keep uninterrupted the possession of the imperial throne. The Albertine branch became extinct on the death of Albert's son, Ladislas the Posthumous, duke of Austria, king of Bohemia and of Hungary, in 1457.

Leopold the Pious (1365-1386) had obtained, in the division of the Austrian dominions, Styria, Carinthia, Carniola, and the Tyrol, together with the old family possessions in Suabia and Alsace. He rounded his dominions by several acquisitions, only one of which, the town of Triest, is of any importance to Austrian history. Weary of the double rule of the Venetian republic and the patriarch of Aquileia, this town voluntarily sought the protection of Leopold in 1382, only stipulating that he should confirm its privileges and its municipal liberty. This acquisition was of great importance to Austria, as it gave her access to the sea and brought her nearer to northern Italy, where she interfered repeatedly in the struggles between the towns and the princes. Less fortunate in Switzerland, where the Forest Cantons rose against him, Leopold lost both victory and life at the battle of Sempach in 1386. This led to the overthrow of the Hapsburg claims to overlordship and to the independence of the confederation.

The reigns of Leopold's immediate successors, William and Leopold IV., have no interest for us. On the accession of Frederick of the Empty Purse, in 1411, the dominions of the Leopoldine branch, after several divisions, were formed into two groups—one including the Tyrol and the Vorlände, those, namely, in southwestern Germany; the other, Styria, Carinthia, and Carniola. Frederick settled himself at Innsbrück, and his brother Ernest, the Man of Iron, at Gratz. Ernest married Cymburga, daughter of the Polish duke of Mazovia. It is said to be from her that the Hapsburgs have inherited the thick, protruding lip which is so characteristic of the family. She was the mother of the Emperor Frederick IV. and grandmother of Maximilian.

Frederick had to maintain a struggle against the nobles of the Tyrol, who formed a strong league against him under the leadership of the lord of Wolkenstein. He sought aid against them among the citizens and peasants. He did his best to remain at peace with the Swiss, but they managed to profit by his troubles. On his way to the Council of Constance Pope John XXIII. had met Frederick at Meran, and had then conferred on him the title of gonfalonier of the church. In return for this honor Frederick helped the Pope in his flight from Constance, and even offered him an asylum in his dominions. For this he was placed under the ban of the empire and excommunicated, and the Swiss, rising in revolt, destroyed the castle of Hapsburg. Frederick was obliged to yield. He gave up John XXIII. to his enemies, and was forced to surrender all his domains and to receive in return from the emperor, as an act of grace, just what he chose to restore to him. " You know the power of the dukes of Austria," Sigismund is said to have exclaimed. " Judge then from what you have seen what an emperor can do." This saying may be coupled with that attributed to Ernest, the Man of Iron: " God be with you, Hapsburg," said the emperor to him in a contemptuous tone. " Thanks, Luxemburg," replied the Man of Iron. That Frederick was not deprived of the Tyrol was due to his brother Ernest, and yet he had more than once to contend against Ernest, as the latter was both ambitious and turbulent. On his death, in 1424, Frederick became the guardian of his two sons, Frederick and Albert, who were minors and who reigned together. Frederick of the Empty Purse died in 1439. The citizens and peasants of the Tyrol, to whom he had granted many privileges, still reverence his memory. His son Sigismund (1439-1496) succeeded to his Austrian possessions, and his nephew, Frederick V., became emperor in 1440, under the name of Frederick IV. (1440-1493). Under him all the Hapsburg lands were again united.

Frederick V. was the father of Maximilian and the great-grandfather of Charles V. and Ferdinand of Austria. It is well

known to what a height of glory the house of Austria, ruler of
Europe and of the New World, attained under these princes. We
shall only notice here those facts in the reign of Frederick which
belong to the history of the hereditary states. He created Austria
an archduchy; he obtained possession of the county of Cilly on the
death of its count, Ulric; and he gained the right of succession to
the territories of his house in Alsace and Suabia, as well as the
Tyrol, for his son, Maximilian, stipulating to pay in return an
annual sum to Sigismund, the son of Frederick of the Empty
Purse. Sigismund had assigned these lands to the house of Bavaria, but Frederick was able to interfere in time. Besides this,
he acquired the town of Fiume, which was one day to rival Triest
on the Adriatic. Himly says: " Possessed of no genius whatever,
but endowed with extraordinary tenacity of purpose, Frederick
knew how to wait, and also how to outlive all his neighbors and
all his enemies. It was thus he was able laboriously to unite the
whole of the territories of the house of Hapsburg, and to secure
to his own line the unbroken succession to the imperial crown."
In his reign we first meet with the famous monogram A. E. I. O. U.
It is to be found on his pottery, on the books of his library, and on
his tomb in the church of St. Stephen. It has been explained as
standing for the proud phrases, " Aquila Electa Juste Omnia Vin-
cit," and also, " Austriae Est Imperare Orbi Universo," " Alles
Erdeich Ist Oesterreich Unterthan" (All the earth is subject to
Austria), and yet again, " Aller Eĥren Ist Oesterreich Voll"
(Austria is full of all honor).

The reign of Frederick was, however, not free from trouble.
Sigismund of Tyrol and Albert VI. of Styria disputed with him
the possession of all or part of the Austrian domains. The citizens
of Vienna allied themselves with his enemies and besieged him in
his own castle, whence he was only freed by the help of the king of
Bohemia, and after he had undertaken to give up Austria to Albert
VI., in return for a yearly sum of four thousand ducats. He did
not keep his engagements, and the quarrel broke out again, whereupon Frederick, as emperor, placed Vienna under the ban of the
empire, and the Pope issued an interdict against it. But notwithstanding the aid of the Pontifical legate and of George Podiebrad,
this struggle went on till the death of Albert VI., in 1463. The
insurrection in Vienna was led by a strange personage, the cattle-
merchant Holzer, who claimed to treat with the emperor as an

equal power. Holzer was in the end betrayed, and died under frightful tortures.

Later on Frederick saw his dominions ravaged by the Turks, who invaded Carinthia and Carniola, and penetrated into southern Styria, in 1472, 1473, and 1493. These new enemies proved, without knowing it, the best allies possible for the house of Austria, as it was mainly owing to the dread of their invasions that the Slavs and Magyars eventually submitted to the common rule of an hereditary monarchy.

PART II

BOHEMIA AND HUNGARY UNDER ELECTIVE KINGS
1310-1526

Chapter X

BOHEMIA UNDER THE HOUSE OF LUXEMBURG
1310-1415.

THE dynasty of the Premyslides became extinct with the assassination of Vacslav III. at Olmütz, and Bohemia has never since been ruled by a really national dynasty. The house of Austria at once took measures to profit by the situation. Albert I., the emperor, treated Bohemia as a fief of the empire, or even as a part of the family estates. He called upon the nobles to elect his oldest son, Rudolf, and enforced his demands by arms, so that the Bohemian nobility was compelled to elect Rudolf, in 1307, and even to guarantee the succession to his brothers in case he died without issue. The emperor further conferred upon him and his brothers an investiture which made an election useless and set at naught the fundamental right of the nobles to dispose of the crown. But a minority of them refused to recognize the new king. He was obliged to employ force, and at the siege of Horazdovce in 1307, he was killed. The estates refused to proclaim his brother as his successor, but appealed to Henry, duke of Carinthia and count of Tyrol, who had married Anna, the daughter of Vacslav III. The Emperor Albert again entered the kingdom, but he was forced to withdraw after the unsuccessful siege of Kuttenberg.

Henry of Carinthia did not long remain in power. He proved incapable, favored the Germans, and provoked revolts. The house of Luxemburg had just attained to the imperial dignity in the person of Henry of Luxemburg, and the nobles of Bohemia offered the crown to his son, John, on condition that he would marry the Princess Elizabeth, the last of King Vacslav's daughters. The marriage was celebrated at Spire, in 1310, and the emperor sent the royal standard of Bohemia to John as a token of investiture. The opposition of Henry of Carinthia was easily overcome, and with the surrender of Prague the whole of the kingdom submitted to John. The occupation of Bohemia by the house of Luxemburg continued for 127 years, from 1310 to 1437, and did much to bind the country to Germany. During it the German element was al-

113

ways favored and enabled to secure a dangerous preponderance in the political life of the state.

King John remained all his life a stranger in the country of his adoption. The national language he learned only against his will, and looked upon Bohemia as a country to be exploited. With a passion for gallantry and adventure, he was a knight-errant rather than a king, and was attracted in turn by France and Germany, according to his caprice. In spite of the fact that he was only fourteen years old at his accession, he began his reign auspiciously. Moravia, which the house of Austria had detached from Bohemia, and a part of Lusatia and the region about Görlitz were annexed, and the suzerainty of Bohemia over a large part of Silesia was secured. Thus the kingdom was largely increased territorially, but internally it was disturbed by the extravagance of the king, the disputes in the royal household, and favoritism to the Germans. Abroad John interfered in all that was going on; it was regarded a good thing to be counted one of his friends, for it was a common saying of the time that nothing could succeed without the help of God and the king of Bohemia.

The number of his expeditions is very great. He helped the king of Bavaria in his struggle against the Hapsburgs, and took Frederick, duke of Austria, prisoner at Mühldorf; tried to secure the Tyrol for his son; took up the cause of the Lombard cities against Martin della Scala, entered Lombardy and subdued the greater part of northern Italy. But this raised up enemies against him on all sides. All the potentates of central Europe, the emperor, Louis of Bavaria, the princes of Austria, and the kings of Hungary and of Poland united against him.

Although often successful, all these wars and exploits were worse than useless to Bohemia. The king wasted the revenues of the crown, and mortgaged its estates: of all the royal castles that of Prague alone was not mortgaged. The visits of the sovereign to Bohemia were always attended by new taxes, new loans, and a fresh debasement of the coinage. The royal authority fell into discredit, and the authority of his lieutenants disappeared. They were no longer obeyed, and the reign of force—*faustrecht*—alone prevailed. The king, when not engaged in warfare, wasted his time on tournaments, and most generally lived on his hereditary domain of Luxemburg, or else at the court of Paris, where he lavishly spent the money extorted from his subjects. During his absence the country was administered by captains, who farmed the crown revenues.

On the death, in 1330, of Queen Elizabeth, who never accompanied her husband, but lived in a solitude worse than widowhood, the hereditary prince, Charles, came to reside in Bohemia. He had been raised at the court of France, where he had learned economy and wise administrative methods. He did his utmost to restore order in the finances, and succeeded so well that after 1333 his father appointed him as co-regent.

Soon after this war broke out over the succession in Carinthia, in which King John opposed the emperor, and with Pope Clement VI. was so far successful as to bring about the election by five of the electors of his son Charles as emperor. But John did not long survive this unexpected triumph. In an expedition against the pagans of Lithuania, in 1337, he had lost one eye, and two years later, through unskillful physicians, he lost the other also. But his blindness in no way robbed him of his warlike ardor. On hearing of the invasion of France by the English he hastened to offer his sword to his relative, Philip of Valois, and was mortally wounded at the battle of Crécy in 1346.

With the election of Charles IV., known in Bohemia as Charles I., the center of gravity of the Holy Roman empire shifted to central Europe, where it thenceforth remained, first in Bohemia and later in Austria. German historians generally have been hostile in their attitude toward Charles IV.; those of Bohemia on the other hand are enthusiastic in their praises of him and call him the father of his country. His father had left behind him enormous tasks, and to these he applied himself with great energy. He regulated the revenues of the crown, freed the domains from mortgages, reorganized justice, suppressed brigandage, divided the kingdom into twelve circles, and revived industry and commerce. The opening of his reign was marked by the founding of the University of Prague, in 1348. According to the custom of the age it was divided into four nations, Czechs, Poles, Bavarians, and Saxons. Many Germans were through it attracted to Prague, where they gradually secured a dominant influence, especially after the founding of the University of Cracow, since the Polish nation was, from that time on, represented at the University of Prague by the Germans of Silesia. Thus the Czechs were at a very early date outweighed by foreigners.

Through its university Prague became the intellectual center, not only of Bohemia, but also of Germany, Hungary, and Poland. A patron of the liberal arts, Charles IV. embellished Prague with monuments which are its pride even to-day. He caused the cathedral of St. Vit to be rebuilt after the style of the Gothic buildings in France, constructed the famous stone bridge at Prague, perhaps the most beautiful in Europe, and built the royal castle of Prague, with its gilded roofs, after the model of the old Louvre, and the castle of Karlstein, near Beroun, to hold the royal insignia and the crown of St. Vacslav. During his reign the first school of painting known to the Middle Ages flourished in Bohemia. A number of works of this school are still extant. Czech literature flourished and produced many knightly romances, chronicles, satirical and elegiac poems, and even attempts at drama. At the king's request the diet consented to the abolition of trial by ordeal, the recognition of the right of the peasant to summon his lord before a court of justice, and some other important reforms. Important improvements were also made in the administration of justice, the relations between vassals and their lords, the status of the bourgeoisie of the towns. To these was often granted the right of managing the internal affairs of the town independent of the diet. The inhabitants of the Czech towns also were admitted to privileges which had up to that time been granted only to Germans.

He induced the diet to establish the principal of primogeniture, which had been customary under the dynasty of the Premyslides, as the law of succession in Bohemia, and thus fix the succession upon the Luxemburg dynasty. Moravia, Silesia, Upper Lusatia, Brandenburg, 'acquired from Otto, and the county of Glatz were declared, by the consent of their respective diets, integral and inalienable possessions of the crown of Bohemia. The see of Prague was made an archbishopric, thus becoming independent of the foreign diocese of Mainz. At the same time a monastery was established at Prague in which the Slavonic liturgy was regularly used.

It is well known how Charles IV. fixed the public law of Germany by means of the Golden Bull in 1346. But even in that famous act he did not neglect the interests of his kingdom of Bohemia. The king of Bohemia figures as one of the seven electors, it is true, but the document states that Bohemia is in nowise to be considered as a fief of the empire. Its king could be elected only by the estates of the country, and not by the emperor. His subjects are free from all foreign jurisdiction, and appeals to any foreign authority are forbidden. Of interest is a special provision ordering that the daughters and heirs of the king of Bohemia learn Latin, Italian, and the Slav language along with German, their mother tongue.

In 1366 Charles IV. concluded a treaty of inheritance with the Hapsburgs, by which it was agreed that whichever house survived the other was to take possession of both Austria and Bohemia. In order to secure Bohemia and the empire to his family, he caused his oldest son, Vacslav, to be crowned king of Bohemia as early as 1363, and in 1376 obtained his election as king of the Romans. Before his death he divided his possessions among his four sons, giving Bohemia, Silesia, the domains of Bavaria, Saxony, and Germany to Vacslav, the eldest; and Brandenburg, Görlitz, and Moravia to the others. He died in 1378 on the eve of the great religious movement which was destined to distract Bohemia for many years.

The glory of the reign of Charles IV. shines the more brightly because the reigns of his predecessor and his successor were unfortunate. His father was a royal adventurer, and his son, Vacslav IV., was a sluggard and a drunkard. The latter was not devoid of all good qualities, however, and his accession gave rise to great hopes in Bohemia. Unfortunately he was of too vacillating a character to rule well during a critical period, when the old institutions were crumbling and the thoughts of men were in a state of fermentation. His reign coincides with two great events of religious history—the great schism in the church and the reform movement of John Huss.

At the time of his accession Vacslav was only seventeen years old, and very far from being the monster he is represented in legend. His education had been sadly neglected, and besides his love for strong drink he had a passion for the chase and for dogs. He was tactless in his treatment of the nobles and clergy, and often bestowed offices upon simple citizens, and even servants of his household and stables. Abroad Bohemia might well have played an important part during his reign because of her family alliances. Vacslav's brother, Sigismund, was elected king of Hungary in 1387; his sister Anne married Richard II. of England, and he himself was in friendly alliance with the court of France. But the first years of the reign were unfortunate. Vacslav aroused the clergy by his violence toward the foremost of the ecclesiastics, notably toward the archbishop of Prague, from whom he demanded one of his castles. John of Pomuk, whose only crime was that he had opposed the royal will in an ecclesiastical matter, he caused to be tortured and thrown into the Moldau, an incident which gave rise to a famous legend in the seventeenth century, when Bohemia had been crushed and the Catholic faith restored. According to it this John Pomuk—St. John Nepomucen—was martyred for refusing to betray the secrets of the confessional, and an unsuccessful attempt was made to substitute his name for that of John Huss among the people.

Many of the nobles, angered by his violent conduct, and by the great influence Vacslav allowed the foreign favorites, rose against him. They claimed to unite for the purpose of restoring the constitution of the land, which was being violated by the king and his favorites, but in reality it was to secure the maintenance and augmentation of the privileges of their order. They had secured the alliance of the king of Hungary and of the Margrave Jost of Moravia, and when Vacslav resisted their demands he was made prisoner and forced to sign what amounted to an act of abdication. But John of Görlitz, the king's brother, supported by the lesser nobles and the inhabitants of the towns, came to his aid. The conspirators were forced to fly into Austria with their royal captive, where they kept him till the following year. In the interval Jost was really regent, and the king of Hungary interfered constantly in the affairs of the kingdom. Vacslav returned in 1396, drove out Jost, and resumed the government. In 1398 he went to France, where he had an interview at Rheims with Charles VI. in regard to the great schism which then divided Rome and Avignon. On his return to Germany he found that the electors had been aroused against him by Pope Benedict IX. In 1400 Rupert, the elector-palatine, was chosen emperor by the three ecclesiastical electors, and he at once declared war on the king of Bohemia. German troops penetrated Bohemia to the gates of Prague. But the city made a stout resistance and saved Bohemia for the king. As a matter of fact he retained only the title of king. Incapable of governing, he was obliged to seek the aid of his brother, Sigismund, king of Hungary. By him he was kept a prisoner in the palace at Prague with the margrave of Moravia, Procopius. Later Sigis-

mund carried both to Vienna, where he confided them to the keeping of the house of Austria. But Vacslav escaped and, through
the aid of that portion of the Bohemians who had refused to obey
a foreign king, again entered Prague in 1402.

These family feuds and the indignities suffered by the crowned
heads must have singularly diminished the respect for authority
among the people. At the same time the scandal to the whole of
Christendom over the existence of two Popes, one at Rome, the
other at Avignon, seriously undermined all religious authority.
Corruption had sprung up among sacerdotal orders. " Among the
priests," says Andrew de Cesky Brod, a contemporary, " there is
no discipline; among the bishops, open simony; among the monks,
countless disorders, and among laymen, there is no abuse which has
not been the habit of the clergy." Besides the Czech nation was
becoming indignant at the constantly increasing preponderance the
Germans were assuming in the kingdom. The peasants began to
find the yoke of serfdom too heavy, especially when imposed by
foreign masters. Respect for the crown was gone, and revolution
became inevitable. It came in the world of religious ideas and
teaching, and its exponent was John Huss.

The religious movement to which the name of Huss has become attached had been prepared even during the reign of Charles
IV., by the eminent preachers, Conrad Waldhauser and Milic of
Moravia. Both had preached the reform of manners and of the
church. Conrad had attacked the monks and the practices of
the age. Among other things he said: " Give to the poor and not
to the monks. They are well off, big and fat, and have more than
they need." Milic attacked the Pope himself and his cardinals.
Both were accused of heresy. Milic had to go to Avignon to defend himself, and died there in 1374. One of his pupils, Mathias
of Janov, the theologian, also endeavored to bring back the clergy
to a sense of their duty. He denied miracles and preached the cor- .
ruption of the church. The Pope and bishops he accused of having
perverted the traditions of the early church in order to advance
their temporal interests. The austere morality of these preachers
is found even in the writings of laymen of the period. Numerous
fragments of the Bible had been translated into the Czech, and
people were beginning to question authority in religious matters.

On the other hand a development of the national literature
aroused in men's minds a desire to be free from the supremacy

which the Germans had usurped throughout the country. The towns had been invaded by them, and, both in the schools and in the churches, their language prevailed over that of the native population, even ecclesiastical positions being not infrequently intrusted to Germans who had no knowledge of the speech of their flocks. The greatness of Huss lies in the fact that he embodied in himself and in his teachings both the moral and national tendencies of his time. As a priest he preached the reform of the church and brought the Divine Word home to the people in their own language; as a patriot he strove to free the Bohemian nation from the intellectual oppression of the German minority. Till the time of Luther no other reformer exercised so powerful an influence over a nation.

John Huss was born in 1369 at Husinec, in the south of Bohemia. He studied at the University of Prague, attained the degrees of Master of Arts and Bachelor of Theology, and held a professorship at the university. As a student of theology he made a deep study of the writings of Wiclif, which had found their way into Bohemia through the intercourse with England brought about by the marriage of the Bohemian princess with Richard II. That he was greatly influenced by Wiclif is easily seen, and he was soon to find himself in violent opposition to the upper clergy. In 1402 he was made dean, and preacher at the Bethlehem chapel, which had been founded by patriotic gifts and where the sermons were in the native language. Crowds flocked to hear him and his sermons on the abuses of the church found a sympathetic echo in the hearts of his hearers.

Unable to refute the charges made by Huss, his adversaries accused him of the Wiclifite heresies. In 1403, at the request of the chapter of Prague, forty-five propositions taken from the works of Wiclif were condemned by the University of Prague. Huss and his followers would not agree to the decision, maintaining that the errors attributed to Wiclif did not exist in his writings, but were falsely read into them. At their suggestion the Bohemian nation of the University of Prague held a meeting in 1408, at which they discussed the forty-five articles, and, notwithstanding the previous decision of the four nations, declared that the condemned articles need not be interpreted in an heretical sense. This declaration was considered by the Archbishop Zbynek as a formal act of disobedience. He ordered a new examination of all known copies of Wiclif's works, and a short time after he had a large number burned. About the same time charges were brought before the archbishop against Huss because of the violence of his preaching.

In the meantime a general council assembled at Pisa to put an end to the great schism in the Holy See. The cardinals most active in bringing about the council planned not only to restore the unity of the church, but also to introduce reforms " as to its head and members." King Vacslav, in obedience to the decision of the council, called upon the clergy of his kingdom to render obedience to the Pope at Rome, Gregory XII. But the Archbishop Zbynek, together with the higher clergy, refused to obey. Vacslav consulted the university on this grave question. It divided, only the Bohemian nation, in which Huss and his friends were in the majority, declaring in favor of the king and the cardinals. Thus the archheretic Huss took his stand on the side of the Roman church, while its representative, the archbishop, declared against it. His opposition to the higher clergy in this matter had the effect also of strengthening his cause at court, for Vacslav had never been on good terms with the higher clergy of his realm, and most of his favorites, from motives of self-interest, looked with favor on the proposed reforms. For the reformers declared that it would be necessary to deprive the church of the greater part of its possessions in order to bring the clergy back to the purity of primitive times. But these possessions once secularized, the king could divide them among his favorites.

Huss seized this favorable moment to procure for the Czech nationality the place which belonged to it by right in the university. He represented to the king the injustice of granting to foreigners an overwhelming preponderance over the natives—a preponderance that manifested itself, not only in decisions on matters of doctrine, but also in the distribution of offices and appointments. " The Czechs," said he, " ought to be first in the kingdom of Bohemia, as Frenchmen are in France and Germans in Germany. The laws of the land, the divine will, and natural instinct demand that they should hold the first offices." In conformity with these ideas the king decreed that henceforth, in all deliberations and elections in the university, the Bohemian nation should have three votes and the foreigners only one. As a result the German professors and students left Prague in a body in 1409, and proceeded to found the University of Leipsic.

This energetic measure on the part of the king made obedience to the decrees of the Council of Pisa easier, and the council, out of gratitude, recognized Vacslav as king of the Romans. But this proved an illusory compliment, for the electors paid no regard to it, and, in 1410, elected Sigismund of Hungary. At the same time, Archbishop Zbynek, by no means crushed by the triumph of Huss, who was now rector of the university, placed the reformer and the city of Prague under an interdict. Huss appealed to the Holy See, and the Pope suspended the interdict in order to give him time to vindicate himself. Zbynek, fearing the anger of Vacslav, fled to Hungary and died on the way.

The Council of Pisa, in order to end the schism, had set aside both the Pope at Rome and the Pope at Avignon, and chosen a new Pontiff, Alexander V. Thus for a time there were three Popes. Alexander V. was to be the restorer of the church, but he lived only a short time, and his successor, John XXIII., possessed none of the qualities and virtues of a reforming Pope. Huss, on the other hand, continued preaching with more ardor than ever, and despairing of reforming the whole church, he directed all his efforts toward the church of Bohemia. Notwithstanding the prohibition, both by the bishop and by the Pope, against preaching in the Bethlehem chapel, Huss continued to do so, and developing the teachings of Wiclif, he denied the authority commonly attributed to the Pope as head of the visible church. The papacy, moreover, just at this time, furnished him with weapons against itself. In 1412 John XXIII., attacked by the king of Naples, who had espoused the cause of his deposed predecessor, Gregory XII., ordered a crusade to be preached for the defense of the Holy See. Full indulgence was promised to all believers who aided with prayers or arms or money. Huss and his followers denounced this as traffic in spiritual favors, both in public disputations and in their preaching. The excited populace gave itself over to excesses against the upper clergy, and the preachers of indulgences were interrupted in the churches by questions from their auditors. Three of the disturbers were seized and beheaded by the councilors of the old town, but the people, far from being intimidated by this severe measure, secured the bodies and interred them, as those of martyrs, in the Bethlehem chapel. The Pope then pronounced an anathema against Huss, and placed every town in which he might live under the interdict. The frightened king besought Huss to leave Prague. Welcomed in the castles of the national nobility, the master found a docile and enthusiastic audience among the country people. From his seclusion he published controversial works, which were read with all the more avidity, not merely because Huss was a true reformer and a defender of the national cause, but also because in his native tongue Huss was a writer of much clearness and force. King Vacslav saw with dismay the spread of the new doctrines in his kingdom, which the Holy See now designated as a hotbed of heresy. He did his utmost to quiet Huss and to reconcile him with Albic, the new archbishop of Prague.

But in the meantime the sale of indulgences had not procured the wished-for assistance for the Pope. Driven from Rome by the king of Naples, he was forced to fly to Bologna, and in this extremity he took refuge in the idea of a general council, which should come to the aid of the ills of the church and the misfortunes of the Holy See. In an interview at Lodi with the Emperor Sigismund it was decided to call a general council to meet at Constance. Vacslav believed that he saw in the council the only means of putting an end to the religious disturbances of Bohemia, which so seriously embarrassed his vacillating mind. The emperor asked Huss to appear at Constance, under an imperial safe-conduct, in order to defend his teaching. The master—so Huss was called by his countrymen—was not the man to recoil before this injunction; he believed himself sufficiently sure of the truth to convince his adversaries, and his enthusiasm made him ready to defend it to the death. He went to Constance accompanied by an escort of Bohemian knights granted him by King Vacslav; he expected to enter the lists with the chance to fight with equal weapons, and relied implicitly on the emperor's promise of safe-conduct. But the council paid no heed to it, regarding it rather as an illegal encroachment of the temporal upon the spiritual power.

Shortly after his arrival Huss was thrown into prison to be judged as a heretic and disturber of church discipline, and the Emperor Sigismund made only a feeble protest. The trial was at first conducted in secret, though later Huss was admitted to defend himself before the council. Many of the accusations against him were false. But in his defense Huss, while not breaking openly with Catholicism, nevertheless defended doctrines which involved the rejection of the Papal authority and placed that of the Scriptures above that of the church. Beyond this the council refused to hear him, and called on him to make a full recantation. This he would not do, and in the session of July 6, 1415, he was declared a heretic and delivered over to the secular authority. By it he was condemned to be burned alive and his ashes to be cast in the Rhine. He walked to the stake with heroic courage and died the martyr's death. One year later the council also caused Jerome of Prague, one of Huss's most faithful adherents, whose fiery eloquence had spread the master's doctrines even in Poland and Lithuania, to be burned.

Huss is frequently known to foreigners only as a famous heretic, admired by some, hated by others, according to the particular religious opinions they hold. Slavic peoples, especially Bohemians, honor him as a writer of genius, a purifier of their language, and an intrepid champion of their nationality. Huss has much in common with Luther; what the latter did for the German language the former did a century earlier for the Bohemian. Not satisfied with making his works models of excellent style, he endeavored to fix the national orthography, took great pains to adapt the Latin alphabet to the soft and sibilant sounds of the Slav tongue, and banished Germanisms from the language as he had banished Germans from the university. "For," he writes, "as Nehemiah chastised the Jewish children for speaking the jargon of Ashdod and being ignorant of Hebrew, so ought all men of Prague be chastised, and all other Czechs whose language is half German, half Czech. We hear them, but we verily do not understand them." His religious and controversial works, as well as his letters written from Constance, are considered models of style to the present day. As a poet, he wrote a number of hymns and himself set them to music, introducing, so the critics say, some excellent innovations in religious music.

But that which most impressed his compatriots was not the genius of the master, but rather the purity of his life, the sweetness of his character, and the heroism of his martyrdom. The council desired to efface all trace of him from the earth. They burned his clothing and scattered his ashes on the Rhine. They believed they had driven out the spirit of reform and subdued Bohemia. But at the fires of the stake at which Huss perished a conflagration was lit which desolated both Bohemia and Germany and was only extinguished in the blood of countless victims.

"Ad majorem dei gloriam."

JOHN HUSS IS LED TO THE FUNERAL PYRE AT CONSTANCE, SWITZERLAND

Painting by Karl Gustav Hellquist

Chapter XI

BOHEMIA AND THE HUSSITE WARS

1415-1437

THE absence of John Huss did not calm the religious excitement in Bohemia. His disciples pushed his doctrines to extremes which their master had not foreseen. Huss had refused obedience to the visible church and proclaimed the right of appeal to the Holy Scriptures only when the church appeared to him in contradiction with the Divine Word. He was not one of those who sought to remake the dogmas and rites according to their own fancy. But the religious imagination of the Middle Ages when once thoroughly aroused would not stop halfway. Dogmas without practical consequences and without moral application, born in the brain of some dreamer, would suffice to excite the passion of the masses whose deepest interest in life was their religion. One of the disciples of John Huss, Jakoubek Steibrsky, or De Stribro, began to teach that communion ought to be given to the people as well as to the priest in both forms, and not in bread only. This teaching was enthusiastically received in all the parishes where Huss had adherents. The cup became the symbol of his disciples, and was to be found on the church steeples and in all public buildings. An epigram of the time says:

> *Tot pingit calices Boemorum turba per urbes,*
> *Ut credas Bacchi numina sola coli.*

The Council of Constance hastened to condemn the innovations of the Utraquists, or Calixtins, as they were called. But the sentence against Huss by this same body was not likely to inspire obedience to the decree against his disciples. The news of the martyrdom of the master, as told by his faithful friend, Peter of Mladenovic, aroused the most violent anger in Prague. The excited masses attacked the orthodox priests, whom they accused of complicity in the judicial murder of Huss; some were robbed, others driven from their homes, and a few murdered. An earthquake and an eclipse of the sun which occurred in 1415 were regarded by the people as a proof of the interest of Heaven in the innocent martyr. In the rural districts the lords and knights who were patrons of livings drove out the priests whom they disliked and replaced them with others, regardless of the authority of bishops or archbishops, though not always from religious zeal alone; many lords despoiled the clergy simply in order to secure the benefices for themselves.

In a large assembly held at Prague, at which 452 lords and knights of Bohemia and Moravia were present, a letter, declaring the execution of Huss to be an affront to the whole Bohemian nobility, was drawn up and addressed to the Council of Constance. They also organized a league which refused obedience to foreign priests, and recognized only the bishops of the national church, provided always that their doctrines conformed to the Scriptures. They even made reservations concerning their obedience to the Pope which the council was about to elect, announcing that they would accept none but the council of professors of the university as authority in matters of faith. A strong minority of the nation, however, composed largely of Germans, whether from conviction or interest, remained faithful to the traditions of the Roman Catholic Church. The rivalry between the two races was, therefore, further intensified by religious differences.

The council took energetic measures. Stribro and the signers of the protest were cited to appear before it, and the University of Prague, the center of heresy, was ordered to be closed and deprived of all the privileges conferred upon it by the Pope. Vacslav, Queen Sophia, and the new archbishop of Prague, Conrad, were warned of ecclesiastical penalties unless they openly disavowed the new heresies. But slight attention was given to the warnings. The report of the death of Jerome of Prague raised the public excitement and anger to its height. The university, far from submitting to the orders of the council, erected itself into a court with jurisdiction in matters of doctrine. Communion in both kinds was declared indispensable to salvation, and Huss was proclaimed a saint and martyr.

But it was not long before dissension, that plague of all independent sects, made its appearance among the Hussites themselves. The masters at the university had declared that nothing should be allowed that would be contrary to the Scriptures. But the Scriptures are not always clear. Thus it came about that sectarians arose who rejected all the sacraments except baptism and the Lord's Supper, denying the authority for the mass, worship of the saints, the doctrine of purgatory, fasts, and the ecclesiastical hierarchy.

The new doctrines spread most widely in the rural districts. The little town of Ousti, not far from the site of the later town of Tabor, became the center for the new religionists. When the University of Prague declared its independence of the council it did not intend to separate from the church permanently. It now assumed the rôle of an orthodox body toward the innovators of Ousti, who had set up a new confession, and pronounced them heretics. But these refused to obey its decisions. Hussism became unfaithful to its principles, for instead of directing its efforts to bringing about the reform of the church, its followers lost themselves in the boundless wastes of theories and dogma. Even in the first period of its enthusiasm constant disputes and quarrels over points of doctrine and dogma occurred among the Hussites themselves.

The Council of Constance broke up in 1418 without having succeeded in reëstablishing the authority of the church in Bohemia. Nor was Pope Martin V., who fell heir to this difficult task, more successful. King Vacslav, at his request, tried to reinstate the priests who had been driven from their parishes, but the people rose against the restored pastors. Rather than enter the churches of the intruders, the peasants, under the guidance of their pastor, would assemble in the open country, usually in the mountains. To these they gave Biblical names, as, for example, Mt. Tabor, near Ousti, on the Elbe. This mountain became the home of the most ardent preachers of the new sect. A new confession of faith was drawn up which aimed at the restoration of primitive Christianity, and maintained the principle of community of goods. Its adherents called each other brother and sister, rejected priestly garb and ritualistic forms of worship, and worshiped in the popular language. These communities who thus separated themselves from the general faith and from the ordinary habits of life awaited only daring leaders to resist not only the church, but also the secular power if it tried to disperse them. These soon appeared in the persons of Nicholas Huss, at Tabor, and the old chevalier, John Zizka of Trocnov, at Prague. The latter had acquired a knowledge of military matters and a hatred of the Germans while fighting with the

Poles against the Teutonic order. Intense religious zeal made of them and their followers, though untrained, the most terrible warriors known to Europe in the Middle Ages.

The struggle began at Prague. In renewing the municipal council of Prague, Vacslav appointed a number of knights hostile to the Hussites. This aroused the people, and led by the priest, John of Zeliv, and Zizka, they invaded the city hall, seized the newly appointed councilors, and hurled them through the windows upon the pikes and lances below. The king, amazed at this popular violence, yielded and appointed magistrates favorable to the people. But he died shortly afterward. King of Bohemia at the age of three, king of the Romans at fifteen, and successor to his father at seventeen, Vacslav had, from the day of his majority, enjoyed all human advantages. But he was not equal to the burdens. Kept a prisoner by his nobles and his brother Sigismund, vacillating between the Holy See and the Hussites, he continued throughout the plaything of his passions, of men and of circumstances, without ever being able to dominate them. His reign marks the beginning of the political decadence of Bohemia. But the Czech nation had arrived at a point in its history when peoples are of greater importance than monarchs, and notwithstanding the excesses inseparable from an age still half-barbarous, we shall see Bohemia accomplishing great things and handing down to posterity a glorious heritage.

The death of Vacslav unchained all the passions which respect for royalty had until then held in check. Churches and monasteries were given over to pillage, Catholic priests driven out and replaced by Hussites. The archbishop and the chapter of the cathedral fled, and many of the rich middle class, especially the Germans, followed their example. Because of the dispositions made by Charles IV., the successor of Vacslav was the Emperor Sigismund, who had so perfidiously betrayed his promise of safe-conduct to Huss. The estates of Bohemia sent ambassadors to him asking him to come to Prague. They demanded the right to communion in both kinds, which, if he acquiesced, meant that he would be obliged, at the very outset of his reign, to place himself in opposition to the council and the Pope. The king gave an evasive answer, and charged the queen-dowager Sophia to carry on the government in Bohemia till his arrival. The regent attempted to disperse a number of meetings and received the support of the nobility, who were beginning to take umbrage at these popular gatherings held under the pretext of religion. But Zizka and Nicholas Huss stirred up the people of Prague; they attempted to take the royal castle by assault, burned a part of the city, and forced the regent to permit the popular gatherings, and communion in both kinds. At the news of these excesses Sigismund promptly decided to come to Prague himself. After receiving the homage of the estates of Silesia and Moravia, he called on the Pope to preach a crusade against Hussites, and prepared to enter Bohemia.

These developments greatly encouraged the Catholics and Germans in Bohemia. The Germans of Kuttenberg began to persecute all the heterodox of the place, seized four hundred and threw them into the mines. A cry of horror arose throughout the entire kingdom. Zizka hastened to Mt. Tabor, organized the brothers gathered on that mountain for military purposes, and made out of the place a fortified town which became the strongest citadel of the Hussites. The improvised army on Mt. Tabor needed special tactics and new weapons; it could not drag about with it the equipment of the knights of the Middle Ages. The flail weighted with iron, the heavy hammer of the blacksmith, were their arms, and clumsy wagons furnished a cover to the combatants and a refuge for the wounded, while an inflexible discipline secured unity of action. Even the Utraquists of Prague, when they saw the emperor take the cross at Breslau, prepared to defend their faith. Cenek of Wartenburg, the burggrave of Prague, issued a proclamation to the Bohemian nation urging them to arm against the common enemy.

In the spring of 1420 Sigismund, at the head of an army, invaded Bohemia by way of Kralove-Hradec and Kuttenberg, and pushed on to the outskirts of Prague itself, where he had himself crowned. He then laid siege to the city, but John Zizka, at the head of the Taborites, marched upon Prague to relieve the city. He occupied Mt. Vitkov, near Prague, which has ever since borne his name, Zizkaberg, repulsed all the assaults of the crusading imperial army, numbering nearly one hundred thousand, and ultimately forced it to raise the siege.

But the emperor's position in Bohemia was still very formidable. He held nearly all the royal cities and towns, and even had possession of the royal castle of Vysehrad, which commands Prague on the right bank of the Moldau. His army was made up of Bohemian Catholics and even some of the Utraquist nobility.

But his treasure was exhausted, and in order to meet the expenses of the war he was forced to pledge a part of the property of the clergy. In the meantime the people of Prague in their turn assumed the aggressive and besieged the castle of Vysehrad. Sigismund tried in vain to relieve it. He was beaten back and forced to abandon it. Shortly afterward conditions in Hungary demanded the emperor's presence, and he had to leave Bohemia, after having organized a provisional government.

The withdrawal of the king greatly increased the courage of the insurgents, who felt that they had the secret sympathy of the majority of the nation. The commune of Prague issued a decree of banishment and confiscation against all those who had joined the king or who refused to recognize communion in both kinds. A portion of the property of the Catholic clergy was also confiscated. In this way the preponderance of the German element in Prague was weakened, and those that remained were converted to the doctrines of the Hussites. The people of Prague, in league with Zizka and the Taborites, now undertook to reconquer the country, and after several months all of the cities except Pilsen and Budweis were occupied, though some of them not till after an energetic resistance. The castle of Prague itself finally succumbed. The Germans generally left the cities after they were reconquered by the Czechs, and have never since regained the preponderance then lost. Many churches, monasteries, and religious buildings were destroyed or damaged during the struggle. The Taborites showed no mercy, but radical measures were necessary. The Utraquist nobility, astounded by these triumphs, ended by abandoning the party of the king and ranging themselves on the side of the people. The archbishop of Prague himself made terms with them, consecrated their priests, and placed a part of the ecclesiastical benefices at their disposal.

The Hussites had triumphed. They met at Prague to adopt their creed and settle upon a constitution for the kingdom. This creed had been formulated by the masters of the University of Prague, and had always appeared at the head of the proclamations of Zizka. It contained four articles: demanding communion in both kinds, free preaching of the Divine Word, the secularization of church property, and the punishment by temporal penalties of mortal sins and offenses against the church, whether committed by laymen or ecclesiastics. A solemn embassy was sent to Vladislav of Poland to offer him the crown, and while waiting his acceptance the country was to be governed by a committee of twenty persons, consisting one-half of representatives from the estates, the other of representatives of the cities and the Taborites. These measures were completed by the acts of a synod which met at Prague under the direction of the university, and which occupied itself particularly with the reform of ecclesiastical discipline. It imposed four councilors upon the Archbishop Conrad, who with him were intrusted to maintain this discipline.

But the Czechs were still far from being united. The Taborites expected to have their own church and had already chosen a bishop (1420) to consecrate their priests, thus separating themselves from the Bohemian church. The Pope, moreover, had interdicted the archbishop of Prague and declared his diocese vacant. The Czech nobility counted on the support of Vladislav of Poland, because a part of the Polish nobility also had adhered to the Hussite doctrines, while an accession of territory to Poland at this time would have been very advantageous because of the king's dispute with Sigismund over Galicia. But the Polish clergy feared that the personal union of Bohemia and Poland would hasten still more the progress of Hussite heresies in the kingdom. The representations of Martin V. led the king to decline the proffered crown. The Czechs then offered it to Prince Vitold, grand duke of Lithuania. They realized how disastrous to their interests the German dynasties had been, and sought to bring about a closer union with their Slav kinsmen.

The danger was great, for Sigismund, together with the German princes, was preparing a new crusade against them. But the Germans entered Bohemia before Sigismund was ready to cooperate with them. Their army numbered 200,000 and counted five electors among its leaders. They laid siege to the town of Saatz, which made a vigorous defense. The crusaders revenged themselves by ravaging the country and massacring the peasants; all who could not speak German were put to death. Zizka hastened to the relief at the head of his Taborites and the men of Prague. The intrepid leader had been blind in one eye for many years, and had lately lost the remaining eye at the siege of the Château of Rabi. But his blindness did not lessen his military skill. His very name carried terror with it. The Germans raised the siege and retired. Sigismund, detained by the Turks on the Danube, finally arrived with an army of 80,000, under the command of the famous condottiere, Pipa the Florentine. Against this force Moravia made no resistance; less fortified by nature than Bohemia, it has also a less warlike and stubborn race. The nobility swore obedience to the king, and renounced communion in both kinds. Their example was followed by some of the Utraquist nobility in Bohemia, and Sigismund pushed forward as far as Kuttenberg, which he seized. But Zizka attacked him unexpectedly, and after driving his army back to the Ford of the Germans, inflicted on him a crushing defeat on the banks of the Sazava, in 1422.

This victory freed Bohemia from the German invasions, and the Czechs were for a number of years comparative masters in their own country. But unfortunately harmony was far removed from their own ranks. Differences over questions of dogma divided the men of Prague from the Taborites, while the Taborites themselves split into various sects. The strangest theories arose among them. Some preached community of goods and of marriage; others (the Adamites) a return to nature, to primitive nudity and unbridled bestiality. Zizka was obliged to denounce these refractory disciples and burned alive those who fell into his hands. At Prague the Taborites had recruited numerous adherents and, under their leader, the monk John of Zeliv, whose eloquence swayed the masses, threatened to take possession of the city. For two years he was the real sovereign in Prague, till some of the wealthy bourgeoisie got him into their power by stratagem and brought about his execution. But a riot broke out as a result, and the conservative Utraquists were expelled from the council and replaced by the followers of the new martyr. But in spite of all these disorders the grand duke of Lithuania decided to accept the crown of Bohemia, and chose for his provisional lieutenant the nephew of the king of Poland, Prince Sigismund Korybutovicz. He assembled an army at Cracow and entered Bohemia by way of Silesia and Moravia, without meeting any resistance. With this people, so divided and so jealous of their freedom, the authority of a freely elected king still preserved all its prestige. The regent put an end to the disorders in Prague and in other royal cities, and restored the administration of these towns to the lords and knights. Unfortunately for Bohemia he did not long fill the rôle of peacemaker. In consequence of a treaty made between the kings of Hungary and of Poland, Prince Vitold renounced the crown of Bohemia, in 1422, and recalled his wise lieutenant. The Utraquist nobility united with the Catholics to place Bohemia again under Sigismund. But Zizka undertook a vigorous campaign, which, as always, ended in the triumph of the Taborites. Sigismund Korybutovicz returned to mediate between the two parties, this time on his own account, and against the wishes of his uncle. His popularity was so great that the two parties agreed to recognize him again as regent.

Soon after these events Zizka died. The few documents by his hand which remain prove his sincere faith, deep religious feeling, and ardent patriotism. In one of his manifestoes he declares that he takes up arms for the defense of Czech and Slav nationality.

The death of Zizka was a serious loss to his party. His courage had enabled the Taborites to resist their enemies within the kingdom. His authority had kept them as far as possible in the paths of reason and moderation. After his death his party divided, the extremists keeping the name of Taborites, the moderates taking that of Orphans. But these two factions, notwithstanding their intestine struggles, were always ready to unite against the Catholics, and by the Treaty of Voszice, in 1425, they obtained the separation of most of the royal towns from Prague and formed an independent confederation under the control of the Taborites and Calixtins. The Catholics themselves consented to a truce, and the lords agreed to tolerate communion in both kinds on their estates. Pilsen was the only town that refused to enter into this agreement.

Moravia had remained more faithful to Catholicism; orthodoxy reigned almost throughout the vast domains of the bishop of Olmütz, and in the royal towns where the Germans were in the majority, and which for the most part Sigismund had pledged to his son-in-law, the duke of Austria. It was only with the help and through the proximity of Bohemia that the Moravian Hussites could hold their own. In the other possessions of the crown of St. Vacslav, in Silesia and Lusatia, the German majority, later so sympathetic toward the doctrines of Luther, was, for reasons more national than religious, hostile to the Hussite movement, while Brandenburg had long ceased to belong to Bohemia. The Emperor Sigismund, always in need of money, had mortgaged it, and in 1415 bestowed it on Frederick of Hohenzollern.

Sigismund still hoped to regain his authority in Bohemia. After vainly seeking aid from the empire, he entered into an al-

liance with his son-in-law, Albert V., duke of Austria, and the
margrave of Meissen, pledging several towns in the north of Bohemia, notably Brux and Aussig, on the Elbe, to the latter. These
the prince at once occupied. But this time the Czechs did not wait
for the invasion of their country; they assumed the offensive, entered Austria to the south, and sent an army to besiege Aussig in
the north. Their leader was again Sigismund Korybutovicz, who
was always faithful to the cause of Bohemia, and Procopius the
Holy, also called Procopius the Shaven, or the Great, a married
priest whom events had made a soldier, and who regarded himself
as heir to Zizka's genius. A bloody battle was fought under the
walls of Aussig, at which the Saxons and Misnians were completely
defeated and forced to retreat beyond the frontier. Albert of Austria fled into Moravia and thence into his own duchy. Thus it came
about that the Hussites became in their turn the aggressors, Sigismund, engaged with the Turks in other parts of his dominions, being unable to check them.

But while victorious over their enemies in the field, the Hussites continued to break up into numerous sects. The divisions
among the Taborites have been noted; these were followed by a
division among the Utraquists. Two parties arose. The one desired a reconciliation with the church, stipulating the right of communion in both kinds. The other adhered to the doctrines of Wiclif, and demanded the abolition of certain Catholic rites and the
use of the national language in the mass for the reading of the
Epistles and Gospels.

Prince Sigismund Korybutovicz sided with the former, because
it favored a reconciliation, and entered into secret negotiations with
the Pope. At this the opposite party rose against him, took him
prisoner, and drove him out of Bohemia, in 1427. The democratic
party triumphed; the men of Prague drew still closer their alliance
with the Taborites, and Procopius the Great became undisputed
head of the Hussites, with even greater power than Zizka had had.

The Holy See, however, continued to preach the crusade
against Bohemia; in 1427 the German princes entered Bohemia
again, this time by way of Pilsen, which had remained faithful to
Catholicism. But at the approach of Procopius the Great their
army withdrew to Tachov, where the Czechs overtook and
defeated them. Procopius now in his turn took the offensive.
He invaded Hungary and ravaged the country as far as Pres-

burg, invaded Moravia, where the Hussites were beginning
to raise their heads again, and by the beginning of 1428 reached
Silesia. There the Czechs occupied and garrisoned numerous
towns, defeated the army of the bishop of Breslau, and
subjected a portion of Silesia. The Hussites likewise penetrated
into Bavaria and Austria, and everywhere put to rout the
troops sent against them. They were invincible, and Sigismund
was obliged to open negotiations. A meeting with Procopius
and his followers was arranged at Presburg. There Sigismund
proposed that all religious differences should be submitted to a
council which was to meet within two years at Basel, and that a
truce should be declared till that time. But the Bohemians had not
forgotten the fate of Huss; they had little confidence in a council.
The proposals were rejected and hostilities were resumed.

Procopius invaded Lusatia and conquered it. Next he led
a great expedition into Meissen and Saxony against Germany. The
army of the elector of Saxony broke in flight before the Hussites.
Meissen, Saxony, Thuringia, and Franconia were invaded, and, according to some historians, seventy cities and several thousand villages were ravaged and burned. The Hussites became the terror
of Germany. The duke of Bavaria, the margrave of Nuremberg,
and many cities purchased peace. The town of Homburg-on-the-
Saale sent a deputation of children to Procopius to beg for pity
from the fierce conqueror.

The exploits of the Czechs filled the mind of Europe with
admiration and terror. The Holy See was all the more alarmed
because the Hussite doctrines were beginning to spread beyond the
borders of Bohemia into Poland, Hungary, Germany, and even
France. From Dauphiny voluntary contributions were sent to the
Czechs, and the bishop of Arras wrote that he dared not leave his
diocese because " he had to watch over his flock in order to guard
them against the Bohemian heresy." Christendom believed the
only remedy for so many evils lay in the convocation of a council,
and the clergy of Germany and of France threatened to meet without the sanction of the Pope. But the Pope had more faith in
arms than in the decisions of theological assemblies. The defeat
of the Bohemians would, he believed, bring the most rebellious
spirits under the authority of the church. Accordingly a new crusade was decided upon at the diet of Nuremberg, in 1431, and
shortly after a new army entered Bohemia from the west. Pro-

copius awaited them at the town of Taus with a formidable force, and once more administered a terrible defeat. Again the Hussites invaded Austria and Hungary.

In the meantime the council of Basel had assembled. The world longed for peace, especially Germany and Bohemia, exhausted by the continual wars. The Bohemian army had largely lost that religious gravity and incorruptible morality which had distinguished the comrades of Zizka, and now included all kinds of needy adventurers. Besides no effective government existed since the departure of Sigismund Korybutovicz. The committee of twelve appointed in 1431 exercised only a very limited authority.

The council of Basel opened in 1431. In October a conciliatory letter was sent to the Hussites asking them to send representatives to Basel. Conrad, the Utraquist archbishop, had died in December of 1430, and if the Bohemians wished to have a clergy they were obliged either to break with apostolic traditions or to become reconciled to the Catholic church. The message of conciliation was received with joy by the estates and the peaceful inhabitants of Bohemia. In a diet held at Prague, in January, 1432, it was decided by the Utraquists and Orphans that negotiations should be entered into to learn how the envoys from Bohemia would be received. They had not forgotten John Huss and the safe-conduct which had saved him neither from the prison nor the stake. The Taborites agreed to negotiate only on the condition that war should be continued till all was settled. Procopius continued to push on his invasion of Germany and ravaged Brandenburg as far as Berlin and Frankfort-on-the-Oder. He then forced Silesia to buy peace from him on exceedingly hard terms. In the year 1432 the Hussites sent an embassy to the court of King Vladislav, which succeeded in arranging a treaty between Poland and the Czechs; in exchange for the aid of the Poles the crown of Bohemia was promised to the young Vladislav Jagellon. Nevertheless the council, nowithstanding the opposition of Pope Eugenius IV., who opposed every compromise with heretics, sent a deputation to the Bohemians to arrange the manner in which their envoys should be received. It was agreed that they should appear not as accused before a tribunal, but as free men with the right to defend their doctrines on the authority of Holy Scripture and the fathers. On this the Hussites decided to send a large embassy to Basel, among whom were many eminent persons.

THE HUSSITE WARS. SURRENDER OF A SILESIAN CASTLE TO PROCOPIUS THE GREAT
Painting by W. Beckman

Procopius, accompanied by one hundred of his co-religionists, entered Basel January 6, 1433. An eye-witness, Æneas Sylvius, afterward Pope Pius II., tells of the impression made on the people by the sight of the Hussites, each of whom, according to their enemies, was possessed by a hundred devils, and of the terror which their chief inspired. " There is the man," the people said, " who has so often put to flight the armies of the faithful, destroyed so many cities, massacred so many thousands, and who is feared as much by his own people as by his enemies." The discussions which now took place, sometimes before the council, sometimes in private conference, and which lasted three whole months, were chiefly upon the four articles quoted above. The majority of the council was favorable to the ideas of reform, and a compromise seemed likely, even on the question of the cup. But the difficulty was to induce the Taborites to accept the principle of authority in the church and the usefulness of the hierarchy. The council, in the spirit of con-ciliation, consented to send a deputation to Prague to treat with the Hussite assembly of Bohemia and Moravia. A special diet then met at Prague, in June, 1433. The church evidently could not agree with all the sects separately, and it was manifestly neces-sary that the Hussites should agree upon a sort of middle doctrine. But the men of Prague and the Taborites could not come to an agreement. The delegates of the council, however, offered to the men of Prague provisional tolerance for communion in both kinds. The other questions were to be settled by the council, in which Bo-hemia would be represented. Above all, it was urged that a truce be declared at once. The men of Prague, on their part, insisted that in order to suppress the various religious sects in the country the cup should be made obligatory in the communion for all Bo-hemia and Moravia. To make this concession was beyond the power of the embassy from the council, and a new Czech delegation was sent to Basel to treat with the council itself. Meantime no armistice was proclaimed; the Hussites continued to ravage Hun-gary, and boldly besieged Pilsen, which had remained the chief stronghold of Catholicism in Bohemia.

The siege of Pilsen dragged, and the besieging army, accus-tomed to live in plenty on the lands of foreigners, dwindled away on the impoverished soil of their native land. An insurrection broke out among the soldiers of Procopius; wounded and made prisoner by those whom he had so often led to victory, he gave up his command to his lieutenant, Czapek of San, who was no more fortunate than he against the bulwark of Catholicism. Meanwhile the Council of Basel had sent a new deputation into Bohemia, which brought to the diet of Bohemia and Moravia proposals of agreement known under the name of the *Compactata*. In these the council offered to grant the cup to those who should ask for it, to consecrate the Utraquist priests, and to admit in principle the other three articles of Prague, reserving to itself only the right of regulating questions of detail, together with the representatives of the Czech church. The Czech clergy, on the question of the *Compactata*, was divided into two parties, the one inclined to accept them, the other holding to obligatory communion under both forms. The latter prevailed and the *Compactata* were rejected. The delegates of the council left Prague in the beginning of 1434, and the war began again more fiercely than ever. Bohemia was now struggling against all Christendom. The council laid a tax on all the Catholic clergy to aid the Czech Catholics and especially the town of Pilsen. This money served to buy off some of the besiegers, and through this treachery the town was revictualed. The permanent committee of the estates called a diet for April, 1434, for the purpose of restoring peace. This diet decreed a general peace, and decided that from this time forward only one army should be maintained at the expense of the nation, and the Taborites and Orphans were called upon to disband their troops or else incorporate them in the new army. This measure for obtaining the proposed end gave the signal for a new civil war. In Prague the new town, inhabited by Czechs and long held by the Taborites, refused to agree to the general peace; the old town, on the other hand, was inhabited by Germans, and accepted the peace. The army which had been raised by the estates entered Prague and forced the rebels to obedience. At this news the Taborites raised the siege of Pilsen and marched on Prague with their old leader Procopius again at their head. But the army of the Utraquists had been reinforced by all the Catholic troops. The two forces met at Lipany in May, 1434. The onslaught was terrible. By simulating flight the Utraquists induced their adversaries to leave their chariots and fight in the open plain. After performing prodigies of valor, Procopius was beaten, tired of conquering rather than conquered, says Æneas Sylvius. He was killed, and with him perished 16,000 of his soldiers, the flower of his army. The Czechs could only be conquered by themselves.

A remnant of these troops, once so formidable, found a shelter behind the walls of Tabor and other of the confederate towns. But many left the side of the confederation and accepted the authority of the estates.

After the victory the estates met in a new diet and entered into communication with Sigismund. They could no longer count upon Poland for support, for Vladislav Jagellon had died, and his son, Vladislav III., found his inheritance contested by a party of the Polish nobility. Sigismund went to Ratisbon to await the delegates from Bohemia. There they also found a delegation from the Council of Basel, but they were not empowered to deal with it. They came to announce to the king that the estates were prepared to be reconciled to him, if he would recognize the liberties of the country and pledge himself to obtain the consent of the council to communion in both kinds for Bohemia and Moravia. Over the first point no difficulty arose, but on the second the king asked them to treat directly with the council. In a diet held on this matter, at Prague, the Utraquists modified their former claims and consented to demand the use of the cup in the communion only in those churches where it then actually existed. But they also demanded that Bohemia and Moravia be given the right to choose bishops and an archbishop.

In 1435 a new interview took place at Brünn between Sigismund, the delegates of the council, and representatives of Bohemia. The council would not recognize the existence of an Utraquist church, and conceded only that in each parish the sacrament might be administered to the faithful with or without the cup, according to the wishes of each. The archbishops and bishops were to pledge themselves to administer the sacrament in either form, and to consecrate both the Catholic and Utraquist priests. The Bohemian delegates, apparently supported by Sigismund, whose conduct was strangely ambiguous, declined to accept these propositions and threatened to quit Brünn. At the instance of Sigismund a new meeting was arranged at Stuhlweissenburg, in Hungary. In the meantime the estates of Bohemia drew up the list of Utraquist and Catholic parishes, and proceeded, in accord with the Utraquist clergy, to the election of an archbishop and two bishops. But the council refused to recognize the election, and appointed one of the delegates temporary administrator of the archbishopric Nevertheless it was at the council at Stuhlweissenburg that the religious peace was finally concluded. Sigismund gave the delegates of the council to understand that the question of prime importance was that he enter into his inheritance, and that later on he would know well the measures to adopt to lead the kingdom back to the true religion. Accordingly the *Compactata* of the Bohemian nation were solemnly proclaimed at Iglau, in Moravia, in 1436. By it the council tolerated for a time the use of the cup, and the existence of the Utraquist clergy, and accepted the four articles of Prague. The emperor-king pledged himself by a royal letter to enforce the observance of the articles of Prague, to permit Hussite preachers at his court, to grant a general amnesty, not to admit foreigners to public office, to carry on the government with the assistance of a committee appointed by the diet, and to take steps to promote the prosperity of the University of Prague. Peace was concluded between Bohemia and Christendom, and Sigismund was at last able to enter Prague, which had not known a king for so many years.

In this manner ended the great conflagration, the first flames of which had arisen about the stake of John Huss. Bohemia had revealed to Europe the astounding spectacle of a people that put its religious faith and its nationality above every other interest, and increased its strength tenfold by its enthusiasm. How did the results of the gigantic struggle compare with the sacrifices it had involved? What had become of the reforms for which Zizka and his followers had struggled so valiantly? The Catholic church in Bohemia did lose a portion of its wealth, but it fell for the most part into the hands of avaricious nobles, upon whom the clergy were thenceforth dependent. The best minds had abandoned the practical ground of morality and discipline in order to engage in discussions of the niceties of dogma. The controversy over the cup had excited men's minds as long before the religious differences had done at Byzantium. Furthermore, the reconciliation of Bohemia with the universal church was far from being complete. The council had by no means granted all the demands of the Utraquists, while these, deceived by the promises of Sigismund, hoped to gain still further concessions. Besides the Pope had not even ratified the *Compactata*.

In the political world the Hussite movement, although securing to the Czech nation a well-founded preponderance, and rolling back for many years the wave of Germanization, had not produced the results one might have expected. It had begun by being popular and democratic. It ended in the triumph of the nobility, which thenceforward became more powerful than ever. A great part of the domains of the crown and much of the possessions of the church had passed into their hands. The balance of power between the crown and the nobility was destroyed. Among other peoples, especially among Catholics, the name of Bohemia became a name of reproach and contempt. What remained to Bohemia was a generous enthusiasm for the Slav nationality, a deep religious fervor, and an austere morality which was later reflected in the writings of its moralists, teachers, and statesmen, and above all in the lofty ideals of the sect of Bohemian Brothers, among whom is to be found perhaps the finest heritage of the Hussite movement.

Sigismund lived only a short time after his restoration; he died before the close of 1437. Even his few months as king of Bohemia were full of bitterness. He found it impossible to reconcile the promises he had made to the council and to the Utraquists. The religious difficulties continued. The bishop of Olmütz, in spite of the *Compactata*, refused to consecrate priests who would not abjure the cup. The archbishopric of Prague remained vacant, and the Utraquist church was governed by an administrator and a consistory of the priests of Prague; factional strife continued and discontent prevailed. Nor were the material conditions in the country such as to improve this. The Taborites had not all laid down their arms. Some of their bands refused to accept the peace, and occupied the Château of Sion, near Kuttenberg. The king captured the place and had the leader with fifty-six of his followers hanged. This roused the Taborites, and Straznice, their leader, had just renewed the war when Sigismund died. With him ended the male line of the house of Luxemburg, from which had come three emperors, two kings of the Romans, numerous minor princes, and, as we have just seen, four kings of Bohemia.

Chapter XII

BOHEMIA UNDER PODIEBRAD AND THE JAGELLONS. 1437-1526

SIGISMUND left no male heir, and with his death, there-fore, the possessions of the house of Luxemburg by virtue of the treaties entered into between the Luxemburg and Hapsburg dynasties, passed to Albert V., of Austria, son-in-law of the emperor. But the agreement had been made in the reign of Charles IV., a period in which the royal power was still at its height. Since then Bohemia had learned not only to dictate to her king, but even to do without a king altogether. Albert V. of Austria had only Upper and Lower Austria, and was not strong enough to seize Bohemia by force. Straznice and the Taborites preferred the young Prince Kazimir, brother of the king of Poland. And as it was to the interest of Poland to unite with Bohemia and thus counterbalance the union of Austria and Hungary, Kazimir was sent into Bohemia with an army, while the king of Poland invaded Silesia and Moravia. Notwithstanding this, and the op-position of a part of the nobility, Albert entered the kingdom, had himself crowned at Prague, and then marched upon Tabor, the center of the resistance. But the Pope, Eugenius IV., intervened and brought about an armistice. A few weeks later, in 1439, Al-bert died, and four months after his death his widow gave birth to a son, Vladislav, called the Posthumous. Him the Bohemians re-fused at first to recognize. The diet offered the crown to the duke of Bavaria, Prince Kazimir of Poland having some time previous renounced all his claims. But the duke of Bavaria declined the offer, and the Bohemian nobility, tired of war, decided to come to an understanding with the queen-dowager, Elizabeth, concern-ing the regency. They asked that the king be brought to Bohemia, as if the mere presence of the king, however young he might be, would maintain order in a country still divided by factions. But his mother refused to send him to Prague, and the country was forced to govern itself; the captains of the circles administered

their provinces as best they could, but did not always do so successfully. The old excitement arose again. The Utraquists claimed
that the promises made by Sigismund were not being kept: communion was not given in both kinds, and the bishop of Olmütz still
refused to consecrate Utraquist priests. As a result the two rival
parties of the Utraquists united against the Catholic party, and they
even proposed to the Taborites to found a church which should embrace all parties. After many discussions the Taborite doctrines
were declared false by the majority of the Utraquists, a decision
which proved the deathblow of the sect; a large number of parishes
withdrew from it, and before long the town of Tabor alone remained loyal to its tenets.

All attempts at uniting the non-Catholic sects had apparently
failed when, in 1444, a new leader appeared in the person of George
of Podiebrad. He was still quite a young man, being only twenty-
four, but he possessed many rare and excellent qualities. According to tradition he had John Zizka as his godfather, and, like him,
he was a valiant soldier and an ardent patriot, full of the desire to
establish order and unity in his native land. " He was," says
Æneas Sylvius, " a short, thick-set man, with eyes full of fire, of
quiet manners, infected, it is true, with the Hussite errors, but a
lover of law and of justice." He induced the heads of the Catholic party to send an embassy to Rome, in 1447, in consequence of
which the Holy See sent the Cardinal Carvajal on a special mission to Bohemia. He arrived in 1448, but with no intention of
conciliation. To the requests that he induce the Pope to accept the
Compactata and confirm John of Rokycana as archbishop of
Prague, he replied by saying that the court of Rome was determined to reject communion in both kinds and to confer the archbishopric upon a person of its own choice. The irritation among
the people burst out anew, so that the cardinal did not deem it safe
to remain longer in the city, and in the confusion which arose
George of Podiebrad marched on Prague and took it by surprise.
He was received in triumph and became the *de facto* governor of
Bohemia.

But his usurpation began another period of bloody conflicts
for his unfortunate country. Ulrich of Rosenberk, the leader of
the Catholic party, took up arms against Podiebrad, and besides his
foreign allies, the duke of Saxony and the margrave of Meissen,
he received the unexpected aid of the Taborites, who had been ex-

pelled from the Utraquist communion. But Podiebrad was as able
a statesman as he was a soldier, and he incited Bavaria and Brandenburg to attack Saxony, while he himself successfully invaded Meissen and established his authority. A diet was agreed to by his
enemies, which was to name a regent. The exploits and power
of Podiebrad marked him as the natural choice of his countrymen,
and in 1451 the emperor confirmed their election. He understood
how to make his authority respected by all, and even reduced the
town of Tabor, forced it to receive Utraquist priests, and cast the
leading members of the Taborite clergy into prison, thus practically
putting an end to the already enfeebled existence of the sect. The
Catholic leader, Rosenberk, was besieged in Budweiss and reduced
to submission.

But the outlying possessions of Bohemia—Lusatia, Silesia,
and Moravia—were almost lost by this time. It was evident that
since their union with Bohemia was so largely through the person
of the sovereign, the coronation of the young king alone could
draw the lines which held them to Bohemia together again. Podiebrad persuaded Vladislav, then fourteen years of age, to come to
Prague and be crowned. The young king recognized him as his
lieutenant for six years, agreed to the *Compactata*, and promised
to keep the engagements entered into by Sigismund. Thenceforth,
with the authority of the king, which had been absent so long, the
regent was able to reorganize the country. He reëstablished the
courts of justice, opened a rigorous inquiry into all the misappro-
priations of lands during the last thirty years, and recovered most
of the estates of the crown. The estates of Moravia, Silesia, and
Lusatia took the oath to Vladislav, excepting only the Catholic city
of Breslau, which was, however, severely punished for its opposition.
The young king had unbounded confidence in Podiebrad in all matters, and loved to call him father. Bohemia became once more
well ordered and prosperous. Vladislav could even offer the emperor an army of forty thousand men for the crusade against the
Turks after the fall of Constantinople. In 1457 the king died when
on the point of celebrating his marriage with Madeleine of France,
daughter of Charles VII.

According to previous treaties the crown of Bohemia should
have returned to the house of Hapsburg. But the people had freed
themselves and did not consider that they were bound by the agreements of former sovereigns. Besides, what need had Bohemia to

seek a foreign ruler when she had the best possible one at home? Podiebrad was the natural choice of his countrymen, and in spite of a great many claimants was elected almost unanimously. Bohemia was once more master of her own destinies. Freed from the control of Austria and Hungary, for the first time since the Premyslides she had a truly national king. Moravia, Silesia, and Lusatia took the oath to the new sovereign. The emperor soon became reconciled to Podiebrad and accorded him the investiture of the kingdom.

As king, Podiebrad continued the work he had begun as regent: the restoration of that peace and prosperity in which the country had been left by Charles IV. The partition and diminution of the royal estates had greatly reduced the army, and the new king did not hesitate to impose heavy taxes upon the estates in order to pay a well-organized force. He acquired throughout Europe the reputation of a wise and powerful sovereign. One of his daughters he espoused to Mathias Corvin, king of Hungary. The other married Albert, prince of Saxony, thus becoming the ancestress of the present dynasty in Saxony.

But the religious troubles still disturbed the country. The Taborites had been suppressed, but they continued their worship in secret, and a new sect arose among them known as the brotherhood of Kunwald, from the place where it had its origin. Later it assumed the name of the Union of Bohemian Brothers, and became known abroad as the Moravian Brothers. It was organized by a poor nobleman, Brother Gregory, and separated entirely from the Roman church, choosing its bishops and elders from the community. Their doctrines were similar to those of the Taborites, but they had one advantage over their fierce predecessors, they refused to defend their faith by force of arms. They preached strict morality and imposed temporal punishments for transgressions of duty. This stood in the way of that rapid growth of the sect which might otherwise have been expected; but in spite of it there were nearly two hundred congregations subject to its bishops and elders in Bohemia and Moravia by the end of the fifteenth century.

But notwithstanding the inoffensive character of the new sect, the king, though himself an Utraquist, was anxious to carry out to the letter the *Compactata*, and treated them with much severity. He hoped to bring about a reconciliation with the Holy See, and to this end sought to crush out all religious innovations. In 1462 he sent an embassy to Rome to beg the Pope to ratify the *Compactata* secured from the Council of Basel. But the reigning Pontiff was Pius II., formerly Æneas Sylvius, who had taken a prominent part in the Council of Basel, and who was resolved to bring Bohemia into complete union with the Western church. Hence, instead of consenting to the demands of the king of Bohemia, he declared the *Compactata* abolished, forbade communion in both kinds, and sent a Papal legate to invite the king to renounce the Utraquist faith. This neither personal inclinations nor political interest would allow him to do, and he cast the legate into prison. Pius II. then declared war against him, and threatened him with excommunication. But the death of the zealous Pontiff in 1468 for a time suspended the effect of the menace. His successor, Paul II., was anxious to gain time and entered into negotiations with the emperor and the Catholic nobles of Bohemia. Finally he hurled his anathemas against Podiebrad: declared him a heretic, backslider, and despoiler of the church, forbade his subjects to obey him, and ordered a new crusade against the Hussites. But he found few of the princes of Germany, except the emperor, disposed to come to his assistance. The sale of indulgences and the hope of plunder did bring together a few armed bands, but they brought but little assistance to the confederacy of Catholic nobles and the few royal towns that joined the rebels.

The king, after trying in vain to come to terms with the Holy See, determined to oppose force with force; he organized a powerful army, threw himself upon his enemies, and captured their principal fortresses. His son Victorin he sent into Austria, in 1468, to chastise the Emperor Frederick in his own possessions. But just at this juncture the Pope raised up a new enemy against Podiebrad in Mathias Corvinus, who was persuaded to take part in the quarrel, less perhaps for the honor of defending the Catholic faith than because of the desire to avenge his personal injuries, and by the hope of uniting the two crowns of Bohemia and Hungary on his head. He forced Victorin to withdraw from Austria, and then suddenly attacked Moravia, where the Catholic towns opened their gates to receive him. He next invaded Bohemia, but was met and surrounded by the Czech forces under Podiebrad, and obliged to sign a truce at Vilemov. Scarcely extricated from his difficulties, he was released from his promises by the Pope and he resumed the war with savage cruelty, cutting off the heads of his Czech prisoners and hurling them back into the enemy's camp with catapults. He even assembled his partisans at Olmütz and had himself proclaimed king of Bohemia. But again a Czech army drove him out and forced him to take refuge in Hungary, though the towns in which he had placed garrisons still held out. Podiebrad, ill and without allies, began to fear the dismemberment of his kingdom. To get the assistance of Poland he entered into negotiations with Kazimir, king of Poland, and persuaded Bohemia to accept him as his successor, notwithstanding the fact that by so doing he was sacrificing the interests of his own house, for he had two sons. This act of disinterested patriotism was the last of his life. He died in 1471 at the age of fifty-one years.

His early death did not permit Podiebrad to carry to completion the great projects he had meditated. He had dreamed of establishing a sort of international tribunal, composed of the sovereign princes, which should act as a court between themselves, their subjects, and the church. He had even sent an embassy to Louis XI. in regard to this project, in 1464, and a quaint account of it in the Czech language has been preserved. He begs the most Christian king of France, as a prince devoted to the general welfare, to convoke an assembly of the kings and princes, which was to work together for the glory of God, the good of the universal church, and the independence of nations—a chimerical dream which Henry IV. was to attempt later on with no better success. Nevertheless, George of Podiebrad, a true son of the Czech nation, by his patriotism and his virtues far surpassed the most illustrious princes of the foreign dynasties that have reigned over his country.

In accordance with the engagements entered into during the lifetime of Podiebrad, the Utraquist estates elected Vladislav of Poland, then aged sixteen, as their king, in 1471. He took possession of the kingdom after swearing to observe the *Compactata,* and brought an army of several thousand men to the aid of Bohemia. Mathias at once invaded the country, but was unable to get beyond Kuttenberg. It would have been wiser had he turned his forces against the Turks, who had conquered the Balkan peninsula and now threatened to overrun the middle Danube valley. Pope Sixtus IV. understood the real interests of Christendom better, and imposed a peace. But Mathias did not long observe it and in 1478 carried on the war until he secured the peace of Olmütz, by which he was given Lusatia, Moravia, and Silesia for his lifetime, and the crown of Bohemia at the death of Vladislav. In case Vladislav survived Mathias he was to have the right to reclaim the lost provinces for four hundred thousand ducats. Thus these wars which had begun in the name of religion, ended in a mere bargain for the possession of certain provinces.

In the meantime the young king of Bohemia had found his kingdom weakened. his treasury exhausted, and a proud and arrogant nobility confronting him. Under George of Podiebrad they had been held in check, that monarch having always looked for his principal support to the lower classes, the *zemane* or squires. But now the nobles got the upper hand, and from the reign of Vladislav Jagellon dates the legalized oppression of the people. Taking advantage of the weakness of the king, the nobles introduced into the law courts the principle that a peasant has no right to enter complaint against his lord. To the already heavy burdens of the agricultural classes they added that of serfdom, by taking from the peasant the right to leave his land. They arrogated to themselves the most extensive monopolies, as, for example, that of making and selling beer to the peasantry, and they even encroached upon the liberties of the towns. These things gave rise to internal struggles in which the young king was often obliged to take part, and which seriously damaged the prestige of the crown and disturbed the peace of the kingdom.

In his dealings with the religious factions Vladislav was more fortunate. In 1485 the Catholics and Utraquists came to an agreement at Kuttenberg by which both parties promised to observe the *Compactata* of Prague and the promises made by Sigismund. These two agreements became from that time forward laws of the state and were added to the coronation oath. But Vladislav's endeavors to secure their confirmation by Pope Alexander VI. proved fruitless. Under the new conditions the Utraquists lost ground rapidly. The bishops of Olmütz had refused ever since the quarrel with Podiebrad to consecrate any priest who would not promise to give up the administration of wine, and Utraquist candidates were obliged to seek consecration abroad or else by tortuous methods at home. Only occasionally could a foreign bishop be persuaded to come to Bohemia to officiate. But while it was thus extremely difficult for the Utraquists to obtain priests, priests without character, sometimes mere adventurers, obtained admission into the

Catholic clergy. The result was a serious decline in the morals of the people. Further, the Utraquist estates asserted the right to nominate the members of the consistories and so reduced their priests to complete dependence.

In the midst of this decay the sect of Bohemian Brothers solved the difficulty about the hierarchical succession by suppressing it altogether, and in the rigorous morality of their daily life were a constant reproach to the official churches. They increased daily in numbers, notwithstanding persecution, for both Catholics and Utraquists denounced the Picards, as the Brothers were called, to the king, and he forbade their worship.

In 1490 Vladislav was elected king of Hungary, and, tired of Bohemia, he went to reside at Buda. He was the first Czech king who did not reside at Prague, and from this time the ancient capital began to lose some of its importance. No great advantage came to either country from the union of the two crowns upon one head. In 1516 Vladislav died. Seven years before he had caused his son Louis, aged three, to be crowned king of Bohemia.

The accession of the young Louis, in 1516, again brought a minor to the throne of Bohemia, and the fact that the succession during this period so frequently fell upon a young prince greatly favored the encroachments of the nobility upon the royal power. On the death of Vladislav the grand burggrave of Prague, with some of the highest dignitaries, assumed the government. Among the estates quarrels and disputes continued. But in 1517 an agreement was reached. The cities—that is, the bourgeoisie—were granted the right to vote with the nobility in the diets of the kingdom, and the representative system thus established continued almost to the present. At this time also the two parts of the city of Prague—the old and the new town—united in order to be the better able to resist the claims of the nobles. This union, known as the Convention of St. Vacslav, did not, however, put an end to the feelings of hatred between the classes. The partisans of the towns and of the nobles frequently came to blows, the castles of the nobles were seized by the citizens, and nobles were beheaded in Prague.

Other troubles also arose. The Turks on the Danube were becoming more aggressive, new imposts were levied, and from the north a new force appeared which stirred up the religious difficulties more than ever. In 1517 Luther published his famous theses and inaugurated the Reformation movement in Germany. By a strange inconsistency his doctrines were enthusiastically received by those very cities of Germany which a short time before had been the strongholds of Catholicism against the Hussites. The Czechs, so long at variance with the Holy See, could not fail to hail the new doctrines with sympathy. They had vainly hoped to retain the use of the cup and still remain in union with the church, for the Papacy had turned a deaf ear to their prayers. Protestantism recalled the traditions of the Hussites; Luther was continuing the work of the martyr of Constance; he did not insist on the stern morality of the Bohemian Brothers, and he had openly broken with the Papacy. His teachings were hailed with enthusiasm. Utraquist priests began to preach his doctrines, and as early as 1523 a Utraquist synod added to their confession several articles borrowed from the Lutheran formularies. A friend of Luther's, the priest Cahera, was appointed administrator of the church of Tyn, at Prague, and the breach with the Roman church increased steadily. The city of Prague became the scene of conflicts and tumults and the new religious controversy in Bohemia became marked by cruel excesses, in which the lawless character of the Czech nobles found ample scope. Indeed, their factious spirit was largely responsible for the death of Louis at the battle of Mohacs in 1526, for they would not come to their sovereign's assistance. But their narrow egotism and lack of patriotism were soon to meet with cruel punishment.

Chapter XIII

HUNGARY UNDER THE HOUSE OF ANJOU, AND THE ELECTIVE MONARCHY. 1308-1444

ON the death, in 1301, of Andrew III., the last of the Arpad dynasty in Hungary, three claimants to the throne presented themselves. The first was Charles Robert of Anjou, closely related by marriage to the Arpads; the others were Vacslav of Bohemia and Otto of Bavaria. Pope Boniface VIII. favored the French candidate, and since he claimed that St. Stephen had done homage to the Holy See, he called on the Hungarian prelates to recognize Charles Robert. Despite the Papal orders, however, Vacslav insisted on his rights, entered Hungary and had himself crowned by the archbishop of Kolsesa. But he was almost immediately recalled to Bohemia by the death of his father, and gave up all claim to Hungary. Otto of Bavaria next presented himself, receiving aid from the German colonists (Saxons) in Transylvania. But he was likewise unsuccessful, and by the year 1310 Charles Robert, who had been crowned in 1308, was recognized as the rightful king. But from the beginning he had to carry on a struggle against one of his powerful vassals, Mathew Csak, of Trencin, really a petty king in the country of the Slovaks.

Abroad the policy of Charles Robert was much more ambitious than that of the Arpads. He could not forget Italy, where his branch of the house of Anjou held sway in Naples, and dreamed of uniting the crown of Naples and of St. Stephen. In this he thought himself successful when he brought about the marriage of his son Andrew with Joan, daughter of the duke of Calabria, who afterward became the notorious Joan of Naples. With Venice he maintained the most cordial relations, and, anxious above all to secure friends in Italy, concluded a treaty of commerce with her in which the towns on the Adriatic were guaranteed her. In the east Poland was his especial concern. In 1320 he married the daughter of Vladislav Lokietek and formed an intimate alliance with him. He never lost hope in his ambition some day to annex Poland, and in 1338 he induced King Kazimir III. to recognize his son, Louis of Anjou, as his heir. Four years later he died.

The character of Louis the Great, the son of Charles Robert, was such that it seemed as if he might realize the ambitious dreams of his father. Shortly after his accession the news of the assassination of his brother, through the instigation of Joan, reached him, and this furnished a good pretext for intervention in the affairs of Italy. Although only temporarily· successful, this first expedition of the Hungarians into Italy served to open a new world of thought and life, of culture and refinement, to them, and the influence upon the literature, the arts, and the manners of the Magyars was great. But although Louis was unable to establish himself permanently in Italy, he was nevertheless successful in securing a firm foothold on the Adriatic. He had married a Slav princess, sister of the ban of Bosnia, a province over which the kings of Hungary claimed a sovereignty they were unable to exercise. Because of his new relations to the Slavs of the lower Danube, the Pope called on him to check the spread of the Patarine heresy in those regions; he came to be regarded as the dread champion of the Roman church in those parts, and the Wallachian adherents of the Eastern church took refuge in Moldavia. In 1358, after a successful invasion of Italy as far as Padua, he forced a treaty on Venice, by which he secured the whole of Dalmatia—an important acquisition because it gave Hungary access to the Adriatic and an opportunity to develop into a maritime power.

In the meantime the Turks had established themselves in the Balkan peninsula and were advancing on Hungary. According to some obscure documents the first battle between the Osmanlis and the Magyars occurred in 1366, near the Iron Gates. In 1375 Sultan Murad took Adrianople, whence he kept watch on Byzantium. The Greek emperor, John Paleologus, visited the court of Louis to implore his aid, promising even to become a convert to the Roman faith. But the Pope, more concerned about matters of dogma than about the dangers to Christianity, persuaded him to put no faith in the promises of the emperor. Louis turned his attention from the empire to Poland, whose crown had so long been the aim of his ambition.

As we saw above he had been chosen heir to King Kazimir. Since then he had lost no opportunity to make himself popular with the Poles by helping them against the Tatars and against the

Lithuanians, who were still pagans. In 1354 he crossed the Carpathians with a considerable army to aid the Poles to hurl back these two peoples, who had invaded Volhynia and Podolia. His services secured him the gratitude of the Poles, and in 1370 he was proclaimed king. But his rule in Poland was not as fortunate as might have been expected; he intrusted the government to his mother, and she was unable to win over this restless, lawless nation. Revolts broke out, and it became evident that Louis would have great difficulty in securing the crown for his successor. He had no son, and after much hesitation married his eldest daughter, Mary, to the young Prince Sigismund of Luxemburg, son of Charles IV., who was sent at an early age to the court of Hungary to study the language and laws of the country. The last years of the reign of Louis the Great were occupied with a struggle against Venice, which ended in the defeat of the Venetians and secured for Hungary the peaceful possession of the Adriatic shore. With the death of Louis the Great, in 1382, the house of Anjou, which had given only two kings to Hungary, became extinct.

It was only natural that these Angevin kings should introduce Western ideas and habits into Hungary. Her institutions began to take on feudal characteristics, though the country never fully adopted the feudal system. "Two things stood in the way," says M. Sayous: "first, the extraordinarily full power of the king over the entire land, which made the growth of large fiefs impossible; and second, the interest taken in politics by the large body of lesser nobility, a class much more numerous in Hungary than in any other country. In a word, the king was too powerful and the people with political rights much too tenacious in maintaining them, for Hungary, notwithstanding its knightly and aristocratic tendencies, ever to become a completely feudal state."

The Angevin princes greatly increased the splendor and luxury of the court, which was held sometimes at Buda, sometimes at Visegrad. They gathered about them a complete hierarchy of great lords, and richly endowed many noble families. Tournaments and the science of heraldry were encouraged; the military forces were grouped in *banderia* about the lords. Those who brought a certain number of soldiers had the right to lead them into battle under their own standards. An hereditary nobility was organized by the law of "atavicity," which forbade noble families selling their estates, which were to descend to the natural heirs, or, in default of these, to revert to the king. Charles Robert and Louis rarely convoked the diet, but as an offset to this they allowed the fullest liberty to the comitats.

The burgher class of the principal cities consisted largely of foreigners: the relations with Naples had attracted a large number of Italians, and the Germans flocked into Transylvania, while trade with Germany increased. Certain cities, known as free cities, enjoyed extensive privileges in return for revenues paid the king. Many of the Jews, whom Louis the Great, in his rôle of champion of Christianity, severely persecuted, emigrated into Austria and Poland. Those who remained constituted a population by itself (*Universitas Judæorum*) entirely dependent on the king and obliged to wear a particular dress. On the other hand, the clergy was overwhelmed with rich donations, which did not increase its morality. Learning increased; Louis the Great, with the consent of Pope Urban V., founded a university at Fünfkirchen, where all the sciences, except theology, were taught. The literary productions of the period are, however, of little value. The works of the Dalmatian historians of this time are the product of the special culture which that country enjoyed because of its more direct intercourse with Italy. Indeed, the literary life of Slavo-Italian Dalmatia was quite distinct from that of Hungary proper, and although not a line has come down to us, we know that there existed at this time a whole cycle of heroic poems.

Prince Sigismund of Luxemburg (1382-1437) was, as we have seen, the heir to the crown of Hungary; but the diet would not voluntarily accept a foreigner. Hungary had no Salic law, and the diet crowned the Princess Mary. *Coronata fuit in regem,* says the chronicler Lucius, and this expression of the fourteenth century may perhaps explain the famous *moriamur pro rege nostro* of the eighteenth. The young princess, with the help of the queen-dowager, Elizabeth, assumed the government. The Poles also refused to accept Sigismund, unless he promised to reside in Poland.

In the meantime Sigismund was seeking a recognition of his rights in Hungary. But it was some time before he was successful. The queen-dowager tried to induce Charles of Orleans to oppose him, and the king of Naples, Charles of Durazzo, actually had himself crowned, but Sigismund succeeded finally, and the diet proclaimed him king of Hungary in 1382. Soon after he abandoned all claim to the crown of Poland, as also the claims of Hungary to Galicia and Lodomeria, which were afterward revived by Maria Theresa.

The beginning of his reign was disturbed by a rebellion in Hungary and Croatia, which was suppressed with severity. On the side of the Turks grave dangers threatened the kingdom. Servia had succumbed at Kosova; the prince of Wallachia acknowledged their suzerainty; Bulgaria had fallen into their hands, and Bosnia had been invaded. Sigismund and the diet determined upon prompt resistance and, as the forces of Hungary were insufficient,.an alliance was sought with the Greek emperor, Manuel II., while embassies were sent to solicit aid from Germany, France, and Burgundy. The disastrous result of this crusade at Nicopolis, in 1396, is well known: the French and Hungarians were defeated and the Ottoman Turks became masters of the lower Danube. Sigismund escaped with great difficulty on the Venetian fleet, and returned to his kingdom by the Adriatic with money furnished him by the little republic of Ragusa.

Within Hungary the reign of Sigismund is marked by two very important events. In 1397 and 1405 the diets of Temesvar and Buda respectively laid the basis for the representative system of government in Hungary. It was provided that each county assembly, or comitat, should send four deputies to the lower chamber, in which the royal cities were also to be represented. The upper chamber was composed of hereditary magistrates and prelates. The county assemblies thus became the real centers of political life, and they very early adopted the plan of instructing their delegates. About this time also the light troops of hussars, specially designed for the warfare against the Turks, were organized, and the Order of the Dragon, whose members were to fight infidels and heretics, was founded.

But Sigismund cannot be regarded as a wise ruler. Melancholy, capricious, overcautious, and cruel, he mortgaged the revenues of the crown, was an inveterate persecutor, and never became popular in Hungary. In 1401 he was seized and imprisoned as a result of a plot, but he was soon afterward released; his action against his brother, Vacslav, king of Bohemia, has been noted; by his unpopularity an invasion by Ladislas of Naples was made possible, and his treaty of succession with his brother-in-law, Albert of Austria, prepared the way for the future rule of the Hapsburgs in Hungary.

Sigismund is better known to history, however, as emperor and king of Bohemia than as king of Hungary. In 1411 he was chosen emperor, and for the first time this dangerous honor was conferred upon a king of Hungary. It proved a great misfortune to her, because thenceforth she was looked upon as an appanage of Germany. Nor did the new dignity make a better king of Sigismund. In 1412 he mortgaged a part of the district of Zips to Poland, and in 1419 he lost the Dalmatian coast, as a result of a war he was waging as emperor against Venice. As a climax to these misfortunes, Sigismund also became king of Bohemia, which proved as fatal to Hungary as it did to Bohemia, for the Hungarians, menaced by the Turks, ought from this time forward to have directed all their energies against the common enemy of Christianity, instead of wasting their strength in useless wars against the Hussites, whose doctrines had, moreover, found numerous adherents among the Magyars themselves.

Had Sigismund been less occupied with the religious war and more attentive to the real interests of the Christian world, he might readily have found a means of indemnifying himself for his territorial losses in the south. Servia, only half subdued by the Turks, had kept its native princes, who, together with the Servian people, many of whom emigrated to Hungary, looked to Sigismund for aid. One of these despots, Stephen Lazarevic, even acknowledged himself as his vassal and did homage to the crown of St. Stephen. He died childless, and according to the terms of the act of homage Hungary got Belgrade and several other towns. They were only given up, however, in exchange for Vilagos, Debreczen, and certain other towns by the new despot, Brankovic.

Toward the end of his reign Sigismund found his kingdom sorely threatened by the Turks on the one side and ravaged by the Hussites on the other. In 1435 the diet of Presburg endeavored to organize the national defense by completing the army: all those who did not already serve in the *banderia* of the prelates or the great lords were in the future to serve in the *banderia* of the county assemblies. The country was divided into seven divisions to facilitate military administration. But this did not prevent internal disorders; revolts of the peasantry broke out in Transylvania, and Hussite doctrine spread among the people. Sigismund died in

1437, after a long reign, without having remedied any of the evils of which he had been either the author or the impotent witness.

Taught by experience, the diet imposed more rigorous restrictions on the new king than those to which Sigismund had submitted. Elizabeth, the daughter of the late king, was declared his heir, and her husband, Albert of Austria, associated with her in the government. At last the house of Austria laid its hand on the throne of Hungary, the long-coveted object of it desires. But Hungary made conditions. The new king must reside in Hungary; he was neither to sell nor give away the crown lands; he was to consult the diet concerning the marriage of his daughters, and he could not nominate the palatine without the consent of the assembly. But neither the monarch nor the assembly had to put this wise agreement into practice. Albert died in 1439, leaving a pregnant wife, and the Turks, masters of Semendria, at the gates of the kingdom. Hungary needed a king, not the infant, Vladislav the Posthumous, who was born shortly afterward. The majority of the nation pronounced in favor of Vladislav Jagellon, king of Poland. Among the supporters of the new monarch was John Corvinus Hunyady, known to history as John Hunyady. He belonged to a noble family in Transylvania, and had already distinguished himself for bravery in the struggles against the Turks. He now supported the king of Poland against the Austrian party, and endeavored to unite all the forces of the nation to fight the infidel.

Sultan Murad had laid siege to Belgrade, which at this time belonged to Hungary, but Hunyady succeeded in raising the siege. Next, when the Turks entered Transylvania, he marched against them and administered a crushing defeat near Hermannstadt, leaving 20,000 on the field of battle. To Brankovic, the Servian despot, he sent the bloody head of a Turkish general, Mesid Beg, as a reward for his aid. Sultan Murad, exasperated by this defeat, sent Schehadeddin and the Janissaries against Hungary. Hunyady attacked them with a vastly inferior force near the Iron Gates, and with his Hungarian cavalry completely defeated them. Murad, terrified, asked for peace, but it was refused. Hungary believed the time had come when the Turks could be definitively driven from her frontiers. In July of 1443 King Vladislav and Hunyady crossed the Danube near Semendria and ascended the valley of the Morava. Here the Turks were again severely beaten and forced to abandon Sophia. The Hungarians then crossed the passes of the Balkans, notwithstanding the formidable defenses of the Turks, and penetrated into the valley of the Maritsa, where they were again victorious. The road to Constantinople lay open to the Magyars. But the severe winter of those rough regions overtook them, and in the midst of triumphs the king was obliged to order the retreat.

For the second time Murad asked for peace, and the diet of Szeged consented on the conditions that a truce be concluded for ten years, that Wallachia pass under the suzerainty of Hungary, that Servia and Herzogovina be restored to the despot Brankovic, and that the Turkish prisoners be ransomed at a heavy price. The conditions were accepted and solemnly sworn to on the Bible and on the Koran. But many believed the peace unwise, especially the surrender of the advantages of the recent victories. Cardinal Cesarini showed that oaths taken to infidels were not binding, and that in the name of the Holy See he might annul them. Consequently Hunyady and the king decided to renew the war, notwithstanding the treaty, and marched upon Bulgaria and the Black Sea. Murad was in Asia, but the Genoese carried his troops to Europe for seventy thousand ducats, and on November 10, 1444, the Christian and Mussulman armies found themselves face to face at Varna, near the Balkans. In order to recall their perfidy to the Christians and to trouble their conscience, Murad had a copy of the broken treaty and the Gospel they had dishonored nailed to a lance and borne before his troops. The battle opened favorably to the Hungarians; their cavalry charged with their usual impetuosity, and King Vladislav, carried away by his enthusiasm, rushed into the midst of the fight, where he fell, and his head, raised on the end of a lance, announced their defeat to the Magyars. The battle ended in hopeless flight, and Hunyady brought back to Hungary only a miserable remnant of his glorious army. The defeat at Varna opened the gates of Constantinople to the Turks.

Chapter XIV

HUNYADY AND THE HUNGARIAN WARS WITH THE TURKS. 1444-1526

THIS time Hungary did not hesitate in selecting a king. The young Vladislav the Posthumous, who was being reared by his uncle, Frederick of Austria, was five years old, and the diet at once proclaimed him king. During his minority the government was to be carried on by representatives of the aristocracy, both lay and ecclesiastic, a veritable republic, and Hungary would have spared herself many misfortunes had she learned by this experience to do without a king altogether. The diet further decided that the young king should be transferred to its authority, in order to be raised in Hungary. But Frederick refused to give up his pupil, and the diet met again on the famous plain of Rakos, and proclaimed John Hunyady governor in the absence of the king. Hunyady became a sort of lieutenant governor in much the same capacity as George of Podiebrad a little later in Bohemia. The first enemy against which he had to defend Hungary was Austria, but the Holy See, recognizing the importance of Hungary in the struggle against the Turks, brought about a reconciliation, and Hunyady again turned his attention toward the Turks. He assembled an army of 25,000, crossed the Danube and penetrated Servia, despite the hostility of the treacherous Brankovic, as far as the fatal plain of Kosovo. Here Murad was awaiting him behind formidable entrenchments, and in 1448 the disaster of Varna was repeated for Hungary. But the popularity of Hunyady and the confidence he inspired continued unimpaired. The house of Austria, however, suspicious of the watchful guardian of the interests of Hungary, raised new difficulties for him. It supported the Czech, Jiskra of Brandyse, hetman of Vladislav, who settled to the north of Hungary, on the slopes of the Carpathians, and occupied those regions for the king of Bohemia. Against this formidable condottiere, who is hated by the Magyars, and regarded by the Czechs as a hero and defender of the doctrines of the Hussites, Hunyady's troops failed. The emperor also continued in his refusal to give up the young king, while the Magyars, always superstitious in their attitude toward the crown and the person of their king, persisted in claiming him. Their envoys even followed him to Italy, where they tried to seize him by surprise. Finally, in 1453, the emperor yielded. Vladislav came to Hungary and Hunyady handed over his authority, receiving with the royal thanks the title of count of Bistrice. But the king did not remain long; after assisting at the deliberations of the diet at Presburg he returned to Vienna.

About this time the Turks again became active on the lower Danube. Constantinople had fallen in 1453, and Brankovic appealed to Hungary for aid. A diet assembled at Buda voted large subsidies, and the *general insurrection,* or a levy of all able-bodied men in case the kingdom should be invaded. Hunyady again entered Servia, ascended the valley of the Morava, where he defeated the Turks near Krushevats, close to the place where they had formerly invaded Servia, and pushed on as far as Sophia. But to expel the Turks from Constantinople would have required the coöperation of all Europe, not Hungary fighting single-handed. Besides, Hunyady had two jealous rivals, the Palatine Gara and the count of Cilly, who did their utmost to turn the young king against him. The brave soldier was obliged to retrace his steps. But he determined at least to save Belgrade, which, from its strength and its position, is the key both of the middle Danube and of the Save. By the Turks it has been called, and with good reason, the Town of the Holy War. Hunyady's brother-in-law was in command of the place and Sultan Mohammed II. had brought together for its capture the most formidable artillery that had ever been seen. In this unequal struggle Hunyady had no ally except the army of 60,000 volunteers which the eloquence of the Monk Capistrano had gathered from all over Europe. A very small force in view of the danger threatening Christendom, but the age of crusades had gone by.

The first battle took place on the Danube, when the Magyar fleet overthrew the galleys of the Turks, and Hunyady and Capistrano were enabled to enter Belgrade. On July 21, 1456, after having destroyed the walls with his formidable artillery, Mohammed ordered the attack by the Janissaries. They broke through the outworks, but on finding themselves confronted by a second line of fortifications their courage failed. Completely repulsed, the sultan fled to Sophia, leaving 24,000 dead and all his artillery under the walls of the citadel. But Hunyady did not long survive this triumph; he died shortly after, whether from a wound or from an epidemic which broke out in the army, is not known. His contemporaries paid the most striking homage to his memory. " With him," said Pope Æneas Sylvius, " have died our hopes." " He was a great man in all things," exclaimed Chalcondylas. And the Polish chronicler, Dlugosz, who is not at all favorable to the Hungarians, is forced to write, " He was celebrated in fight, and possessed of great worth as a leader of armies. His death was a calamity not only for Hungary, but for the whole Catholic world."

King Vladislav was not worthy of such a subject. Besides his previous ingratitude, he now allowed himself to be prejudiced against the noble warrior, even after his death, by the count of Cilly. Hunyady's son, Vladislav, and his brother-in-law Szilagy came into possession of a letter written by the favorite to the despot of Servia, in which he proposed to him to exterminate " these Wallachian dogs," as he called the Hunyadys. They resolved to anticipate him, and when Cilly came to Belgrade with the king they caused his assassination. This was but an act of justice according to the customs of the time, but the king never forgave it, and at the instigation of Gara had Vladislav Hunyady cast into prison at Buda, and condemned to death in 1457. The headsman, in his agitation, struck three times without reaching the neck of the noble victim. " The laws forbid striking more than thrice," said the son of the man who had saved Belgrade. But the king, inflexible in his vengeance, ordered the execution of the sentence. And as if to complete his own dishonor, he issued an edict declaring John Hunyady a traitor and a scoundrel. But Vladislav did not long survive his shame. He died a few days after his victim, Vladislav Hunyady. Magyar poetry has found a fertile field in these tragic events and is full of the memory of these sad scenes.

The memory of John Hunyady received a glorious vindication. Vladislav Hunyady had perished at the hands of the hangman, but he left a younger brother named Mathias. Him the Hungarian diet, at Pesth, in January, 1458, elected by almost unanimous choice as king. Szilagy, his uncle, was chosen governor for five years, and after pledging himself to respect the liberties of the nation, raised an army of 40,000 in support of the young king. But Podiebrad, the newly elected king of Bohemia, whither

Mathias had been sent by Vladislav the Posthumous, refused to let him return except for a heavy ransom, and on condition that he marry his eldest daughter Catherine. For the first time in many years Bohemia and Hungary each had a native king, and the Holy See and the house of Austria were alike astonished and enraged at this innovation, which paid so little regard to their rights, and still less to their claims.

The young king was worthy of his lofty dignity; he had received a remarkable education; he spoke Hungarian, German, and Slav, and from his father he inherited warlike instincts and the art of ruling. He began by putting the military forces of Hungary on a good footing. Then he took up the task of reducing the strength of the great nobles who disputed the royal authority, and among whom were his uncle, Szilagy, Gara, Jiskra de Brandyse, and Ujlaky. In this, too, he was successful, notwithstanding their alliance with Frederick IV., who still had possession of the sacred crown and who now took the title of king of Hungary. The emperor finally yielded, recognized Mathias as his adopted son, and returned the sacred crown. In return he obtained his own recognition as heir to the throne, in case Mathias died childless.

This left Mathias free to pursue the traditional policy of the Magyars against the Turks, who had been gaining ground steadily. In 1463 Bosnia was completely conquered by them; its king and the greater number of the nobles beheaded, 30,000 young Bosnians enrolled in the Janissaries, and 200,000 carried into captivity. In Wallachia, too, they had completely established their rule. Mathias sent ambassadors to Vienna, Venice, and to the Pope, and with the aid received from them was able to recover a part of Bosnia and drive the Mussulmans back from Belgrade. Once again the frontier of Hungary on the Save was safe. But much more remained to be done; it was necessary to drive the Turks from the Slavo-Hellenic peninsula, and in this work Hungary would naturally be the sword of Europe. Still a proposal for a general council and a grand league of Christendom against the infidel made by France and Bohemia was rejected by Mathias, who suspected both the motives and the plan. He had always retained a certain animosity against Podiebrad, and he had little faith in a council, remembering, perhaps, the sad consequences of the Council of Constance. Besides, he regarded Podiebrad as a Hussite, and, encouraged by Pope Pius II., he now turned his arms against Bohemia, thus beginning an anti-Christian crusade against the very king who cherished the grandiose designs of a European coalition against the infidel.

For a time the war was delayed, first by the intervention of the emperor, always eager to interfere in the internal affairs of Hungary, later by the revolt of Transylvania. But in 1468 Mathias assembled the estates of Hungary at Eger to prepare for the fratricidal struggle against Bohemia—" A war," says the Hungarian historian, Boldenyi, " the most unjust and fruitless that Mathias could have undertaken from the standpoint of Hungarian interests. What glory, what triumphs would not have been assured to Christendom in an intimate alliance of Hungary with Bohemia against the Mussulman. The face of eastern Europe might perhaps have been changed! " Nothing could have been more favorable to the interests of the Turks and the Austrians than this conflict. The Hungarian diet hesitated at first, but the Papal legate, the bishop of Breslau, and the envoy of the emperor urged them on. War was determined upon, and the Pope's legate wrote, " The church owes eternal praise to the king of Hungary."

The details of the war belong to the history of Bohemia. After a struggle frequently interrupted by negotiations and a partial reconciliation with Podiebrad, Mathias had himself crowned king of Bohemia at Olmütz, in 1469. The death of Podiebrad, however, changed the situation. The Czechs elected Vladislav Jagellon, the king of Poland, and against this rival, who commanded the forces of two kingdoms, Mathias had little chance of holding the crown he had usurped in Moravia. Besides, he found himself threatened by an invasion of the Turks in southern Hungary. A treaty was soon (1475) concluded, by which Mathias was granted Moravia and a part of Silesia. But these gains brought but little advantage to Hungary. Indeed, the first part of the reign of Mathias is wretched enough; the second part is greater and nobler. The king, inspired by a wiser policy, directed his attacks against the two real enemies of his kingdom—the Turks and the emperor. And it was high time that attention should be given the Mussulman advance. While Mathias was warring in Bohemia, Mohammed II. had built the fortress of Shabats on the Save, which commands that river above Belgrade. Against this fortress the king led his forces and captured it, while his lieutenant, Batory, aiding Prince Stephen of Moldavia, drove the Turks from that province.

Against the emperor he was equally successful. The house of Hapsburg, always jealous of Hungary, could not leave Mathias in the peaceful enjoyment of the spoils of the struggle with Bohemia, and a war broke out. It was, however, of short duration: the Hungarian cavalry invaded Austria, carrying all before it, and the emperor having fled to Linz, recognized the right of Mathias to the free possession of Moravia and Silesia in 1485.

But notwithstanding these successes, Mathias, constantly pressed by the Turks, was beginning to reap the fruits of his mistaken policy. At the very moment when he was most in need of allies he found himself isolated. In 1479 a formidable Turkish army invaded Transylvania. The king sent Batory against them, and on the plain of Kenyer-Meso—the field of corn—this general, despite his smaller forces, scored a brilliant victory. He himself was wounded six times during the battle and finally saved only by the heroism of Kiniszy, the intrepid commander of the hussars. The tents and baggage of the enemy fell into the hands of the Hungarians, who celebrated their victory with extravagant rejoicings. Kiniszy himself, according to the chroniclers, " throwing aside his usual gravity, executed the Hungarian dance, holding a dead Turk in his teeth and one in each arm." The death of Mohammed II. increased the hopes of the Christians still further. The conqueror of Constantinople was succeeded by Bajazet II., and he offered a truce for five years. This Mathias accepted, and at once turned to take up the struggle with the Emperor Frederick again. Frederick was forced to fly to Nuremberg. But the Germans of Vienna were not inclined to submit to the Magyars, and a long siege was necessary to reduce the city in 1485. Already in possession of Silesia and Moravia, the mastery over the archduchy of Austria gave Mathias a state almost as large as Austria of to-day, if we except Bohemia and Galicia. But his dominions were far from being consolidated, and while the house of Austria extended its influence by marriages, Mathias had no legitimate heir. And in 1490 a sudden death carried him off before he had made final arrangements for the disposition of his possessions. He wrote his own proud epitaph: " Austria conquered bears witness to my power. I was the terror of the world. The emperor of the Germans and the sultan of the Turks trembled before me. Death alone could conquer me."

Hungary mourned her hero, and Mathias Corvinus remains

to-day one of her most honored and best remembered kings. He did not belong to a foreign house, but was one of her own sons. He accomplished great things, but he was not a great man, and the meanness of his ambitions has done more harm to Hungary than the courage and variety of his enterprises profited her. As a law-giver and a patron of art and letters his greatness is less questionable. Few sovereigns have had more respect for the constitution. Every year he convoked the diet, including not only the prelates and barons, but also the representatives of the comitats; or, as a contemporary expressed it, the " commonalty of the kingdom."

" The political life of the comitats was very active during his reign: these county assemblies met frequently, and Mathias looked to them for support against the great nobles, who strove to make themselves independent of the crown. The king had the right to name the chief count of the comitat, but his deputy had always to be chosen from among the nobles of the comitat. The functions of the palatine were lessened and he was deprived of those judicial powers which made of him the chief justice of the kingdom. Although very religious and devoted to the Holy See in a somewhat capricious manner, Mathias restrained the clergy and prohibited appeals to Rome. But above all he tried to restrain the privileges of the upper nobility. " Mathias is dead and justice is fled " is a Magyar proverb that has come down to our times. The king also took great pains to encourage and protect commerce, and invited foreigners to his kingdom, especially the Servians, who came in great numbers, after the death of Brankovic and the final ruin of the old Servian empire.

Mathias had a well-cultivated mind, and possessed that ready wit which makes a king popular. " He is a wise and learned king, and of great dignity of speech. He says only what is necessary and in reason and eloquence he surpasses all the princes I have known," wrote the Papal legate. His second wife, Beatrix, brought from Italy the traditions and influence of the Renaissance; many Italians lived at the court of Buda and embellished the kingdom with beautiful buildings. The royal palace was magnificent and filled with precious objects. Mathias founded at Buda the first royal library, the famous Corvina, which is said to have possessed fifty thousand manuscripts, an enormous number for that time. Agents were sent everywhere to buy manuscripts or make copies, and thirty copyists were constantly at work in Buda itself. He gathered about him poets and writers, but unfortunately their works, which were in Magyar, have perished; the only manuscripts of the time that have been preserved deal with theology. The national language had not yet attained its true place in literature.

The treasures of the Corvina library were unfortunately scattered and lost during the succeeding centuries; the kings of the Jagellon dynasty sold some and the Turks carried off others. Some found their way to Paris, notably a Ptolemy and a St. Jerome; others to Vienna and Pesth, while recently some volumes were restored by the Turks on the occasion of the expressions of sympathy between the two countries during the Russian war of 1877. But the era of manuscripts was about to end: printing was introduced from Germany in 1473, and by the end of the century Buda had as many as thirteen bookstores. To this time also belong the beginnings of a learned society called "Sodalitas litteraria Hungarorum." Most of the writers of the time are Italians and Greeks, though some are natives, notably John Thuroczy, the author of the "Chronicles of Hungary." Mathias contemplated founding a large university at Buda, but death prevented the realization of the project, though an Academia Corviniana, comprising the two faculties of theology and philosophy, existed down to the time of the battle of Mohacs.

The reign of Mathias Corvinus is the highwater mark in the history of Hungary: from this time forward we shall see her hopeless decay. After the death of Mathias the diet, unable to find a native king, and divided between rival factions, turned to a foreigner. Vladislav II., king of Bohemia, and the old rival of Mathias, was elected, thus uniting the two crowns of St. Vacslav and St. Stephen, a union which Mathias had so ardently hoped to bring about by his deplorable war.

It was by no means the common interests of the two kingdoms that had prompted the choice of the diet, for Vladislav was feeble and insignificant. He was called the "King Dobre," which expresses inertia, a characteristic which recommended itself strongly to the violent nobility, anxious for a brief respite from the harsh rule of Corvinus. "He neither liked nor knew how to command, and, if he had, the country would have refused to obey. His head was empty, and his purse was even more so. He must fumble at the very bottom to find a solitary coin. Insects and the weather had eaten the fur from his garments, and his clothes were so worn that they had lost their color."

The beginning of his reign was not fortunate; Maximilian recovered the Austrian provinces, and John of Poland declared war on his brother and obliged him to surrender a part of Silesia. Maximilian also invaded Hungary, consenting to withdraw only after a treaty had been signed which assured the succession in Hungary to the house of Austria in case Vladislav died without children. This treaty, in which the king disposed of the kingdom without consulting it, raised a storm of indignation.

Meanwhile the Turks were crowding in upon the southern frontier. Failing in his attempts to capture Belgrade, in 1492, Bajazet II. had entered the valley of the Save and defeated the disorganized Hungarian forces. The diet of 1493 complains bitterly of the cowardice and inertia of a king who preferred " the repose and pleasures of the chase to the stern duties of war." The finances of the kingdom were in the greatest disorder; the great lords quarreled over the possession of power. In 1505 the diet came to a remarkable decision. " This kingdom," declared the manifesto, " has often been governed by foreign kings and never has it suffered so much as under their rule. . . . Concerned only with the interests of their families instead of studying the manners and customs of this Scythian people, who have made themselves masters of the soil they occupy at the price of their blood, these foreigners have given themselves up to idleness rather than the toils of war. Thus we have lost Servia, Galicia, Lodomeria, Bulgaria, and Dalmatia. . . . This dismemberment of our frontiers may well cause us fear lest the enemy will ultimately invade our land itself, if the nation, out of love for its native soil, does not choose from among its own a capable king." It was somewhat late for this expression of patriotism. The nobles had only themselves to blame if Hungary had so often been ruled by foreigners. The manifesto was sent to all the comitats. It was mainly the work of the prothonotary, Stephen Verböczy, an ardent patriot, who devoted his life to the study of the public law of Hungary. But unfortunately legal formulas, however eloquently expressed, avail nothing against brute force.

Vladislav had one son, Prince Louis. Entangled in the network of Austrian diplomacy, he had affianced him in his cradle to Mary of Austria, the sister of the future Charles V., agreeing further that if his son should die first to bequeath the kingdom to his daughter Anne, who was betrothed to Ferdinand of Austria. And he cared so little for the interest of Hungary that he did not even take advantage of the League of Cambray to regain Dalmatia from Venice. An insurrection among the peasantry, accompanied by appalling Jacqueries, added still further to the sadness of this miserable reign. Hungary was essentially an aristocratic country. The great barons did their utmost to crush the lesser nobility, and these in their turn exploited the peasants. Deep-seated hatred was nourished by the rural classes, and awaited only a suitable opportunity to burst forth. In 1513 Cardinal Bakracz came from Rome with a bull for a crusade against the infidel. The peasants armed as if against the Turk, and then turned upon their lords. The leader of the movement, Dosza, was a peasant from Transylvania and a Szekler. Armed with a scythe, he led the peasants in what he proclaimed a holy crusade, or *kurucz*, against their infidel lords. In the first encounter he was successful, but the nobles chose John Szapolyai, the voïévode of Transylvania, as their leader, and defeated Dosza near Temesvar. Their revenge upon the captured leader was terrible. The king of the peasants was seated on a throne of fire and a red-hot crown was placed on his head. His wonderful fortitude under torture has made his name a popular one in Hungary, and tradition tells how Szapolyai was smitten with blindness for two years as a punishment for his cruelty.

In the celebrated work presented to the diet in 1514 by Verböczy, entitled " *Decretum bipartitum juris consuetudinarii,*" the public law of Hungary is compiled. This work, so to speak the last will and testament of independent Hungary, furnishes ample evidence of the wretched social conditions which underlay the *kurucz* and the numerous revolts that convulsed Hungary at this time. It recognizes one legal class only, the nobles, descended from the ancient conquerors of the soil. As for the Jobbagyones, the serfs, Verböczy declares that the revolt under Dosza " marks them forever as infidels and condemns them to perpetual servitude."

The impotent Vladislav died in 1515. The reign of his infant son, Louis II., is marked by two great catastrophes, the loss of Belgrade, in 1516, and the defeat at Mohacs, in 1521. The young king was corrupt and dissolute and quite incapable of governing, while his guardians were not men to rise to the occasion. The finances were disorganized and the nobles quarreled over the shreds of sovereignty still left. These disorders were of great service to the Turks. While Hungary was giving herself up to anarchy, Turkey was ruled by her great sovereign, Suleiman the Magnificent. A pretext to declare war was afforded him by the arrest of a Turkish subject accused of being a spy. He assembled his troops at Sophia, captured Shabats, and laid siege to Belgrade. The place surrendered in 1521, and the key to the Danube became thenceforward a Turkish fortress. Even in the presence of this danger Hungary remained disunited and divided.

Meanwhile King Louis sought help on all sides. To the king of England he wrote, " If help from your Majesty does not arrive promptly, our kingdom is lost," and he even tried to induce a Persian prince to make a timely diversion in the extreme East. The Austrian princes offered their assistance, but they were too feeble, even when combined with Hungary, to undertake the struggle with Suleiman the Magnificent. On April 25, 1526, Suleiman had started from Constantinople with 100,000 men and 300 cannon. He marched not only against Hungary, but also against the empire, one of the pretexts of the expedition being the captivity of Francis I., for he came, he said, to rescue " the beg of France " from the hands of his enemies. He crossed the Save near Essek, captured Peterwardein and came up with the Hungarians at Mohacs, on the right bank of the Danube. The Hungarians were commanded by the king in person, assisted by Paul Tomory, archbishop of Ka-losca, one of the warlike bishops of whom Hungary affords many examples; George Szapolyai, and by Peter Pereny, bishop of Great Varadin. Pereny wished to temporize in order to wait the help from Croatia and Transylvania, but the impetuous Tomory led to a decision in favor of immediate action, on August 26, 1526. The opening of the battle seemed favorable to the Hungarians, but Suleiman had ordered his first ranks to fall back before the Hungarian cavalry that the main body might then close in on them. Thus deceived, the Magyars were overwhelmed at close range by the Ottoman artillery; forced to retreat, they rushed into the marshy lands, where many were engulfed. The king was lost, Tomory was slain, 7 prelates, 22 magnates, and 22,000 men remained dead on the field. The road to Buda was now open to the invaders, and laying waste the country on their way, they pushed on to the Magyar capital. There they pillaged and destroyed the rich treasures collected by Mathias Corvinus, sending much down the Danube to enrich and adorn Constantinople. Little by little the tide of invasion ebbed, leaving behind it a land of devastation and ruin.

With the death of Louis II. the independent existence of Hungary came to an end. Henceforward it was to oscillate between Austria and Turkey for a century and a half, and then be entirely under Austrian suzerainty till the time when the feeling of nationality had become sufficiently strong to enable it to be once more a self-governing nation.

PART III

THE ACQUISITION OF BOHEMIA AND HUNGARY, AND THE UNIFICATION OF THE MONARCHY UNDER THE EMPERORS. 1493-1740

Chapter XV

THE AUSTRIAN EMPERORS. 1493-1740

THE real greatness of the house of Austria dates from the reign of Maximilian from 1493 to 1519. At his accession he united under his rule all the domains of his family: Austria, properly so-called, Styria, Carinthia, Carniola, and the Tyrol, and his territories reached to the sea at Triest and Fiume. In 1500 he inherited Gorica, Gradiska, Mitterburg, and the Pusterthal, and although he lost the seaports on the Adriatic in his war with Venice in 1509, they were soon recovered. The war with the Swiss ended less fortunately for Austria. After a severe struggle, during which the Confederates, with their long pikes and halberds, had invaded Austrian Suabia and the Tyrol, destroyed over two hundred villages and towns, and slain more than twenty thousand men, Maximilian agreed to the peace of Basel in 1499, by which the Swiss were finally released from all obligations to the house of Hapsburg and the emperor. But this loss was really a gain. By concentrating her power, Austria strengthened herself. In 1505 Maximilian, by his successful intervention in the disputes over the Bavarian succession, secured a number of towns from that state, notably Kufstein, and the lordships of Rottenberg and Kitzbühl, giving him a foothold on the sources of the Drave and the Isonzo. Thus at this time the Austrian dominions formed a sort of half-circle, touching the southern frontier of Germany from Silesia to Switzerland, while she also had scattered possessions in Suabia, Alsace, and the Black Forest. Among her subjects were Germans, Slavs, and Italians; but then, as now, the Germans, thanks to the proximity of Germany, to the innate tenacity of their race, and to the prestige of the imperial crown, were the dominant element.

The most important event in these hereditary provinces during Maximilian's reign, apart from the invasions of the Venetians, the Swiss, and the Turks, was the peasants' war which broke out in Carniola in 1515 and rapidly spread throughout the neighboring provinces. Contemporaneous with the revolt of Dosza, in

Hungary, this insurrection also was caused by famine and the exactions of a selfish nobility. The Slovene peasants of Carniola adopted as their watchword *stara pravda*—our old rights—and, like the Magyar *kurucz*, declared that they revolted not against the sovereign, but against the nobles. The insurrection spread rapidly, and, if contemporary accounts are to be believed, they set on foot an army of 80,000 men, spreading terror everywhere, taking castles, and hanging nobles. But like the peasants' revolt in connection with the Lutheran Reformation a little later, the movement was suppressed with ruthless cruelty.

Maximilian was always in need of money, and frequently summoned the diets of the hereditary provinces to ask for subsidies, which were often refused. The provinces were poor, but the monarch was still more so, and out of his necessity he was obliged to promise not to make war without the consent of the estates. Under his reign, also, the provinces were drawn more closely together by the organization of general diets, to which they sent their representatives, as, for example, the diet of Wiener-Neustadt, in 1502, in which Upper and Lower Austria, Styria, Carinthia, and Carniola were all represented.

Many of the affairs of Austria, however, during the reign of Maximilian, as indeed during that of many of his successors, are intimately wrapped up with those of the empire. In 1493, on the death of his father, Frederick IV., Maximilian was chosen emperor. He hoped to make the imperial dignity hereditary in his family, and to use it to further Hapsburg interests. These he believed to lie in the acquisition of the Netherlands, regaining Hungary and Bohemia, the defeat of the French king in the dispute over the rich inheritance of the dukes of Burgundy, the reassertion of his claims in Italy, and the admission of Austria into the electoral college. The electors, who were deeply impressed at this time with the need of reforms within the empire, gave him but a lukewarm support, and, on the matter of admitting a new member into their college, refused flatly to comply with his wishes. Thus the Hapsburgs, although for centuries the wearers of the imperial crown, were excluded from the body which conferred it, though they later entered the electoral college as kings of Bohemia. Nevertheless, Maximilian continued his other projects, and lost no opportunity of identifying the interests of his family with those of Germany. Before a diet held in 1506 he declared that he hoped

"Tu Felix Austria nube!"

THE SOLEMN DOUBLE ENGAGEMENT OF THE GRANDCHILDREN OF EMPEROR MAXIMILIAN I IN THE CATHEDRAL OF
ST. STEPHEN, VIENNA, JULY 22, 1515

Painting by V. Brozik

some day to add the crowns of Bohemia and Hungary to the empire, if he were properly aided. It is chiefly through his wise family alliances that he contributed so much toward the increase in prestige and power of the house of Austria. By his own marriage with Mary of Burgundy, in 1477, he had prepared the way for the extensive dominions of Charles V. and the acquisition of possessions and influence in the Netherlands, Burgundy, and Italy. By the marriage alliances entered into with the reigning houses in Bohemia and Hungary he laid the basis for the Austrian state as it exists to-day, and to no Hapsburg ruler is the well-known distich more applicable than to Maximilian:

> *Bella gerant fortes: tu felix Austria nube;*
> *Nam quæ Mars aliis, dat tibi regna Venus.*

In 1515 the marriage of his grandchildren, Ferdinand and Mary, with Louis and Anne, the children of Vladislav, king of Bohemia and Hungary, was arranged, and at this time Vladislav and his brother, Sigismund, king of Poland, paid a visit to Vienna, during which the ancient treaties of inheritance between Austria, Hungary, and Bohemia were renewed. Thanks in a large measure to these treaties, Austria was to become the dominant power in the middle Danube, and the house of Hapsburg unite under its scepter Bohemia and Hungary as well as Austria. Unfortunately the rôle she thus came to play in European matters from the sixteenth century onward has too often led historians to forget the internal history of the peoples with whom her destinies have since been so closely associated.

Maximilian died in 1519, and was buried at Innsbruck, his favorite residence, for he was a great hunter and passionately fond of the mountains of the Tyrol. Of all the Austrian sovereigns none since Rudolf has lived so long in the popular memory. He himself contributed to perpetuate his name with posterity through the two poems, " *Theuerdank* " and " *Weiss König,*" which he inspired and perhaps wrote in part. He was fond of artists and learned men, and became the patron of the *Sodalitas Danubiana,* a kind of academy founded at Vienna by the humanist Konrad Celtes. Indeed, Vienna and Austria enjoyed a renaissance of learning and culture during his reign. It is the age of the German renaissance of Erasmus and Hutten of the activity of the newly discovered art of printing, and of all that great social and economic unrest that preceded the Reformation.

Maximilian was twice married, but had only one legitimate son, Philip the Handsome, born to him by Mary of Burgundy. Philip married Joanna the Insane, daughter of Ferdinand and Isabella of Spain. He died in 1500, leaving two sons, Charles and Ferdinand, to divide the empire of Europe, and carry the name of Austria to the savannahs of the New World.

On the death of Maximilian I. his two grandsons, who had been reared and educated away from Austria, Charles in the Low Countries, Ferdinand in Spain, fell heir to his possessions. Charles was elected emperor in 1519, and two years later, in 1521, he came to an agreement with his brother concerning a division of their lands. By this settlement Charles V. conferred on his brother all the Austrian possessions with the title of lieutenant of the empire, reserving to himself that of duke of Austria. This prince, one-half Spaniard, was not received with confidence in a country where he was so little known, and the foreign advisers whom he brought with him were extremely unpopular. Disturbances arose in Vienna, but were suppressed and the two ringleaders executed. On May 27, 1521, at Linz, Ferdinand celebrated his marriage with the Princess Anne, sister of Louis, king of Bohemia and Hungary, and at the same time Louis, then aged fifteen, married Mary, the sister of Ferdinand, thus carrying into execution the wise matrimonial plans of Maximilian.

The name of Ferdinand I. is completely obscured by that of Charles V., but in reality Ferdinand's reign marks the beginning of a state which plays an important part in the destinies of Europe even to-day, while only the memory of the wide dominions of Charles V. remains. The Spanish branch of the house of Hapsburg attained its highest power at the Treaty of Château-Cambrésis in 1559, while the Treaty of Vervins, in 1598, already marks its decline. The power of the Austrian branch, on the other hand, owing to its possession of the hereditary states, Bohemia, Hungary, and after 1558 the imperial crown, increased steadily.

In 1526, at the death of Louis at Mohacs, Ferdinand became king of Bohemia and Hungary. At his coronation at Prague and at Buda he swore to maintain the rights and privileges of the two kingdoms. Five years later he was elected king of the Romans, in spite of the opposition of the Protestants, and in 1558 emperor.

From this time the imperial crown, with one unimportant exception, remained in the house of Austria.   A staunch Catholic, Ferdinand opposed the Reformation, and did all in his power to prevent
the movement from entering his dominions.   As was the case in
Germany, it coincided with a formidable peasants' war; Salzburg,
Styria, and the Tyrol rose in insurrection, and a popular assembly
which met at Meran drew up a manifesto the boldness and audacity

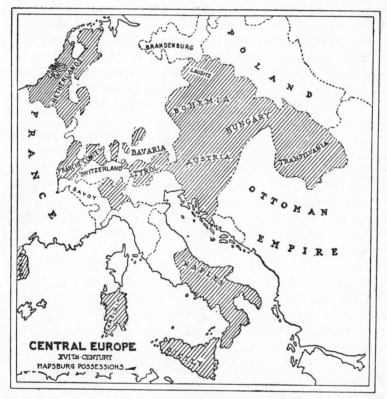

of which astonish us even to-day.   " In the Tyrol," says this document, " there will be henceforth but one law, and that the law of
the land; there shall be no Roman law, foreign and unintelligible
to the poor people.   The government sitting at Innsbruck shall be
composed only of natives.   There shall be no distinction of person before the tribunals.   Bishops, monasteries, and begging friars
shall be suppressed; priests shall not be allowed to hold more than
one living.   The surplus of the revenues of the church shall be

devoted to the needs of the poor. The estates of the clergy shall be secularized and the revenues of the monasteries shall be collected by the servants of the king and employed for the public good. The king may choose only his financial agents, all officers of justice shall be appointed and dismissed by the people. Fishing and hunting shall be free to everyone, the great trading companies shall be dissolved in order that the prices of commodities may be decreased. All custom houses except those belonging to the crown shall be suppressed; likewise the seigneurial dues and forced labor. Uniformity of weights and coinage shall be decreed." The peasants also took great pains to declare that they fought against the privileged orders and not against the king. Ferdinand was obliged to yield. He granted pardon to the insurgents and the execution of those clauses of the articles of Meran which did not affect the property of the church.

The Reformation made rapid progress in other hereditary provinces. In Austria proper there were ardent disciples as early as 1520, and thirty years later the procession of *Corpus Christi* could not be held at Vienna. Two hundred parishes had no priests, and 268 had become Protestant. The same progress was made in Styria; in 1552 the procession of *Corpus Christi* was suppressed at Gratz. In Carniola, among the Slovenes, one result of the Reformation was the emancipation of the national language; several theological works were printed in Slavic at Tubingen under the direction of Primus Truber, who also undertook the translation of the Bible into the native tongue. The new doctrines penetrated as far as Triest and Gorica, and in the Tyrol the Anabaptists almost succeeded in causing another uprising among the peasants. On several occasions the diets themselves gave expression to the need for liberty of conscience, and Ferdinand, who had begun by forbidding the use of Luther's Bible, was obliged finally to allow communion in both kinds.

But the spread of the Reformation was not to continue long without more serious and better organized opposition. At the famous Council of Trent, which met in the Tyrol from 1545 to 1563, under the protection of Ferdinand, the doctrines of the Catholics were clearly formulated, and in 1547 Ferdinand set up a censorship of the press in his dominions. About the same time the Society of Jesus was founded for the special object of combating the Reformation, and it was not slow in entering the Austrian lands, for in 1552 the Jesuits established themselves in Vienna, in 1560 in the Tyrol, and in 1564 in Styria.

But the religious difficulties were not the only troubles Ferdinand experienced. He had to witness the ravaging of his territories by the Turks; Vienna was besieged in 1529, and thirty years later Carniola was devastated by them. Amid all these difficulties Ferdinand had the satisfaction of seeing his son Maximilian chosen king of the Romans and to have him crowned king of Bohemia and Hungary. The principle of primogeniture had not been fully established in the house of Austria, and Ferdinand divided the hereditary states between his three sons, Maximilian getting Austria, Ferdinand the Tyrol, and Charles Styria, Carinthia, and Carniola.

Ferdinand died in 1564. He has been praised by many. He had received an excellent education; he knew Spanish, French, and German, and he was fond of men of letters and science. Although a devout Catholic, he was not a fanatic, and might in other times have made a good ruler for the hereditary provinces. But imbued with the idea of absolutism, he could not understand the constitutions of Bohemia and of Hungary. In Bohemia especially his memory is detested. From his reign dates the High Council of War, the first institution common to the whole group of states.

Maximilian II. was a tolerant and liberal-minded prince for his time. His preceptors had been the learned Wolfgan Schiefer (Severus) and Collatin, who were secretly attached to Protestantism. It was in order to correct their influence that Ferdinand sent the young prince to Spain and he even talked of excluding him from the succession.

When Maximilian assumed the reins of government in 1564 he had already shown his goodwill toward the Reformation, and this policy he continued during his reign. He corresponded with Melanchthon, and even maintained a Lutheran preacher at his court, greatly arousing the suspicion and anxiety of the court at Rome. When the news of the massacre of St. Bartholomew reached him he denounced the perpetrators in no unmeasured terms. Nevertheless, he declined to yield to the request of the estates of Austria to expel the Jesuits, and would allow the nobles only to practice the Reformed religion, refusing to grant liberty of conscience to the towns. He had married his cousin, Mary, the daughter of Charles V., who, faithful to her Spanish blood, brought up

their children with a horror of heresy. Two of his sons, Rudolf
and Mathias, reigned after him. The former he had caused to
be crowned king of Hungary in 1572 and of Bohemia in 1575.

Rudolf II. was more mindful of the zealous devotion of his
mother than of the tolerance of his father. In more than one
respect he resembled Philip II., for he had the fierce fanaticism and
the morose disposition of that prince, though he lacked his strength
of will. He has become notorious for his love for the occult sciences, and for his obstinate indolence. Prague, which owes to him
much of its splendor, he chose as his place of residence, and there
he lived in retirement in his castle of Hradcany, surrounded by
astronomers and astrologers, among whom were Tycho-Brahé.
But the dangerous fancies of this weak emperor ended by disturb-
ing his reason, and his brothers decided to proclaim Mathias head
of the family. In 1608 he was given the title of governor of
Austria, Moravia, and Hungary.

In the hereditary provinces the reign of Rudolf was marked
by a peasant war, caused by the agrarian difficulties and the demand for liberty of conscience, the two causes of discontent which
are intimately associated with each other during this period. But
the Jesuits and the upper clergy worked hard to suppress the demand for reform, and the spirit of their methods is well illustrated
by the following couplet addressed to the emperor in 1581:

> *Utere jure tuo, Cæsar, servosque Lutheri*
> *Ense, rota, ponto, funibus, igne neca!*

In Styria the Archduke Charles was no less zealous to restore
Catholicism. He established the Jesuits at Gratz, and by 1572 the
religious processions, suppressed twenty years before, were resumed.
The protests of the Lutheran nobility were ignored, and the
counter-reformation progressed rapidly. A Catholic printing-press
was set up at Gratz, and a Jesuit university, which exists still, was
founded there in 1586. The nobles were compelled to send their
children there for instruction under pain of disgrace and punishment, while they were, at the same time, forbidden to allow their
children to attend the heretical schools of Germany. But the
burghers, peasants, and diets harassed the archduke incessantly
with their petitions, and he died in 1591 of weariness and chagrin.
His work was continued by his successor, Ferdinand, afterward em-

peror and king of Bohemia and Hungary. On a pilgrimage to Loretto this prince had taken a vow to exterminate heresy, and he remained true to his word. He began by driving the Protestant preachers from Gratz and other towns, then he seized their schools, burned their books, and compelled all members of the Reformed religion to sell their property and emigrate. The Capuchins were sent for to help the Jesuits to lead the people back to the faith. Later on Ferdinand had an opportunity to apply these methods of conversion on a larger scale in Bohemia.

In Austria the Archduke Mathias was obliged to treat with the estates and to renew the agreements of Maximilian, which granted liberty of conscience on the seigneurial estates, but not in the towns. In the Tyrol the Archduke Ferdinand, who must not be confused with Emperor Ferdinand II., labored with equal energy for the restoration of Catholicism. But his administration was good. The province owed to him the *Landesordnung,* a code of laws which remained in force for more than two centuries, an improved system of coinage, and wise measures for the development of commerce and industry.

Rudolf, whose weak mind had, as we have seen, led his brothers to assume the administration of his affairs, never married, and he was succeeded in 1612, in Austria, Bohemia, and Hungary, by Mathias. The latter's thirst for power and constant activity stand in striking contrast with the indolence of his brother, but he was devoid of greatness. The chief interest of the reign of Mathias centers in the beginning of the Thirty Years' War. Without direct heirs, his principal concern was to secure his inheritance to his family. He chose his cousin, Ferdinand, of the Styrian branch, as his heir, and obtained an act of renunciation from his brothers, Albert and Maximilian, and from the king of Spain. The Bohemian and Hungarian estates ratified this agreement and Ferdinand was crowned in the two kingdoms.

It may seem somewhat surprising that this transaction should have been so readily accepted in Bohemia and Hungary, but it should be remembered that in all essentially aristocratic countries the nobles prefer to obey a stranger to one of themselves, even if the latter were a Mathias Corvinus or a Podiebrad. Besides, there was the constant menace of a Mussulman invasion, and both countries instinctively felt that it was to their interest to secure the support of the princes of a house already powerful by

itself, and who could, in case of necessity, bring to their assistance
the forces of all of Germany. Unfortunately, the Hapsburgs were
overzealous as protectors of Catholicism, neglected the interests
of Bohemia and Hungary, and associated themselves completely
with Catholic intolerance. Adherents of the reform doctrines,
whether of Huss, Luther, or Calvin, were as hateful to them as the
Turks. Besides, they identified all spirit of independence with
heresy, and ruthlessly crushed out liberty, making absolutism the
basis of their policy.

Ferdinand II. (1618-1637), a fervent Catholic and a despot,
was the first and one of the best examples of this class of Austrian
rulers. He had been educated at Ingolstadt under the direction of
the Jesuits and his pious uncle, William of Bavaria, and had at
different times expressed his desire to become a Jesuit himself.
His policy in Styria, noted above, shows how he carried the pre-
cepts of his instruction into practice. Bohemia and Hungary
afforded a much larger field for his religious ardor. His reign was
a golden age for the Catholic church in Austria. He founded sixteen Jesuit colleges, besides numerous convents for the Barnabites,
Capuchins, Carmelites, Augustines, and Benedictines, at the same
time greatly increasing the estates of the clergy. Outwardly a
strict observer of the Christian virtues, Ferdinand was always prac-
ticing ostentatious acts of charity in matters not touching the
treatment of heretics. His second son, Leopold William, was
destined for the church, and at the age of eleven was already
possessed of two bishoprics and four abbeys. Under Ferdinand all
the hereditary provinces had again been united, but in 1623 he
ceded the Tyrol to his brother Leopold, who married the beautiful
and talented Claudia de' Medici.

Ferdinand II. naturally assumed the leadership of the Catholic party in the Thirty Years' War, and at his death, in 1637,
bequeathed this enormous struggle to his successor, Ferdinand III.
(1637-1657). This war was to strike a rude blow at the prestige
of the house of Austria in Germany. It was during its progress
that the remarkable pamphlet on the Holy Roman Empire, by
Hippolytus a Lapide (Philip Chemnitz), appeared. According to
this famous pamphlet the only way of saving the empire from
certain ruin was to exclude Austria from Germany. She had never
exercised any but a disastrous influence there; she had become
powerful at the expense of the empire, and she ought now to allow

Germany to form a federation without her, under the tutelage of France or Sweden. The Peace of Westphalia, in 1648, in assuring liberty of conscience to Germany, made no stipulations for the subjects of Austria, excepting the Silesians, among whom the extensive spread of Protestantism was to be an important factor in the later separation of that province from Austria and its assimilation by Prussia. In the hereditary provinces the counter-reformation was continued with greater energy than ever. But in spite of its efforts, sympathy for the Reformation continued, particularly in Upper Austria, and a number of families of the noble class emigrated to secure liberty of conscience. Uprisings by the peasants were ruthlessly suppressed. Yet Ferdinand III. was not cruel or wanting in intelligence. The Venetian ambassador in his correspondence represents him as an enlightened, gentle, and moderate sovereign. He simply carried out the ideas of his age and the traditions of his family. The early death of his oldest son, Ferdinand, left the succession to his second son, Leopold, whose long reign, from 1657 to 1705, occupies the second half of the seventeenth century.

At the accession of Leopold I. the Austrian state was much smaller than at present. Galicia still belonged to Poland and the Dalmatian shore to the republic of Venice; the Tyrol to a cadet branch of the house of Austria, and scarcely a third of dismembered Hungary yielded obedience to the king. On the other hand, Bohemia still included most of Silesia. But Leopold soon acquired the Tyrol, while the victories of Eugene secured for him nearly all of Hungary, Croatia, Slavonia, and Transylvania. Altogether the Austrian dominions, which numbered only 6800 square miles at Leopold's accession, had been increased to 9100 at his death.

And yet this prince, who thus increased his inheritance by a third, was not of a warlike temperament, and never commanded an army. He had been educated by the Jesuits Müller and Neidhard, and was to have entered the church. He brought to the throne the merits and defects of his early training, great purity of life, extreme humility, and a spirit of inexorable intolerance. He had absolutely no decision of character and followed the advice of the most divergent councilors, especially of his Jesuit confessor, Müller, whom Puffendorf calls "a pedant of the schools who understood nothing of practical affairs." He led a melancholy, monotonous life in his castle at Vienna, only partially relieved by the study of music, painting, literature, and some of the mechanical arts. More than once placards were found on the doors of the palace which implored him to be a Cæsar, not a musician or a Jesuit. "In Leopold," says Sayous, "were united and intensified all the faults of his ancestors, without any of their greatness. The haughty Austrian lip had become a real deformity in him and made him look like a veritable caricature of Charles V. Leopold founded two universities, one at Breslau, the other at Innsbruck. He reformed the courts of justice, substituted the German for the Latin language, and organized a regular police in Vienna.

Leaving aside the part played by Leopold as emperor in the affairs of Europe, his reign in Austria presents but one event of importance, the siege of Vienna by the Turks. In 1683 the grand vizier, Kara Mustapha, supported by the Hungarians, marched upon Vienna. The emperor, with his family and the court, and the larger part of the nobility, hastily withdrew to Linz, leaving the capital with a feeble garrison and dismantled fortifications. Under such circumstances it seemed as if it could not hold out long, but Duke Charles of Lorraine and Count Stahrenberg exerted every effort to put it in a state of defense, and the inhabitants displayed a courage bordering on the heroic. Students, merchants, and citizens turned soldiers and themselves burned the outskirts of the city lest they should be used as shelter by the enemy.

The Turks were soon masters of the outer works, and after establishing a magnificent camp, settled down to a regular siege. At least eighteen attempts were made to take the city by storm. The situation became rapidly desperate; added to the danger from without was the steadily approaching famine within. Fortunately the great Polish king and hero, John Sobieski, whose very name was already a terror to the Turks, appeared in time to save the city from its terrible fate. Supported by the Pope, Innocent XI., Sobieski succeeded in persuading the Polish diet to send its army against the Turks. Sobieski, knowing the peril of Vienna, at once pushed forward by forced marches to its relief. On the Danube he was joined by the army of the duke of Lorraine and the contingents from Saxony and Bavaria, and when he reached Vienna he had about 80,000 men under his command. On September 12 he appeared on the heights of the Kahlenberg. The attack was at once made; the shock was terrible. The infidel gave way, Kara Mustapha fled, and more than 20,000 Turks perished.

The next day the conqueror entered Vienna, enthusiastically greeted by the populace, which had witnessed the departure of the emperor with much indignation. On September 15 Leopold in his turn came back to the capital, and soon the meanness of his character manifested itself. More jealous of Sobieski than grateful for his help, he at first avoided an interview, and then ended by contriving means of humiliating his benefactor. He wasted much time trying to determine how an emperor ought to receive the elected king of the Polish republic. "With open arms," the duke of Lorraine had replied; but to Leopold the great question was whether he should stand to the right or to the left. The interview at length took place in the open field, and it was decided that the two sovereigns should stand facing each other. After the exchange of a few commonplaces, Sobieski rode off, saying he would direct his generals to show the emperor his army if it would please him.

In his letters to Maria Kazimira, his wife, he tells with eloquence and much bitterness the painful impression made upon him by Austrian ingratitude. "The palatine of Red Russia," he wrote, "displayed our army to the emperor, but our people are much annoyed and complain loudly because the emperor did not deign to thank them even by a bow for all the pains and privations they have undergone. They give us neither forage nor provisions; our sick are lying on dunghills, and our many wounded cannot obtain boats to carry them down to Presburg, where I could more easily provide for them at my own cost. They will not bury our dead in their cemeteries, not even the superior officers. . . . They steal our baggage and carry off those of our horses which are in the rear. Except for the oats found in the camp of the Turks, all our horses must have perished. We should be less miserable if they constructed a bridge across the Danube and allowed us to go and live among our enemies. There we would at least find provisions: but here these Viennese gentlemen put off everything from one day to another, and now that they are saved give themselves up to the excesses for which God had rightly punished them. Because many of our men, on account of the lack of provisions in the country, hurried to the city to find food, the commandant has given orders to exclude them and to fire upon them. After so great a battle, in which we have lost so many people of our most illustrious families, we are treated like plague-stricken men whom everyone avoids. Nothing remains but to see our army waste away, not under the blows of the enemy, but by the fault of those who owe us all. So I shall march away to-day, perhaps to find a greater famine, but I wish to get away from Vienna, where they fire upon my men. We are here upon the banks of the Danube, like the Israelites formerly on the shores of the Euphrates. We weep for the loss of our horses, for the ingratitude of those whom we have saved, and for so many chances of victory lost. Finally, everybody is discouraged and some even go so far as to regret that we brought aid to the emperor at all."

After leaving the emperor at Vienna Sobieski pursued the Turks into Hungary and captured Gran, and in December he re-entered Cracow.

Before taking up the reign of Joseph I., it is important to study briefly the general organization of Austria under Leopold. All political and judicial matters were at this time intrusted to a Council of State or Secret Conference, matters of finance and commerce to the Court Chamber (Hofkammer), and war to the Council of War. But the powers of the different councils were not very clearly defined. The Secret Conference never numbered more than twelve members. It assisted the emperor in all important matters. The practice of intrusting ministers with special departments did not yet exist. There was no minister of foreign affairs and all negotiations were conducted with a slowness that had become proberbial. *"Vienna vult expectari"* was a widespread proverb in the diplomatic world. Nor could any member of the council ever boast of having as much influence with the emperor as any one of his numerous confessors.

The High Council of War had been established in 1556, and under Leopold it was composed of about a dozen members, presided over by a president. At the head of the army was a lieutenant general dependent upon the council. At the beginning of the reign Austria did not yet possess a standing army. The celebrated General Montecuculli was the first to demand that one should be organized, and although his wishes were not conceded, he nevertheless induced the emperor not to disband all the troops after a war, and to make some effort to retain veterans in the service.

The army, not counting the garrisons or the Hungarian and Croatian troops, numbered on an average about 30,000 men. In the Turkish wars from 50,000 to 90,000 were put in the field, but of these the German princes furnished from 20,000 to 30,000. After 1680 the continuance of war had for its immediate result the permanence of the army, and its organization along definite lines. The first infantry regiment dates from 1680, and by 1705 there were twenty regiments of cuirassiers, eleven of dragoons, and thirty-six of infantry, besides the irregular troops. An infantry regiment numbered from 2000 to 2500 men, those of the cavalry from 500 to 1000. Recruiting was done, as elsewhere throughout Europe at this time, by recruiting officers and sergeants who allured men to becoming soldiers by the promise of money and booty. In case of extraordinary need the provincial diets voted special levies, and vagabonds and prisoners of war were forcibly enrolled. Old soldiers married and brought up their children in the profession of arms, so that oftentimes three generations might be found in the ranks, while the armies were always followed by an immense number of women and children.

Toward the end of the seventeenth century a small fleet was established on the Danube, commanded by an admiral and manned by sailors from Holland and the Baltic. In time of peace the garrisons were always weak; Vienna never had more than 2000 soldiers. In Hungary the government maintained 10,000 men aside from the national militia, but they were poorly fed and badly paid, and often obliged to pillage the enemy's country to obtain food. Indeed, pillaging of this kind had become a regular custom, even the Turks agreeing that if the frontier was not crossed by more than 500 men and so long as they were without artillery, peace was not violated. War was, moreover, still very poorly organized; supplies were never ready, and the expeditions against the Turks always set out too late. Regiments were often farmed out or rented by the colonels or other officers for their own profit; the treasury paid poorly and pay was at times half a year in arrears, which accounts for the frequent insubordination of the troops. In 1698 a commission was appointed to remedy these evils; its deliberations were numerous, but it accomplished nothing. There were also other deplorable influences at work in the army. Not infrequently the appointment of officers depended upon the king's confessor; there was no guarantee for their obtaining a technical education, and it became necessary to have recourse to Prussian, French, and English officers for this purpose. No military school existed. The care of the sick and wounded was neglected. In

1696 a lottery was established as a means of founding a military hospital, and the lottery has since remained a recognized financial institution in Austria.

The greater part of these miseries was due to the bad state of the finances. The whole of the ordinary revenues by direct taxation was made up of more or less equal subsidies, voted each year (in Hungary every three or four years) by the different diets. Thus, Lower Austria paid on an average two hundred thousand florins, Upper Austria one hundred, Bohemia, Silesia, and Moravia twelve hundred thousand. Extraordinary subsidies took the form of voluntary gifts. The indirect taxes were often burdened with debts contracted toward the various provinces of the empire. But the treasury was very clever at finding sources of revenue. As early as 1676 it laid a tax on billiards, playing-cards, and hair-powder; later on the monopoly on tobacco and stamped paper was introduced; in 1691 a capitation tax was laid, from which neither nobles nor ecclesiastics were exempt, and then finally, under pretexts of philanthropy, the lottery was established. Toward the end of the reign the total revenues from the three groups, Austria, Bohemia, and Hungary, approximated the sum of twelve million florins.

For purposes of administration the country was divided into different groups: Lower Austria, comprising the Austrian lands on both sides of the Enns; Middle Austria, Styria, Carinthia, Carniola, Gorica, and Istria; Upper Austria, the Tyrol, Outer Austria, and the possessions of Austria in Germany; Bohemia, which included Silesia and Moravia; and Hungary and Croatia, which formed one group. Three chief chanceries were maintained at the court, one for Bohemia, one for Hungary, and the third for the hereditary states. But these did not prevent the continuance of the local institutions autonomous to each. For example, Hungary had its chancery at Vienna, while the emperor was represented in Hungary by the palatine, and in Croatia by the ban; but every effort was made to bring the financial and military administration under the control of Vienna. Bohemia, crushed in 1620, retained only its chancery.

The Hapsburgs have always had absolutist tendencies, and the prestige of their imperial title made them more readily forget their duties as kings, counts, or archdukes. Nevertheless, their rule was based on the principle of representation. Each province had its estates, in which sat the deputies of the nobility, the clergy, and the towns. It is true the government did not always consult them in matters of civil and criminal legislation or on questions of commerce; it looked to them to levy the taxes, and left them the direction of internal affairs, the lower courts and the appointment of the provincial officers. Customs barriers existed between all the provinces, imposing burdensome shackles on commerce. Legislation busied itself with absurd details. A police ordinance of 1671 divided lay society into five classes and defined minutely what each should wear and eat. Another ordinance in 1688 reduced the number of classes to three, and tailors and cooks were called upon to denounce all those who infringed upon the provisions laid down by the authorities with respect to the garments and food of the three classes. Very suspicious in certain matters, the police was lax and utterly negligent in most things. Vienna was dirty and badly kept; the plague which broke out in 1679 was as terrible as the great epidemics of the Middle Ages. The Emperor Leopold fled before it, as four years later he fled before the Turks. More than fifty thousand persons are said to have perished.

This paternal absolutism, added to a series of perpetual wars, for the most part foreign to the interests of the different parts of the country, to the wretched state of the finances, and to the great influence of the Jesuits, readily explains the backwardness of Austria at this time from the literary and artistic standpoint. The teaching of the Jesuits and of the Piaristes, who settled in the country after 1656, was confined to the formulas of the schoolmen, and the importation of books in which foreign ideas were found was strictly prohibited. The Latin, in which instruction was given, was execrable, and the German was no better. Nor were the sorry conditions in Bohemia and Hungary more favorable for the development of a national literature.

And yet Leopold meant to encourage letters: he set aside considerable sums for the court library, and after the annexation of the Tyrol brought a part of the collections of the castle of Ambras to Vienna. He also collected what remained of the scattered library of Mathias Corvinus and caused a catalogue of the manuscripts in the imperial library and the works of the physicist, Father Kirschner, to be published at his private expense. He founded the University of Innsbruck, and of Breslau, and began the collection of the paintings which now form the Vienna gallery. But de-

spite these praiseworthy efforts, men of genius are entirely wanting in his reign.

The short reign of Joseph I., from 1705 to 1711, was entirely
occupied on the one hand with the struggle against France over
the Spanish Succession, and on the other with the conflict with the
Transylvanian, Rakoczy. He has been praised for his tolerance
toward the Reformed faith. He even forbade Catholic priests
from attacking the Protestants in their sermons. Toward the
Jesuits he showed himself much less favorably disposed than his
predecessors, and if the doubtful testimony of Joseph II. can be

accepted, entertained the idea of expelling them from the empire.
Nor was he afraid to oppose the Pope in the matter of benefices.
Clement XI. issued a bull against him, in which he reproached the
emperor " for having forgotten the hereditary piety of the house of
Austria."

At the death of Joseph I. his brother, Charles, was in Spain,
where he had been engaged for several years in an unsuccessful
conflict with Philip of Anjou over the possession of that kingdom.
Charles now left Spain and returned to Austria. The final settlement of the War of the Spanish Succession, in the treaties of
Utrecht and Rastadt, in 1713 and 1714, is well known. The house

of Austria renounced its claim to Spain, but obtained by way of compensation the Low Countries, Naples, Milan, and the *presidios* of Tuscany and Sardinia. The history of these ephemeral possessions, which contributed less to strengthen than to weaken Austria, is designedly not treated in this volume. It would have been a much wiser policy, for Austria had she sacrificed them and pushed on without relaxation the extension of her dominions at the expense of the Turks.

Charles VI. (1711-1740) succeeded to the empire and to the kingdoms of Bohemia and Hungary without dispute. His brother, Joseph I., had left two daughters, but the will of Leopold I. excluded women from the throne, and provided that in default of male heirs the younger brother should succeed the elder. It declared further that in default of male heirs by Charles VI., the daughters of Joseph I., that is, daughters of the older son, should take precedence over daughters of the house of the younger. Charles VI. had only one daughter, Maria Theresa. Immediately after his accession he began a series of negotiations with the object of reversing the order of succession established by Leopold I., and of securing to his daughter the succession of the Austrian dominions in their entirety. These negotiations extended over the greater part of his reign, and resulted in the celebrated act known as the Pragmatic Sanction. Its principal features are found in the following three articles forming a summary of a solemn declaration read by the emperor to the Secret Council at Vienna on April 13, 1713:

1. All the Austrian dominions form an indivisible whole.

2. Male heirs in the house of Austria succeed each other according to the law of primogeniture.

3. In default of male heirs, daughters are to succeed according to the following order: first, those of Charles VI.; second, those of Joseph I.; and then those of Leopold I.

The council had only to record the will of the sovereign without discussing it. But Charles wanted further guarantees and he next obtained the renunciation of their rights by the princesses interested; then he set himself to secure the ratification of the agreement by the different states over which he ruled, beginning with the more docile. These, one by one, gave their adhesion, Hungary alone offering any serious obstacles. For at his coronation Charles VI. had subscribed to a number of agreements, one of which was that in default of male heirs the Hungarians would

have the right to choose their own king. But the Hungarian diet
finally gave its consent in 1722, and Charles VI. then proclaimed
the Pragmatic Sanction in the Low Countries and Milan. It still
remained to secure the acceptance of the plan by the European
powers, and in this he was likewise successful. Prussia and Russia
recognized the Pragmatic Sanction in 1726; England and Holland
in 1731; Germany in 1732; Poland in the year following; while
France, Spain, and Sardinia gave their adhesion in 1735, after
the Treaty of Vienna. But as Prince Eugene wisely said, a
well-filled treasury and a good army is better than all these guarantees on paper, for the latter in nowise prevented the powers from
attacking Maria Theresa as soon as she mounted the throne.
The chief significance of the Pragmatic Sanction, however, lies
in the more or less voluntary consent given to it by the different
parts of the Austrian state, some out of a sentiment of loyalty
to the reigning house, others because they were tired of continually struggling and felt themselves incapable of sustaining
an existence outside of Austria. Thus this pact, which is looked
upon as a mere bit of historic parchment abroad, remains to-day
the basis of the public law in Austria. In his anxiety to establish
the principles of the Pragmatic Sanction Charles VI. often sacrificed more vital interests. The War of the Polish Succession
ended in the Treaty of Vienna in 1735, by which Austria lost
Lombardy and ceded the Two Sicilies to Don Carlos in exchange for
Parma and Piacenza. More serious losses were sustained in the
war against the Turks. By the Treaty of Belgrade, in 1739, Charles
was obliged to restore to the Porte nearly all that Hungary had
gained by the Treaty of Passarovitz. He did not long survive, and
died in 1740 at the age of fifty-six.

Charles VI. is celebrated for his love of the fine arts, particularly music. He induced the foremost Italian musicians, Scar-
lati and Caldara, to come to Vienna. He embellished the city,
founded academies for painting and sculpture, and enlarged the
collection of medals. An enthusiastic admirer of Italian, he appointed Muratori as his historian and Metastasio as his poet
laureate. He adopted effective plans to develop commerce; he
built many roads, some of which bear his name to-day; he founded
an Eastern Trading Company at Vienna in 1719, a Company
of the Levant at Triest, and an East India Company at Ostend,
which latter, however, he soon sacrificed to the jealousy of the

maritime powers of the north in order to secure their adhesion to the Pragmatic Sanction. Triest and Fiume were made free ports, and a small fleet was created on the Danube to protect river navigation. Mention should also be made of Charles VI.'s efforts to improve the administration of justice. His clemency secured for him the name of Titus among the courtiers, but it did not extend to matters of religion, for during his reign many Protestants were forced to emigrate to Germany and Transylvania.

Chapter XVI

BOHEMIA: HER FIRST HAPSBURG KINGS
1526-1619

THE death of Louis at the battle of Mohacs in 1526 had left the elective throne of Bohemia vacant. Ferdinand of Austria laid claim to it on the basis of the treaties concluded between Vladislav and the Emperor Maximilian; but the estates of the realm stubbornly refused to recognize their validity, and insisted that the throne could be ascended by none but a freely elected sovereign. Rivals of Ferdinand appeared in Sigismund of Poland and William and Louis of Bavaria, but by adroit methods of bestowing gifts and promises upon the influential persons in Bohemia, Ferdinand was finally chosen, being unanimously elected by the twenty-four electors to whom the estates had intrusted the decision. He immediately confirmed the privileges of the estates, and the *Compactata* of Sigismund, and signed a *revers,* in which he acknowledged that he owed his election to the free choice of the estates; at the same time he agreed to make his residence at Prague. The diet held immediately after the accession of the new king decided upon some of his prerogatives. It authorized him to crown his successor during his lifetime, provided he was the legal heir to his kingdom; it recognized the exclusive right of the king to convoke the diet or the assemblies of the circles, and it voted subsidies to aid him in his war against John Szapolyai and his allies, the Turks. By his tolerance and firmness Ferdinand at first won the good-will of his new subjects; he endeavored to put an end to the quarrels between the religious factions, and reduced the nobles, who had maintained a veritable tyranny on their estates, to obedience. He solemnly pledged himself to protect the Utraquists and to afford them equal rights with the Catholics. But this tolerance did not apply to the Bohemian Brothers, who were always proscribed, nor to the adherents of the new Lutheran doctrines, whom the Utraquists tried in every way to win for their cause. He restricted the privileges of the royal

194

cities by forbidding meetings of the municipal assemblies except by the permission of the king. He restored regularity into the administration of justice, and put an end to the private wars which had for years been wasting the country.

A sincere Catholic, Ferdinand was naturally strongly opposed to the Lutheran innovations, but circumstances would not allow him to proceed against them in Bohemia with the rigor he might have wished. He forbade them the use of the churches, but he could not prevent the spread of their worship and doctrines on the estates of the lords and the knights. In order to combat the new heresy more effectively, he endeavored to bring about a union between the Utraquists and the Catholics, in which he was naturally unsuccessful. The Lutherans on their part tried to profit by the difficulties Ferdinand encountered in Hungary, by working for a more definite organization among themselves, but the king made no concessions. On the contrary, expeditions against the Turks or the Hungarians afforded him a pretext to procure numerous additional grants of money over and above the annual subsidies.

Charles V. called on his brother Ferdinand for assistance in his struggle against the Protestant league of Smalkalde. But the king of Bohemia could not raise troops without the consent of the estates, and the Utraquist members did not judge it expedient to furnish soldiers to fight against their coreligionists. The king was obdurate and ordered the members of the estates to assemble with their troops at Leitmeritz in January, 1547. Many refused to cross the frontier except in defense of the country, and only a docile minority accompanied Ferdinand against Saxony.

The moment the king had left the kingdom the dissatisfaction broke out. Notwithstanding the royal prohibition, the consuls of the city of Prague were obliged to call the citizens together. A league for the defense of the liberties of the country was formed, and the Utraquist barons and knights espoused its cause, some of the Bohemian Brothers becoming its chief orators. Under their direction were drawn up the articles to be presented to the king, in which he was called upon to divest himself of all the prerogatives he had acquired from the crown to the detriment of the kingdom during the twenty years of his reign. According to these articles the Utraquists were to have the right to organize their church as they wished and to form alliances for the defense of their interests. The diet of the kingdom and the assemblies of the circles had the right to meet, if they saw fit. The king was to surrender the concessions made him in 1545 with regard to the succession, and agree to appoint only such officials as the diet would approve. Messengers were dispatched to Ferdinand to ask for the convocation of a diet to deliberate upon these measures, while the estates of Moravia, Silesia, and Lusatia were invited to adopt similar programmes. Overtures were received from the elector of Saxony and a victory of his forces over the imperialists encouraged the estates in their demands. They placed an army in the field to coöperate with him if he continued successful, but his defeat at Mühlberg in 1547 destroyed their hopes. Ferdinand reëntered at the head of an imperial army and the estates had not the courage to resist him. By a promise of amnesty to all barons and knights who gave in their submission he still further wrought their dissolution. They hastened to Leitmeritz to pay their homage to their sovereign, and then marched with him upon Prague. The terrified capital surrendered at discretion, and other towns followed the example. The king took special vengeance on the towns, confiscating their property and curtailing their independence by the appointment of royal judges and captains. The estates of only a few of the nobles were confiscated. Two knights and two burghers were executed, and the king announced that the cities had forfeited the right of representation in the diet, but that notwithstanding he would in his clemency only restrict or suppress their privileges. Thenceforward no communal meeting could be held except in the presence of a royal judge. Thus this attempt at revolution, badly planned and badly carried out, resulted solely to the profit of the dynasty. It increased the royal domain, which had been much reduced during the last reigns, and it weakened the power of the diets, in which the bourgeoisie could appear only by the royal favor, and, so to speak, under the supervision of royal officers.

These energetic measures made it possible for Ferdinand to go to Augsburg, at which place Charles V. had just convoked the German diet. He left his second son, the Archduke Ferdinand, as regent. At Augsburg the German princes demanded that the crown of Bohemia be subjected to the same charges as the rest of the empire, but Ferdinand maintained the rights of his kingdom and its independence against Germany. A short time afterward he established a royal court of appeal for all the possessions of the Bohemian crown; repressed the jurisdiction of the municipal courts at Prague and Leitmeritz; prohibited the further use of the code of Magdeburg, and brought about the unification of the law throughout the whole kingdom. In the same year he renewed the persecution of the Picards and the Bohemian Brothers. He broke up their community and forced the Brothers to join either the Catholics or the Utraquists. Those who refused were forced into exile, and more than eight hundred emigrated to Prussia and Poland.

At the diet of 1549 Ferdinand proposed fresh measures against the Lutherans, but he met with a strong resistance from the estates of Bohemia and Moravia, and the energy displayed by the German Protestants obliged him to renounce his plans. The Peace of Augsburg in 1555, which secured the triumph of the Reformation in Germany, gave fresh courage to the Evangelicals of Bohemia. To resist them Ferdinand threw himself passionately on the side of the Catholics; he called the Jesuit society to Prague, founded an archbishopric for the Catholics, and negotiated with the Council of Trent for the admission of the Utraquists into the Catholic church. In 1564 he obtained from Pope Pius IV., and from the Council of Trent, the sanction for the use of the cup throughout the kingdom of Bohemia, and thereafter the Jesuits, and the archbishop himself, might be seen administering the sacrament in both kinds.

Maximilian II., Ferdinand's successor, was, as we have seen, favorable to the Reformation, and ascended the throne in 1564 with ideas of toleration which he applied as much as the spirit of the century would permit. On the request of the Utraquists he permitted them to govern themselves, not according to the *Compactata*, but according to "the word of God." The Evangelicals, however, were not able to obtain his recognition of the Confession of Augsburg, and consequently united with the Bohemian Brothers, who still existed in secret, to elaborate a kind of national confession of faith. But this also failed to obtain the recognition of the sovereign, and the Lutheran church remained without clergy and without organization. This led to a condition of disorder and moral anarchy which wasted the energy of the best minds, and the wearisome quarrels which resulted fill most of the reign of Maximilian.

Externally Bohemia was at peace during the reign of this

prince and his predecessor. Some levies were furnished against the Turks and Hungarians, but no foreign enemy was seen on the native soil. This long period of peace, constantly troubled by theological discussions and religious quarrels, seems to have enervated the Czech nation, for it lost many of those warlike qualities which had been its glory in the previous century. The national literature became verbose and pedantic, and more remarkable for the quantity than the quality of its productions. A large number of foreigners, especially Germans, again settled in the capital, and the policy of the sovereign was always prompted by the interests either of his own country or of Germany, never by those of the kingdom itself.

Rudolf II. (1576-1612) had more taste for the arts and sciences than for theology, and, like Charles IV., he made Prague one of the most learned cities of Europe. Czech literature attained a remarkable development. The Bohemian Brothers published a translation of the Bible, which was for Bohemia what Luther's was for Germany. Nevertheless foreigners increased in number in the kingdom. Educated in Spain, Rudolf gathered about him Spaniards and Germans and never learned the Czech language. But although very favorable to Catholicism, he was so much of a dreamer and so indolent that he remained for a long time either ignorant of the religious quarrels of his subjects or else indifferent to them. The Jesuits made great progress in the schools, and acquired considerable influence with the Catholic nobility, till finally they succeeded in obtaining an overpowering influence over the enfeebled mind of Rudolf himself. In 1602 he renewed the persecutions against the Bohemian Brothers, whom the Utraquists tried in vain to defend. The Jesuits and Catholic fanatics became masters of the kingdom. All state officials were obliged on pain of dismissal and exile to sign a confession of the Catholic faith, and it is even told of a certain lord that he hunted his peasants to church with his dogs and forced them to receive the sacraments. The archbishop of Prague assembled a provincial synod for the avowed purpose of bringing back all of Bohemia to the Catholic union. Religious dissensions broke out worse than ever when the feeble Rudolf had to defend his power against his brother Mathias, who was impatient to rule over the whole of the Austrian states, and who had found allies in the Bohemian Brothers in Moravia. The leader of the latter was Charles of Zerotin, an important personage in Moravian history, who had previously served with Henry IV. of France. He convoked the estates of the kingdom at Caslav and entered Bohemia, but the Bohemian estates remained true to their lawful king and flocked round him at Prague. The incident, however, gave the Utraquists the opportunity successfully to demand the redress of their religious grievances and the adoption of sweeping reforms. Rudolf promised all they asked and purchased peace from Mathias by the Treaty of Libno, 1608, by which he ceded Moravia to him. /At the diet held in 1609 the Evangelicals and the Bohemian Brothers renewed their demands, calling upon the emperor to recognize the Bohemian confession; to admit them into the consistory of the Utraquists and to intrust to them the management of the University of Prague. The emperor refused these demands, whereupon they constituted themselves into an independent diet in the town-hall of the new town of Prague and formed an armed league for the protection of their religion. At the head of their forces they placed Count Mathias of Thurn, a German who had shortly before settled in Bohemia, appointing with him a committee of seventy-five directors who were charged with the defense of their interests. The league was joined by the estates of Silesia.

The emperor-king, alarmed, begged the elector of Saxony for his mediation, and ' offered to allow the formation of a special consistory for the Bohemian Brothers. They refused his offer and drew up their demands in the form of a letter of majesty, or fundamental law, which Rudolf signed in July, 1609. This celebrated document secured the recognition of the Bohemian confession, the admission of the Evangelicals and the Bohemian Brothers to the Utraquist consistory, and their right to govern the university. They were empowered, moreover, to choose a certain number of defenders of the faith from among the lords, knights, and citizens to watch over the maintenance of their privileges. About the same time a treaty was concluded between the Catholics and the Utraquists, which declared that henceforth religious parties were mutually to give due respect to each other's confessions. Thus there was brought about a definite recognition of the rights of liberty of conscience, so far as it was understood in that epoch—a kind of Edict of Nantes, which secured the religious peace of Bohemia for the future. Rudolf, however, had been an unwilling party to the agreements, and neglected no opportunity to revenge himself. At his instigation the Archduke Leopold, the younger brother of Ferdinand of Styria, threw an army of 12,000 into Bohemia, capturing Tabor and several other towns of the Evangelicals. But the diet soon assembled an army and dispersed the invaders, after which they besieged Rudolf, whom they suspected of complicity in the affair, in his royal castle and forced him to abdicate. Mathias was then elected in his stead, Rudolf dying the following year.

The Protestants and the Utraquists did not know how to make use of the liberties which they had forced from Rudolf. By an agreement between the Evangelicals and the Brothers the consistory was renewed and the dignitaries chosen from among members of both confessions. But no serious measure was decreed to increase the number of the clergy or to improve church discipline, while the differences between the teachings of Luther and Calvin divided the Reformers into the two rival camps. They took possession of the University of Prague, but in this case, too, it was shown how much easier it is to destroy institutions than to build them up. They shrank from the necessary sacrifices, and the school of John Huss no longer enjoyed the renown of former times. The efforts of the estates aimed less at religious improvement of the nation than at the increase of political liberties. At his coronation they presented the following conditions to Mathias: they claimed the right to hold diets without the consent of the king; to summon the army when they deemed it advisable; to maintain the union entered into with the estates of Silesia in 1600 for the defense of the common faith; to conclude similar treaties with neighboring countries, and, finally, to renew the treaties concluded formerly by Podiebrad with the Protestant electors of Saxony, the Palatinate, and Brandenburg, so that the estates might invoke the assistance of these princes in their conflicts with the king. Of these demands Mathias ratified only the third and postponed the discussion of the others, hoping that he might win over the leaders of the opposition by favors and dignities. But in this he was unsuccessful, and the Reformers sought for allies among the Hungarians and the Protestant princes who were interested in the humiliation of the house of Austria. The emperor-king tried to avert the crisis which threatened him by bringing forward the proposal of a war against the Turks, and invited delegates from the different diets of the Austrian dominions to assemble at Linz in 1614. But they refused the men and subsidies for which he asked. Under the same pretext he convoked the general diet of the Bohemian provinces at Prague, which contented itself by adopting rigorous measures to maintain the Czech language as the official language of the kingdom, and in order to avert the threatened danger from German immigration, decided that in the future no foreigner should be admitted into Bohemia unless he spoke Czech.

Mathias, having no heir, proposed to the estates that they recognize his cousin, Ferdinand of Styria, as his successor to the throne of Bohemia. After some opposition, due to the fact that it was well known that Ferdinand was the enemy of the new religion and a determined defender of Catholicism, they agreed.

An incident of minor importance which occurred about this time again aroused the slumbering religious passions. The Utraquists, on the strength of the letter of majesty, had built several churches on the domains of the abbey of Brevno and of the archbishopric of Prague. The letter of majesty had, however, only proclaimed tolerance within the royal cities, and the abbot and the archbishop ordered the closing of these churches and appealed to the king, who supported them. The Defenders of the Faith, on learning this, convoked the Protestant estates, who declared that the government had violated the letter of majesty, and dispatched messengers to Vienna to demand the restoration of the churches. Mathias refused and ordered the assembly to be dissolved. This reply raised the anger of the estates to a high pitch, and after some hesitation they decided to declare their independence and to break with the sovereign in a most startling manner. On leaving the country Mathias had appointed ten lieutenants to govern it in his absence. It was now resolved to hurl these from the windows of the castle of Hradcany at Prague. May 23 was the day fixed for the revolt. The leaders of the conspiracy were the counts of Thurn, Schlick, and William of Lobkovitz. Fully armed, they entered the castle and found four of the royal lieutenants, the grand burggrave Adam of Sternberg, with his son-in-law, Jaroslav of Martinitz, burggrave of Karlstein, the chief justice William of Slavata, and the grand prior of the Knights of Malta, Diepold of Lobkovitz. With them was Fabricius, the secretary, an obscure person whom this day was to make famous. The room, which is still shown in the castle of Prague, was small and admitted only a limited number of the conspirators. They angrily questioned the lieutenants, asking them to state whether they had inspired the threatening letter which Mathias had written to the diet, and when the lieutenants refused to reply, they declared that they would not withdraw without having obtained an explanation, saying, " You are to know, Jesuit dogs, that you have not to deal with women now." All the conspirators agreed that Martinitz and Slavata had inspired the imperial letter, and in spite of their protestations they were declared enemies of the country and without the pale of the law. After this summary judgment Sternberg and Diepold of Lobkovitz were thrown out of the door, while the two other lieutenants were seized and hurled from the windows of the castle. The secretary, Fabricius, who was hiding among the attendants, shared the same fate. But by a peculiar chance the three men escaped death, although they fell from a height of more than forty yards. The rubbish in the ditch of the castle broke their fall; Slavata alone was slightly injured, and all escaped. The secretary, Fabricius, hastened to carry the news of the catastrophe to Vienna, where he was raised to the nobility as a reward of his fidelity and received the appropriate title of Hohenfall (Lord of the High Fall).

The defenestration of Prague was the signal for a terrible war. On the very day of this act of rebellion the estates organized a provisional government of thirty directors and assembled an army, the supreme command of which they intrusted to Count Thurn. They sent to ask German princes for their alliance, exiled the Jesuits, and banished the archbishop and abbot of Brevno. The emperor, surprised by this unexpected revolt, at first hesitated. His favorite, Cardinal Khlesl, counseled moderation, and the weakly Mathias dreaded the war which his future successor, the proud Ferdinand, urged upon him. He sent a commission to Prague in the hope of coming to an understanding with the rebels, but the mission failed. The royal lieutenants of Prague were kept under strict surveillance. Besides, it was by no means an easy task to bring together sufficient forces against Bohemia. The diet of Hungary, in which the recognition of Ferdinand was just being discussed, was far from tractable, while the estates of Upper Austria and of Moravia refused to furnish troops against the Czechs. The Bohemians on the other hand did not wait to be attacked. They marched against the Catholics, who remained faithful to the dynasty, and besieged the city of Budweis. Finally, in order to compel Mathias to act, his two brothers, Ferdinand and Maximilian,

HAPSBURG KINGS 203

seized Cardinal Khlesl and shut him up in the castle of Ambras. Deprived of his habitual counselor, Mathias left the conduct of affairs to Ferdinand. An army of 10,000 men commanded by Henry of Dampierre entered Bohemia, and Thurn was obliged to raise the siege of Budweis. Nevertheless he repulsed Dampierre in two engagements, and obliged him to retire into Austria. The imperial army was soon reinforced, however, by Spaniards brought up by General Buquoi. But the Czechs on their part also received assistance. All the Protestants of Germany were the enemies of Austria, and the Bohemian revolt was the signal of a European reaction against the excessive powers of this house, which held Europe and the Reformation in check. Charles Emmanuel of Savoy and the princes of the Evangelical union sent an auxiliary army, led by Ernest of Mansfeld, to aid the estates. He entered Bohemia and captured the city of Pilsen, which had refused, as in the time of the Hussites, to recognize the authority of the estates. He then defeated Buquoi and compelled him to shut himself up in Budweis.

At the beginning of the winter the elector of Saxony tried to mediate: a congress was assembled at Eger, but it ended in failure. The plenipotentiaries of the estates demanded that Mathias definitely accept the four articles concerning which negotiations had been carried on ever since his accession. On March 20, 1619, he died.

Chapter XVII

THE THIRTY YEARS' WAR AND THE OVER-
THROW OF BOHEMIA. 1618-1648

FERDINAND II. (1619-1637) at once took up the struggle
with the estates and displayed much more energy than his
predecessor. He began his reign by a letter addressed,
not to the estates, but to the old royal lieutenants, announcing to
them that he would respect the letter of majesty and those privileges to which he had sworn at his coronation, and promising
further to establish peace and order in the kingdom. At the same
time he caused an offer of truce to be made to the rebels, but the
estates refused it. In the spring of 1619 Thurn invaded Moravia,
but found the estates of this province very reluctant to support
the Bohemian revolt. At the head of the party of moderation
was the leader of the Bohemian Brothers, Charles of Zerotin, who
exercised an indisputable influence. He had been on more than
one occasion the subject of national intrigues and the victim of
base persecution, but, notwithstanding, he went to Prague the day
after the defenestration to counsel moderation and obedience. And
though his brother-in-law, Wallenstein, and one of his sons-in-
law were among the revolutionists, he continued loyal to his sovereign. The arrival of Thurn in Moravia, however, gave a head
to the malcontents of that province, and the estates joined the confederation concluded between Bohemia, Silesia, and Lusatia.
Thereupon Thurn marched upon Vienna, where the Protesants
had risen in their turn and demanded the free exercise of their
religion. But a defeat of Mansfeld by Buquoi recalled him to
Bohemia.

In the meantime, however, Bohemia could not remain without a sovereign. It was contrary to the ideas of the time that a
nation could be capable of governing itself, and the patriotism of
the Bohemian nobility was not sufficiently enlightened to choose a
national sovereign. Three foreign candidates became rivals for
the throne, the young Elector-palatine Frederick, who was the

chief of the Protestant German Union, John George, elector of Saxony, and Charles Emmanuel, duke of Savoy. On September 26, 1619, Frederick was elected by a general diet of all the countries of the Bohemian crown. This so enraged the elector of Saxony that he became reconciled to Ferdinand, who had just been elected emperor. Frederick arrived in Prague and was crowned by the Utraquist administrator in the Church of St. Vit. He promised to agree to the four points formerly proposed to Mathias, and by which the sovereign was completely subjected to the estates. All the Catholics had opposed the election, but the invasion of

THE AUSTRIAN STATE
AT THE BEGINNING OF THE
17TH-CENTURY

Hungary by Bethlen materially aided the new king. Buquoi was compelled to leave Bohemia and to march against the Transylvanian troops, Thurn following him as far as the Danube. At Presburg a treaty was concluded between the Czechs, Hungarians, and Transylvanians against the house of Austria. The contracting parties even sent an embassy to Constantinople to come to an understanding with the Turk, but Bethlen soon made peace with Ferdinand and the emperor employed the winter of the year 1620 in collecting his forces. The king of Spain, the Pope, the elector of Bavaria, who was the head of the Catholic League, and the elector of Saxony all furnished soldiers. Even Sigismund of Poland promised to send assistance. The Protestant princes of Germany, on the other hand, were deterred from coming to the aid of Bohemia by the presence of the Spaniards in the Low Countries, so that Bohemia found herself without allies. Frederick was not the man to rise to the situation. A fanatical Calvinist, he favored the sect of the Bohemian Brothers to the prejudice of the Lutherans, whose anger he excited. He transformed the national cathedral of St. Vit into a cold, barren Protestant sanctuary, and by the preference which he constantly showed for his foreign advisers he estranged his best generals, Thurn and Mansfeld.

In the spring of 1620 the Bohemian army invaded Lower Austria, but it was unable to score a decisive victory, while Ferdinand and his allies began to act with an energy which soon dashed all its hopes. Maximilian of Bavaria and Tilly entered Upper Austria, the elector of Saxony, Lusatia, and the Cossacks of the king of Poland pushed forward as far as Lower Austria. Very soon Maximilian and Buquoi entered Bohemia by the south with a force of about 50,000 men, while the Bohemians had only 25,000. One city after another fell into the hands of the imperialists, and the Bohemian army after retreating first to one point, then to another, finally awaited a decisive engagement upon the plateau of the White Mountain to the west of Prague, where they entrenched themselves. Here the two armies of the enemy attacked it with terrible fury, and put it to flight, despite the heroism of the Hungarians and Moravians, who fought to the very last. Ten thousand dead were left on the field of battle, and the camp of the Czechs fell entirely into the hands of the enemy. When the battle began Frederick was quietly feasting in his palace, and on being notified that the engagement was on, started for the scene of action only to meet the ruins of his army precipitously rushing into the city, November 8, 1620.

But all hope was not yet lost. Prague might defend itself. Eight thousand Magyars sent by Bethlen had just reached the frontier. Moravia and Silesia were in arms; and Mansfeld still held several strongly fortified cities; only Lusatia, occupied by the Saxon troops, had succumbed. But Frederick looked upon the contest as hopeless, and retired to Breslau. The estates, forsaken by the sovereign whom they had chosen, opened the gates of the city and gave themselves up to the mercy of the conqueror. Ferdinand intrusted the administration of Bohemia to Charles of

Lichtenstein, while Buquoi pushed on to Moravia to complete the submission of that province. In the meantime the elector of Saxony reduced Silesia, and Frederick was obliged to leave Breslau. His able general Mansfeld, who had continued his resistance for some time in the west, was forced to quit Bohemia.

So long as Ferdinand was not absolutely sure of victory he observed a prudent reserve and gave no inkling of his intentions with regard to his revolted subjects. As soon, however, as he felt himself master of the situation his vengeance burst forth. He gave orders for the arrest of all the old offenders, the directors, and all those who in any way had taken part in the revolt. He threw into prison all those who, trusting in the royal clemency, had remained in the capital, and the most terrible reprisals began. All the Calvinist preachers and the Bohemian Brothers were banished; an extraordinary tribunal was established in Prague under the presidency of Lichtenstein, and after summary judgments the executions commenced.

On June 21, 1621, before the city hall of the old town, twenty-seven of the principal leaders were put to death. Among them was the rector of the University of Prague, Jensenius, who had been condemned to be quartered, but whose sentence was commuted to having his tongue cut out. Some were beheaded, others were hanged; all died heroically confessing their faith. The heads of the victims were exposed on the tower of the bridge of Prague. This day was for Bohemia what later on the bloody day of Eperies was for Hungary. On the following day the punishments decreed for those who had not been condemned to death and torture were pronounced; they were flogging, banishing and imprisonment. The property of the victims was confiscated to the king, his generals, and courtiers—Spaniards, Italians, Walloons, and Germans. Indeed, it is at this time that there were established in Bohemia a crowd of foreign families such as the Colloredos, the Piccolomini, the Wallis, the Gallas, the Lichtensteins, etc., whose descendants may still be found in Austria or Bohemia. One can readily understand how these intruders, enriched by the royal munificence at the expense of the Czechs, should be little disposed to champion the rights of the kingdom. Another portion of the confiscated property was devoted to pious foundations, especially in favor of the archbishopric of Prague and the Jesuits, for whom the emperor had a particular fondness. One of their number, Father Carafa, who was intrusted with the organization of the counter-reformation in Bohemia, has himself characterized the system which he adopted by the following naïve avowal: "We have long ago recognized that there is only one method of enlightening the Bohemians and leading them back into the good way, namely, by persecution." To these persecutions Ferdinand put an end in 1622 by a mandate under the name of a general pardon, a document which affords us a measure of his clemency. All those who had taken part in the revolt, the pardon says, deserve to be punished both as to their lives and their goods; but the emperor in his mercy pardons them as to their lives, contenting himself with the confiscation of their property if they consent to recognize their faults. Seven hundred and twenty-three lords and knights accepted this mockery of an amnesty which left them either partially or completely ruined.

But the great concern of Ferdinand II. was the reëstablishment of the Catholic religion throughout the entire kingdom. The University of Prague was taken away from the Utraquist professors and handed over to the Jesuits, who now took over the direction of instruction throughout practically all of the kingdom. The elector of Saxony made a vain attempt to intervene in favor of the Lutherans, his coreligionists. In 1624 an imperial mandate definitely proscribed all the Bohemian Brothers and organized the Catholic restoration. The churches were handed over to priests, many of whom had to be brought in from foreign lands, especially from Poland. Those who would not profess the Catholic religion could enjoy no civil rights or exercise any occupation: and the rights of marriage and of burial were withheld from them. Neglect of fast days, holidays, and the mass was punished by fines. The new lords installed by the imperial favor on the confiscated properties persecuted their peasantry in order to bring them into the true faith. But with it all these measures were insufficient. At Prague it became necessary to exile the greater portion of the influential citizens, and in other of the royal towns recourse was had to quartering of troops upon the inhabitants. The indomitable tenacity of the Czechs was increased rather than diminished by persecution. The Lysa inhabitants burned their town and emigrated in a body rather than yield. In other sections incipient revolts broke out, but were easily suppressed, and order was reëstablished by means of executions and tortures. The horrors and crimes committed during this epoch form one of the saddest episodes in the history of religion.

After the religious reaction came a reaction in politics. Immediately following his victory Ferdinand brought to Vienna the original drafts of the royal charters of Rudolf and the letter of majesty, and had them torn to pieces and thrown in the fire. He was determined that Bohemia, being now exhausted, should be reduced once for all to servitude. In 1627 he published a new constitution. It begins by declaring the throne of Bohemia hereditary in the house of Hapsburg in the male and female lines. To the representatives of the three estates of the Bohemian diet (lords, knights, and burghers) a fourth was added, namely, the clergy, which ranked them all. It comprised, besides the archbishop of Prague, the primate of the kingdom, all those ecclesiastics who held royal benefices. The diet was deprived of all legislative functions, which were henceforth reserved to the emperor. It retained only the right of giving its consent to the taxes, but without the power of imposing any condition whatsoever upon the sovereign. It could deliberate only upon questions submitted to it by the king. The supreme tribunal was deprived of all legislative power and was to comply with the decisions of the executive; trials were to be held in secret, and the German language was to be used equally with the Czech in the law courts and in all public acts. A few weeks after the publication of this decree a new order crowned the work of unification. It granted a period of six months to all those who had not yet been converted, to accept the state religion.

The emperor himself came to Prague to supervise the execution of his orders, to hold a diet according to the new constitution, and to have his son, Ferdinand III., crowned. A certain number of conversions took place, but many were insincere. The pretended Catholics continued to practice the religion dear to their consciences in the secrecy of their own firesides or in the shades of the forest. Great numbers of Czechs left their country and sought in Protestant lands the liberty of conscience denied them at home. It is estimated that no less than thirty-six thousand families emigrated, founding colonies at Dresden, Pirna, and Meissen in Saxony and at Leszno in Poland.

Moravia was treated with no less harshness than Bohemia. Dietrichtstein, who had been appointed commissary-general of this province, began by recalling the Jesuits, casting the leaders of the revolt into prison, and confiscating their estates. Non-Catholics were forbidden to hold landed property, and emigrations were proportionately as numerous as in Bohemia. Among the voluntary exiles ought to be mentioned the celebrated teacher, John Komenski (Comenius), who took refuge first in Poland, finally in Holland. His works have had a considerable influence on education and are still regarded as classics. His countryman, Charles of Zerotin, took refuge in Silesia. Czech literature was regarded as heretical and mercilessly persecuted, Czech books and manuscripts being sought out even in private houses, and burned by the zealous proselyters. Thus the Thirty Years' War, the signal for which had been given by Bohemia, was to secure liberty of conscience for the rest of Europe, but to Bohemia herself it brought nothing but ruin.

Exhausted as she was by the harsh measures of Ferdinand II., Bohemia was nevertheless called upon to furnish soldiers for the armies which Wallenstein was leading into Germany. This famous soldier of fortune was born in the north of the kingdom, of a family which belonged to the Bohemian Brothers. Left an orphan at an early age, he was educated by the Jesuits and became a Catholic while still a boy. His brother-in-law, Charles of Zerotin, had recommended him to the Emperor Mathias, and his first experience in warfare was received against the Turks and against Venice. During the rebellion against the emperor he remained faithful and took part in the Battle of the White Mountain. No one profited more than he by the ruin of Bohemia. By way of payment for certain debts which he had contracted in the service of the emperor, he received the principality of Friedland, which contained no less than nine towns and fifty-seven villages. To these he added a large number of confiscated estates bought in at a low price, and in this manner constituted, with the emperor's sanction, what virtually amounted to a petty sovereignty, with the right even of administering justice and of coining money. When in 1626 the king of Denmark came to the help of the Protestants in Germany, Wallenstein offered to raise and maintain an army at his own expense for the service of the emperor, an offer that was accepted. He collected 30,000 mercenaries and entered Germany, ravaging the whole country through which he passed, and securing from the emperor in return for his services first the duchy of Sagan in Silesia, next that of Mecklenburg, together with the title of Admiral of the Baltic. Wallenstein inspired the Germans of the seventeenth century with the same terror that they had felt for Zizka and Procopius in the fifteenth. Even the emperor's allies were terrified by his success and asked for his recall. He returned to Prague, where he built himself a magnificent palace. At Jiciu he entertained a court as brilliant as a king's, being waited upon by sixty pages and constantly attended by a bodyguard. Men of family even quitted the service of the emperor to enter his.

When the king of Sweden took up the cause of Protestantism, and it was found that Germany had no general able to resist this formidable adversary, the emperor was advised to send for Wallenstein. He agreed to take up arms only on condition that he was to have the supreme command, both military and political. The Saxons, the allies of Gustavus Adolphus, had already penetrated into Bohemia as far as Prague, and with them had returned a large number of Bohemian emigrants, who drove out the Jesuits and prepared to show the last honors to the Protestant martyrs whose heads still remained exposed on the tower of the bridge at Prague. But Wallenstein, who had assembled his army at Znaim in Moravia, also entered Bohemia, drove out the Saxons, and followed the Swedes through Bavaria and Saxony. A battle was fought at the tragic field of Lützen, where Gustavus Adolphus fell, November 16, 1362, but the Swedes stood their ground and Wallenstein withdrew to winter in Bohemia. But during all this time, while fighting the enemies of the emperor, Wallenstein was negotiating with them in the hopes of realizing his boundless ambition of securing territorial sovereignty in Germany and perhaps the crown of Bohemia. These negotiations excited the suspicions and the fears of the court, and he was assassinateed on February 25, 1634. It is difficult to determine how far he was guilty or who gave the order for his assassination. What is certain is that Ferdinand, while ordering three thousand masses to be said for the repose of his soul, divided the greater part of his estates among the men who had taken part in the plot against him. Wallenstein, whose tragic end has inspired one of Schiller's great plays, has left behind him a name which inspires astonishment and contempt, and his countrymen curse his memory. The year of Wallenstein's death saw the Swedes again before the walls of Prague, but they were unable to enter the city, and were soon obliged to leave Bohemia.

The elector of Saxony, Frederick, concluded a peace with the emperor, and received from him the province of Lusatia, which he held as a fief from the crown of Bohemia, and which has remained ever since a part of Saxony. Indeed, the province was already largely Germanized in the sixteenth century, and to-day there are but few remains of the old Slav population to be found. Under Ferdinand III. (1637-1657) the Swedes again returned to Bohemia under their leader, Banner. The land was left to its fate by the emperor, and suffered terribly from those who twenty years before had been its allies and who now remained for a whole year as its conquerors. Region after region was ravaged and the enemy carried off everything they could lay their hands on. But in 1640 the imperial army returned and the Swedes were forced to retire. Ferdinand himself came to reside in Prague in order to organize the defense of the kingdom in person. But in 1645-1647 the Swedes under Torstenson again invaded the country and crushed the imperial forces, following the retreating Austrians into upper Austria. In 1648 the new Swedish general, Königsmarck, got into Prague itself by stratagem, but was forced to withdraw because of the desperate resistance of the inhabitants. He then besieged the city, but the siege was interrupted by the Peace of Westphalia, and Prague was saved.

No country had suffered more cruelly during the Thirty Years' War than Bohemia. Towns and villages were destroyed or depopulated, the people starving and wretched, the land untilled and trade ruined. A kingdom which—without including Lusatia, Moravia, and Silesia—counted three million inhabitants before the war was reduced to seven or eight hundred thousand. Deprived of its independence by the new constitution and exploited by a rapacious foreign aristocracy, Bohemia seemed to have received its death-blow. The sovereign resided at Vienna, and the government was carried on by high civil and judicial functionaries, who formed a sort of regency. The high chancellor lived at Vienna, and the chancery of the kingdom of St. Vacslav sank into a subordinate position. The principal dignitaries were the president of the court of appeal and the chancellor. The other functionaries had merely honorary titles, with offices filled only on the occasion of a coronation. Finances were in the hands of the royal chamber in Vienna, and the army was made a part of the imperial forces. The royal cities, it is true, retained their civic guard, but these were not a military body. The country was still divided into circles, each governed by two captains, one selected from the lords, the other from the knights. Towns had their burgomasters and their consuls, but they were under the strict surveillance of the captains and the royal judges, while the peasants were serfs and absolutely under the rule of their lords. Indeed, this was the only one of their ancient privileges which the nobles had been able to keep, though it must not be forgotten that these nobles were for the most part not the old Czech nobility, but foreign adventurers hostile to the Czechs and devoted to the sovereign whose creatures they were, so that servitude under them was far harsher than it had ever been under the native aristocracy. Religious unity had been established by means of persecution, as we have seen, but in spite of it some followers of the old sect remained long afterward, and down to the very end of the eighteenth century the proscribed rites were secretly celebrated in rural districts. " I remember," says the refuge Holyck, " when I was about seven years old, going with my parents to a vast and gloomy forest. We were sitting upon a cart under the snow-covered trees while several hundred of the faithful rapidly gathered and began to build themselves huts of branches. Not far off a bell, hung between two trees, was rung for divine service, and I still remember as in a dream hearing the preachers preach and seeing the communion administered to the crowd. . . . Watchful sentinels were placed at the corners of the woods, and then all sang joyfully the praises of the Lord. The communion took place after the sermon round the stump of a rudely fashioned tree. How sweet and sublime sounded those holy hymns in the depths of the forest! "

Two bishoprics, those of Leitmeritz and Hradic, were added to that of Prague in order to watch over the maintenance of the Catholic faith. But the most active agents of the Catholic restoration were, of course, the religious orders, especially the Jesuits. Bohemia became the special province of this celebrated order. Indefatigable missionaries and professors, they possessed themselves of all public education and conducted a bitter warfare against heretical books and traditions. Veneration and pilgrimages were encouraged, and new orders of monks settled in Bohemia, no less than 179 new convents being built. So great was the growth of the Jesuits that the court of Vienna became alarmed at their influence, and made them surrender to the government the control of the faculties of law and medicine.

Czech nationality suffered cruelly from all these trials. Many of the domains of the lords were abandoned by the old inhabitants, who were replaced by German colonists. These brought with them their language, which from that time on became the dominant tongue in the frontier lands to the north and west. Indeed, it is from this period that the real German invasion of Bohemia dates. Germans then occupied and have held down to our own times almost a third of the soil of the kingdom, and their language, favored by the government at Vienna, became more and more that of the upper classes. The national literature fell into neglect. Indeed, the greater part of the productions of Bohemian literature had already been destroyed, either by the Jesuits or the Swedes, while the new Catholic literature which took its place had neither the vigor nor the originality of the old. It was, however, tolerably prolific, and proves the vitality of the national language, which in spite of its harsh experiences is more flourishing to-day than ever. The religious works of this period fill in the gap between the brilliant period of the Hussite movement and the literary renaissance of the eighteenth century.

Between this renaissance and the period of decadence which began under the reign of Ferdinand II., the history of Bohemia presents few points of interest. She has not, like Hungary, tumultuous diets at Presburg or revolts in Transylvania. One or two events only need be mentioned. In 1680 an agrarian revolt broke out in the circle of Caslav. The peasants took up arms and sent delegates to Prague to complain of the tyranny of the lords. They declared that they were treated more harshly than if ruled by Turks or Tatars, and demanded alleviation of their misery. The delegates were thrown into prison and two regiments were sent against the revolted peasants. Upon this the revolt broke out worse than ever in the circles of Leitmeritz and of Pilsen, and it was only with great difficulty that the movement was suppressed. In the War of the Spanish Succession Joseph I., as king of Bohemia, concluded a treaty with the German princes by which he undertook to contribute for Bohemia to the common expenses of the empire, and in return the princes guaranteed the integrity of his kingdom. But the crown of Bohemia remained independent of the empire. This treaty is sometimes regarded as the prologue to the one which later included Bohemia in the Germanic Confederation. It was concluded without any reference to the opinion of the diet of the kingdom. Charles VI. paid more attention to the estates, for he wished to secure the crown for his daughter, and laid before them the famous Pragmatic Sanction for their approval, which they adopted on October 16, 1720. The same monarch appointed a permanent committee of the diet in Bohemia to administer those current affairs which properly fell within the jurisdiction of that assembly.

Chapter XVIII

HUNGARY DIVIDED. 1526-1564

IN Hungary, as in Bohemia, the defeat of Mohacs left the field free to Austrian ambition. A great number of patriots, Verboeczy at their head, thought that a national king should be chosen. Meeting in a diet near Tokay, they proclaimed John Szapolyai, under the name of John I. The Szapolyais had already played a great part in the history of Hungary. Stephen Szapolyai had taken Vienna in 1425, and had been lieutenant of Mathias Corvinus in Austria. His son John was voïévode of Transylvania, and in crushing the jacquerie of the *kurucz* had rendered to the Magyar aristocracy signal services. Under the reign of Louis he had, together with Verboeczy, and the Archbishop Bakracz, exercised a veritable regency. It has been asserted that he was even then aspiring to the throne, and that if he did not go to the aid of King Louis it was because he desired a disaster that would give free scope to his own ambitions. Be that as it may, he was crowned, in 1526, by the bishop of Nitra; but another diet had assembled at Presburg which proclaimed Ferdinand of Austria. Ferdinand had the advantage of having been crowned with the true crown of St. Stephen, for which the patriotic Magyars have always had a superstitious veneration. The troops of Ferdinand drove back those of Szapolyai and compelled him to take refuge in Poland; a united diet met at Buda and declared Szapolyai and Verboeczy enemies to the fatherland. Szapolyai then turned to the side from which it would seem that Hungary might least dream of hoping for aid: he sent his agent to the Sultan Suleiman.

Suleiman promised his coöperation in exchange for the homage of Hungary; he deigned, according to his own words, " to cede to Szapolyai a kingdom which belonged to the conqueror of Mohacs by the rights of war and of the saber." On the other hand, King Francis I. agreed to a treaty that gave to the young duke of Orleans the succession of Szapolyai, in case the latter left no male child. He accorded to the king of Hungary an annual

216

subsidy of twenty thousand crowns. At the same time Friar Martinuzzi, of the Croatian family of Utiesenovic, prior of the famous Polish sanctuary of Czenstochowa, traveled through Hungary striving to make enemies for Austria and adherents for Szapolyai.

In the spring of the year 1529 Suleiman entered Hungary, this time not as a conqueror, but as a suzerain. Not far from Mohacs Szapolyai appeared before him and kissed the hand that had inflicted such terrible disasters on his country. He allowed the holy crown, that palladium of Hungarian independence, to be carried away by the Ottomans, and accepted the Turkish garrisons which established themselves at Buda and at Gran. But the troops which Suleiman led to the aid of Hungary made almost as many ravages in this vassal country as in that of an enemy. " The Magyars," says one of their historians, " scarcely knew which they should hate the more, the Austrians who came to attack them or the Osmanlis who came to defend them." Suleiman failed at the siege of Vienna, and in 1531 a truce was concluded between the two kings of Hungary. After long conflicts an agreement was reached between the two pretenders. By the Treaty of Varad (1538) Ferdinand and the Emperor Charles V. recognized Szapolyai as king of Hungary. In return he guaranteed to Ferdinand the succession, even in case he should have a son.

Two years later Szapolyai died, leaving a young son. Verboeczy and the queen-dowager, a daughter of Sigismund, refused to disinherit him, and appealed for aid to the sultan. The Ottoman sovereign welcomed this opportunity for intervening in the affairs of Hungary. He recognized the son of Szapolyai as king, and himself marched to his assistance. Ferdinand, reduced to conquering his kingdom, was besieging Buda and had invested it rigorously. The city was on the point of surrendering when Suleiman arrived; the Austrians, taken between two fires, were crushed; their general, Roggendorf, died of his wounds. But the grand seigneur was resolved to be paid dearly for his succor; he had the little king of Hungary brought to him, covered him with caresses, and recommended his sons to love him as their own brother. Meanwhile his troops occupied Buda. Once master of the place, Suleiman declared that he would continue to occupy it, since John Sigismund was not of an age to defend it. He assigned him Transylvania as a residence, of which he named him voïévode.

The queen-dowager protested in vain against this humiliation. It was necessary to set out for this exile, whither the Monk Martinuzzi accompanied them. The court of the young prince was established at the château of Lippa. "From this time," says Sayous, "there were three Hungarys: western Hungary, the kingdom of Ferdinand; central Hungary, occupied by the Turks and governed by the pasha of Buda; and eastern Hungary, which formed the independent principality of Transylvania."

The principal church of Buda was transformed into a mosque, and Verboeczy had the humiliating honor of being appointed the supreme judge of the Christians of Buda, subjects of the grand seigneur. He died a short time afterward.

The success of Suleiman was not only a defiance to the ambition of the Austrian claimant, but also to the peace and security of the whole Christian world. The German princes offered their aid to Ferdinand; the noblemen of the greatest families put themselves at his service; Martinuzzi, always much occupied in holding the balance between the German and the Turk, the interests of Hungary, and his own personal ambition, renewed the Treaty of Varad, in 1541, joining to it one stipulation, however, that Ferdinand should expel the Ottomans. But the expedition of the Germans did not succeed; in vain the Hungarian diet asked for further assistance from them. Suleiman made himself master of Gran and of Stuhlweissenburg. To the misfortune of Hungary, the struggles of Protestants and Catholics then divided Germany. The greater part of the Hungarians, treated with relative mildness by their Mussulman conquerors, accustomed themselves to their domination. Martinuzzi, "that monk of wicked and unfortunate caprices," as Ferdinand wrote, negotiated anew with Suleiman.

In the midst of this agitated period Martinuzzi was the true master of the country. He continued between the three sovereigns, Ferdinand, Szapolyai, and Suleiman, that see-saw policy which betrayed his double education, Slav and Italian. He offered Transylvania to Ferdinand, and drew upon that unfortunate country a Turkish invasion; then he turned anew against the Austrians, and persuaded the dowager-queen to renounce the crown to Ferdinand. She gave up the royal insignia at the diet of Klausenburg. But the Austrian king had little confidence in this equivocal personage, who knew how to play so many parts at once. He sent the condottiere Castaldo, assisted by unscrupulous Italians, who could be depended upon for a hazardous stroke, into Transylvania to watch him. And notwithstanding the fact that he had recently been made a cardinal, he was soon assassinated, struck down by sixty-six blows delivered by these hired assassins. So ended this curious personage, who has been compared, not without reason, to Wallenstein. The court of Rome launched her thunderbolts against the assassins guilty of having laid violent hands on a prince of the church; but Ferdinand, who did not dissimulate the part he had taken to " despatch Friar Georges," succeeded in obtaining from Pope Julius III. absolution for the murder.

The death of Martinuzzi did not deliver Hungary from the scourge of war. Temesvar succumbed, in spite of an admirable defense. Eger defended itself with no less heroism. Summoned to surrender, the besieged, as their only response, planted on the rampart four pikes surmounted by a coffin draped in black. The Turks made an assault four times on the intrepid city, where the women rivaled the men in valor; more than 8,000 of the defenders perished under the walls, in 1552. Isabelle Szapolyai, in the midst of these miseries, in despair of reconquering the whole of Hungary for her son, after having sought and obtained the promise of aid from France to secure Transylvania for him, died in 1559.

The situation of Hungary proper was in all respects deplorable. Ferdinand left vacant those offices, like that of palatine, which had to be filled by natives, put the administration in the hands of Germans, and gave the military command to foreigners. He had to conclude, in 1562, a treaty with the Turks, which recognized the possession of their conquests and promised them an annual present. It was, in effect, only a disguised tribute. Ferdinand had at least the consolation of seeing his son Maximilian crowned, in 1563, at Presburg.

This prince (1564-1576) continued his father's policy. The peace concluded by Suleiman and Ferdinand had but a short duration. In 1566 Suleiman attacked the town of Szigeth, west of Mohacs, north of the Drave. It was commanded by the Croat Zrinyi or Zrinski, the old ban of Croatia. The waters of the river Almas surrounded like a lake this little city, of which the garrison numbered no more than 2,500 men. The suburbs burned, Zrinyi took refuge in the castle; there the Turks endeavored to force him to surrender, sometimes by terror, threatening to cut the throat of his son George, whom they held prisoner, sometimes by the most

seductive promises.   Suleiman, in an access of fury, died before the
impregnable city.   The Vizier Sokoli, however, concealed his death
from the besieged.   Meanwhile the castle fell to pieces under the
artillery; Zrinyi clothed himself in his most magnificent garments,
put gold in his pockets, " so that something might be found on his
corpse," and at the head of his remaining soldiers threw himself
into the midst of the Turks.   There he found the death which he
sought.   That of Suleiman was only revealed to the troops after
the reduction of the town.   Szigeth, of which both Slav and Hungarian poetry have chanted the tragic fate, remained in the hands
of the Turks till 1689.   Maximilian also allowed the town of
Gyula to be taken, and in 1568 signed two treaties with the new
Sultan Selim, which sanctioned once more the dismemberment
of Hungary.

The condition of those parts of Hungary that were under
Turkish domination became almost as miserable as that of the
Servian and Bulgarian provinces; the orders of the pashas often
began with this formula: " In the name of the all-powerful emperor, know that if you disobey, the punishment is ready and the
funeral pyre awaits you."   The towns occupied by the Turks were
covered with ruins; the Janissaries kidnaped the young Hungarians
in order to make them enter the army of the grand seigneur; the
imposts were heavy, sometimes crushing, and collected by chance.
From the administrative point of view the country was divided into
twenty-five *sandjaks,* redivided later into four *eyalets* (those of
Buda, Eger, Kanisza, and Temesvar).   The autonomy of the
comitats, however, was respected, and they had, in certain respects,
especially from the religious point of view, more liberty than those
in the Austrian parts of the kingdom.

Maximilian also recognized the sovereignty of John Sigismund Szapolyai in Transylvania.   The young prince renounced
the title of king and contented himself with that of Most Serene
Prince.   He died in 1571, and with him ended the dynasty of
Szapolyai.   The Transylvanian diet elected as his successor the
wise Stephen Batory, who was called to high destinies; Poland
had given kings to Hungary: Transylvania, in 1575, gave to Poland one of her most remarkable sovereigns.

The throne of Poland had become vacant by the departure of
the French king, Henry of Valois.   Maximilian II. and Batory
announced their candidature; Batory was elected.   The Poles con-

sider his reign one of the most glorious of their history. He took with him to his new kingdom some Hungarians, who improved the military service, especially the artillery. Maximilian did not long survive this blow. He took care before his death to have his son Rudolf crowned at Presburg. Maximilian, whose tolerant and liberal spirit was not popular in the kingdom which he showed himself so incapable of defending, was, nevertheless, when compared with his immediate successors, one of the best sovereigns of mutilated Hungary.

The condition of Austrian Hungary during this period was but little better than that of Ottoman Hungary; continual warfare prevailed. The national militia being naturally insufficient, the Austrian prince covered the country with foreign troops, who were often as oppressive as the Mussulmans. Each comitat recruited soldiers for the national defense, and we have seen how these native troops, the *honveds*, distinguished themselves at the defense of Eger and Szigeth.

Another important fact ot this period was the spread of the Reformation among the Magyars. In spite of the political antagonism between Hungary and Bohemia, the doctrines of Huss had filtered into the kingdom of St. Stephen and prepared men's minds for religious changes. The causes which predisposed the Catholics of Hungary to this change were the same as in the neighboring countries. Abuses had grown up within the church. Hungarian genius, less original and cultivated than that of Bohemia and Germany, had not in itself energy enough to bring about the Reformation; yet it was supple and docile enough to accept it. The German colonies of Transylvania formed, besides, a sort of transition between Germany and Hungary. As early as the reign of Louis II., one year before the battle of Mohacs, the diet, at the instance of the terrified clergy, decreed the punishment of heretics by fire. The dismemberment of Hungary favored the extension of the new doctrines; the diverse masters who divided the kingdom among themselves were not able to give the persecution that unity necessary for a successful struggle against heresy. In Transylvania Pastor Honter early multiplied books and schools; in Hungary the first Reformer was Devay, who had known Luther personally at Wittenberg. He translated the epistles of St. Paul into Magyar. Some of the nobles became adherents of the new doctrines, and after 1548 the diets ceased to pass laws of persecution. The Evangelical church freely organized itself on the basis of the Confession of Augsburg. But it was Calvinism that especially established itself in the center of Hungary, in the valley of the Theiss. *Calvinista hit, Magyar hit:* the Calvinistic faith is the true Magyar faith, says a proverb. Lutheranism was of German origin, and as such suspected by patriots. It was at Debreczen that the new sect established itself; it had as a leader Pastor Juhasz, who, following the fashion of the time, Grecianized his name into that of Melius. He translated the Scriptures, composed songs, and entered into relations with Theodore de Beza. In 1567 the Synod of Debreczen formulated in seventy-four articles the creed of the Magyar Calvinistic church. John Huss had renewed Czech prose, and Luther German prose; the Hungarian Reformers, Devay, Erdoesi (Johannes Sylvester Pannonicus), Gaspar Heltai, and Karoly, rendered the same service to their country. In spite of the Catholic and Ultramontane dynasty, Protestanism became for Hungary a new force.

The reign of Rudolf (1576-1612) did not tend to make the house of Austria any more popular. At the beginning of his reign the diet made known the grievances of the country. It demanded guarantees from the sovereign and wished that the relations with Turkey might be regulated by national ambassadors, and not by Germans or Italians, strangers to the interests of the kingdom. Rudolf was so wounded by this language that he left Hungary and never returned. For four years he did not convoke the diet, and did not have a palatine appointed. A friend of the arts and occult sciences, imbued with absolutist doctrines, he did not love the barbarous, independent spirit of Hungary; he consulted it only when in need of subsidies. A Venetian ambassador sums it up thus: "The Hungarians detest the house of Austria; they consider themselves not only as conquered, but as scorned by her, since they have imposed upon them the government of the Germans, their natural enemies."

Meanwhile the war continued with the Turks. In order to hold in check the Mussulman invaders, the emperor accorded to Servian colonists certain districts between the Unna and the Kulpa, charging them with the defense of the frontier. Those abandoned districts, called by contemporaries *desertum primum, desertum secundum,* were thus repeopled by a population at the same time agricultural and warlike, and we have here the beginning of the military frontier which has lasted to our own time. In 1577 the fortress of Karlstadt was constructed in order to defend Croatia against Mussulman invasions. In 1592, Hasan, pasha of Bosnia, was defeated under the walls of Sisek. In 1595 the town of Gran was captured by the combined troops of the empire and Hungary. This advantage was unfortunately neutralized for by the loss of Eger. Defended by natives, this town had been impregnable; confided this time to a garrison composed in great part of Walloon mercenaries, it capitulated. Other engagements mark the war, but the ardor of the Turks was diminishing, and in 1601, after their victory before Kanisza, they agreed to a peace by which they kept their possessions. During this war, in which the Austrians had introduced Walloons, Spaniards, and Italians into the country, and the Turks the Tatars, the Magyars suffered as much from their allies as from their enemies.

It is in Transylvania, that trilingual Hungary, with its Magyars, Germans, and Wallachians, that the conflict for control during the next few years takes place. Stephen Batory governed the principality ably from 1571 to 1575, but in introducing the Jesuits he prepared for grave religious conflicts. One of his successors, Sigismund Batory, feeble-spirited and dominated by the Jesuits, themselves entirely devoted to the emperor, consented in 1597 to cede Transylvania to Rudolf, in exchange for the principalities of Oppela and of Ratibor, in Silesia. But upon the advice of his uncle, Cardinal Andrew Batory, he revoked this decision. A conflict with Austria ensued, and at the same time Michael, voïévode of Wallachia, attacked the principality in the hope of being granted it by the Ottomans. Weary of war, Sigismund abdicated and retired to Prague, where he died in 1613. Transylvania was then invaded by the imperialists and governed by General Basta, whose occupation has left most execrable memories. The exactions of the Austrians made Mussulman domination almost desired; the Protestants, whom the Turks had left in peace, were systematically persecuted. Such violence could scarcely fail to excite a bloody reaction. The Transylvanians arose, in concert with the Magyars of Upper Hungary, exasperated by the brutalities of the imperial lieutenant, Belgiojoso. All these foreign adventurers treated the kingdom as a conquered country, and made the Austrian dynasty detested. The Transylvanians had at their

head a great lord, full of audacity and of military talent, Stephen
Bocskai; he was seconded by the young Gabriel Bethlen. The imperialists were defeated before Kaschau (or Kassa), which opened
its gates, and the diet proclaimed Bocskai voïévode of Transylvania. The new voïévode showed himself to be as skillful a diplo-
matist as he was a valiant general; he negotiated with the Turks
and assured himself of the support of the sultan, Achmet II., who
even offered to recognize him as king of all Hungary. Bocskai
was prudent enough to decline that dignity. By the Peace of
Vienna, in 1606, his rule was recognized not only over Transylvania, but also over a part of northern Hungary; should he die
without heirs these provinces were to return to the house of Austria. The Peace of Vienna stipulated, besides, liberty of conscience
for Protestants, the obligation for an archduke to reside in the
kingdom in the absence of the king, and the engagement to reserve
to natives alone military command and the public offices.

The kingdom of St. Stephen, with Transylvania, Croatia,
Slavonia, and Dalmatia, included at this time 5163 square miles.
The house of Austria held 1222, the Porte 1859, and Bocskai 2082.

The Treaty of Vienna was brought about by the efforts of the
Archduke Mathias, who strove to make up by force of energy for
the indolence of his brother, Rudolf. Once governor of Austrian
Hungary, he attempted to claim the discontent of the nation. He
did not succeed, however, in annexing Transylvania after the sudden death of Bocskai in 1606. The diet of that province, meeting
at Klausenburg, elected Sigismund Rakoczy, and then Gabriel
Batory, after Rakoczy had voluntarily renounced the princely
title, in 1608.

That same year Mathias, it will be remembered, compelled his
brother to cede Austria and Hungary to him. His reign did not
carry out all the hopes to which his efforts as archduke had given
rise. But he restored to the kingdom its national dignitary, the
palatine, and engaged himself never to leave that important office
vacant; he restored the holy crown, withdrew the foreign garrisons,
and recognized liberty of conscience. In his absence the palatine,
the royal council and a treasurer exercised sovereign authority.
These concessions appeased the sorrows of Hungary, without causing them to be completely forgotten. Henry IV. of France was
not ignorant of them, and, in the political plan which he meditated,
and which death prevented him from putting into execution, he

intended to enter Hungary. He wished, to use the words of Sully, " that the Hungarians might be put in possession of their ancient freedom, of the right that they had of themselves electing their prince or of changing the form of the state and manner of government as they might think proper."

After the coronation of Mathias the Protestant Thurzo was elected palatine; this choice was a strong guarantee for religious toleration; but the traditions and the usual counselors of the house of Austria rendered its maintenance difficult. Besides, among the Hungarians themselves the Reformation had decided adversaries. At their head was Cardinal Pazmany, a pupil of the Jesuits, a fiery prelate, ingenious and eloquent, who brought back to Catholicism the representatives of some of the greatest families of the kingdom. For an instant, after the tragic death of the voïévode Batory, the violence of which had provoked Austrian intervention, Mathias conceived the hope of reconquering Transylvania. But the Transylvanians held even more to their liberty of conscience than to their political independence; they elected the Protestant Gabriel Bethlen (1613-1629). This enlightened prince made tolerance flourish in religion, discipline in the army, and good order in the administration of the country. Not without reason has he been compared to Mathias Corvinus. Like that great king, he had a taste for the arts and possessed a fine education. He held the balance equal between Protestants and Catholics, as between Austrians and Ottomans. But when Ferdinand II. (1619-1637) had mounted the throne and the Thirty Years' War broke out, Bethlen understood that the interests of Protestantism were gravely menaced, and that Magyar nationality would perhaps be struck the same blow that menaced Bohemian nationality.

The emperor attempted at first to assure the neutrality of the voïévode by sending to him Nicholas Esterhazy, one of the most skillful diplomats and best patriots of Austrian Hungary. Esterhazy was one of those who, like Francis Deak later, accepted freely the Hapsburg dynasty and demanded only, in exchange for loyal submission, respect for the wishes of the nation. A sincere but liberal Catholic, he held, so to speak, a middle course between Cardinal Pazmany and the Protestant Bethlen. That great prince, after having hesitated some time, took the part of Bohemia. He circulated everywhere a manifesto entitled " The Complaints of Hungary," and convoked all the comitats in a general diet. This assembly met at Kassa, named him governor, and put George Rakoczy, as captain general, at the head of the comitats of the north. Bethlen sent to Count Thurn a body of 10,000 auxiliaries, assured the independence of the diet, which met at Presburg, and decided to carry aid to Bohemia, in 1620. The diet proclaimed Bethlen king of Hungary, at about the same time that Bohemia chose the elector-palatine; unfortunately the Protestant cause, which the new sovereign represented, found then no support either in France or Poland; even the Turks themselves seemed disinterested in the affairs of Hungary. The defeat of the Czechs at the White Mountain ruined the hopes of Transylvania. Bethlen treated with Ferdinand, and by the Peace of Nicolsburg renounced the crown of Hungary. But he kept Transylvania and the administration of the seven comitats of the north. He received, besides, the title of prince of the empire, and an annual subsidy of fifty thousand florins.

But this treaty was only provisional; Bethlen had the highest ambitions. He hoped to find allies, and negotiated with the governments of Holland, England, and Venice through their ambassadors at Constantinople. He established close relations with northern Germany and married the Princess Catherine of Brandenburg. He had under his orders an entire diplomatic staff. From 1623 till 1629 he negotiated with the French ambassador at Constantinople, De Césy, who encouraged him to march against Austria. Yet all these efforts, and even an attempted campaign against Wallenstein, had no positive result; Bethlen died in 1629, without in any way having modified the situation which had brought about the Peace of Nicolsburg.

Chapter XIX

HUNGARY FREED FROM THE TURKS AND RECONCILED TO AUSTRIA. 1629-1746

GEORGE RAKOCZY was chosen to succeed Bethlen in spite of the pretensions of the Princess-dowager Catherine of Brandenburg, sustained by the courts of France, Holland, Sweden, and Brandenburg. During the Swedish period of the Thirty Years' War Transylvania was tranquil. In Hungary the palatine, Esterhazy, strove to maintain public liberty against the encroachments of the sovereign, but he was not able to prevent Cardinal Pazmany from establishing the order of Jesuits. They founded a university and took in hand the education of the Catholic youth. Under Ferdinand III., who succeeded in 1637, the discontent of the Protestants of Hungary was increased by a series of incessant violations of the Treaty of Vienna. Rakoczy believed the occasion favorable for declaring war on Austria; in spite of the supplications of Esterhazy, who begged him not to weaken Hungary before the Turks, he treated with France and Sweden. They promised him as a reward for his coöperation a yearly subsidy of twelve hundred thousand crowns, and the religious liberty and political independence of Hungary and Transylvania. In 1644 he commenced hostilities. Making himself master of Kassa, he advanced to Eperies, where he issued a proclamation inviting the Hungarians to revolt. But checked by the imperial troops, he had to return to his own states. He did not wait for the conclusion of the negotiations which led to the Treaty of Westphalia, but treated for himself. The emperor, in the Peace of Linz, 1645, ceded to him the possession of the comitats of the north, which Gabriel Bethlen had already possessed, and two fortresses.

Transylvania prospered greatly under the reign of this prince, who introduced at his court and into his army the principles of the Reformed religion. He had for successor his son, George Rakoczy II. (1648-1660), whose ambition nearly compromised the destinies

of the principality. He hoped, with the aid of Sweden, to reach the
throne of Poland, like Batory, his predecessor. But the Porte
would not allow so powerful a state to be established on its frontiers.
Hence followed a series of wars and invasions, during which
Transylvania was cruelly ravaged, and George was killed in the
struggle. John Kemenyi, one of his principal lieutenants, and one
of the best writers of the time, succeeded him and attempted to
repulse the Turks, this time with the aid of the emperor. He perished in his turn, and the Transylvanians, as much afraid of the
imperial alliance as of the ravages of the Ottomans, accepted the
voïévode, Michael Apafy, whom the Porte imposed upon them.

The reign of Leopold I. (1657-1705) left the saddest memories in Hungary. At the coronation of this prince the diet had
exacted that the dignity of palatine should be reëstablished and foreign troops removed from the country; the Protestant party furthermore pleaded in favor of liberty of conscience, so often violated.
The invasion of the Turks in 1664, under the Grand Vizier
Kiuprili, united for a moment all the forces of Hungary and the
empire; the imperialists were commanded by the celebrated Montecuculli, the worthy adversary of Turenne, and the Hungarians by
Zrinyi, a descendant of the famous hero of Szigeth. Zrinyi accomplished prodigies of chivalrous valor, while Montecuculli represented the severe school of the great tacticians of the Thirty Years'
War. The battle of St. Gothard, called the battle of Körmend by
the Magyars, was fought on Hungarian soil, August 1, 1664, and
was for the Turks a formidable defeat that rejoiced all Christendom. Hungary, however, profited nothing by this triumph. The
peace which was soon concluded at Vasvar, without the participation of the diet, did not free a foot of Hungarian soil; a
truce of twenty years was concluded. Indeed the Turks received
several other fortresses, notably Great Varadin.

It seemed as though the treaty had been concluded in the interest of Turkey and Austria against Hungary. The Emperor
Leopold, led by the Jesuits, and inspired by the double fanaticism
of intolerance and monarchical absolutism, proposed to destroy at
the same time the Reformed religion and the liberties of the kingdom. "I will make Hungary a captive, then a beggar, and after
that a Catholic," has long been attributed to him, though history
finds no evidence to support the accusation. He attempted at
first to suppress the diet and replace it by an assembly of nobles and

of prelates meeting at Vienna; but that body resisted and thwarted his projects.

But the danger to Hungarian liberty continued, and she could hope to find succor only in the help of the foreigner. In 1665 Frankopan, a Croatian magnate, allied to the illustrious family of Zrinyi, addressed to the elector of Mainz a memorial in which he said: " The kingdom of Hungary has arrived at such a state of ruin and of misery that, if God does not inspire the Christian princes to defend it, all is at an end with this bulwark of Christendom and of all the nations. . . . The upper comitats of Hungary have reached such a degree of despair that they see no other safety except to put themselves under the protection of the Turks. . . . The Hungarians, by a national antipathy, have always had a horror of the domination of the Turks. . . . However, to-day extreme necessity reduces them to such thoughts." Apafy remained indifferent; Zrinyi and Frankopan attempted, however, to incite Hungary to insurrection; they collected some troops, and soon laid down their arms upon the promise of a complete amnesty. Arrested, as was also their accomplice Nadasdy, they were imprisoned, and, contrary to the laws, judged without the territory of the kingdom, Nadasdy at Vienna, Zrinyi and Frankopan at Wiener-Neustadt, and were condemned to death, the emperor, " by his pure grace imperial and royal" sparing them from having the right hand cut off.

The execution of the three counts was, moreover, the signal for atrocious persecutions directed in turn against the patriots and against the Protestants. Many were exiled, put to forced labor, or sold to the viceroy of Naples to row upon his galleys. But these severities did not stifle the Magyar spirit of independence, the name of the *kurucz* reappeared; and Louis XIV., who was at war with Austria, ended by giving aid to the malcontents. The French ambassador in Poland passed over to them both men and money. The insurrection had found a formidable chief in the person of Emerich Toekoeli, who had married the widow of George Rakoczy II., the valiant Helen Zrinyi. Toekoeli, whose flag bore the device, *" Pro aris et focis,"* succeeded in raising an army, which pushed its way vigorously into Moravia. He coined money bearing his own effigy, and exercised a real sovereignty. He wished to be king of Hungary and counted on finding allies in the Turks, who were then marching on Vienna. He went to meet Kara

Mustapha, and invested Presburg while the Ottomans were besieging the Austrian capital. The defeat of the Turks by Sobieski was also a defeat for him, who was called the king of the *kurucz,* and he was reduced to carrying on a guerrilla warfare. Meanwhile the imperial army, victorious over the Ottomans, penetrated into Hungary and seized some of the principal places, and finally Buda itself, which was recovered after so long an occupation. The Turks were pursued as far as Mohacs, where they expiated by the loss of 20,000 men their former victory on these plains. Kara Mustapha, attributing his reverses to Toekoeli, had his old ally arrested and imprisoned in Belgrade; his captivity put an end to the movement, and the partisans of the king of the *kurucz* dispersed, surrendering the places they occupied. The fortress of Munkacs alone held out, defended by the wife of Toekoeli, the intrepid Helen Zrinyi, whose heroism has often been sung in Hungarian poetry.

The insurrection at an end, and Hungary partially regained, it would seem that mercy should have been the first duty of the conqueror. But Leopold and his lieutenants were not of this opinion; an amnesty was proclaimed and violated immediately, the Italian general Caraffa becoming the unpitying executioner of imperial vengeance. Established at Eperies, he instituted in that city a tribunal whose horrors recall the most bloody exploits of Spain in the Low Countries. During thirty consecutive days thirty hangmen submitted the victims, innocent or guilty, to the most refined tortures and the most horrible deaths. The " Butchery of Eperies," as it is called, is the most tragic memory in Hungarian history. The Emperor Leopold pretended, it is true, to justify himself by saying that these horrors had taken place without his knowledge.

After having thus terrorized Hungary, he had the right to hope for every concession. Till this time, in spite of persecutions, the crown had remained elective; now he decided to make it hereditary. The diet of 1687, in conformity with the wish of the sovereign, proclaimed the crown hereditary in the male line of the house of Hapsburg. The proceedings in Hungary had been the same as in Bohemia; at first executions, and then changes more or less freely consented to by the people. The king had to take oath to the fundamental laws of the country; but article 31 of the Golden Bull, or the constitution of Andrew II., was abolished. It was the one which proclaimed the right of insurrection. The diet, in

ENTRY OF THE VICTORIOUS AUSTRIAN TROOPS INTO THE FORTRESS OF BUDA

Painting by Gyula Benczur

granting all these concessions, stipulated that executions should cease and the prisoners be set at liberty, so a general amnesty was proclaimed. Toekoeli had already retired to Nicomedia, in Asia, and Helen Zrinyi surrendered the fortress of Munkacs.

Now that all Hungary was regained the Austrians were in a position to free the country from the Turks. In 1688 they crossed the Danube and captured Belgrade and Nisch. But the Turks under their new leader, Mustapha Kiuprili, had awakened from their lassitude, pushed up the Danube and regained both places. Mustapha next invaded Hungary, but there he was defeated and slain by the Austrians under Louis of Baden in 1691. But the war continued, and with the aid of Toekoeli, who had returned, the Turks entered Transylvania, where they held their own till Prince Eugene of Savoy assumed command of the imperialists. This young prince, who became so formidable an antagonist of the Turks, was in upper Hungary in 1697, when he heard of the approach of the Turks by way of the valley of the Theiss. He immediately threw a bridge over the river at Zenta, and was preparing to attack the enemy, when he received orders from the emperor, by courier, forbidding him to fight. He found the position of his troops, however, such as to justify disobedience, and the brilliant victory of Zenta justified his audacity. More than 10,000 Turks perished, a great number being thrown into the Theiss; the sultan fled to Temesvar, and thence to Constantinople. Winter prevented Prince Eugene from following up his advantages, and the emperor, preoccupied with the succession to the throne of Spain, granted peace to the Ottomans in 1699. A treaty was concluded at Carlowitz, by which the sultan agreed not to help the Hungarian malcontents, and to abandon all claim to Transylvania. Of all her old possessions in Hungary, Turkey was allowed to keep only the small territory of Temesvar, the emperor getting the rest—Hungary, the larger part of Croatia, Slavonia, and the suzerainty over Transylvania. A special clause in this Treaty of Carlowitz stipulated for the maintenance at Buda of the tomb of a Mussulman monk, Gul Baba, " the Father of Roses "; this tomb exists in our day, and is still the object of pious pilgrimages among Mohammedans. Latterly the Hungarians have kept it in repair at their own expense in order to show their sympathy for Turkey.

In the month of April, 1690, Leopold laid claim to Bosnia and Bulgaria on behalf of Hungary, and called upon the Slavs in Tur-

key to take up arms.   A little later he invited the Servian patriarch
of Ypek to settle in his dominions, promising the Servians the free
exercise of their religion and a separate government.   In 1691 the
patriarch accepted this offer, and from thirty-five to forty thousand
families were settled on the banks of the Maros, in Sirmia, in
Slavonia, in the district of Backa, and even in the outskirts of Buda;
and these colonists, owing to their special privileges, formed a distinct nation.   The soldiers which they furnished the Austrians,
like those Servians who had settled in Hungary before, rendered
great services to the Hapsburgs in the wars against the Turks.   The
descendants of these Servian colonists are still to be found in the
south of Hungary, where their influence is considerable.

   After the departure of Toekoeli Transylvania had become an
Austrian province, and during the campaigns against the Turks
the Austrian generals had garrisoned most of its towns.   The
young Prince Michael Apafy had been taken to Vienna to be
educated, and the principality was governed by imperial lieutenants.   The Treaty of Carlowitz obtained recognition for this new
state of things from the whole of Europe, and the same year, by
a special charter, Leopold recognized the rights and privileges of
the principality and granted the free exercise of the Protestant and
Orthodox religions.   But the Transylvanian nobility did not accept
at once this annexation, which, while uniting the province to the
mother country, also subjected it to a brutal soldiery and an oppressive government.

   The malcontents found a leader in the person of Francis
Rakoczy (1706-1711), who brought to their cause an inheritance
of heroic traditions and hereditary hatreds.   His mother was the
daughter of that Count Zrinyi who had perished on the scaffold,
and the widow of George Rakoczy and of Toekoeli; his father,
George Rakoczy, had taken part in the conspiracy of the three
counts, but, more fortunate than they, had escaped the scaffold.
At the age of twelve Francis Rakoczy himself had been taken to
Vienna and educated in the Catholic faith.   It had been intended
that he should become a priest, but obtaining permission to return
to Hungary and to travel, he married, while still quite young, a
princess of Hesse-Rheinsfeld, whose heroic courage harmonized
well with his adventurous temperament.   To great bodily vigor
Rakoczy joined rare moral energy and an extraordinary ambition.
His first conspiracy did not succeed, and he was seized and thrown

THE ARREST OF FRANCIS RÁKÓCZI II, CHIEF OF HUNGARY AND VOIÉVODE OF TRANSYLVANIA

Painting by Gyula Benczur

into the prison of Neustadt, whence he found means to escape, and took refuge in Poland. There, although the emperor had confiscated his property and put a price on his head, he entered into relations with the French embassy, which allowed him a subsidy. In 1703 he returned to Hungary.

A peasant revolt had just broken out in the neighborhood of Munkacs, and the irritation was great throughout the kingdom, for the attempts of the court of Vienna to destroy Hungarian liberty had been increasing. Only recently the emperor had called before him the great nobles and prelates, to whom he proposed the suppression of a part of the Hungarian nobility, that *petite noblesse* which played so active a part in the public life through the comitats. On the other hand a great number of families were indignant at the clauses of the Treaty of Carlowitz forbidding the return to the kingdom of those Hungarians who had emigrated into Turkey during the recent revolts. The insurrection of 1703 was therefore more than a simple movement of the *kurucz;* some of the representatives of the greatest families and even Catholics joined the revolted peasants. By the beginning of 1704 the insurrection had spread over Transylvania, crossed the Vah, and even made some progress in the neighborhood of Vienna. At this moment began the War of the Spanish Succession; the Bavarians, allies of France, invaded Austria, while Prince Eugene was busy fighting the armies of Louis XIV. The king of France corresponded with Rakoczy, calling him " my cousin," and sent him French officers.

In spite of some military reverses, Rakoczy organized a government, and a diet named him chief of the Hungarian nation. A second diet proclaimed him voïévode of Transylvania, and the greater part of the kingdom of St. Stephen soon came under his command, though he would gladly have come to terms with the emperor on condition of being allowed to keep only Transylvania. But the exasperation of the Hungarians was so great that they had resolved to break once for all with the Hapsburgs. At the diet of Onod thirty-one confederated comitats—the kingdom then contained fifty-two—proclaimed Joseph I. no longer king of Hungary. They dared not go on and offer the crown to Rakoczy, but at the suggestion of Louis XIV. offered it to the elector of Bavaria, who refused it, and precious time was lost in negotiations. In the meantime Heister, the imperial general, defeated the insurgents at Trencsin, in 1708, and retook a part of Hungary. These successes were followed up by Stahrenberg and Sickingen. Louis XIV., exhausted by defeats, suspended his subsidies; Rakoczy, finding himself unable to continue the struggle, left the country and took refuge in Poland. The diet accepted the Treaty of Szathmar, which stipulated for a general amnesty and the reëstablishment of Hungarian liberties. Later Rakoczy went to Paris and visited the court of France, which had formerly treated him as a sovereign. This circumstance has done much to popularize his name, which one sees constantly in the contemporary documents and memoirs, especially those of St. Simon. As the Austrian government finally became disquieted over his sojourn in Paris, Rakoczy went to Turkey. There, in conformity with the Treaty of Passarowitz, the Porte assigned him as a residence the château of Rodosto, near the Sea of Marmora. Even in this retreat he did not entirely renounce his ambitions, and made several unsuccessful attempts to interest France and Turkey in his cause. To while away his time he wrote his "Memoirs on the Hungarian Revolutions," which were published at The Hague in 1732. The name of Rakoczy has remained attached to a celebrated march, the author of which is unknown. It is certain, however, that it was often played in his armies, and that it has become for the Magyars a national hymn, the Marseillaise of their revolutions. Whenever Hungarian liberty has been stifled its use has been rigorously forbidden by the Austrian Government. In our time it has been adapted to the orchestra by Berlioz.

Hungary, defeated, was definitely reconciled with Austria by the Peace of Szathmar, and it is Joseph I. who had the honor of accomplishing this great work. After having been proclaimed in 1707 unworthy of reigning over Hungary, he had permanently established his dynasty on the throne by his death in 1711. This prince, who died at the age of thirty-three, was of so gentle and tolerant a character that he would doubtless have won the lasting affections of his reconciled subjects had he lived longer. His successor, Charles VI., who was Charles III. of Hungary, bound the Magyar nation still more closely to the dynasty. After his coronation he recognized by a special law the right of the Hungarians to elect their own king in case the male line of the house of Austria should become extinct. The Pragmatic Sanction proves, however, how little he held himself bound by this concession to Magyar pride. The first years of his reign were devoted to establishing order in the country, but evil traditions were not abandoned; the amnesty was limited in its application, and religious intolerance continued, with less brutality in its forms, it is true, but with quite as much obstinacy. It attacked equally the Hungarian Protestants and the new Servian colonists of the Orthodox faith. But the court of Vienna was not alone to blame for these persecutions; the greater part of the Magyar Catholics joined in them.

The reign of Charles VI. saw the final expulsion of the Ottomans. In 1716 the grand vizier of Sultan Achmet III. crossed the Save and marched on the town of Peterwardein. There Prince Eugene awaited him and won the victory of Peterwardein, which resounded throughout Christendom. The Hungarians fought gloriously in this battle, which cost the grand vizier his life and restored to the conquerors the town of Temesvar and the last possessions of the Turks in Hungary. The next year, 1717, the redoubtable fortress of Belgrade was also taken, and with its fall all danger from the Turks in the middle Danube came to an end. The loss of the fortress was a fatal blow to their power, and the sultan consented to sign the Treaty of Passarowitz, abandoning entirely the right bank of the Danube, Belgrade, and a part of Servia and Wallachia. These conquests delivered into the hands of Austria the keys of the Ottoman empire. She might then, by following up her successes in this direction, have given liberty and civilization to the Servian and Rumanian populations, and gradually annexed them. But to accomplish this the Hapsburgs would have had to direct their undivided energies to the lower Danube. They chose instead to make acquisitions on the more distant Rhine in Germany, and even in Italy. Against the Turks a weak defensive policy was followed, which had most unfortunate results in the next war.

When in 1737 war with Turkey again broke out, the husband of the then archduchess, Maria Theresa, Prince Francis of Lorraine, was put in command of the imperial army. He was severely beaten in an attempt to invade Bosnia and Wallachia, and forced to retire into Transylvania. In May, 1738, the Turks captured Oesova, and Belgrade, the only place left the Austrians on the right bank of the Save, was in imminent danger of being captured. Under these circumstances Charles VI., though in alliance with Russia, agreed to the Peace of Belgrade, 1739, in which Belgrade and the whole of Servia was again restored to the Turks. Austria's unique opportunity in the Balkan peninsula was lost. In the negotiations for peace the presence of France as a factor in the international relations of Turkey was conspicuously felt. Thenceforward France, Russia, and later England were all too deeply interested at Constantinople ever again to allow Austria a free hand in the Balkan.

The internal history of the territory reclaimed for Austria under Charles VI.'s reign was far from happy. Hungary had lost her political vitality, and the diet was very compliant. It voted the Pragmatic Sanction on the promise of the king to convoke the diet at least once in three years, to reside in Hungary whenever circumstances permitted, to arrange the business of the country in person with the help of the Council of Regency presided over by the palatine, and to make Fiume a free port. The Servian colonists, who had entered Hungary, were reduced to the condition of serfs, and persecuted for their Orthodoxy. In 1734 the Servian and Hungarian peasants, victims of persecution and oppression, rose in rebellion. They were joined by some Hungarian Protestants who were likewise suffering, but the movement was suppressed by the army and cruelly punished.

PART IV

THE STRUGGLE FOR THE UNITY OF THE MONARCHY. 1740-1792

Chapter XX

MARIA THERESA. 1740-1780

THE Archduchess Maria Theresa, heiress of Charles VI., had married Francis Stephen, duke of Lorraine, whose family had been allied to that of Austria by marriage since the preceding century. At the close of the War of the Polish Succession, in 1735, he had been obliged to give up Lorraine to Stanislas Leszczynski, and had obtained in exchange the grand duchy of Tuscany, left vacant by the death of the last of the Medici. Tuscany was not annexed to the dominions of the reigning house of Austria, but became an inheritance for younger sons, and at the death of Francis passed, not to his oldest son, Joseph II., but to the younger, Leopold.

Maria Theresa was the first woman who had ruled over all the Austrian states, and she could not, like her predecessors, succeed to the imperial crown, which seemed by this time to have become hereditary in the house of Austria. As queen of Bohemia, however, she had a vote in the electoral college. She made her husband co-regent, but gave him only a slight share in the government; the active and imperious spirit of the young princess would not permit a partition of her authority, and at the beginning of her reign Francis Stephen was no more than the husband of the queen. Her accession seemed a favorable opportunity for the enemies of Austria; no one believed in the permanence of the Austrian state, as it had been created by Charles VI. with the help of the Pragmatic Sanction, and nothing seemed easier than to dismember it. The French Marshal de Belle-Isle even arranged a plan which gave the Low Countries to France, Bohemia and the imperial crown to Bavaria, Silesia to Prussia, and Tuscany, Parma, and the Lombard possessions to Spain and Sardinia. Only one thing embarrassed the marshal, and that was what to do with Moravia. Maria Theresa was to think herself lucky to keep Hungary and the Austrian provinces.

It seemed as if no state could be more easily broken up than this polyglot empire, which had no other tie than the person of the sovereign and the more or less faithful adhesion of the diets to the Pragmatic Sanction. Besides, a new power had arisen in north Germany, full of vigor and ambition, which now for the first time assumed its place as the rival of Austria among the German states. Prussia, erected into a monarchy early in the century, now had for its sovereign a prince as enterprising as he was unscrupulous, Frederick II., known to history as Frederick the Great. For his invasion of Silesia he claimed rights no better founded than were those upon which the dismemberment of Poland was afterward based. Austria protested in vain: Frederick had on his side the final argument of kings, and the occupation of Breslau and victory of Molvitz decided the cause in his favor in 1741. He had at his command an army in admirable condition, and the money that had been carefully hoarded by his predecessor, while the Austrian treasury was empty and the army in a wretched state.

The success of the Prussian king seemed a proof of the weakness of the edifice which had been so laboriously raised by Charles VI. The young queen found herself surrounded by enemies on every side—Bavaria, France, Spain, the elector palatine, and the elector of Cologne. Charles Albert, duke of Bavaria, married to a cousin of Maria Theresa, now laid claim to a part of the Austrian dominions as the descendant of Anna, daughter of Ferdinand I., who had married one of his predecessors, Albert V. The will of Ferdinand I. ran thus: " In case our sons should die without heirs male, our daughters shall have a right to a part of the inheritance." According to Charles Albert, as soon as females were allowed to succeed the oldest daughter of Ferdinand I. and her descendants ought to take precedence of all later heiresses. He also claimed Austria by virtue of certain rights of the house of Bavaria antedating the year 1156. Augustus III., elector of Saxony, who had married the oldest daughter of Joseph I., based his claim partly on that of his wife and partly on a distant relationship to the house of Babenberg. The other powers, without alleging any other right than that of the strongest, wished simply to dismember Austria in order to aggrandize themselves. At first Maria Theresa tried to negotiate; she offered Louis XV. the duchy of Luxemburg if he would persuade Spain to content herself with the Low Countries, and the elector of Bavaria with a part of Upper Austria; but these

MARIA THERESA

attempts at negotiation failed, and it was necessary to have recourse to arms.

An alliance was concluded between France, Spain, Bavaria, and later Saxony and Prussia. It has been recently shown that the Treaty of Nymphenburg under the form in which it has come down to us, is apocryphal. But it is an incontestable fact that France put her troops at the disposal of the elector of Bavaria. Charles Albert, with the help of the French army, took Linz and pushed into Bohemia, while Frederick occupied Silesia and the Spaniards attacked Italy. The support of the Hungarians and the subsidies of England were all that saved Maria Theresa in this crisis. After an interregnum of two years the elector of Bavaria was chosen emperor of Germany, and it seemed that the house of Hapsburg-Lorraine had lost the imperial crown. England paralyzed the efforts of Spain in Italy, and forced Frederick II. to sign the preliminaries of Breslau and the Peace of Berlin. Maria Theresa ceded to her fortunate rival upper and lower Silesia, the Bohemian county of Glatz, the lordship of Kostcher in Moravia—in all more than 650 square miles. She kept of Silesia only the principality of Teschen and some parts of those of Troppau Jägerndorf, and Neisse. This was a considerable loss; Silesia, conquered by Frederick II., not only brought Prussia to the frontiers of Bohemia, but deprived Austria of a million of her German population, thus still further increasing the proportion of the Slav and Magyar elements. Besides being German, the population was almost entirely Protestant, and therefore but little regretted the Austrian rule.

Saxony, which had hoped to annex Silesia and a part of Moravia, now left the league and concluded a treaty of alliance with Maria Theresa, in 1743. For a moment the fortune of war seemed to turn to the side of Austria. The French were obliged to evacuate Bohemia and the Austrian troops entered and occupied Bavaria, forcing the new emperor to retire. He had had himself crowned at Prague. In her turn the queen of Bohemia and Hungary now received the homage of Bavaria, and established a royal lieutenancy at Munich. France and Bavaria proposed peace, but it was refused. France therefore attacked Austria in the Low Countries, while Frederick II. took up arms again in July, 1744, entered Bohemia, and defeated the Austrians and Saxons in several engagements.

In the meantime Charles VII. returned to Bavaria, though

only to die. His son signed the Treaty of Füssen and recognized
the Pragmatic Sanction. Francis of Lorraine, husband of Maria
Theresa, was then chosen emperor, and the imperial dignity returned to the house of Austria. Finally the mediation of England
brought about the peace of Dresden between Prussia, Austria,
and Saxony, in which Prussia recognized the imperial dignity of
Francis I., and the states of Prussia and Austria mutually guaranteed one another's possessions. We shall not follow here the
events of this war in the Low Countries and in Italy. Notwithstanding the support of England, and even of Russia, which sent
some troops as far as the Rhine, the armies of Maria Theresa were
generally defeated. The Treaty of Aix-la-Chapelle, in 1748, terminated this series of campaigns more advantageously than the
empress-queen had had a right to hope. She ceded to Sardinia
upper Novara and Vigevano, and to Don Philip of Spain, Parma,
Piacenza, and Guastalla. Except for the loss of Silesia, however,
the Austrian states remained intact.

The acquisition of Silesia had given Frederick II. a strong
position on the very frontier of Bohemia. Russia had begun to
take a share in the affairs of Europe, and her alliance was in future
to have great weight in the disputes that occurred between Vienna
and Berlin. From the year 1746 a treaty of defensive alliance had
existed between Austria and Russia, by which each power undertook to furnish an army of 60,000 men in case Frederick should
attack Poland, Austria, or Russia.

But Austria could not be sure of keeping her Spanish or Italian
possessions so long as France was her enemy. In 1753 Maria
Theresa summoned to her counsels a remarkable man, the Count
Kaunitz, who succeeded in putting an end to the long-standing
rivalry between the houses of Bourbon and Hapsburg, and brought
about a definite understanding between the courts of Vienna and
Versailles. Kaunitz, a member of an old family of Bohemia, was
born at Vienna in 1711. He had at first been destined for the
church, but the death of his older brother had thrown him back
into the world. He had studied at the universities of Vienna, Leipzig, and Leyden, and had traveled in Holland, England, France,
and Italy. He had married a Stahrenberg, a descendant of the
leader who had defended Vienna, and had entered the public service while still very young. Under Charles VI. he had been a
member of the imperial council; and on her accession Maria

Theresa had intrusted to him several diplomatic missions, sending him first to Italy, then to Brussels, and at last to England, where he showed himself possessed of rare qualities. He represented Austria at Aix-la-Chapelle, and was, from 1751 to 1753, Austrian ambassador in Paris. Upon his return to Vienna he pointed out very forcibly to his sovereign the necessity of a French alliance. France, who could throw her troops at once upon Belgium, the Rhine, and Italy, was, he argued, far the most dangerous enemy of Austria, and her alliance should be secured, if possible. In spite of the opposition of the emperor and the majority of the council, an alliance with France was determined upon. Kaunitz was appointed chancellor and placed at the head of foreign affairs, and from this time all his efforts were directed toward a reconciliation between the two countries whose rivalries had for centuries dominated the alliances of Europe. Unfortunately England and France were at this time in the midst of a colonial dispute, and Austria could scarcely expect to retain the support of England and be at the same time in alliance with France. Kaunitz at first tried to remain neutral, but he soon decided that an alliance with France would be far more useful against Frederick II. Besides, fearful of the security of Hanover, England had made overtures to him. After much diplomatic maneuvering, Kaunitz finally succeeded in procuring the French alliance, the conditions of which were expressed in two treaties at Versailles. The second of these, known as the Second Treaty of Versailles, was signed in May, 1757. It constitutes one of the most remarkable agreements ever made between two great powers, and is in every way a signal triumph to the Austrian queen and her able minister. France pledged herself to support Austria with a large army of 105,000 men, and an annual subsidy of twelve millions of florins so long as the war should last, and all she stipulated to receive in return was a portion of the Netherlands. The war was to continue till Prussia was dismembered, and Austria had reconquered Silesia and her former Italian possessions. Russia had already entered the alliance, and the Treaty of Versailles therefore marks the complete abandonment of the traditional grouping of the powers, so that it has quite appropriately been called the Diplomatic Revolution.

It has been said that Maria Theresa, in her anxiety to gain the friendship of Louis XV., entered into direct relations with Madame de Pompadour, and wrote her a letter styling her "dear friend and fair cousin." The proud princess never used such language. "You are mistaken," she wrote, October 10, 1763, to the electress of Saxony, "if you believe that we have ever had anything to do with the Pompadour. Not a letter has been written, not an interview has been granted our minister through means of her; they have paid court to her, like all the rest, but there has been no intimacy. Such a go-between would not suit me." On the other hand, she was intensely eager for the success of the negotiations.

Frederick II., apprised of the coalition against him, without delay invaded Saxony, seized Dresden, and then pushed into Bohemia, advancing as far as Prague, May, 1757. But there the defeat of Kolin compelled him to withdraw from this kingdom. He had at last found in Marshal Daun a worthy adversary. Pressed on the west by the French, on the east by the Russians, who had just occupied eastern Prussia, and on the south by the Austrians, who had reëntered Silesia, Frederick's affairs seemed desperate. But the brilliant victory over the French and imperialists at Rossbach relieved him from the most imminent danger, and rushing from Rossbach back to Silesia he inflicted a terrible defeat on the Austrians at Leuthen, in December, 1757. The details of the war furnish a series of victories and defeats for Frederick in which, like a lion at bay, he rushes from one antagonist to another, though gradually weakening under the strain of contending against such overwhelming odds. In 1760 he was still holding his enemies at bay. In 1762 Peter III. withdrew from the Austrian alliance, France entered into negotiations with England, and Maria Theresa, fearful of being left alone to fight her formidable antagonist, agreed to the Peace of Hubertsburg, in 1763. Austria acquiesced in the retention of Silesia by Frederick II., and he in turn promised his electoral vote in the approaching imperial election to the Archduke Joseph.

The Seven Years' War was an excellent school for the Austrian army, which improved greatly during its progress. Among the generals whose bravery and talent appeared most conspicuously were Joseph Daun, who organized the School of Cadets at Vienna and who recalled the severe methods of Montecuculli; the Livonian Loudon, who after having offered his sword in vain to the king of Prussia, won in the Austrian service a glorious name that is not yet forgotten; and the two Irishmen, Brown and Lacy. The

FREDERICK THE GREAT ADDRESSES HIS GENERALS BEFORE THE BATTLE OF LEUTHEN

"If any among you fears to share the last danger with me, he may resign now, without hearing a word of reproof from me"

Painting by Arthur Kampf

victories of Kolin and of Hochkirch, of Kunersdorf and of Maxen, showed that Austria was to be counted from that time among the military states of Europe. Thereafter the great powers were anxious for her alliance.

A short time before the Treaty of Hubertsburg the Emperor Francis I. had died. By his marriage with Maria Theresa he had no less than sixteen children, and through their marriages the house of Austria became allied with many of the reigning families of Europe. The Princess Maria Christina married Albert of Saxony; Marie Amelia, Duke Ferdinand of Parma; Maria Caroline, Ferdinand, king of the Two Sicilies; and the Archduke Ferdinand, the hereditary princess of Modena. These unions still further increased the interest that the house of Austria had always had in the affairs of Italy. Then the marriage of Maria Antonia (Marie Antoinette) with the dauphin of France in 1770 seemed as if it would make permanent the alliance which Kaunitz had succeeded in bringing about between the houses of Bourbon and Hapsburg-Lorraine. The correspondence of Maria Theresa with the dauphiness and with De Mercy, Austrian ambassador at the court of France, has been preserved. It shows what an interest the empress attached to the maintenance of the most cordial relations between the two countries, and reflects great honor to the character of Maria Theresa, whether considered as a sovereign or as the mother of a family.

After the death of Francis I., his son, Joseph II., was elected emperor, in 1765. His mother associated him with her in the government and confided the direction of the army to him, but he played no more active a rôle in the actual government of the country than did his father.

The empress-queen, in spite of the reverses that Frederick II. had inflicted on her, had reason to be proud of the prosperity of her states and the splendor of her house. An opportunity which the government at Vienna did not allow to escape soon presented itself for repairing, by a new acquisition, the loss of Silesia. Poland had for many years been falling more and more into a state of anarchy. The deplorable system of electing sovereigns, practiced by a tumultuous and anarchical nobility, could not but bring the country under foreign domination. The *liberum veto,* or the right of the individual noble to veto laws, made legislation impossible and practically legalized anarchy. For years, therefore, strong government was entirely wanting in Poland. Society consisted of the nobles, most of whom were sadly impoverished, and their serfs; there was no middle class. To ambitious neighbors pretexts for intervening were not wanting. Undoubtedly Maria Theresa would not of herself have planned the dismemberment of Poland, but when Russia and Prussia were preparing to claim or conquer at least part of the kingdom by virtue of real or imaginary rights, the empress was easily persuaded to yield to reasons of state.

The first idea of the partition should certainly be attributed to Frederick II. In 1772, on the occasion of the success of the Russians over the Turks, a success which had called for the mediation of Austria, he proposed to offer Russia compensation in Poland. Catherine II. was easily won over to this plan, and Joseph II., after two interviews with the king of Prussia, in which it was agreed that Austria should share in the partition, was also won over. But Maria Theresa was at first troubled by these propositions, so repugnant to her devout and loyal spirit. To her minister at Berlin she wrote: "I admit that it is hard for me to decide upon a thing of which I am reassured neither as to its justice nor its utility, and which I do not even find useful. What right has one to despoil an innocent nation that has always before been so gladly defended and helped? Why are there so many great and costly preparations and so many noisy threats regarding the equilibrium of the north? The most plausible reason, that of not remaining alone among the other powers, and so deriving no advantage from the situation, does not seem to me to suffice, nor even to be an honorable pretext, for joining two unjust usurpers in order to ruin, without just cause, a third. I do not understand the politics that permit, in case two make use of their superiority to oppress an innocent one, that a third may and should, simply as a precaution for the future and a convenience for the present, imitate them and commit the same injustice, one that seems to me insufferable. What will France, Spain, and England say if we suddenly ally ourselves with those whom we have so much wished to restrain, and whose proceedings we have declared unjust? That would be giving the lie to all that has been done during thirty years of my reign. Let us endeavor rather to diminish their pretensions than to think of sharing with them under conditions so unequal. Let us pass for feeble rather than dishonest."

Again Maria Theresa seeks to explain the reasons that have forced her to agree to the partition: "The interest of our own safety and that of all Europe," she writes, "demand that we take, though to my regret, the part of seeking to counterbalance the increase of power that Russia and Prussia are obtaining, by reserving for ourselves that part of the land in dispute to which we have incontestable rights." By these last words it can be seen that state policies have crowded out the Christian scruples of the queen.

The treaty of partition was signed July 25, 1772. It has been said that Maria Theresa wrote with her own hands the following words below the report deciding on the adoption of the treaty: "*Placet,* since so many clever and learned men wish it so, but long after my death will be seen the results of having so despised all that which hitherto has been counted holy and just." These words, of which the original has not been found, appear to be apocryphal. The real sentiments of the empress after the partition are found in the texts quoted above and in a letter to Mercy, the Austrian ambassador at the court of France. Maria Theresa regrets at the same time being associated in the affair and having profited too little. "They have indeed led us by the nose," she writes regarding her accomplices, "and I am inconsolable. If I could indeed console myself it would be with the fact that I was always opposed to this iniquitous partition, so unequal, and to an alliance with these two monsters. . . . I have yielded, not wishing to make war, but quite contrary to my convictions. I hope that the monarchy may not feel the effects of this after my death."

On the other hand she wrote to Kaunitz: "When all my possessions were menaced I had confidence in my right and in the assistance of God. But in this affair, where not only the right cries to Heaven against us, but where all equity and good sense are also against us, I realize that nothing else in all my life has caused me so much anguish. What an example we are giving the world in prostituting our honor and our reputation for a piece of Poland or of Moldavia and Wallachia. I see well that I am alone and no longer vigorous; that is why I allow things to go their way, but not without the greatest chagrin." Frederick II., with his habitual cynicism, spoke of the pangs of Maria Theresa in quite a different tone. "She is always weeping and always taking." She herself has characterized the situation by these words, which have at least the merit of sincerity: "We wish to share with Prussia and we wish at the same time to appear honest."

The presentiments of Maria Theresa have been in part realized. The possession of Galicia has caused many embarrassments to the Austrian Government; and yet through an unlooked-for change, the Poles have become to-day the most loyal subjects of the Emperor Francis Joseph.

The partition once resolved upon, it was necessary to find a plausible pretext for carrying it out. The queen of Hungary and Bohemia invoked certain rights, fictitious or real, that the two kingdoms might have over the territory of Poland. At first, in 1770, claim was made to the thirteen towns of the county of Zips, which had been pledged in 1412 to Vladislav, king of Poland, and which had remained in pledge 359 years. Definite possession of these was taken November 5, 1772, in the name of the queen of Hungary, to whom the annexed villages owed homage.

In September, 1772, Austria presented new claims. "Russia and Prussia having resolved to make good their ancient pretensions to certain districts of the kingdom of Poland," the empress-queen had new territories occupied. A special manifesto explained the rights of Hungary to Little Russia and Podolia, and those of Bohemia to the duchies of Ausschwitz and Zator. So Austria acquired Red Russia, a part of Podolia, and the palatinates of Sandomir and Cracow, with the rich salt mines of Wieliczka and Bochnia, the whole comprising an extent of 1500 square miles and 2,500,000 inhabitants.

The new possessions received the official title of the kingdom of Galicia and Lodomeria. The title of king of Galicia and Lodomeria had already been borne by the kings of Hungary. Meanwhile Maria Theresa, in spite of her honest intentions, was careful not to attach these reannexed countries to Hungary or to Bohemia, whose independent spirit she feared, but made of them an immediate possession of the crown. The capital of the new kingdom was established at the town of Lemberg. In the course of the year 1773 a royal rescript organized the administration of the country, and in December the estates, the clergy, the nobility, and the bourgeoisie took the oath to the Austrian dynasty. The administration was confided to German officials. In 1775 the country was divided into eighteen circles; in each of the chief places of these was established a normal school for the propagation of the

MARIA THERESA 249

German language, which was that of the administration, though Latin remained everywhere that of the courts. The organization of the estates was based on that of the kingdoms of Bohemia and Hungary. Joseph II., who had taken much more interest in the dismemberment of Poland than had his mother, and who certainly had not had the same scruples, visited the new provinces in 1778, without doubt in order to study the results of the Germanizing system which he was intending to apply to his other states.

Another acquisition, less important than that of Galicia, was that of Bukovina, as a result of the war between Russia and Turkey. Austria and Turkey had been at peace since the Treaty of Belgrade, but when Russia seized the Crimea and was approaching the Danube, Maria Theresa became disquieted, assembled an army in Hungary, and insisted as early as 1772 on imposing her mediation. In 1774 the Porte made peace with Russia in the important treaty of Kutchuk Kainardji. Austria took advantage of these circumstances to occupy certain parts of Moldavia. The reasons given to the Porte to justify this sudden occupation were no better than those by which the partition of Poland was authorized; the invaded territories were necessary to Austria for communication between Galicia and Transylvania in order to prevent the desertions of soldiers, and, after all, a part of Moldavia had once belonged to Podolia, now an Austrian possession. Turkey protested, while Russia and Prussia demanded explanations. But Turkey, without allies, had to yield, and in 1775 the treaty of cession was concluded. The ceded territory comprised about 189 square miles, 4 market towns, and about 60 villages; but it was very important from the strategic point of view. The hospodar of Moldavia, Ghika, whose principality was dismembered by this cession, attempted to prevent the inhabitants from swearing fealty, and was seized and beheaded by order of the sultan. The Rumanians, however, still venerate his name as that of a martyr to independence. The population of Bukovina is composed for the most part of Little Russians and Rumanians. In 1875 the Austrian Government celebrated the centennial of the annexation by founding a German university at Czernowitz, by which it was expected to hasten the Germanizing of the country.

Thus Maria Theresa and her son practiced in their turn the rounding out of territories that Frederick II. had set the fashion for by the conquest of Silesia. Joseph II. had in these matters the same principles as the king of Prussia. In 1779 the elector of Bavaria, Maximilian Joseph, the last of the Wittelsbachs, died. Joseph II. put forward a claim to the electorate and determined to sustain it, if need be, by force of arms. The legitimate heir, the elector palatine, Charles Theodore, was so frightened by the threats of Austria that he consented to a treaty which left him scarcely half of Bavaria.

But Frederick II., who dreaded any aggrandizement of Austria, took up arms and entered Bohemia. This war, feebly carried on, had no especial military importance. The Austrians called it "the skirmish of plums"; the Germans, "the war of potatoes"; while old Loudon, accustomed to heroic struggles, growled about this "beast of a political war." The mediation of France and Russia led to the Peace of Teschen, in 1779, by which Maria Theresa kept only a small part of Bavaria, the district of the Inn. The Treaty of Teschen was the last diplomatic act of the reign of Maria Theresa. She died a short time afterward, in 1780, leaving the Austrian state larger and stronger than at her accession.

Chapter XXI

THE INTERNAL HISTORY OF AUSTRIA UNDER MARIA THERESA. 1740-1780

IN the reign of Maria Theresa Bohemia, already so cruelly tried, became once more the battlefield of the jealous leagues against the house of Hapsburg. In 1741 the elector of Bavaria pushed forward as far as Prague and summoned the estates. About four hundred nobles and knights whose lands were occupied by his troops appeared and took the oath of allegiance to him in the cathedral of St. Vit. The Czechs had little reason to be attached to the Hapsburg dynasty, and the change of masters was a matter of small consequence to them. Only the great functionaries quitted the capital and remained loyal to the queen. Charles of Bavaria instituted a provisional government, established a chancery for Bohemia at Munich, and convoked a diet in order to obtain supplies for the prosecution of the war. After this he returned to Germany and ceded the county of Glatz to Frederick, a cession which Maria Theresa was obliged to ratify. Later Bohemia was invaded by the French under Marshal Belle-Isle, and Prague occupied by them. Not till April, 1743, did Maria Theresa enter Prague and receive the crown from the archbishop of Olmütz. In order to prevent the crown of Bohemia from resting in the future on the head of a stranger, and in order to efface its historic traditions as much as possible, it was carried to Vienna.

In the cession of Silesia the kingdom of St. Vacslav lost one-third of its territory. But Bohemia still had other sacrifices to make. The diet gave up all control exercised by it over the administration and the maintenance of the army; agreed that appeals could be carried to Vienna; that the chancery of Bohemia should be absorbed in the high chancery of the court, and that the criminal law of Bohemia should be made uniform with that of the rest of the Austrian dominions. An archbishopric of Olmütz was created, and Moravia was by this means removed from the spiritual jurisdiction of Prague. The German language was introduced into all

schools and offices as the sole official language of administration
and instruction. These were hard blows to the Czech nationality.
On the other hand, Maria Theresa gained some popularity in Bohemia by her edict of 1773 concerning forced labor. The peasants
did not at first understand it; they imagined that the queen had freed
them from all dues, and that her agents hid the truth from them.
They marched in bands upon Prague to see the royal documents, and
burned and pillaged the castles as they went. It took a large army
to reduce them, and General Wallis had great difficulty in protecting the capital. After the loss of Silesia, Maria Theresa had two
fortresses built—that of Theresienstadt and that of Josephstadt—
to protect the country from invasions. A census taken in the reign
of Maria Theresa gave the number of males in the kingdom as
1,200,000, implying a population of about 2,500,000, while immediately after the Thirty Years' War it had been only 800,000.

" It has been seen how the house of Austria never ceased to
oppress the Hungarian nobles. They knew not how valuable they
would one day be to it. It sought among that people money which
it had not, and did not see the men which it had. When a throng
of princes divided its territories among themselves, when the various parts of the monarchy became motionless and inert, so to
speak, the only life left was among that nobility, which, becoming
indignant, forgot all in order to fight, and believed that it found
its greatest glory in pardoning and dying for those who had injured it." These words of Montesquieu express with that author's
habitual brevity the feeling of admiration aroused throughout
Europe by the devotion of the Hungarians to Maria Theresa.
Those who do not know the Magyar temperament can see in this
devotion only the expression of chivalrous feeling, but the Magyars are legists as well as knights. Nevertheless the legendary and
picturesque episode with which are associated the famous words
" Moriamur pro rege nostro Maria Theresa" require explanation
in some detail.

Charles VI. had not contented himself with the recognition
of his daughter as his heir by the kingdom of Hungary; he had also
wished that his son-in-law, Francis of Lorraine, should enter into
closer relations with the Magyar nation, and for this reason he
had, in 1732, bestowed the title of royal lieutenant upon him.
Now the Hungarians were exceedingly jealous lest they should be
confounded with the hereditary states. On the death of Charles

MARIA THERESA, EMPRESS OF AUSTRIA
(Born 1717. Died 1780)
Painting by Wm. von Camphausen

VI. his successor had not yet been crowned. If Francis of Lorraine ascended the throne of Hungary with his wife, and if he, as was already evident that he would be, were elected emperor, Hungary would run great risk of becoming a mere appanage to Germany. If, on the contrary, the crown of St. Stephen were placed on the head of Maria Theresa alone, the historic individuality of Hungary would have much greater chance of being preserved. On the death of her father, Maria Theresa had intrusted the lieutenancy to John Palffy, an old companion in arms of Prince Eugene. She gave him full power, promised to respect the liberties of the kingdom, and shortly to convoke the diet. This diet was actually opened on May 18, 1741. The debates were very animated, the majority being strongly opposed to the idea that the husband of the new queen should be associated with her on the throne of Hungary. Some days later at Vienna the queen received a deputation bringing her the congratulations of the diet, not only on her accession, but also on the birth of her first son, the future Joseph II. This deputation received renewed assurances that the privileges of the kingdom would be respected, and that the queen would very shortly come to Presburg. On July 19 she embarked on the Danube in a boat decorated with the national colors of Hungary—red, white, and green—and as she passed the frontier she was saluted with a cry " Vivat domina et rex nostro! " The title rex had been given by the Hungarians to the only woman who had reigned before her in Hungary. On the 21st she received the homage of the diet in the castle of Presburg, and in a Latin speech renewed the promises which she had made to Palffy. She promised to maintain all the rights and privileges of the kingdom, with the single exception of the thirty-first article of the Golden Bull, which proclaimed the right of insurrection, to leave the sacred crown in Hungary, and to renew all the clauses of the Pragmatic Sanction.

The diet was quite sympathetic toward the young queen, whose graceful manners conciliated even the fiercest; but it was careful not to sacrifice any of the privileges of the kingdom. It demanded that the nobles should be free from taxation; that the peasants and not the land should be taxed; that Transylvania should be indissolubly united to Hungary, and that Hungarians alone should hold office. The deliberations were turbulent, but by good fortune the diet elected as its palatine Palffy, who was chivalrously devoted to

the queen. He won over the most troublesome members and persuaded the diet that the questions still pending should be decided
after the coronation. This ceremony, which had always excited
the enthusiasm of the Hungarians, so jealous of their autonomy
and so impassioned for the sacred crown, took place now under
circumstances of unusual interest. It was a young and beautiful
princess whose brow the hereditary diadem now encircled, and
who, mounted on a fiery charger, brandished the sword of St.
Stephen to the four quarters of the globe from the top of the
King's Hill.

" She was one of the most beautiful women in Europe," writes
an English eye-witness. " Her figure was elegant and her bearing majestic, and her eyes were expressive and full of gentleness.
It was only a short time before that she had given birth to a son, and
a look of delicacy, which still remained, lent a new charm to her
features. Everything about her was charming. This portrait,
which is not in the least flattered, should always be kept in mind
when one recalls the enthusiasm which the princess inspired in the
Hungarians."

Nevertheless, after the coronation the disputes recommenced.
Even the hundred thousand florins which were to be a gift on
her " joyful accession " were made the subject of bargaining, and
the Magyar spirit for legal form expressed itself in numberless
quibbles which drew tears from the young queen. It was on September 13, 1741, that the first scene of the theatrical episode which
contemporaries have exaggerated took place. The queen had summoned the two *Tables* to the castle of Presburg, and there she
appeared before them, dressed in mourning, the crown upon her
head and the sword of St. Stephen by her side. The dangers
threatening the queen and Hungary were set forth by the chancellor, Louis Batthyany, after which the queen, in a short Latin
speech, called upon the assembly to provide for the safety of herself, her children, and her crown. Her words, mingled with tears,
excited considerable but suppressed emotion. This was greatly
increased during the reply of the primate, who was frequently
interrupted by cries of " *vitam et sanguinem* "; and a levy of
100,000 men was at once decided on. The prince-consort was
accepted as co-regent of the kingdom, and he took the oath September 21, promising to devote his blood and his life to the queen and to
Hungary. It was on this occasion that Maria Theresa showed her

young son to the estates, and that the celebrated cry broke forth—
"*Moriamur pro rege nostro Maria Theresa!*" It was by no means
a sudden outburst of chivalrous sentiment, but the result of negotiations long-continued and of emotions skillfully called forth. Contemporaries themselves were deceived, and saw in this a single
episode of a moment, ignorant of the details that had preceded.

As a matter of fact this diet, which ended on October 29, had
devoted itself almost entirely to the preservation of Hungarian
interests. The queen had agreed to all its demands, which were,
moreover, quite legitimate; she had consented to the suppression
of some military frontiers, and had obtained in exchange for these
concessions the help she needed to continue the war. On the other
hand the enthusiasm of the Hungarians did not pass away with the
circumstances which had given it birth. Maria Theresa owed to
them some of her best troops: the Servians and Croats who, commanded by Baron Trenck, gained an almost legendary reputation
for their valor and cruelty. These fierce *pandours,* accustomed to
war with the Turks, and now suddenly thrown into the midst of
civilized Europe, brought with them the semi-barbarous habits derived from their frequent contact with Asiatic hordes. The devotion of the Magyars to Maria Theresa was shown upon many fields
of battle; their horsemen penetrated as far as Berlin, and even to
Alsace. Frederick the Great, with the adroitness common to Prussian ambition, tried to destroy the fidelity of the Hungarians to
their queen by recalling to them their past insurrections, and the
services which Brandenburg had then rendered them; but his efforts
failed.

This exchange of services between the Magyar nobles and the
court of Vienna formed a tie between them such as had never
previously existed. The great nobles were assiduous in their at-
tendance at the palaces of Vienna, Schönbrunn, and Laxenburg,
where contact with the Bohemian and Austrian nobility and the
gentle influence of the empress-queen led them to renounce their
national costume so dear to their traditions, to acquire the habit of
speaking German, and to seek the foreign titles of prince, count,
or baron. It was at this time that the bodyguard of Hungarians
was formed at Vienna, and that the Order of St. Stephen was
founded. By means of ingeniously arranged marriages and a
system of cleverly devised temptations, the greater nobility was
by degrees Germanized. But the lesser nobility—the landed

gentry—remained incorruptible, and in the discussions of the *Lower Table,* and in the meetings of the comitats, they continued to defend with indomitable obstinacy the privileges of the kingdom. The disputes between the queen and the chambers turned upon two essential questions: the condition of the peasants and the constitution of the military frontiers. The peasants were serfs of the soil in Hungary, but in the eighteenth century ideas of philanthropy, and more particularly the financial condition of the kingdom, required the abolition of serfdom. The queen asked for a reform of the old system, but the nobles replied by a series of complaints against the encroachments of the German administration, against the council of regency, against the powers of military commanders, and against the title of *landtag* (local diet), which had perhaps been designedly given to the Hungarian diet instead of that of *reichstag,* or diet of the kingdom. But in spite of opposition the queen issued an edict, which she was able to enforce by dint of perseverance, regulating the life of the peasants. This law remained a fundamental law of the land down to 1832. According to it the peasants were henceforth free to move from place to place and to bring up their children as they pleased, while all legal cases in which they were concerned were in the future to be tried before the courts of the comitats. These liberal measures were accepted by the nobles only with great reluctance. They were afforded, however, some compensation in the matter of the military frontiers.

The old system of the court at Vienna had aimed at the complete separation of the frontier lands from Hungary. They had been freed from the rule of the Turks by the imperial arms, it was urged, and therefore they belonged to the emperor. Besides the Slavs of these regions, strangers to the Hungarian nation, were in no wise anxious to be reunited to the Magyars. They preferred their obligations of military service to the condition of Servian serfs oppressed by the comitat. They had, besides, certain privileges, such as the holding of an assembly of their own, and of choosing their bishop. But in spite of all this Maria Theresa was obliged to yield to the demands of the Hungarians, and to consent, in 1750, to the suppression of the frontiers of the Theiss and the Maros. As a result of this one hundred thousand Servians left the country and settled in Russia. The Austro-Hungarian army lost some of its best soldiers by the exodus, and the *gränszer* (soldiers of the frontier), who did remain, rose in rebellion in 1755. A further concession was made to the Hungarians when, in 1776, the Servians were forbidden longer to maintain an agent at Vienna to look after their interests; and finally, in 1779, all the territory between the Maros, the Theiss, the Danube, and the Carpathians was incorporated in the kingdom and formed into three comitats. In this manner Hungary gradually recovered the territory Vienna had taken from her.

In 1765 Maria Theresa associated her son Joseph with her in the government, with the title of co-regent. The philosophic mind of this prince would seem to have inspired some of the measures decided upon soon after, as, for example, the suppression of the right of sanctuary and of the mendicant orders, and the assistance given to public instruction and the establishment of numerous village schools. The Hungarians are grateful to him to this day for having given them the port of Fiume, which had formerly been dependent on Triest, although it is still a question in dispute whether the city of Fiume was united to Croatia or to Hungary proper. The possession of the town has been claimed most energetically by the Croats, but the government of Vienna has finally decided that it belongs to Hungary.

On the whole the kingdom was in a flourishing condition at the death of Maria Theresa. From the national point of view, however, it was enfeebled, and had lost the greater part of those ancient rights the maintenance of which was so dear to patriots. The diet of the kingdom, which according to the terms of the Golden Bull should have met every year, was convoked only three times during the entire reign.

In the hereditary provinces of the Austrian group, as well as in the kingdoms of Bohemia and Bavaria, Maria Theresa zealously sought to develop the authority of the prince and to diminish that of the estates. Almost all the executive power had hitherto been in the hands of the prelates, lords, knights, and a number of privileged towns; justice was administered by the towns or the lords; the roads were bad, and the militia not based on any regular system. Under Maria Theresa the government began to interfere with the churches and schools, and tried to secure to the citizens of the towns the position which had hitherto been denied them. On her accession the queen retained the principal advisers of her father, but after the Treaty of Aix-la-Chapelle she made Haugwitz, who rendered her most important services, chancellor. Chotek was intrusted with the reform of the finances, while Kaunitz was given charge of foreign affairs. The following are some of the principal measures adopted to increase the power of the central government: The right of voting certain of the indirect taxes, such as the tax on salt, on tobacco and on stamped paper, were taken from the diets; the estates were required to present their budgets to the court of accounts at Vienna; they were deprived of all political power, which was vested in the royal lieutenant; the corvées and the seigneurial dues of the peasants were diminished. The division of administration among chanceries of Austria, Bohemia, and Hungary and Transylvania was abolished; the patent of May 14, 1749, separated the administration of justice from the legislative and executive functions of government, and decreed the union of the two chanceries of Austria and Bohemia in one supreme power called, at first, the directory of the interior, afterward, the united chancery of the imperial and royal court. Thus did absolutism take the first step to bring about the arrangement now in force under the parliamentary system of Cisleithenia. Maria Theresa also instituted, in 1760, a council of state, whose business it was to watch over the whole administration. By degrees administrative power was withdrawn from the permanent committees of the provincial diets and vested in the representatives of the sovereign, and the estates were only allowed to meet for the purpose of voting upon the measures proposed by the crown. Royal officials were appointed in the circles, from which they had hitherto been excluded. Here they were the representatives of the central authority and required to protect the peasants against their lords.

The peasants, without being serfs—except in Hungary—were almost entirely dependent upon their territorial lords. They were not the proprietors of the soil, but had merely the usufruct of their holdings; they could neither quit the estate, marry, nor bring up their children to any other business than that of laborer without the consent of their lord, and they were bound to numberless services comprised under the name of robot-corvée. Maria Theresa undertook to ameliorate their condition. In order to regulate the territorial taxes she caused a new land survey to be made and suppressed the exemption from taxation which the land of the lords had hitherto enjoyed. These measures suited not only the needs of the treasury, but also the humanitarian ideas coming into favor at the time. They were applied to all the Cis-leithenian states except the Tyrol, Gorica, Gradisca, and Triest, where feudal institutions had never taken deep root. It was the policy of Maria Theresa to improve the conditions of the peasants in order to weaken the nobles; to attract the great lords to Vienna in order to diminish their influence; and to unify the aristocracy of the different portions of the empire in order to unify the monarchy.

The reform of the communal system presented considerable difficulty. Down to the middle of the eighteenth century there were the most radical differences in the constitutions of the various communes. Some depended upon a lay, others upon an ecclesiastical lord, while others, especially cities and towns, were under the immediate authority of the sovereign. Some enjoyed almost complete freedom, while others were constantly tyrannized over by the lords or by the agents of the monarch. Some of the towns even possessed the right of representation in the diet. Their constitutions differed as much as those of the Italian republics. Here the municipal government was aristocratic, there a pure democracy; here municipal offices were hereditary, there elective. The institutions of the Middle Ages, as, for example, the guilds, were still vigorous; there were burgesses of the towns, and "burgesses of the suburbs," "great burgesses," and "small burgesses"; while in those towns which were under Italian influence, such as Triest and Gorica, there existed a patriciate, or hereditary aristocracy. But these patriarchal institutions began to disappear after 1748. A law passed in 1776 proclaiming freedom of trade attacked the principles upon which the corporations and guilds were based. The administration of justice was also intrusted to a body of magistrates, who replaced the old local courts.

In the middle of the eighteenth century the law of the land consisted solely of prescriptive rights and local customs, the deficiencies of which were supplied from civil or Roman law, from canon law, and in some provinces from imperial decrees. The basic principle in all was that every citizen should be judged by his peers. Clergy, universities, nobles, public officials, citizens, peasants, and Jews, all had their special tribunals. There was no appeal from the lords or the magistrates in the towns. Punishments were still barbarous, those most in vogue being branding, mutilation, the wheel, and the stake, and these terrible penalties were usually imposed by ignorant and superstitious judges. Civil suits dragged on indefinitely, and often no final decision was rendered at all. In 1753 Maria Theresa resolved to bring about uniformity of the law in all parts of the monarchy. The work of compilation took many years. The commission appointed by her produced eight folio volumes in 1767. These were afterward abridged, and the first volume of the new edition appeared in 1776. In 1768 the " *Constitutio criminalis Theresina* " had been published. It retained the barbarous penalties of the Middle Ages, admitted torture, and punished blasphemy. But in 1777 torture was finally abolished and trials for witchcraft, although not entirely suppressed, were at least considerably checked. By a patent of 1749 the administration of justice had been separated from purely provincial business and a minister of justice appointed for all the non-Hungarian states. Some of these praiseworthy reforms, it must be admitted, had the Utopian features characteristic of the eighteenth century, as, for example, the so-called commission of chastity, whose office it was to prevent unlawful amours.

Though a sincere Catholic, Maria Theresa never sacrificed the interests of the state to the church. She suppressed the ecclesiastical penalties which the priests had been in the habit of imposing; forbade the various religious orders from sending money out of the country; the Papal nuncio to travel in her dominions, and the bishops to correspond directly with Rome. She also prohibited priests from assisting in the making of wills, and in 1773 the Order of Jesuits was suppressed in Austria, as it was about this time in many other countries. Down to 1740 public instruction was entirely under the control of the clergy; scarcely any elementary schools existed, and teaching in the higher schools was extremely poor. Austria was in a pitiable condition of inferiority as regards education when compared with France, or even northern Germany. A foreigner was intrusted with its improvement—Gerhard van Swieten, a Dutch professor of medicine at the University of Vienna —who was physician to Maria Theresa, and also the reactionary president of the commission for the censorship of the press. The schools were placed under the control of the state, and a law was passed in 1749 reserving the sole right of choosing the professors of the University of Vienna to the government, while a little later the schools belonging to the Jesuits and the Piarists were placed under the state. An imperial resolution of September 24, 1740, contained the following words: " The organization of schools is and must always remain an affair of the state " (*Das Schulwesen ist und bleibt allzeit ein Politicum*). This principle, pushed to its extremes, had some singular consequences. The universities were not open to everyone, and no one could study abroad without the sanction of the state. Even theological works were submitted to the government censorship, a censorship that was very rigorous and often quite as intolerant as that of the ecclesiastics. It prohibited even such classical works as those of Machiavelli. A great number of schools for the young nobility were founded during the reign of Maria Theresa, among them the Theresianum, which exist at the present time.

In 1766 the commission of instruction and of the censorship of the press was founded. The suppression of the Jesuits had considerable influence on education, but at first the majority of the professors had to be chosen from among ex-Jesuits, as the number of other teachers was not sufficient. A new code of education, published in 1775, continued in force down to 1850.

The most meritorious act of Maria Theresa was the foundation of elementary schools. Before 1770 primary education, properly so-called, did not exist, all education being dependent upon the church. In May, 1770, the first normal school was opened at Vienna, and a royal edict of the same year established schoolmasters independent of the priests. The suppression of the Jesuit order and the sequestration of their property had placed ample funds in the hands of the government and enabled it to convert many of the classical into elementary schools. In 1774 the celebrated Silesian teacher, Felbinger, was summoned to Vienna to introduce good methods of teaching. At the same time higher education, especially at the University of Vienna, rose rapidly, the faculties of medicine and of law taking rank among the first in Europe. In literature not much was done: poetry was still halting and clumsy. The rococo style dominated in architecture and sculpture, and was represented at Vienna by the Italian Canova. The only great art in which Austria excelled was music, and under Glück, Haydn, and Mozart it attained a development previously unknown. Their works, moreover, reveal clearly the influences of the races among whom they were composed; they combine the melodious brightness of the Italian, the depth of harmony of the German, and the melancholy of the Slav.

Francis I., the husband of Maria Theresa, devoted himself

especially to the finances, a work in which he was assisted by Chotek, a Czech noble. He was well acquainted with financial questions, and his first care was to reduce the expenses of the court. On the accession of Maria Theresa the treasury was exhausted; it is stated that the young queen found only eighty-seven thousand thalers. One of Chotek's first measures was to levy a tax on property, then one on persons, which affected everybody from the prince who paid six hundred florins to the maid who paid four kreutzers. All exemption from taxation was abolished.

Chotek was also the first to show the use that could be made of Triest as a seaport for Austrian commerce, for under his direction the town grew rapidly. Dutch, Neapolitan, and Greek merchants established trading houses there, and commerce was carried on with both hemispheres. By 1763 Austria had twelve large ships trading with India, one of which took possession of the Nicobar Islands in 1776. Triest itself was frequented by six thousand vessels annually. Twenty-five consulates were established in the Atlantic and Mediterranean, seven in Italy, thirteen in European and Asiatic Turkey, one at Ragusa, one at Alexandria, one, at Tripoli, and one at Lisbon. The Oriental Academy, founded at Vienna in 1754, furnished capable and well-educated men as consuls. The board of trade established in 1766 did much to develop commerce, the cloth of Moravia especially being widely in demand.

Roads and canals were improved, and the customs of the interior reduced or abolished. Postal arrangements were also perfected. Chotek created a reserve fund for unexpected circumstances, and raised the credit of Austria by his punctuality in paying the interest on the public debt. Under Charles VI. the public revenue had scarcely reached the sum of thirty million florins; by 1773 it amounted to almost fifty-six millions, and by the death of Maria Theresa it exceeded eighty millions. A patent bearing date of 1751 reorganized the lottery, which was bringing in not less than eight hundred thousand florins by the end of the reign.

The system of centralization was also applied to the departments of war and foreign affairs. Each state, however, retained the right of voting its contingent for the army. The total number of troops rose to 113,000 men, not counting the irregulars furnished by Hungary. Military schools were established, and Maria Theresa took special pains to watch over the welfare of the soldiers. During the War of the Austrian Succession a special medal was struck in her honor, bearing the well-deserved inscription "*Mater castrorum.*" Some reforms were borrowed from the Prussian system, as for example, marching in time; and the corps of sappers and miners was introduced. The artillery, directed by Prince Lichtenstein, was considered the best in Europe. In 1772 conscription was introduced in Bohemia, Austria, Moravia, Carniola, Carinthia, and Galicia. During the Seven Years' War there were no less than 200,000 men under arms. "A woman," said Frederick the Great, "has carried out measures worthy of a man." The navy of Austria at this time was composed of nine ships of war, carrying 110 guns, and six galleys of 36 guns each. "On the accession of Maria Theresa," wrote Sonnenfels, "the monarchy had neither external influence nor internal vigor. There was no emulation or encouragement for ability; the condition of agriculture was wretched, trade small, the finances badly managed, and no credit. At her death she left to her successor a state improved by her many reforms, and raised to that rank which its size, fertility, and the intelligence of its inhabitants ought always to insure." Certainly Maria Theresa has greater claims to the title of Great than Catherine of Russia.

Chapter XXII

JOSEPH II. 1780-1790

JOSEPH II. was forty years old on his accession to the throne. He had been emperor of Germany for fifteen years, and in a certain measure his mother had associated him with her in the government of the Austrian states. He had visited the courts of Russia, France, and Italy, and was enthusiastically devoted to the philosophical ideas of the century, awaiting with considerable impatience the time when he could apply its formulas in his own dominions. Among the contemporary sovereigns he seems to have sought an ideal in Frederick the Great. During the lifetime of Maria Theresa, however, he was forced to conceal his aspirations. There existed an avowed antagonism between the old court of the empress and the young court of the emperor, while the young prince, so long confined to the domain of pure theory, little realized the difficulties that would arise with the practical application of his ideas. The Prince de Ligne said of him some months before his accession, " He will be a man of weak desires, which he will never satisfy; his whole reign will be a constant desire to sneeze." It has been well said of the greater portion of the innovations or reforms of the French Constituent Assembly that they had first been tried by Joseph II. But the violent reforms of the Revolution were applied to a homogeneous people much more enlightened than were the Austrian peoples, and even in France many of them would probably never have been accepted if they had not been enforced by the terrorism of the convention and the despotism of Napoleon. The philosopher king Joseph II. looked upon men as so many pawns, ready to be moved about at will, so much inert matter to be experimented upon and molded by the royal pleasure. Of the many reforms he tried during his reign some came too soon, others too late. Too soon, because the majority of the people were not yet ripe for the ideas of liberalism and religious tolerance which the sovereign desired to grant them; too late, because the consciousness of their separate nationality was beginning to awake among the different peoples of the monarchy, whom the sovereign desired to civilize by Germanizing. Restricted by his mother to the direction of military affairs, Joseph II. believed that he could govern his states as he would a regiment. The work of the encylopedists and of the French economists, especially the physiocrats, were his favorite studies, and he aimed at making philosophy the lawmaker of his empire. But he could find in Austria no such men to aid him in carrying out his plans. Those whom he did have belonged mainly to the secret societies of the Freemasons or the Illuminati, organizations which had been obliged to conceal their existence under Maria Theresa. Under Joseph, however, they were tolerated, and by 1785 Freemasonry was officially recognized.

The programme of Joseph II. was very simple. It may be summed up in this formula: to destroy everything not in harmony with his philosophical doctrines, without regard either to historical or religious traditions. His most ardent desire was to bring about a complete similarity of language among the various peoples over whom fate had placed him to rule. To a Hungarian noble who protested against the introduction of the German language in that country he wrote, " Every proposal should be based upon the irrefutable arguments of reason. . . . The German language is the universal language of my empire. I am emperor of Germany. The states which I possess are provinces which form one whole with the state of which I am the head. If Hungary had been the most important of my possessions I should not have hesitated to make all the others speak Hungarian."

In his warfare with the past Joseph II. found religious tradition and faith on the one hand and historical tradition and a sense of nationality on the other, the greatest obstacles. We shall see how he provoked a patriotic reaction in Bohemia and Hungary, the results of which are felt to-day, while even in his struggle against ultramontanism he did not always have right on his side.

From the very beginning of his reign Joseph declared war on the Holy See and the religious orders. " We must lessen the influence of the Ulemas," he wrote in a letter addressed to Cardinal Herzan, his minister in Rome. " I despise superstitions and Sadducees; I must free my people from them. The principles of monasticism are in flat contradiction to human reason." On another occasion he wrote to the archbishop of Salzburg, " The monks

are the most dangerous and the most useless subjects of a state."
In accordance with these ideas he transferred the right of granting
marriage dispensations, previously reserved to the Holy See, to
the Austrian bishops; forbade religious orders to recognize as their
head any person residing in a foreign land; the publishing of Papal
bulls without the imperial sanction; the teaching of the two Papal
bulls, " *Coena Domini* " and " *Unigenitus,*" which defined the prerogatives of the Pope; the use of titles conferred by the Roman
chancery; that young men go to Rome to study at the German college; and the sending of money to Rome.

All these measures were enacted in the first year of his reign.
The year following Joseph attacked the convents. At a single
blow he suppressed more than six hundred monasteries of those
orders which made religious contemplation their sole object, and
decreed that their property should be applied to charitable works.
He had them sold at a low price, not excepting even the works
of art or the sacred utensils; the number of monks, which had
been about sixty-three thousand, was reduced to twenty thousand,
and these were strictly forbidden to retain any relations with
foreign countries. The monarch even intervened in the details
of public worship, forbidding the placing of the votive offerings
in the churches, the reading of more than one mass at a time,
and the setting apart of altars with special privileges in the matter of indulgences or the organization of pilgrimages. He also
forbade the use of metal candlesticks and wooden coffins, a simple
sheet being declared sufficient for burial. These two prohibitions
were the result of an idea of economy, the king maintaining that it
was useless to waste so much silver, copper, and wood.

The Edict of Toleration, also published in 1781, granted the
exercise of their religion to Lutherans, Calvinists, and non-Uniate
Greeks. They were granted the right to have schools and churches,
but without towers or bells and without doors open to the public
road, excepting in Hungary and in Transylvania, where liberty of
conscience was always more or less in vogue. Members of the
different sects were granted the right to acquire property and
to hold public office. The condition of the Jews was ameliorated;
they were allowed to attend the university and to practice medicine.
For more than a century and a half toleration had been entirely
unknown in Austria, and now when it was proclaimed Hussites,
Utraquists, and Bohemian Brothers immediately reappeared in

Bohemia. But Joseph II. had a fashion of himself determining what was meant by religious tolerance, and kept it within official bounds. A sect of Deists having been organized in Bohemia, he issued a decree of which one of the articles reads as follows: " If a man or a woman inscribes himself in the lists at the chancery of the circle as a deist, the person must immediately receive twenty-four blows from the stick, not because he is a deist, but because he pretends to be something about which he knows nothing." This conception of liberalism closely approaches that entertained by Peter the Great, and yet these incomplete and absurd measures dealt terrible blows at Catholicism. The Archbishop of Vienna and Pesth protested vigorously, as did the clergy in general, and Pope Pius VI., believing that he would be able to avert the dangers which threatened the Austrian church, took the unheard-of step of making a journey to Vienna. On his arrival he was lodged in the imperial castle and treated less as a guest than as a prisoner, not being allowed to communicate even with the Austrian bishops, and although received with the most enthusiastic veneration by the Viennese, he failed utterly to move the skepticism of the prince.

After the departure of the Pope, Joseph II. renewed his campaign against religious institutions with redoubled energy. He suppressed all the convents of the mendicant orders, even those of the Trinitarians, whose mission it was to ransom captives from barbarous peoples. He would no longer permit, said he, the sending of money abroad—he had provided for the interests of his subjects by treaties and the establishment of consuls. A still severer blow to the church was struck in the decree concerning marriage, published in January, 1783. It made marriage a purely civil contract, and allowed divorce. The emperor also deprived all foreign bishops of their property in Austria and annexed them to his dominions; at the same time he compelled the Austrian bishops to surrender all possessions which involved dealings with a foreign power. As an offset to all this he greatly increased the number of country curates and primary schools. Finally, however, the continual protests of the Holy See bore some fruit. The emperor journeyed to Rome, and in an interview with the Sovereign Pontiff conceded some relaxation in his attitude toward the church.

Josephinism, as this policy has been called, preceded by nearly a century the Kulturkampf of modern Germany. The universities were as harshly treated as the church upon which they had so long depended. They were deprived of their property and made state establishments. But Joseph II. was essentially utilitarian, and expressed little serious interest in education except for primary instruction. On the other hand, Austria owes to him many philanthropic establishments, such as hospitals and schools of medcine and surgery. In 1783 a German university was founded at Lemberg for the purpose of Germanizing Galicia. Everything that recalled a past hateful to the emperor was treated with merciless brutality. Thus the palace of Hradcany, at Prague, was turned into cavalry barracks, the objects of art which adorned it being abandoned to downright pillage. A list of the latter drawn up by his agents describes Titian's " Leda " thus, " Item, a naked woman bitten by a wild goose." Most of the legal measures of the emperor recall the excesses of the Reformation or those of the French Revolution.

An enemy of feudal rights, and an enthusiastic philanthropist, Joseph II. abolished serfdom in Moravia, Galicia, and Hungary, and granted to the emancipated serfs the complete ownership of the lands they cultivated. The powers of the *kreisämter* (officials of the circles) were augmented so as to completely destroy those of the lords. Everything was done to Germanize Bohemia and Hungary and to reduce them to the position of simple provinces. The whole of the Austrian possessions were divided into thirteen governments, and subdivided into circles with a captain (*kreishauptmann*) at the head of each. They were Galicia; Bohemia; Moravia and Silesia; Lower Austria; Inner Austria (Styria, Carinthia, and Carniola), the Tyrol; Outer Austria (possessions in southwestern Germany); Transylvania; Hungary; Croatia; Lombardy; Gorica, Gradiska, and Triest; and the Low Countries.

Diets were no longer convoked, and the privileges of the royal towns were entirely suppressed. Each town had a burgomaster, aided by two or three councilors, who were really state officials. Imbued with the theories of the physiocrats, Joseph II. undertook a thorough reorganization of the system of taxation. His ideal was to be able ultimately to obtain an average of forty per cent. upon all articles for the use of the treasury; until this could be accomplished he contented himself with establishing an impost levied on the income from land calculated upon the average yield of the last ten years. He decreed that thirty per cent. of the net produce of the land should be set aside for the use of the state, and neither nobles nor priests were to be exempt from payment. Two commissions of taxation were created, one for Hungary, the other for the rest of the monarchy, and a government survey at an enormous expense was undertaken.

The efforts of Joseph to enrich his people through commerce were especially directed to the Low Countries, which possessed excellent harbors for merchant vessels. His attempt to establish the free navigation of the Scheldt, in which he failed because of the combined resistance of the Dutch and the French, is worthy of note. He was more successful on the Danube, and the natural riches of Hungary—wheat, wine, and cattle—were sold with much greater profit than formerly. A road, called after him the *Via Josephina,* was constructed to unite the town of Karlstadt with the ports of Zeng and Bag, and the ports on the Adriatic, especially Fiume, were improved. Owing to the friendly terms with the Porte the emperor saved Austrian ships from the attacks of the Barbary corsairs, and reciprocal treaties of commerce were concluded with the emperor of Morocco, with Turkey, and with Russia. In these commercial enterprises Joseph was aided by the director of commerce, Count Zinzendorf, who had been governor of Triest. Trade with the Levant acquired a degree of prosperity previously unknown. Factories were even established in China and the Indies, and Joseph secured from Hyder Ali the possession of the Nicobar Islands. The time had passed when it could be said that the Viennese did not even know how to weave a pair of silk stockings. Numerous manufactories arose, and the emperor did his utmost to develop home industries and to restrict the importation of foreign commodities. He was anxious that the merchants of his dominions should no longer be merely " the agents of the English, French, and Dutch." A law of 1784 established a thorough-going protective system, by which the importation of foreign products was entirely forbidden. Private persons only could bring in articles of food on payment of heavy duties, in many cases amounting to sixty per cent. Even the importation of salted fish was forbidden, and in order to set a good example the emperor had all the foreign wine of his cellars distributed among the hospitals. This system naturally developed smuggling and informers, but it was rigorously enforced. It should be noted also that the greater part of the manufactories thus established were erected by foreigners—Swiss, French, and English—who carried off a large portion of the millions which the emperor was thus trying by force to keep in his dominions.

The legislative work which was done by Maria Theresa was continued by Joseph. He published a civil code, which formed the basis of that of Francis II., the code still in use in the Austrian dominions. His penal code bears the stamp of his own philosophical ideas. The cruel punishments retained by Maria Theresa for blasphemy and sorcery were abolished and the criminal courts were reorganized. The punishment of death was reserved for rebellion alone, and trials for witchcraft were abolished. But this code, so humane in some respects, still allowed imprisonment in irons for thirty years, the condemned being chained to the wall of the prison. Some penalties were absurd, others of Draconian severity. Criminals were condemned to be chained in pairs, whatever their rank, and forced to sweep the streets of Vienna or to drag the boats which came up the Danube.

In foreign affairs Joseph II. adhered faithfully to the policy of rounding out his territories, after the example of Frederick the Great. Hence, while seriously interesting himself in the Low Countries, he understood perfectly that they were a source of weakness rather than of strength for Austria. In 1785 he tried to exchange them for Bavaria, but Frederick the Great spoiled the plan, and the project had to be abandoned, the Prussian king uniting the leading German princes in an alliance known as the *Fürstenbund* against the ambitions of Austria in Germany. Four years later, in 1789, trouble broke out in Belgium. These provinces, wearied by the imperial despotism which attacked both the national liberties and the religious institutions dear to a population strongly Catholic, rose and proclaimed their independence. This movement was not suppressed till after the death of Joseph II. Against Turkey he took up again the traditional policy of Leopold I. and Charles VI., which involved a close alliance with Russia. In an interview with Catherine II., in 1786, he had formed a plan with the empress which involved the total expulsion of the Turks from Europe, and the partition of their lands between France, England, Austria, Spain, and Russia. When the war broke out between Turkey and Russia he took part without hesitation. He sent his troops against the Turks " in order to recover those lands which unfortunate circumstances had separated from his empire," and because he was determined not to allow the Russians to be the sole heirs of the ruins of Turkey. In a letter addressed to the king of Prussia he announced his intention of Germanizing his conquests.

About this time the people of the Balkan peninsula began to bestir themselves and to dream of their former independence. Signs of the coming Servian revolution appeared, and the first Servian national poet, Dositei Obradovic, greeted the Austrian army enthusiastically. His poem of "Servia Delivered" had a frontispiece representing Joseph II. breaking the chains of the southern Slavs. "Noble sovereign, Joseph the Great!" cried the poet, "extend thy protection to the Servian race. Turn thy beneficent face toward the people dear to thy ancestors, to wretched Servia and Bosnia, who suffer miseries without number. Glory of the world, illustrious monarch! restore to Bulgaria her boyars, to Servia her heroes of old time, and to Greece her Pindars!" But the hour for the emancipation of the Christians of the Danube had not yet sounded, and the Austria of Joseph II. was hardly the instrument fit for this purpose. It would have brought them only the doubtful benefit of Germanization. Nevertheless, extensive preparations for war were made —245,000 infantry and 36,000 cavalry were set on foot. But this vast army was not concentrated, but scattered from the Dniester to the Adriatic. Joseph II. himself took command, but becoming ill returned to Vienna, after having lost 45,000 men from disease and fighting. Loudon was left in command and carried on the war with vigor, capturing Belgrade September 29, 1789, and then pushing on into Bosnia.

But the emperor did not long survive these triumphs. The revolt in the Low Countries and the concessions which he was obliged to make to Hungary affected his generous but poorly balanced mind. He had been forced to humiliate himself before Pius VI., whom he had formerly defied, in order to induce him to exhort the Belgians to return to their obedience. To the Hungarians he restored their confiscated privileges, and sent the crown of St. Stephen to Pesth. On February 20, 1790, he died at the comparatively early age of forty-nine, and it is said he composed the following epitaph for his tomb: "Here lies a prince whose intentions were pure, but who was unfortunate in all his undertakings."

The word Josephinism has remained in the language of Austria to express those ideas which he endeavored to introduce, and which failed because of the tenacity of historical and religious prejudices. Nevertheless, his philanthropy and his love for his people, manifested in so many instances, have assured his name a memory of considerable popularity. In a Moravian village a monument is still standing on the spot where the emperor with his own hands guided the plow, to show his interest in agriculture. The peasants celebrate his good deeds even in our time, and for many years they refused to believe in his death.

Historians both of Hungary and Bohemia regard the reign of Joseph II. as a disastrous period for their respective countries. From the very outset he adopted a series of measures which deeply irritated the Magyars. With his philosophical ideas he looked upon the crown of St. Stephen as a bauble and the liberties of Hungary as the mythical relics of barbarism. The political customs of the country pleased him no more than its manners, and he took great delight in ridiculing the long beards and soft boots of the magnates. He never would be crowned nor would he appoint a palatine. He irritated the prelates by his measures against the convents, without satisfying the Protestants by his tolerance, because it was always tyrannical. He refused to unite Galicia to Hungary despite the fact that that province had been regained on the plea of the rights of the crown of St. Stephen. He began by concentrating all the business of the country in the Hungarian chancery and the council of lieutenancy established at Buda. In 1784 he ordered that the holy crown should be brought to him at Vienna to be kept in the imperial treasury. To confiscate this symbol of Hungarian independence was to the Magyars the same as an attempt to suppress the nation itself, and the affront was deeply resented. Up to that time the official language of the kingdom had been Latin, a neutral language between the various idioms used in Hungary. Joseph believed he was proving his liberal principles by substituting German, and the diet, which was no longer convoked, was unable to complain against this arbitrary and impolitic act. But the comitats gave utterance to bitter complaints. Joseph II. soon learned that it was not wise to attack the dearest prejudices of the nation, and the edict which proscribed the Hungarian language was the very act which gave the signal for its revival.

Magyar literature had existed for some time. Among the young Hungarians who composed the Hungarian guard of Maria

JOSEPH II

Theresa were several, notably the poet Bessenyi, who had cultivated the national poetry with much enthusiasm. Historical collections in the Hungarian language had been begun, and now the attacks of Joseph II. gave fresh vigor to the new movement. Other measures helped to excite the nation, and the spirit of patriotism increased. Joseph decreed a general census, which was to serve as a basis for recruiting the army. In this no distinction was made between classes, and the comitats were entirely disregarded. The dissatisfaction became serious, and troops had to be sent to protect the officers in charge of the work. It was still worse when Joseph proceeded to meddle with the comitats themselves. He suppressed their meetings and placed at their head an officer named by himself. The country was divided into ten circles, each governed by a captain (*kreishauptmann*), a name which is still hated in Hungary. These imprudent measures were to some extent atoned for by the liberal reforms which accompanied them, as, for example, the suppression of the feudal courts; but the Hungarians were too irritated to appreciate them. Moreover, the nobility was not sufficiently enlightened to share the ideas of the sovereign concerning taxes which made the land and not the peasant the basis of taxation, and the efforts of Joseph to obtain an accurate survey of the land met with much resistance. At the time of the Turkish campaign the comitats refused to supply men and provisions, and the issue of the campaign was not sufficiently brilliant to appeal to them on the basis of military prestige and glory. On all sides the convocation of the diet was demanded. Some of the comitats declared the demands of the king illegal; others suppressed the royal order, while the general discontent was so great that several opened negotiations with the king of Prussia. Joseph, ill and wearied of the ten years' struggle, yielded and in an ordinance of January, 1790, recalled all his reforms, and restored everything to the conditions of 1780, with the exception of his measures for religious tolerance and the improvement of the condition of the peasants.

In Bohemia likewise he refused to be crowned, and he insulted the Bohemians in their most cherished national feelings by turning the palace of his predecessors into a barracks. The religious tolerance which he granted was undoubtedly a blessing to the kingdom, but those of his subjects who would not join the official sects were severely persecuted. Deists were flogged and exiled into Hungary, and their children torn from them in order to be educated in the state religion, while the number of those who declared their adhesion to the Augsburg Confession did not exceed forty-five thousand. Entrance to the gymnasium was denied all those who did not possess a knowledge of German, and this language was substituted for Latin in the teaching of the faculty of philosophy at the University of Prague. The functions of the court of appeal at Prague were restricted to Bohemia, and no longer allowed to extend to Moravia, while Prague was deprived of its title of *residenzstadt,* which was henceforth reserved to Vienna. The functions of the diet were considerably diminished, the emperor forbidding the estates to dispose of their own fund or special budget without the sanction of the court chamber (*hofkammer*) of Vienna. In 1783 he suppressed the standing committee of the diet and transferred its authority to the central government. Indeed, the only one of their ancient rights the estates retained was that of voting taxes, although the manner in which they were to be raised was taken from their control. Finally, in 1788, Joseph announced to the diet that it was to limit its deliberations to matters submitted to it by the sovereign, and that it would be convoked only at his pleasure. The estates protested, and when the new patent concerning taxes was published, in February, 1789, the high chancellor of Bohemia and Austria, Count Rudolf Chotek, refused to sign it and sent in his resignation.

After so many attacks on its independence and its nationality, it might seem that Bohemia would have been entirely crushed as a separate nation, and that she was ready to become a German province of the Austrian state. But the moment of her deepest humiliation was precisely the moment of her regeneration. This revival was closely linked in certain of its phases to the general reaction which followed the death of Joseph II. Its first symptoms appeared almost directly after the coronation of his successor. " The oppression of Joseph II.," says Count Caspar Sternberg in his memoirs, " has awakened the spirit of nationalism which had slept for a long time. The emperor, who wished to centralize everything, desired also to suppress the Bohemian language, but no people would allow the palladium of its national existence to be snatched from it. At the coronation all those who speak Czech might be heard using that language in the very corridors of the palace." The Czechs themselves date the new birth of their na-

JOSEPH II   275

tionality from the reign of Joseph II. Bohemia owes to this prince only one benefit—the foundation of the Royal Society of Sciences, which flourishes to-day, and which from its very beginning became the center of those historical researches which contributed so powerfully to the revival of Slavism in Bohemia.

The new sovereign, Leopold II., who reigned only two years, from 1790 to 1792, had been serving in Tuscany an apprenticeship in the art of governing since 1765, and the wisdom of his administration, which was both intelligent and paternal, had rightly called forth the praises of economists and philosophers. On his accession he yielded gracefully to the violent reaction already setting in against the policy of his brother. He began by declaring that he considered the estates of the provinces as the pillars of the monarchy, that he would restore their privileges, and that he would labor hard with them to bring the interests of the people into harmony with those of the sovereign. He suppressed those measures of Joseph II. which had caused most irritation, suspended the system of taxation which held the commune responsible for the taxes of all the inhabitants, opened the frontiers to foreign products, and redressed many of the real grievances of the Bohemians and Hungarians. He restored many of their most important rights to the clergy, especially those of regulating the liturgy, holding synods with the sanction of the government, and organizing the administration of the parishes. On the other hand he retained the measures which prohibited the publication of bulls without the royal sanction, which deprived the bishops of the administration of the funds of the dioceses, and which subjected ecclesiastics to the jurisdiction of the ordinary courts. This policy satisfied and disarmed the clergy.

But Leopold II. was less fortunate in his dealings with the revolted Netherlands. He made the most liberal promises, offering them complete amnesty, and promising no longer to intrust public office to strangers, to give the control of the army to the estates, and to make no law without their consent. They refused to yield, and he was obliged to have recourse to arms. An army of 30,000 men was brought together in Luxemburg and sent into the Netherlands. Namur and Brussels were soon taken, and Belgium was reconquered, only to become in a few years the battlefield for the struggle against the French Revolution.

In the meantime the war against Turkey continued. The success of the Austrian arms made England, and especially Prussia, uneasy. The latter mobilized an army on the borders of Silesia and encouraged the malcontents of the Low Countries. But in spite of this Leopold entered into negotiations with the king of Prussia concerning the restoration of conquests on the Danube by Austria and Russia, for compensation to be found at the expense of Poland, Prussia to get Thorn and Danzig. Old Kaunitz indignantly rejecting these insolent proposals, a congress met at Reichenbach, in 1790, in which Prussia, Austria, England, and Holland were represented. The congress ended in the Treaty of Sistova, by which Austria surrendered her conquests, retaining only Orsova, and the Unna district on the borders of Croatia, and agreed not to support Russia in any war which might arise between her and the Porte. Thus Austria once more gave up the substance for the shadow; she sacrificed by this agreement the territory which would have consolidated her real frontiers, in order to preserve the Belgian provinces which were not only distant and unruly, but a constant temptation to the greed of France.

It would have been impossible for Austria to remain indifferent to the progress of the French Revolution. As emperor, Leopold was under obligation to defend the feudal rights of the German princes in Alsace, Franche-Comté, and Lorraine, which were suppressed by the National Assembly, and as the brother-in-law of Louis XVI., he witnessed with anxiety the progress of democracy and the decline of the royal authority. In July, 1791, he published a circular, dated from Padua, calling upon all the sovereigns of Europe to intervene in favor of the king of France against his revolted subjects. A little later he issued, with Frederick William II. of Prussia, the celebrated Declaration of Pilnitz, in which the two sovereigns agree to employ the most effectual means " to place the king of France in a position to establish with absolute freedom the basis of a monarchical form of government, which shall at once maintain the rights of sovereigns and promote the welfare of the French nation." In February, 1792, Leopold concluded a definite alliance with Prussia in regard to their relations with France. On March 1 he died unexpectedly, leaving to his son, Francis II., the inheritance of the most formidable struggle which the Austrian state had ever had to maintain. On April 20, 1792, France declared war on " the king of Bohemia and Hungary."

PART V

AUSTRIA DURING THE REVOLUTIONARY AND NAPOLEONIC ERAS. 1792-1815

Chapter XXIII

FRANCIS II AND THE WARS AGAINST THE REVOLUTION. 1792-1804

A BRIEF survey of the Austrian monarchy at the opening of the great European war in which she played so conspicuous a part is essential. "If we omit Tuscany and Modena," says M. Himly, "territories over which the younger branches of the house of Hapsburg were already reigning, or expecting to reign, the empire covered an area of 11,600 square leagues (German) and numbered about 24,000,000 inhabitants. Geographically they fell naturally into two parts of about equal extent; that portion which belonged more or less completely to the empire had a population of over 10,500,000, and occupied about 86,000 square miles; the provinces outside of the empire had a little less than 14,000,000, spread out over nearly 164,000 square miles. Each of these two great divisions consisted of three groups of countries which were themselves historically and politically distinct. On the one side were the two circles of Austria and of Burgundy, and the territories of the crown of Bohemia; on the other the Polish, Hungarian, and Italian possessions.

The kingdom of St. Stephen, that is to say, of Hungary, with the kingdoms of Croatia, Slavonia, Hungarian Dalmatia, and Transylvania, was estimated at about 125,800 square miles and at 9,100,000 souls; the kingdom of Bohemia, with Moravia and Silesia, had 4,300,000 inhabitants spread over 31,000 square miles, while Galicia and Bukovina had about 3,300,000 on about 33,200 square miles.

Milan and Mantua, with the imperial fiefs of Liguria, were reckoned at about 4700 square miles and 1,350,000 inhabitants, and the Austrian Low Countries at 2,000,000 on 10,100 square miles. A sixth group comprised the imperial domains, properly so-called —that is, the circle of Austria and a number of minor possessions in Suabia and the Lower Rhine; together these measured about

45,000 square miles and comprised in the neighborhood of 4,300,000 inhabitants.

In actual size the Austrian monarchy came next to Russia and France in 1792. It was somewhat larger than the present Austrian empire, but it was so scattered as to be an easy prey to an enemy. Bohemia, Galicia, Hungary, and the hereditary states formed a compact group, but the Milanese and the Mantuan districts were separated from it by Venetia. The Breisgau and Austrian Suabia were practically surrounded by the innumerable states of Suabia, while Belgium was entirely isolated from the other provinces, and her people were eager to throw off the foreign yoke. It was upon these outlying positions that the effect of the war was sure to be felt first.

The Austrian army at this time consisted of 270,000 men; there were 77 regiments of infantry, 39 of which were furnished by the German possessions and by those Slav lands not included in Hungary, 11 by Hungary and Transylvania, 5 by the Low Countries, 2 by Italy, and 17 by the military frontiers. Garrisons were supplied by two regiments set apart for that purpose, and there were two regiments of artillery. The army was recruited by a system of conscription established by Joseph II. in all his states except in the Tyrol, the Low Countries, and Hungary. In the latter country the emperor was offered in case of need the *insurrection* and special levies.

The prince who had to take so prominent a part in the long struggle of this period had reached the age of twenty-four at his accession. He had been brought up in Tuscany with Leopold, and had later lived at the court of Joseph II., who did his utmost to inculcate his own ideas of reform into him. During the short reign of Leopold II. he had seen how good sense and patriotic feeling had reacted against the excesses of Josephinism, and a peaceful reign would perhaps have given him the opportunity of displaying those worthy bourgeois characteristics with which nature had endowed him. But in the prolonged struggle against the Revolution he became gradually gloomy and despotic.

When the war broke out Francis II. had been crowned at Buda and at Prague, but he had not yet been elected emperor. Accordingly the French declared war against the king of Bohemia and Hungary. They first invaded Belgium, and after the battle of Jemmappes on November 6, 1792, the Austrian Low Countries as

FRANCIS II 281

far as Luxemberg fell into their hands. In the following spring
the Austrian victory at Neerwinden opened France to the imperialists for a short time. But Austria's ally, Prussia, gave but
a lukewarm support, for she was more interested in the second
partition of Poland in 1793, and in which Austria failed to share
because of the war with the French republic. Finally, in June of
1794, as a result of the battle of Fleurus the Netherlands were
definitely lost to Austria.

The execution of Louis XVI. was an act of defiance to the
kings of Europe, and the execution of Marie Antoinette a challenge

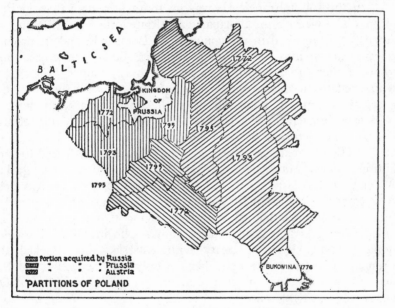

PARTITIONS OF POLAND

to the house of Austria in particular. But Francis II. was neither
able to rescue nor avenge the unfortunate sister of his father. For
in 1795 his ally, the king of Prussia, signed the Treaty of Paris
with the French, and withdrew from the war, and he was reduced
to seek compensation for the loss of the Low Countries in what
remained of unhappy Poland. With Prussia and Russia the third
partition was agreed upon, and Austria secured the palatinates of
Sandomir and Lublin, together with some portions of Cracow,
Masovia, Podlachia, and Brest, as far as the junction of the
Bug with the Vistula. This territory was given the official name
of Western Galicia. The reasons given for this new desmem-

berment of Poland were poor enough. Poland, it was urged, had become the seat of anarchical and revolutionary ideas which threatened to become dangerous to the adjacent countries, and since Austria could not prevent the seizure of Polish territory by the other two great neighboring powers, it became her duty to look after her own interests. No pretended historical right was invoked, as in the first partition, and expediency alone was urged in extenuation of this inglorious conquest. By this partition Austria acquired about 1,100,000 inhabitants and 1800 square miles of territory.

In the south Francis II. was no more fortunate than in Belgium. The victories of Bonaparte at Montenotte and Millesimo, in April, 1796, resulted in the conquest of Lombardy and its prompt reorganization into the Cisalpine republic, Bonaparte proclaiming to the Italians that he was waging war only against "the tyrant who tried to enslave them." Who would have said then that the greatest tyrant of them all was the future father-in-law of Napoleon himself? The troops of Francis made heroic efforts to resist the victorious march of the armies of France, but without avail. His commander, Wurmser, was defeated and forced to shut himself up in Mantua, and after the defeat of the Hungarian Alvinzy at Arcola and Rivoli, he was forced to capitulate, in February, 1797. The road to Vienna lay open. Just at this moment the aristocratic republic of Venice, believing that it could save its independence and guarantee itself against the invasion of revolutionary ideas, signed a treaty with Austria, and attacked the French. This imprudence cost her not only her liberty, but reduced her to a servitude which formed one of the saddest episodes of the history of the next century.

After the capitulation of Mantua, Francis, realizing that his southern territories were in danger of being overrun by the French, suddenly recalled from the army of the Rhine the ablest of his generals, the Archduke Charles, to oppose the victorious French. In the Tyrol and in Bohemia levies en masse were ordered, and the insurrection was voted by Hungary. The archduke did all in his power to reorganize the Austrian army, and took up a position behind the Tagliamento in order to defend Triest, but Massena had obtained possession of the Col de Tarvis, over which the main road from Verona to Venice passes. This gave him the key to the passage of the Alps, and Vienna was in great danger. But

FRANCIS II 283

the patriotism of the luxurious city rose to the occasion. The entire population took up arms, the fortifications were repaired, and the war, which had at first been only one of cabinets and of principals, became, with the approach of the enemy, a national struggle. Evidently it would be dangerous for Napoleon to venture into a country so deeply aroused, without having effected a junction with the armies on the Rhine. He opened negotiations, and an armistice was agreed upon, followed by preliminaries of peace, in which Austria ceded to France Belgium and her Italian possessions on the right bank of the Oglio, and received in exchange a part of the Venetian possessions situated on the Adriatic. Venice obtained Romagna, Bologna, and Ferrara as compensation.

It was while these negotiations were being conducted that the anti-French feeling broke out in the republic of Venice. At the news of *les Paques Veronaises* the French troops again invaded Venetia and besieged the city of the doges, which dared not, or knew not how, to defend itself, even though protected by the sea, against generals who had not a single vessel at their disposal. In May Venice was occupied by the French, and a tree of liberty was planted. A few months later, in November, 1797, definitive peace was signed at Campo Formio. Austria renewed her concessions and recognized the Cisalpine republic. France retained the Ionian Islands and the Venetian possessions in Albania, Austria receiving as compensation the territories of Venice and her territory as far as the Adige. The duke of Modena, who had been dispossessed, was to be indemnified for the loss of his duchy by the cession of the Breisgau, which Francis II. gave up to him. In the secret articles of this treaty the emperor engaged himself to help France in the acquisition of the left bank of the Rhine, demanding in exchange the latter's good offices in the acquisition of Salzburg and that part of Bavaria situated between the Inn and the Salza, which intercepted the communication with Tyrol. One of the consequences of this treaty was the setting at liberty of Lafayette, who had been a prisoner at Olmütz since 1792.

On the whole Austria came out of this war very fortunately, considering her defeats. She had held her own against France even after Prussia had withdrawn from the struggle; she was less weakened by the loss of the Low Countries than strengthened by the acquisition of Venice and Dalmatia. Her new territories contained 16,625 square miles and about 3,000,000 inhabitants, and although the French, before evacuating Venice, had destroyed the fleet of the republic, the maritime importance of the new acquisition was very great. The Adriatic became almost wholly an Austrian sea, and the Dalmatians were skilled mariners and brave soldiers. This province, which had formerly been so much coveted by the kings of Hungary, now fell to the Hapsburgs without their having struck a blow for its conquest. From this time forward it shared the fate of Austria. It had been a Roman province, colonized by the Slavs, and formed a part of the kingdom of Croatia. In the tenth century the Venetians began its conquest, which was not completed until the end of the fifteenth, and even then the interior of Dalmatia continued a part of Croatia till it fell into the hands of the Turks. Thanks to Venetian colonization, the Slav towns took on a distinctly Italian character, which they retain even to-day. The government was exclusively in the hands of the Venetians and the native population was both pillaged and persecuted. A decree of the republic forbade the marriage of Venetians with Slav women.

The administration of the province had been intrusted to a *proveditore,* who was always a Venetian senator, and who held office for three years. The civil, judicial, and military power was exercised by him, and he resided at Zara. The country was divided into twenty-two circles, all governed by Venetian nobles, whose administration was both servile and corrupt. The army was composed of natives, but all the officers were Venetians. Little was done for public instruction; Venice was not anxious to develop an independent civilization, and directed her efforts rather toward Italianizing her Slav subjects. Nevertheless, in spite of this Italian influence, a national literature struggled into existence, though it found a real home only in Ragusa, which continued throughout to maintain a position of independence owing to the protection of the Porte.

The Treaty of Campo Formio did not end the work of Austrian diplomacy. She sent three representatives to the congress of Rastadt, where the affairs of Germany were still to be arranged. After the congress, which closed in April, 1799, two of the French representatives were murdered by Austrian hussars, and this made war almost inevitable. Another circumstance which complicated the situation and estranged the two countries was the fact that Bernadotte, the French ambassador in Vienna, assumed an attitude altogether unlikely to conciliate a population irritated by recent defeats. He even presumed to attempt to prevent the celebration of a military fête in the capital, and caused the tricolor flag to be displayed from the balcony of his hotel, the flag of that revolution which had beheaded Marie Antoinette. It was torn down by an enraged populace, and Bernadotte demanded his passports. The French asked for an apology, which Austria refused, and it became apparent that a new conflict was imminent. In March, 1799, the Directory declared war. Cobenzl, who had just succeeded Thugut as minister of foreign affairs, bent every energy to obtain allies. The second coalition was formed with Russia, England, Portugal, Naples, Turkey, and Austria all in league against France. The struggle began simultaneously in southern Germany, Switzerland, and Italy. The coalition had brought together a large force of men. The victories of Archduke Charles and Mélas, which continued after the assumption of the supreme command by the Russian general, Suvarov, need not be related. The return of Napoleon to Italy brought victory again to the standard of France. Marengo stopped the onward march of Mélas, in June, 1800, and after the capitulation of Alessandria he was forced to fall back upon the Mincio. In western Germany Moreau was also successful against his adversary Kray, and Austria, worn out by the useless struggle, consented to peace. But her allies urged her to continue the struggle. The defeated generals were relieved of their command and others appointed, but the victories of the French continued. At Hohenlinden, in December, 1800, they were entirely victorious, and another cruel blow was struck to the Austrian arms. The Archduke Charles, who had been in retirement since his victories of the previous year, again assumed command to save the Austrian cause. But he found only the ruins of the army which he had recently led to victory. The French were marching on Vienna, and it was necessary to yield. On December 25 an armistice was concluded, tracing a line of demarkation. Cobenzl went to Lunéville, where he negotiated the terms of peace with Joseph Bonaparte.

The terms of the Peace of Lunéville were very like those of the Treaty of Campo Formio. Francis II. consented to recognize the Batavian, Helvetian, Cisalpine and Ligurian republics, and the surrender to France of the ancient Hapsburg possessions on the left bank of the Rhine, along with other minor territories. The Archduke Ferdinand II. exchanged Tuscany for the new electorate of

Salzburg, the formation of which cost the dynasty of Hapsburg nearly a million people.

Nor had Francis II. succeeded in guaranteeing the integrity of Germany. France held the left bank of the Rhine, and the dispossessed princes turned toward Paris to urge their claims for indemnity. By the secularization of ecclesiastical states the clerical princes who had been the most faithful supporters of the Hapsburg dynasty had disappeared.

Perhaps the most important result of this extended struggle is the fact that it gave rise among the peoples of Austria, and especially in her army, to a real feeling for the unity of the monarchy. Her soldiers, drawn from so many different nations, had fought side by side for ten years, and a feeling of brotherhood was naturally engendered. Corps of officers grew up embodying in their organization the idea of one fatherland. In 1848 a Viennese poet wrote to Radetzky, " It is in the camps of your army that Austria is to be found." Even in 1800 this was practically true. As a matter of fact the Austrian monarchy was essentially a military one. It was the army which held the various parts of this bizarre state together.

In the struggle against the French Revolution the nobility of the different provinces vied with each other in their enthusiasm; Hungary twice voted the *insurrection.* In 1796 and 1797 the Tyrolese and the inhabitants of Lower Austria took up arms *en masse.* In Bohemia the militia of the country was organized in 1796, and Moravia and Silesia raised a corps of chasseurs in 1800. During a visit of the Archduke Charles in Bohemia a special legion was raised as a consequence of the enthusiasm he inspired.

The direction of military affairs continued in the hands of the Council of War (*hofkriegsrath*). It consisted partly of officers and partly of civilians, and sat at Vienna, but despite the zeal of its members it rendered very mediocre services. It wished to conduct military operations from a government office. In the campaign of 1799 Suvarov declined to communicate his plans to it. In 1801 the emperor made the Archduke Charles its president, and the year following the unlimited military service was reduced to fourteen years.

The direction of foreign affairs during almost all of this stormy period was in the hands of the famous Thugut. Kaunitz, who had conducted the affairs of the foreign chancery for three reigns, and who had the satisfaction of effecting a reconciliation between the two hostile courts of Versailles and Vienna, had retired in 1796. Thugut, who had had an extended career in the foreign service, especially in connection with the early years of the French Revolution, was throughout a bitter opponent of the French republic, and his dismissal was one of the conditions insisted upon by France in the secret clauses of the Treaty of Campo Formio. In 1800 he, too, retired to private life. He was succeeded by Joseph Cobenzl, who had filled the post of Austrian ambassador at Berlin and St. Petersburg, and by his clever diplomacy had succeeded in keeping up the most cordial relations between Austria and Russia for sixteen years. After bringing about the Peace of Lunéville he continued at the head of foreign affairs till 1805, conducting the affairs of his office like a clever courtier rather than a great statesman.

At home the struggle between the partisans and opponents of Josephinism still continued, but the foreign wars diverted attention from the ideas of reform. A special ministry for finance for Galicia and a new commission of public instruction had been appointed, but no general plan of reform was adopted. We may judge of the general confusion existing at this time from an extract from a memorandum addressed to the emperor by Count Chotek: "The reign of your majesty," he says, "is marked by a series of mutations; a special department (*hofstelle*) has been made of the police; the chamber of accounts established in 1761 has been dissolved; the old distinction between the different nationalities has again been recognized, and expediency has been allowed, first to direct politics, then to control the state. A new commission of instruction has been created, and the two legislative commissions which formerly existed have been made into one, besides many other changes which have been made since the Treaty of Campo Formio. The management of the finances has been taken from the control of the united *Hofstelle,* and Count Saurau has been appointed president of the court chamber and minister of finance. The supreme control of justice has been vested in the Austro-Bohemian chancery, and a special department created for Galicia, which controls both judicial and political matters. These two changes evidently defeat their object; on the one hand two new departments are created for provinces whose constitution is the same, on the other a minister is overburdened with duties

absolutely heterogeneous. In 1801, after Count Saurau was appointed to a new office, a ministry or board of control for the
bank and a secret board of credit were created, and the finances
once more joined to the department of political affairs. There
was only one minister for the two departments of justice and
political matters. As head of the ministry he had control of justice,
and in his capacity as minister controlled the finances, an amount
of work beyond the capacity of any man. And this system of administering the finances was adopted at the very moment when their
precarious condition demanded central and united control.

"As soon as peace was restored," continues Chotek, "the
emperor tried to establish a more permanent organization. He
instituted a central bureau (*Conferenzministerium*), in which all
the branches of the administration should meet, and from that time
onward the home, foreign, and military affairs of the monarchy
have been under a common direction. . . . In civil matters
it was necessary to make the entire country immediately dependent
upon one minister. It was necessary to determine the power of
each official, from the village magistrate to the minister, in such
a way that it would be impossible for any one of them to go
beyond the limits of his authority, and that each should know
precisely over what matters he had jurisdiction, and what must
be referred to the higher officials, so that in the end the emperor
should always be in a position to obtain complete knowledge on
important matters without being troubled with useless details.
But this result has not been attained. The internal administration has been badly organized. Matters of small importance
are continually brought to the attention of the emperor and the
conference. The proposals that have been made have gone no further than fragmentary attempts at legislature and temporary measures concerning the finances and other matters. No attempt has
been made to organize the departments; to study the wants of the
estates as a whole, or the means of satisfying those wants; to
improve the condition of the country by trade and commerce, or
to found really useful schools. In these matters there has been
none of that unity of action for which the *Conferenzministerium*
was created." What Count Chotek asked for, since popular parliamentary government was not to be had, was a council of ministers similar to that now existing in all European countries. But
the times were too troublesome for these reforms.

Eight years of war could not fail to exhaust the finances of the empire, considering the poverty of Austria-Hungary at that time. The emperor mortgaged his private estates in order to obtain money; provinces and corporations, and even private persons, vied with each other in their zeal and their sacrifices. All sorts of expedients were resorted to; the amount of paper money was increased, forced loans were raised, the duties on merchandise were maintained at a percentage which was absolutely intolerable to trade, and the protective system continued in full force with all its abuses. Internal freedom of trade, which Joseph II. had introduced, was destroyed, and a line of custom-houses was once more established between Hungary and the rest of the Austrian dominions.

The construction of roads was pushed on with great activity, especially in Carniola, Croatia, Bohemia, and Moravia, and a canal was made between the Danube and the Theiss. The emperor was proud of his fondness for agriculture, and founded several special schools for its study. He took great pains to develop the rural economy of Galicia, where, it must be owned, Polish neglect had left much to be done. In 1799 serfdom was abolished, and gradually some degree of order was introduced into that province. Many charitable institutions were founded in this reign.

The work of codification, which had been begun in the reign of Maria Theresa, was continued and additional volumes of the code were published. Unfortunately, Francis II. did nothing for public instruction; he had neither the time nor the wish to do so. The dread lest the ideas of the French Revolution should make their way into Austria led him to apply to freedom of thought a prohibitive system even more strict than that which weighed so heavily on trade. The censorship of the press was taken out of the hands of the professors to be placed in those of the police, and a tax on printed matter was introduced. In many ways the reign of Francis II. was the opposite of that of Joseph II. In his horror of liberal ideas, Francis believed that he could not combat them better than by strengthening religious institutions and by increasing the influence of the clergy. Nevertheless he maintained the laws providing for religious toleration. A commission was appointed in 1795 to inquire into the condition of education, but the alterations proposed by it were not very liberal in spirit and based solely on the principle of expediency.

Chapter XXIV

FRANCIS II AND THE WARS AGAINST NAPOLEON. 1804-1815

A FTER the Peace of Lunéville the house of Hapsburg-Lorraine was bereft of all its German possessions except the archduchy of Austria, and the authority of the emperor in the German states existed only in theory. It possessed no other power save that derived from its own dominions. These were henceforth divided into five groups, the hereditary provinces, the kingdom of Bohemia, the kingdom of Hungary, Galicia, and Venetia. The first three belonged to the emperor by hereditary right or by contract mutually agreed to; the last two had been recently conquered, and were retained by force. It was therefore only natural that the old titles of archduke of Austria, of king of Bohemia and of Hungary, should be insufficient for the owner of so many possessions, and Francis II. desired to adopt a title that would both impress Europe and be at the same time more in accord with the actual facts. The Hapsburgs had long been known as the house of Austria, and their territory, although far from being homogeneous, had been definitely grouped around the dynasty by the Pragmatic Sanction. The Magyars had accepted the principle of hereditary succession and Bohemia, exhausted by long struggle, seemed pacified.

Accordingly after the establishment of the imperial dignity in France by Napoleon, Francis II. decided to adopt the title of Emperor of Austria. A letter to the people announced his decision in the following paragraph:

" Although we have been by the grace of God and the choice of the electors of the Romano-German empire raised to such a degree of splendor as leaves us no title to desire, nevertheless our solicitude as ruler of the house of Austria induces us to strive for the maintenance of complete equality between our imperial title and hereditary dignity and those of the other sovereigns and most illustrious powers of Europe, in a manner befitting the ancient splendor of our house and the greatness and independence of our dominions. Therefore we claim for the house of Austria, after the example of the imperial court of Russia in the last century, and of the new sovereign of France, an hereditary imperial title for its own states. And we have determined, after mature deliberation, to take solemnly for ourselves and our successors for all our kingdoms and lands the hereditary title of emperor of Austria, after the name of our house. At the same time we declare that each of our kingdoms, principalities, and provinces shall nevertheless preserve its title, constitution, and privileges."

This measure was the reward of long, patient work on the part of the house of Austria, but in reality it made no change in the condition of any of the provinces. Even Francis II., and his successor, Ferdinand IV., were still crowned kings of Bohemia and Hungary, and renewed the engagements to these countries, while no Austrian sovereign has ever been crowned emperor of Austria.

By the foreign courts the new title was recognized without demur. Francis II. made no attempt to break the ties which bound some of his states to Germany; indeed, he solemnly declared to the German diet that he would not do so. Nor did the assumption of the new imperial title make any great impression on the people, who had been accustomed to seeing the title of emperor joined to that of king on all public documents. Nevertheless, by thus declaring the historical unity of the Austrian realms, Francis added to the Pragmatic Sanction a corollary that Charles VI. would not have ventured to add in the eighteenth century.

At the time of his assumption of the imperial title Francis II. was thirty-six years old, but events had aged him before his time; he had become timid and suspicious. Among the sciences he understood only natural science, and of the arts only music, the one great art that has really flourished in Austria. The philosophical ideas of the eighteenth century were unknown to him. His main strength lay in that persistent patience which is regarded as the chief characteristic of the Hapsburgs. He affected that patriarchal mode of life and popularity not infrequently combined with ideas of absolutism and love of tyrannical power. He wished to be the father of his people, but a father who would not willingly allow his children to reason for themselves. He meant to exercise unlimited power, and the great trials he met with only served to confirm him in his ideas of absolutism. He took for his motto the words " *Justitia regnorum fundamentum*," but he explained its meaning after his own fashion. The only power in the state outside of the emperor was that bureaucracy which had been made the motive power of all government by Joseph II. The Hungarians retained their independence, but Bohemia had not yet awakened, and the Austrians prided themselves on seeing absolutism incarnate in their emperor. " *Es giebt nur ein Kaiserstadt, es giebt nur ein Wien.*" " There is only one imperial city, there is only one Vienna." This popular saying flattered the self-love of the Viennese just as their music lulled their indolent minds to sleep.

From 1801 to 1805 foreign affairs were conducted by the vice chancellor, Louis Cobenzl. He was, as we have seen, a politician of the old school, tricky and courteous, but by no means so able as the young ambassadors Stahrenberg, Metternich, and Stadion, who served under him. After 1803 he secured the services of Frederick Gentz, the ablest political writer of Germany, and one of the most formidable antagonists of German unity. Gentz was a Silesian, born after the conquest of that province by Prussia, and had studied at the University of Königsberg. Owing to the miserable state of public education and the antagonism of her various nationalities, Austria could rarely find the men she needed among her own subjects, and was forced to seek them abroad—a curious phenomenon, seen even in our own day, when Count Beust was called from Dresden to reconstruct the empire after Sadowa. The ministry of Cobenzl contained no men of mark, save perhaps the Archduke Charles. After 1801 he was field marshal and president of the council of war. He had introduced many reforms and enjoyed a widespread popularity throughout Austria, being the only general who could oppose Napoleon with any chance of success.

The relations between Austria and France since 1801, in appearance at least, had become quite cordial. The Austrian ambassador at Paris showed marked attentions to the new emperor, and at Vienna a saying of Cobenzl's was frequently heard, " The monarchs of Europe have a colleague in Napoleon for whom they need not blush." In reality, however, the heir of the revolution could not be other than the enemy of Austria, and Bonaparte inspired in the court and the nobility a hatred which could only result in renewed hostilities. Hence England and Russia had no difficulty in drawing Austria into a new alliance for the purpose of curbing the aggression of France. In case of success she was to receive an extension of frontier to the Po and the Adda, Salzburg, and the reëstablishment of the *secundo genitur* in Tuscany, while England promised to pay one million, two hundred and fifty thousand pounds sterling for every hundred thousand men Austria would place under arms. On these conditions Austria furnished three hundred and thirty-five thousand men. The Archduke Charles opposed the idea of fighting Napoleon, intoxicated by his recent successes, and resigned his presidency of the council of war.

The plan of campaign involved the simultaneous attack of the French by three armies, one in Italy, one in the Tyrol, and one in Bavaria. The war was popular in Vienna. "It is touching," writes Gentz, "to see the good feeling which animates the entire country; this time our cause is so just, so holy, that no one dares murmur; all feel that the present situation cannot last." The Archduke Charles took command of the army of Italy, the Archduke John that of the Tyrol, while the emperor in person commanded the army of Germany, leaving its direction to General Mack. The latter's disastrous capitulation to Napoleon at Ulm on October 17, 1805, with his entire army, is well known. It was a terrible blow for Austria. Summoned before a council of war, Mack was relieved of his command and condemned to ten years' imprisonment. "The blow which has overwhelmed us," writes Gentz, " is one of those which crushes heart and mind." The emperor tried hard to keep up courage. In a manifesto of October 28 he said: " The Austrian monarchy has always risen triumphant from every misfortune that has befallen it in times past. Its strength is still unconquered, and in the hearts of the brave men for whom I fight the old spirit of patriotism still lives." Negotiations were entered into with Prussia in the hope of gaining her mediation, and perhaps her assistance, but other reverses still awaited Austria. In Italy the Archduke Charles had accepted the command of the troops who were to oppose the army of Massena, and, although successful, the capitulation of Mack necessitated his recall to help the threatened German provinces. With 24,000 troops he pushed northward into Hungary by way of Styria, abandoning the Tyrol to Ney.

In the meantime the French had occupied Vienna, having entered it on November 13. Napoleon took up his headquarters at Schönbrunn, where he received the deputation from the capital, which begged him to spare their city and presented him with a serv-

ice of plate, an act of servility that did not save them from a heavy
fine and the usual requisitions of war. It was the first time since
the days of Mathias Corvinus that a conqueror had entered Vienna.
Meanwhile the emperor of Austria had joined the Russian forces
under Alexander in Moravia. The united armies numbered nearly
90,000. Napoleon had about 65,000 men to meet this force, and on
December 2, 1805, administered a crushing defeat at Austerlitz.
This battle decided the fate of the campaign.

Hostilities ceased and a definite peace was signed at Presburg on December 26, 1805. Austria recognized all the changes
made by France in the Italian peninsula, and ceded to the kingdom
of Italy, Venetia, Istria, and Dalmatia. The new kingdoms of
Bavaria and Würtemberg were increased at the expense of Austria.
Only the duchy of Salzburg fell to Austria as a compensation for her
many losses, and most of this she has retained ever since. The
monarchy lost the Tyrol, with its brave and loyal inhabitants, and
the forelands of the Alps, which had assured Austrian influence in
Germany, all her possessions on the Rhine, in the Black Forest, and
on the upper Danube, altogether nearly three million people. She
no longer touched Switzerland or Italy, ceased to be a maritime
power, and was obliged to pay an indemnity of forty millions, at a
time when her treasury was already exhausted.

In January, 1806, the Emperor Francis returned to the capital,
where he was enthusiastically received, and the Viennese returned
to their luxurious and easy life, for to console them in their misfortunes had they not the greatest musicians in the world in their
Haydn, Beethoven, Salieri, and Clementi?

Following closely on the defeat of the allies, Napoleon organized Bavaria, Würtemberg, Baden, and eleven other states into the
Confederation of the Rhine, and on August 1, 1806, these states
notified the diet at Ratisbon that they regarded the empire as dissolved. The rôle of Austria in Germany seemed to have come to
an end, and, in recognition of the fact, Francis, on August 6, 1806,
publicly declared that he resigned the imperial throne and absolved
all the officials of the empire from their allegiance. Thus the
scepter of Charlemagne fell from the hands of the dynasty which
had held it with but one slight interruption since 1438. It was
naturally not surrendered without regret. For even though
Francis ruled over more than fifteen millions of non-German subjects, his education had been purely German, and to maintain the

FRANCIS II   295

domination of the Hapsburg house in Suabia and on the banks of the Rhine, the Scheldt, and the Po was a cherished ideal. To their German ambitions and sympathies they had on more than one occasion sacrificed their duties and obligations to the crowns of St. Vacslav and St. Stephen.

Hence, notwithstanding the end of the Holy Roman Empire, all the aspirations of the Austrian government continued to turn toward Germany and Italy. It was, moreover, very difficult for Austria to remain neutral and disinterested in the face of the incessant attempts of Napoleon to control Europe. Most of the court nobility held estates in Germany, and thought only of retaining them. Under these circumstances the relations between Napoleon and Metternich at Paris became very much strained. Still Austria dared not venture to support Prussia and Russia in the war which broke out in 1806. But Napoleon did not feel any gratitude to her for that. He properly divined the hostile intentions of Francis II. " What would your sovereign have? " he brusquely demanded of Metternich at a reception in August, 1808. " He would have his envoy respected," dryly replied the diplomat. When the Austrian General Vincent brought a letter of congratulation to the emperor at Erfurt from Francis, the latter roughly reminded him that he had been in a position to destroy Austria entirely, and that she owed her continued existence to his indulgence. The basis for this irritation of Napoleon lay in the Austrian armaments.

The Archduke Charles had set himself vigorously to increase the efficiency and morale of the troops, and to fortify the frontier on the German side. He abolished corporal punishment in the army, and organized a provincial militia as a reserve for the regular army. This *Landwehr* drilled on holidays and assembled in corps once a month. The diet of Bohemia voted a million and a half florins for the support of this militia, while the diet of Hungary made like sacrifices. At the same times measures were taken to provoke a national uprising. Indeed in all the provinces of the monarchy the national enthusiasm was marked. One warlike meeting succeeded another; Arndt and Körner as well as other poets of less note wrote patriotic hymns, which became immediately popular, as, for example, the poem by Collin, which is a sort of Marseillaise for the Austrian monarchy: " The throne of the Hapsburg will remain unshaken, Austria will not perish! Arise, O ye people! form your battalions, to arms, to the frontier! "

Napoleon's costly expedition into Spain was well calculated to arouse the boldest hopes. In March, 1809, war was again declared against France. The Archduke Charles was appointed generalissimo, with powers such as no head of the army had had since the days of Wallenstein and Prince Eugene. The available troops numbered 283,000 men, while the *Landwehr* and the *insurrection* in Hungary, according to the most trustworthy calculation, could furnish 310,000 more, a grand total of over 500,000. But the actual strength of the field army at the beginning of the war was no more than 265,000.

Three armies were to attack Napoleon simultaneously, the first in Bavaria, under the Archduke Charles, the second in Italy, under the command of the Archduke John, and the third, of 35,000 men, under the Archduke Ferdinand, was to invade Poland. Minor bodies of troops were to drive the French out of Dalmatia and Triest. Never in all her history had Austria placed on foot such an army. She posed as the champion of the independence of peoples, and of the liberty of Europe, which the Archduke Charles declared in his proclamation had taken refuge under Austrian banners. "Soldiers, your victories will break its fetters. Your German brethren to-day in the ranks of the enemy await only their deliverance." There is no proof that the Czechs, Slovenes, Hungarians, Croats, Rumanians, and Poles were fired with this interest in the deliverance of their German brethren. But the archduke was only repeating the traditional phrases of the monarchy. It was a question, above all, of impressing Europe, and especially Germany, with the idea that the destiny of the Germanic race was bound up with that of the house of Austria. "We fight to maintain the independence of the Austrian nation," said a manifesto addressed to the German people, "to secure that independence and that national honor which belong to her. Our resistance is her last hope, our cause is hers. With Austria Germany has been independent and happy. She can become so again only through her."

The first episode in the war was the insurrection in the Tyrol against Bavaria. These rude mountaineers were devoted in their fidelity to the house of Austria. Through a long series of reigns they had maintained their privileges and their patriarchal customs. At the time of their annexation to Bavaria Maximilan Joseph had promised them not to change one iota in these privi-

THE LAST CALL TO ARMS OF THE TYROLEAN PEASANTS DURING THE NAPOLEONIC INVASION

Painting by Albin Egger-Lienz

leges, but scarcely a year had passed when the Bavarian minister undertook to reorganize the new province. The estates of the Tyrol were dissolved; the religious administration overturned; the pastors displaced without cause, and festivals and pilgrimages suppressed. Under different circumstances and if carried out in a different manner, some of these reforms would have been most excellent; but being thus brutally imposed by foreign rule they drove these simple people to the verge of desperation. They had never severed their relations with Vienna, where the Tyrolese Hormayr valiantly represented their interests. Early in 1809 three patriots, Hofer, Hüber, and Nessing, went to Vienna to arrange a plan of insurrection with the Archduke John. On their return they organized the revolt. Innkeepers, peddlers, and laborers were the principal agents, but the secret was admirably kept.

Among the heroes of the struggle three are worthy of the special attention of the historian, Andrew Hofer, the innkeeper of Passeyer, Speckbacher, and the Capuchin, Haspinger. The innkeeper and horsedealer, Hofer, was known throughout all the Tyrol. He had been a member of the diet, and in 1796 he had led the Tyrolese in Italy against the French. Although the father of seven children, he never hesitated to leave them for the service of his country. Speckbacher had taken part in the previous campaigns, and developed a real military talent. The Capuchin Haspinger, better known as Father Joachim of the Red Beard, had accompanied the Tyrolese in all their expeditions as chaplain. He never shed blood himself, but no one knew better than he how to incite the soldiers to battle and heighten their patriotism by their religious faith.

On April 9, 1809, the Austrian general crossed the Tyrolese frontier. He was triumphantly received everywhere, and Hofer called his compatriots to arms. When the Austrians reached the Pusterthal they did not find a single Bavarian. Hofer and his peasants had already driven the foreigners out. Some days later Innsbruck was captured, but the captors sullied their victory by pillaging the houses of the Jews and Bavarian officials. On the following day 3500 Frenchmen laid down their arms in the presence of these rude mountaineers. Hormayer, who had arrived with the Austrian army, reëstablished the old administrative system. But in the south the struggle was more severe. There the French general with 8000 men for some time held their own against the

army of Hofer and his Austrian allies. Then he slowly withdrew
into Italy, and by the end of April all of the Tyrol except the
citadel of Kuftein was in the hands of the Austrians. But these
unexpected successes filled the Austrians with confidence which
after events by no means justified.

Napoleon had left Paris on April 13, and hastened to meet
the Archduke Charles, who had entered Bavaria. The Austrian
lines extended from Munich to Ratisbon. By the victory of
Afensberg Napoleon cut them in two, seized Lándshut, and crushed
the main body at Ekmühl and Ratisbon, on April 22 and 23. The
stand of the Austrian army had been heroic, and it lost nearly
40,000 men in killed, wounded, and prisoners. These heavy
losses were by no means compensated for by the successes of
the Austrians in Italy, where they occupied Friuli, and in Poland,
where Warsaw capitulated to the Archduke Ferdinand. The
Archduke Charles had been forced to fall back on Bohemia in
order to reorganize his army, leaving the way to Vienna open,
and on May 13, after a brief bombardment, the French entered
the Austrian capital for the second time.

But the campaign was by no means ended. After the occupation of Vienna the right bank of the Danube from Linz to the
Hungarian frontier was in the hands of the French, while the left
bank was held by the Austrians. Napoleon caused bridges to be
thrown across the river beyond Lobau in order to dislodge the
enemy. The troops of Massena and Lannes seized the villages of
Aspern and Esslingen, behind which the Archduke Charles, com-
manding 95,000 troops, awaited them. On learning of the passage
of the French he issued an order to his troops, which recalls the
famous words of Nelson at Trafalgar: " To-morrow is the day
of battle; the destiny of the monarchy depends upon you; I will do
my duty and I expect the same from the army." For two days
he made an attempt to drive the French into the Danube. The battle was not decisive and the French troops were obliged to entrench
themselves in the island of Lobau. The two days had cost the
two armies more than 40,000 men in dead and wounded, and
Marshal Lannes had been killed. Victory seemed to hesitate between the two forces and Napoleon was forced to recognize that
he had at last found a foeman worthy of his steel. By the Austrians Aspern is regarded as the most glorious victory since
Zenta and Kolin. The Emperor Francis sent his special congratu-

lations to the archduke, and Napoleon said later, " Those who did not see the Austrians at Aspern have seen nothing."

After the battles of Aspern and Esslingen Napoleon fortified the island of Lobau, transforming it into an entrenched camp whence he could easily pass to either shore. His most serious danger lay in the arrival of the Archduke John from Italy. The latter had been gradually driven in by Eugene Beauharnais, but had turned aside into Hungary to aid the *insurrection*. Beauharnais did not follow him thither, but joined his forces to Napoleon at Vienna, and thus reinforced Napoleon crossed to the left bank of the Danube with 150,000 men and 550 cannon. The Archduke Charles, whose forces had been raised to only 135,000 men, considered it inadvisable to dispute the passage. He awaited the French upon the heights of Wagram. The results of that bloody day are well known, and again 40,000 men were left upon the field of battle. After most brilliant fighting the Archduke Charles was forced to abandon his position and retreat into Moravia. From there he asked for an armistice, which was granted. The execution of the armistice was instructed to the Archduke John, to whom was given the command of the army, a slight to the Archduke Charles which led him to resign. He thenceforth lived in retirement except for a brief period in 1815. Since the days of Wallenstein and Prince Eugene no Austrian general had so great an influence over his soldiers.

The final treaty of peace was signed at Schönbrunn on October 14. On the day following Napoleon ordered the demolition of the fortress of Vienna, the Viennese having in vain prayed for the preservation of their old walls, which had formerly protected them against the Turks. The territories of Salzburg, the section of the Inn, and some other districts were ceded to Bavaria. To Napoleon Francis surrendered what had been left of Gorica, with the county of Montefalcone, Triest, and Carniola, the upper part of Carinthia, and all of the right bank of the Save, from its source to the Turkish frontier—that is, Croatia, Fiume, and Austrian Istria. Lusatia was given to Saxony, and western Galicia rounded out the territory of the duchy of Warsaw, while the circle of Tarnopol went to Russia.

The Austrian monarchy sustained a loss of over 3,500,000 of its subjects, her population being reduced to less than 21,000,000. The secret articles of the treaty limited the army to 150,000 men, and provided for an indemnity of 85,000,000 francs. But of all these sacrifices, the abandonment of the Tyrol was the most painful. Despite all his promises to these brave mountaineers, Francis was obliged to surrender them to Bavaria. Hofer and his companions had never despaired of victory. They had successfully opposed both Bavarians and French, alone, unaided, sometimes without any news whatever from the capital; they had placed their country in a state of defense, manufactured arms, ammunition, and cannon, and forced the French to evacuate Innsbruck. They now decided to continue the struggle on their own account. The 30,000 Frenchmen, Bavarians, and Wurtemburgers were repulsed and crushed by rocks hurled down upon them in the narrow mountain passes. The resistance was heroic and more stubborn even than that of Spain. General Lefèbvre was obliged to retire into Carinthia in August, 1809, leaving Hofer master of the country. The latter established himself in the imperial palace as commander-in-chief, and never did a leader receive more implicit obedience. But the arrival of fresh troops from Italy and Baravia made further resistance useless, though the struggle was prolonged till December, and the Tyrolese leaders were forced to fly or go into hiding. Spechbacher and Haspinger succeeded in crossing the frontier, but Hofer, upon whose head an award of 100,000 florins had been placed, was betrayed in 1810, and taken to Mantua. The commander of the fortress was that same Bisson who had had occasion to appreciate the military talent of this intrepid soldier, and who had endeavored to secure his services for Napoleon, only to be rebuked by the answer of the simple mountaineer: " I remain faithful to my Emperor Francis." A council of war condemned him to death, and on February 21 he was shot. In 1823 a number of Tyrolese officers disinterred his bones and brought them back to Innsbruck. The tragic death of Hofer contributed in a remarkable degree to the awakening of national sentiment in Germany. The revenge of the conqueror was not turned aside by the death of the hero. In order to crush all resistance the Tyrol was dismembered, a part being given to Italy, a part to Illyria, and the remainder to Bavaria. The University of Innsbruck was closed and its young men enrolled under foreign banners.

Napoleon's relations with the Illyrian provinces were more fortunate. He revived the classic name of Illyria for all the countries bordering on the Adriatic—Carinthia, Carniola, Gorica, Istria,

and part of Croatia and Dalmatia—and divided them into provinces. The name of Illyria excited most lively enthusiasm among
the Slav peoples, only recently oppressed by Germanism, and now
grouped for the first time into a national unity such as they could
not even hope for under the Austrian government. The national
language was encouraged and a Slav liturgy developed. " The
people," says a Slovene historian, " were particularly impressed
with the precise and prompt justice accorded by the French courts.
General security was greater than at any other period, and the
Slovenes still have most excellent recollections of the French gen-
darmes. The imposts were regulated and collected with more system, and communal liberties increased. It would be a long story
to narrate all the benefits the French rule brought to these countries. During the four years over which it lasted the French language rapidly spread among the people, and at Laibach there were
none with any pretense to enlightenment that did not learn French.
Even to this day the Slovene peasant calls the imposts *Franke*
in remembrance of the French financial administration. Charles
Nodier, who was appointed librarian at Laibach, published a polyglot sheet, the *Illyrian Telegraph*. The poet Vodnik translated the
grammar of Lhomond into Slovene, and sang the praises of Napoleon in the well-known ode, " Risen Illyria," in which the aspirations and hopes of his native land are set forth. " Napoleon has
said, Awake, Illyria! arise! She wakes and sighs, ' Who calls me to
the light? O noble hero, it is thou who hast awakened me! thou
wilt give me power, wilt lift me up. Our race shall be glorified, a
miracle is preparing! I dare prophesy to the Slovenes. Napoleon
has come, and an entire generation springs to earth. Resting one
hand on Gaul, I stretch out the other to Greece to save her. At the
head of Greece is Corinth, in the center of Europe is Illyria. Corinth is the eye of Greece, Illyria shall be the jewel of the world.' "

In Dalmatia likewise the French government favored the national language, which had been suppressed by the Venetians, and
had the official journals of the country published in both Slav and
Italian. Schools were created and a great road was constructed
which bore for many years the name of " Napoleon's Road." Indeed it is a direct result of the French occupation of these regions
that Austria now possesses Ragusa, and that in her official documents she still retains the fiction of the kingdom of Illyria.

Austria came out of this struggle weakened and almost ruined.

Only a policy of patient and wise moderation could now enable her to reëstablish her finances and reorganize her army. At the moment peace was signed, Francis had taken as his first minister Count Clemens Metternich, and after the dismissal of Stadion he intrusted him with the management of foreign affairs. Metternich, like so many others, came from a family strangers to Austria proper, the name coming from the little village of Metternich in the Rhenish provinces. In 1630, at a period when that country was being exploited by the Germans, a branch of the family had settled in Bohemia. Metternich's father had been Austrian minister at the courts of the Rhenish electors. His son, who was born in 1773, had married a granddaughter of Kaunitz, and entered the diplomatic service at an early age. Since the peace of Presburg he had represented Austria at Paris. It was he who had prepared the disastrous campaign of 1809, but in spite of its failure the emperor deemed it necessary to place the direction of affairs in the hands of the one man who best understood Napoleon.

It was Metternich who brought about the union between Napoleon and the Archduchess Marie Louise. He saw in this union the best means of securing to Austria the alliance of her powerful enemy, and Francis II. was obliged to give his consent to the marriage of his daughter to the upstart Cæsar, who spoke of the Austrian emperor as " this skeleton, Francis II., who has been placed upon a throne through the merit of his ancestors." Public opinion received this new humiliation with much grief. For an Austrian emperor to accept as his son-in-law the crowned heir of the revolution which had beheaded Marie Antoinette was an even greater humiliation than Wagram. On the evening of the marriage, which took place by proxy, and at which Napoleon was represented by the plebeian Berthier, the " Sacrifice of Iphegenia " was played at the court theater, and the courtiers could not forbear comparing their sovereign with the barbarian Agamemnon and the archduchess with the Greek heroine. Unfortunately the meanness of Marie Louise's character has deprived her of much of the sympathy her position would naturally inspire. Metternich accompanied the young princess to Paris, where he obtained some accommodation regarding the payment of the indemnity and the waiving of the humiliating clause of the treaty which reduced the Austrian forces to 150,000 men.

The most serious matter for Austria after 1809 was the finan-

FRANCIS II

cial situation. From 1793 to 1810 the public debt had risen from 377,000,000 to 658,000,000 florins. It had been necessary to have recourse to forced loans and at times to the suspension of payment on official salaries. A patent of 1809 ordered all private citizens to deliver their precious metals, in exchange for which they received bonds and lottery tickets. The issue of paper money increased steadily. In 1792 it amounted to 200,000,000; in 1810 it had passed the milliard mark. Bills for 30 and 15 kreutzers were issued, and paper money depreciated in the inverse ratio to the quantities issued. In 1809 the florin had depreciated to one-fourth its full value, and the banknotes from the provinces ceded to the French contributed still further to this depreciation. Prices became higher and higher, and to pay the indemnity to Napoleon it was found necessary to melt down the precious vessels of the churches.

In 1810 a sinking fund had been created, and a tax of one-tenth was laid on all property, real or personal. By 1811 the total amount of the banknotes issued had reached the appalling sum of 1,060,-798,753 florins, and nothing was left the government but bankruptcy. On February 20 of this year all notes were reduced to one-fifth of their face value, which brought about a terrible financial catastrophe, and many families were ruined. This special patent fixed the value of paper money from 1799 to 1810, taking into consideration the date on which debts had been incurred. Persons who had borrowed 100 florins in 1803 paid 129 florins in paper; in 1806, 148; in 1809, 234; and in 1811, 500. The Hungarian diet agreed to a reduction of fifty per cent., but refused the *scala*, which was nevertheless insisted upon by the government. It was only in 1816 that order was restored in the finances.

The reign of Francis II. was more successful in legislation than in finance. In 1803 the penal code was published, and in 1811 the new civil code. Both were animated by the spirit of humanity and justice to which the eighteenth century had given birth. The penal code suppressed confiscation, the galleys, and the dragging of boats. It retained hanging as the death penalty, and imprisonment in three degrees of severity—hard labor, the pillory, and fasting, which is even now inflicted. It did not provide for the appointment of a minister of justice nor allow prisoners to have counsel, and yet this penal code was one of the best of this time, and continued in force down to 1852. The civil code of 1811 was the result of fifty years or more of work which had been begun by Maria Theresa. On January 1, 1812, it came into use throughout the whole empire, excepting in Hungary and Transylvania. It recognized special legislation for the church, for the Jews, and for large landed estates in their relation to the provincial estates, and while it left the peasants in subjection, it did not recognize serfdom, admitting the principle that every citizen was capable of enjoying civil rights.

This adoption of a uniform code for all the provinces except Hungary aided materially to bring about that political unity which has always been the chief aim of the dynasty. Only the Magyars held to their independence, refusing to accept it, notwithstanding the superiority of the new code over the *jus tripartitum* then in force.

So long as Napoleon remained at the head of the French empire there could be no peace in Europe; nations must be either his allies or his enemies. Francis had chosen to be his ally, and it was not long before he was dragged into his wars. In the struggle tween Napoleon and Russia he had to submit to the necessity of helping his son-in-law, as he had formerly submitted to the humiliation of giving him his daughter. Austria, reduced to the rôle of land power, was surrounded on all sides by states created by the conqueror: Switzerland, the Confederation of the Rhine, Italy, and the duchy of Warsaw were all creations of Napoleon, and even Austria herself was in a state of vassalage. " God and his avenging angel are destroying us," wrote Gentz. When Radetzky was the chief of staff he formed a plan for making of the standing army a body in which the whole male population should be trained, after the model of the Prussian *Landwehr*, and Metternich had given his approval; But Count Wallis, president of the Hofkammer, opposed it on the basis that " Austria was in so enfeebled a condition that she could not dream of going to war for the next ten years, perhaps not for thirty."

Metternich was determined to maintain cordial relations between the two empires, and so despite his desire to remain at peace, Francis was forced to ally himself with Napoleon against the Tsar. He promised 30,000 troops and 30,000 reserves, and in case of success he was to receive a territorial compensation in exchange for these sacrifices. Considering the situation of Austria these were very honorable conditions indeed; it again put her in a position to come forward as a mediator should circumstances allow it. But the nation was discontented with an alliance with Napoleon; plots were organized to deprive him of the Illyrian provinces, while English and Prussian agents journeyed throughout Austria rousing the people against France. In May, 1812, Francis II. and his son-in-law met at Dresden. Metternich, who accompanied his master, endeavored to turn Napoleon aside from the Russian campaign, an enterprise which he saw was full of danger. But his efforts were in vain. The Austrian army assembled at Lemberg under the command of Schwarzenberg, and the reserves were assembled in Transylvania. There was little enthusiasm among the Austrian soldiers, and Schwarzenberg's proclamation clearly expressed his perplexity: " We are fighting for an object which is common to us with other powers—those powers are our allies. We are fighting with them, not for them. The army will show that virtue which is the best of all military virtues, namely, to sacrifice itself in order to fulfill the object which the sovereign has proposed to himself." The army did fulfill its duty, and marched into the duchy of Warsaw. Schwarzenberg penetrated some distance into Lithuania, but he did not take part in the expedition against Moscow or in the disastrous retreat which followed, and hence was able to bring back his troops almost intact. It was plain that it was not the business of Austria to continue, on her own account, a struggle in which the grand army had failed. The war had been unprofitable from the beginning, and now it was more so than ever. Metternich, who was regarded as the author of the fatal expedition, was loaded with abuse: public opinion demanded an open alliance with Napoleon's enemies. Upon the express orders of the Emperor Alexander the Russians refused to recognize the Austrians as enemies. " We are waging war," they said, " only against the French and the Poles." A diplomatic agent was even sent to Schwarzenberg to propose that he should recognize an armistice, and although the proposition was refused, Schwarzenberg consented to cross to the left bank of the Vistula.

At Vienna the excitement was intense when it was learned that the king of Prussia had left Berlin and publicly formed an alliance with Russia. Vienna had become the rendezvous of many Prussian and German *emigrés,* among whom was the poet Körner, who had become attached to the theater at Vienna as dramatic poet. Even at the time of the French alliance Körner wrote songs which could not fail to arouse hatred against France. This is especially true of his ode on the victory of Aspern, which, according to him, was a German victory. " This battle have the German people fought." He had addressed some enthusiastic verses to the Archduke John. " My German pride bows down before the German hero who has rekindled the flame upon the altar of victory." He invoked the shade of Hofer, the Tyrolese hero, in ardent language : " They have captured thee, the slaves of the tyrant, but thou hast looked to heaven as a place of victory ; and hast entered to liberty through death." The burning of Moscow he celebrated in these words : " The phœnix of Russia flung itself into the flames only to rise younger and more beautiful than ever ; already St. George is brandishing the victorious lance."

Francis II., without daring to show his sympathy for the passions raging round him, proposed nevertheless that Napoleon make peace, and to that end offered his mediation, which was accepted. Metternich was becoming suspicious about the aggrandizement of Russia, which only recently had annexed Finland and Bessarabia, and he also believed that the time had not yet come when Napoleon could be safely attacked. In order that Austria might be able to intervene with some chance of success, it was necessary that she should be well armed, and a considerable force was accordingly assembled in Bohemia. Schwarzenberg was sent to Paris with instructions, as Metternich said, " to offer to Napoleon not merely mediation, but rather the intervention of an ally who is weary of the war and desires to put an end to it." But the arrogant speech of Napoleon at the opening of the Corps Législatif in February, 1813, left but little hope for peace. In the meantime, public feeling grew more and more violent at Vienna, and when the king of Prussia declared war on Napoleon, it could no longer be restrained. The government concluded a secret agreement by which the Austrian army in Poland returned into Galicia and remained neutral. Napoleon endeavored to interest Austria in the war against Prussia by the promise of Silesia, and, if need be, the surrender of the Illyrian provinces ; but these vague promises were not sufficient, and thenceforth the only bond that united France to Austria was the slender tie of the marriage between Marie Louise and Napoleon. When Napoleon left Paris he was anxious to determine the value of the Austrian alliance, and issued orders for the Austrian auxiliary troops to march with Poniatowski. The order was not obeyed. The Austrians, who had begun to withdraw from the left bank of the Vistula, continued their retreat. Still Francis, desiring to save appearances, could not make up his mind. The English agents were ordered to leave Austrian territory, and he ostentatiously refused to receive the Prussian General Scharnhorst, who was coming to propose an alliance with Prussia and Russia. Secretly, however, he sent Stadion to the Russian camp, while he congratulated Napoleon on the victory of Lützen. He levied a special tax, called an anticipatory tax, amounting to twelve times the value of an ordinary tax, a sum approximating 45,000,000 florins. Never did the old adage, *Si vis pacem para bellum,* receive a more complete application.

The command of the army assembled in Bohemia was given to Schwarzenberg. His principal officer was Joseph Radetzky, who later was to play a very important rôle in the military history of Austria. The emperor, accompanied by Metternich, set out for Bohemia in order to be near the scene of military operations. After an interview with Alexander, and the king of Prussia, Metternich went on to Dresden to see Napoleon. He endeavored to make the French emperor agree to a European peace. He proposed that Napoleon surrender the Hanseatic towns and the Illyrian provinces, abolish the duchy of Warsaw, and the Confederation of the Rhine, and restore Prussia to the position she had occupied in 1805. But intoxicated by victory, the conqueror refused to listen to the proposals. The utmost that he would concede to preserve Austrian neutrality was the cession of the Illyrian provinces. After the departure of Metternich, however, he authorized Maret, his minister of foreign affairs, to enter into negotiations with Austria, and even to accept proposals for a conference which was to meet at Prague to arrange a European peace. But in the meantime Austria, Russia, and Prussia had signed the Treaty of Reichenbach, on June 27. Consequently, the conferences which were opened at Prague were not of a serious character. Napoleon had granted an armistice with the sole object of gaining time to organize his forces. But while the congress was in meeting, the military representatives of Russia, Prussia, Sweden, and Austria met in Silesia to determine upon a common plan of operation against Napoleon. In order to flatter Austria, the supreme direction of affairs was intrusted to Schwarzenberg, at this time in the prime of manhood. He had entered the army at the age of fifteen, had fought against the Turks under Joseph II., and had participated in the campaigns of the Low Countries and the Rhine, as well as in all the wars against France. He well knew the enemy he had to deal with, and Napoleon, too, recognized in him a worthy adversary. The choice of Schwarzenberg, therefore, as the leader of the allied army may be attributed as much to his military talent as to deference to Austria. Two Austrian armies took the field, one on the frontier of the Illyrian provinces, the other on the side of Bavaria. Too late, Napoleon decided to make overtures. His courier arrived on the morning of August 11, and on the previous evening Metternich had sent a note to Caulaincourt announcing the alliance of Austria with Prussia and Russia. The army of Austria was to play a decisive part in the campaign which was now opening.

The Austrian army found a secure base of operations in Bohemia, protected on all sides by mountains. On August 17 Schwarzenberg's forces began to pass the defiles into Silesia, and crossed the Saxon frontier on the 22d. The proclamation of the generalissimo expressed the situation succinctly: " Russians, Prussians, Austrians! you are fighting only for the liberty of Europe, and for the independence of your native land! All for one, one for all! Let this be your battle cry, and victory is yours." Thus was ushered in the memorable campaign of 1813, and throughout it all the military history of Austria is intimately associated with that of France and Germany. Some fighting on the southern frontier of Austria, the great victory at Leipzig—fought on the days of October 16, 18, 19, 1813, and commonly called the Battle of the Nations—the retreat of Napoleon, the campaign in France, and finally the taking of Paris, in March, 1814, mark the successive stages of the conflict.

On Austrian territory itself considerable fighting occurred, but as all depended on the outcome of the principal campaign, this is of slight importance. Two attempts on the part of the French to enter Bohemia were repulsed by the allies and served only to bring Austria more closely into union with Russia and Prussia in the Treaty of Teplitz. In the southwest the military operations resulted in the occupation of Karlovac and Fiume without resistance. A division was sent into Dalmatia and one into the Tyrol by the Pusterthal. In Upper Austria the conflict was not serious, despite the presence there of the Bavarians, the allies of the French. The former had been invited by Russia and Prussia to join the alliance, and after some hesitation the Bavarian general signed an agreement, on October 8, placing his army at the disposition of the allies. As a result of these developments the French were forced to abandon Laibach and the Illyrian provinces, the governor general, Fouché, taking refuge on Venetian territory.

The news of the agreement arrived at between Austria and Bavaria was welcomed in the Tyrol with the most lively satisfaction, and the Austrian troops received an enthusiastic welcome at. Innsbruck, on their way to Italy. On their way southward they seized Trent and pushed forward into Italian territory. The southern Tyrol was now entirely in the hands of the Austrians, and the Tyrolese of Innsbruck, jealous of the fortunate fate of their countrymen, rose and drove out the Bavarians. In Dalmatia the towns still faithful to the French were seized with the help of the troops from an English squadron. The last place to hold out for the French was Ragusa, and against it the Servian, Milutinovic, was sent. After a slight resistance the town surrendered. Thus by the beginning of 1814 Austria was again mistress of the Adriatic coast, and the reannexation of Dalmatia and the Illyrian provinces and the restitution of the Tyrol were to her by far the most important results of that gigantic struggle which was only to be finally closed by the battle of Waterloo.

These successes were more easily attained because of the disasters which befell Napoleon at the beginning of the campaign in Germany. The battle of Leipzig, won chiefly by the very capable generalship of Schwarzenberg and his superior numbers, especially after the defection of the Saxons, compelled the French to beat a hasty retreat to the Rhine. Immediately before the battle of Leipzig Schwarzenberg wrote to his wife: " As I stand at my window and reflect that I have opposed to me one of the greatest generals of our times, the veritable emperor of battles, it seems as if my shoulders were too weak and that they must succumb under this terrible burden. But when I look at the stars I say to myself that He who directs their course has likewise traced my path. If it is His wish that right shall triumph, His wisdom will give me light and strength. If it is the will of Providence that we should succumb, my personal loss will be the least of all our misfortunes. Whether defeat or victory is ours, I have already conquered all self-conceit, and the judgment of the world will bring me neither reward nor punishment." From the very beginning of the battle

of Leipzig Napoleon saw the merit of Schwarzenberg. " It was I,"
he said to the Austrian General Merveldt, who had been brought to
him as a prisoner, " it was I who first drew the attention of your
sovereign to Schwarzenberg. If he is going to beat me, he is certainly going about it in the right way." He sent Merveldt back to
propose an armistice on the basis that the Austrians were to retire into Bohemia, the Prussians and Russians behind the Oder,
the French behind the Saale, and Saxony was to remain neutral.
But it was too late. Francis declined to receive the overtures of
Napoleon, and the victory which followed justified his decision.
After the battle the emperor conferred the grand cross of the Order
of Maria Theresa upon Schwarzenberg, the field-marshal present-
ing his commander's cross to Radetzky, saying, " Loudon wore it,
and I cannot give it to one more worthy." Nor was the diplomat
who brought about the coalition forgotten in the distribution of
imperial favors. To Metternich was granted the title of hereditary
prince. The Austrians also took part in the battle of Hanau, in
which they tried, with the help of the Bavarians, to cut off the retreat
of Napoleon. One by one the states belonging to the Federation of
the Rhine, Würtemberg, and Hesse-Darmstadt joined the coalition. Francis II. entered the town of Frankfort, where twenty
years before he had received the imperial crown, and where
Schwarzenberg now established his headquarters.

The allied armies were now on the borders of France, and Metternich, desiring to keep the humiliation of Napoleon from being
carried too far, tried to open negotiations in Frankfort. He sent
for the French minister at the court of Weimar and dictated to
him the terms on which a treaty might still be arranged. France
was to surrender Holland, Italy, and Switzerland, and to accept the
natural frontier of the Pyrenees, the Alps, and the Rhine as her
boundary. To these propositions Napoleon replied in vague and indefinite terms, proposing a conference at Mannheim for November. This the allies, encouraged by their recent success, particularly
in Spain and Holland, declined to entertain, and it was decided to
march upon Paris. Nevertheless even in the thick of the first conflict of the campaign in France, negotiations between Metternich
and Caulaincourt continued. A congress early in February of
1814 at Châtillon-sur-Seine resulted in the demand by the allies
that France should return to her limits of 1790. Napoleon, intoxicated by a few temporary triumphs, endeavored to enter into

direct negotiations with Francis, offering to divide the empire of
Europe with him. He believed that victory had again returned to
his banner. " I am nearer Vienna than the allies are to Paris! " he
exclaimed in his arrogance. His overtures were rejected, and on
March 1 the representatives of the allies—Metternich, Nesselrode,
Hardenberg, and Castlereagh—signed the Treaty of Chaumont,
in which the powers agreed not to lay down their arms until they
had restored the peace and liberty of Europe. This treaty was to
last for twenty years. None of the signatory powers was to
make peace on its own account. The congress at Châtillon broke
up without coming to any definite conclusion, and Schwarzenberg
decided to march directly upon Paris. On March 30 the allies
entered the French capital, their success being due to the wise
temerity of Schwarzenberg. Napoleon once said to the Austrian
Koller, who accompanied him to the island of Elba: " An ordinary
general would have been anxious over his return, and would have
worried over his lines of communications; a good general would
do nothing but just what Schwarzenberg did. I knew that he was
capable of doing this, but I expected him to solicit the advice of the
sovereigns and that he would thus allow the favorable moment to
escape." Blücher confirmed the judgment of Napoleon when, some
time later, during a visit to Carlsbad, he drank " to the hero who
in spite of the presence of three monarchs led us to victory." The
courts of Europe loaded the happy conqueror of Paris with every
distinction. The city of London voted him a sword of honor, the
University of Oxford made him a doctor of civil law, Bohemia
erected a statue to him, and the Emperor Francis granted him a
permission to quarter the arms of the house of Austria with
his own.

Francis II. did not enter Paris with his two allies, but he
gave his consent to their arranging the affairs of his son-in-law
and daughter, not allowing his feelings to interfere in matters of
state. When he reached Paris, on April 15, the Treaty of Fon-
tainebleau had already been signed. By this treaty the island
of Elba was given to Napoleon, and Parma, Piecenza, and Guastalla to Marie Louise, the daughter of the Cæsars not caring to accompany her husband into exile.

In Italy Eugene at Rome and Murat at Naples, both creatures
of Napoleon, were unable to maintain themselves against the coalition. While Eugene was fighting the Austrians on the Adige,

Murat tried to establish his authority throughout all central Italy, but the English and Austrians seized Tuscany, and the latter entered Milan. Two months later the Treaty of Paris gave Italy north of the Po and east of the Ticino to Austria, and thenceforward Austria gradually assumed the rôle of policeman in favor of legitimacy throughout all the peninsula. Austrian troops reëstablished Francis IV. on the throne of Modena and Reggio, Ferdinand in Tuscany, and Ferdinand IV. in the kingdom of the Two Sicilies. But the story of Austrian domination in Italy does not enter into the scope of this work.

On May 3, 1814, Louis XVIII. entered Paris; the war was over; Schwarzenberg laid down his command, and the work of diplomacy commenced. It was no easy matter to come to an agreement over the partition of the spoil. From the outset it had been agreed that the grand duchy of Warsaw should be divided among the three eastern monarchs, but now Alexander, who coveted all of Poland, raised objections, and won over Prussia to his side by promising her Saxony. In the diplomatic negotiations which resulted Metternich showed much cleverness and perseverance in defending the interests of his sovereign. He induced the powers to arrange the terms of peace with France, and then postponed all other questions till a congress could be called at Vienna.

In the month of September, 1814, Vienna became the rendezvous of the crowned heads of Europe. The kings of Würtemberg, Denmark, Bavaria, and Prussia, and the emperor of Russia all attended the congress, at which festivities were throughout more in evidence than business. The words of the Prince de Ligne, " Le congrès ne marche pas, il danse," are well known. The first anniversary of the battle of Leipzig was celebrated by a gigantic review, at which Alexander paid solemn homage to the military skill of Schwarzenberg. " It is to you, after God," said he, " that we owe our success." The preliminary arrangements were not easy. The question of Poland gave the diplomats much embarrassment, and caused more than one disagreement. Metternich, although supported by Castlereagh and Talleyrand, had to withstand much violent opposition in the preliminary congress. But it was never a real congress, rather a succession of committees where questions which affected particular countries were discussed by the representatives of those countries. The subjects of discussion were not merely those which had resulted from the great war against Na-

THE CONGRESS OF VIENNA

After the crayon drawing of Jean Baptiste Isabey

poleon, but included also such general questions as the navigation of the rivers of central Europe, the slave trade, and the pirates of the Mediterranean. The congress was divided into a number of sections and was looked upon as if it were a European tribunal, before which all who had suffered in the revolution might come to demand redress for their injuries. The Order of the Knights of St. John appealed to it for the restoration of the island of Malta, which they lost twenty years previous, while all the petty princes of Germany urged their claims upon the congress.

But the great stumbling-block was the Polish question, and on more than one occasion it threatened to break up the congress. Russia had taken possession of the grand duchy of Warsaw and treated it as conquered territory. At one time it looked as if the negotiations must break up, Austria, England, and France even going to the extent of forming an alliance against the pretensions of Russia and Prussia. At last Nesselrode worked out a plan which seemed to satisfy all, and according to which Poland was divided much as she is now. The serious difficulties over the claims of the king of Prussia, who demanded Saxony, which Austria and France would not consent to, were also adjusted. A committee was appointed, consisting of the representatives of Austria, France, England, Russia, and Prussia, to settle the disputed points. This committee became the real congress. Indeed, it was the beginning of that system of the five great powers which directed the destinies of modern Europe for a quarter of a century after the congress. This committee induced Prussia to renounce most of her claims to Saxony, and arranged the final partition of Poland.

It was in the midst of these negotiations and festivities that Vienna received the news, on March 4, that Napoleon had landed on the coast of Provence. By a strange coincidence the very evening that the news arrived a comedy entitled " The Interrupted Dance " was being played at the court theater. The Austrian troops were at once ordered to take up their march toward France, and a few days later it was publicly declared that Napoleon Bonaparte, having violated all law, was an enemy to the public peace, and placed under the ban of the nations.

On March 25 the allies renewed the Treaty of Chaumont, and declared themselves resolved to carry on the war until Napoleon should be deprived of all power. The plan of campaign was worked out at the house of Schwarzenberg, the sovereigns of Russia and Prussia and the Duke of Wellington taking part. Three great armies were formed, one in the Low Countries under Wellington and Blücher, comprised of English, Dutch, and Prussians; one on the Rhine under Schwarzenberg, including the Austrians, Russians, and Germans; and an Austrian army in Italy to check Murat, who was advancing with 80,000 men. While the armies of the coalition marched against Napoleon, Marie Louise remained quietly at Schönbrunn. This commonplace princess merits very little attention from the historian; unfaithful to her husband even during his lifetime, she died in 1847, the dupe of Metternich's policy and the willing accomplice of Neipperg. The war did not seriously interrupt the negotiations of the congress; indeed, the arrival of Napoleon rather served to hasten a final settlement. On May 3 the treaties regarding the final partition of Poland were signed. In June the constitution of Germany was drawn up, and on June 11 the sittings of the congress terminated. The war began in Italy in the month of April, when Murat advanced into the Po valley and was defeated by the imperial troops at Rimini, at Anco, and at Solentino. He fled to Naples, whither he was pursued by the Austrians and forced to take refuge in France. On the Rhine the Austrian troops found but little to do. They entered Alsace, took Huningue, and held the small army of Rapp in check at Strassburg. On June 30 the allied monarchs took up their quarters at Hagenau, where they received a deputation from the French, headed by Lafayette. He was told that no steps toward peace could be taken until Napoleon had been surrendered to the allies. The main body of the army of Schwarzenberg then marched upon Paris, which he entered, this time without resistance. No Austrian fought at Waterloo on the memorable day of June 18, where the last hopes of Napoleon were dashed. On November 20, 1815, the second Treaty of Paris was signed, by which France was required to pay an indemnity of 700,000,000 francs and to submit to the frontiers of 1790 and the occupation of her eastern provinces by 150,000 men for a period of five years.

It may well be asked what were the results of so many battles and so much diplomacy. No other of the Hapsburg dynasty had passed through such a series of reverses and triumphs. Four times Francis II. had had to accept humiliating peace from his arrogant conqueror; twice he had seen the enemy enter his capital, and he had lost the Low Countries, the lands in Suabia, and the duchy of

Milan, receiving in compensation Venice, Dalmatia, Salzburg, and western Galicia—only to lose them again. He had had even to sacrifice the hereditary provinces, the loyal Tyrol, Istria, Triest, Gorica, half of Carinthia, Carniola, and a part of Croatia. He had had to surrender that imperial crown which had been for centuries the ornament and glory of his house. And yet after the Treaty of Vienna he found himself in possession of a more vigorous and more compact empire than before the Revolution; while his army and diplomacy excited the envy and admiration of Europe. He had the hegemony both in Germany and in Italy, the younger branches of the house of Hapsburg-Lorraine having been reëstablished in Tuscany and Modena. The Empress Marie Louise was to have Parma, Guastalla, and Piacenza for life. In Germany, Austria regained all which had been taken from her by Bavaria, with the exception of Wurzburg and Aschaffenburg. She had given up the troublesome possessions of the Low Countries, the Breisgau, Suabia, and western Galicia. To sum up, in place of 24,000,000 inhabitants in 1792, scattered from the North Sea to the Danube, over an area of 266,000 square miles, she now had 28,000,000 on a compact area of 277,637 square miles. Every portion of the empire was contiguous, except at one corner, where the Turkish districts of Klek and the Sutorina interrupted the coast line of the Dalmatian possessions. The empire of Austria now included five kingdoms of different origin, Bohemia, Hungary, Galicia, Illyria, and the Lombardo-Venetia.

Francis II. had declined all proposals to assume again the imperial crown of Germany, but he by no means wished to give up his position in the German world. It was Austria which had made Germany, it was at Vienna that the final reconstruction of the .German states had been made, and in exchange for these services Metternich successfully claimed that his monarch should be president of the diet of the Confederation of German states at Frankfort. But in order that Austrian domination should be successfully maintained in Germany, it was necessary that the largest possible number of her subjects should belong to the Confederation. Francis therefore declared that all of his provinces which had at any time belonged to the Holy Roman Empire were now included in the Germanic Confederation. Of these provinces only Austria, Salzburg, the northern Tyrol, and Vorarlberg, containing at the most three or four millions of people, were purely German. In order to make up the needful number these were augmented by the addition of Bohemia, two-thirds of whose population was Slav; Moravia, with four-fifths of hers Slav; Styria, one-half Slovene; Carinthia, Carniola, Gorica, and Gradiska entirely so; Istria and Triest, half Slovene, half Italian; the southern or Italian Tyrol; Austrian Silesia, half Slav; and the Polish duchies of Auschwitz and Zator, in Galicia. Thus by her diplomatic triumph Austria forced six or seven millions of pseudo-Germans into the Germanic Confederation, and from the point of view of numbers made a good showing at Frankfort. In order to justify her pretensions as a German power she had to work harder than ever to Germanize her people, and in so doing opposed the natural development of their genius and political freedom. But the extension of her influence in Germany and the consolidation of her territory was not the only result of the twenty years' war. Her internal organization had been greatly strengthened by the creation of an army such as had been unknown in the days of Joseph II. or Maria Theresa. There had been developed in this army the spirit of discipline and brotherhood in arms which had drawn together and inspired with the same feelings those of the most diverse lands—Germans, Slavs, and Magyars. And this army was to be on more than one occasion the bulwark of the empire; to enforce that obedience, which comes from fear, or all sorts of peoples, and to spread ideas of fidelity to the flag and to the monarchical principle which has given new vigor to the Austrian empire. But in spite of this the government has not succeeded in stifling the aspirations of the various states for liberty and national autonomy, for the realization of their historic rights, always ignored by the sovereign, but always claimed by the people.

PART VI

THE PERIOD OF REACTION AND THE AWAKENING OF THE NATION-ALITIES. 1815-1848

Chapter XXV

FRANCIS II AND METTERNICH. 1815-1835

THE treaties of 1815 seemed to have brought to an end the era of revolution. The years which followed mark a period of implacable reaction, in which the sovereigns of Europe, rejoicing over the fact that they had rescued their crowns and their lands from the Revolution, united in a common effort to resist the ideas of 1789.

Among those princes who undertook to lead his subjects back to the doctrines of the old régime none was more zealous than Francis II., and none was so ably served in this respect as he, in his chancellor, Prince Metternich. Francis II. had a commonplace mind and a mean character. He had no capacity for understanding great things, and attached an undue importance to trivial ones. He had a passion for writing documents and for holding audiences. Fond of games and chamber concerts, in which he liked to take part himself, he was always, says Springer, on the lookout for anyone who would be of use as a member of the quartet. He was envious of anyone who, like the Archduke Charles or Radetzky, had won the popular favor by his services. On one occasion, in a fit of suspicious jealousy, he went even so far as to have the private locks of the archduke broken open. This same characteristic sometimes drove him to act with extreme cruelty. In 1820 a riot took place among the students at Prague, and, being unable to find the culprit, he compelled all those who had had bad marks to enlist in the army. A harsh selfishness was the nautral consequence of his theory of absolutism, which led him to look upon his people and provinces as if they were his private property. Like his predecessors, however, he knew how to clothe his despotism in patriarchal form, which always pleased the simple people. In the absence of representative government an inquisitorial police acted as an agent between the sovereign and his subjects. Like Louis XV., he took much pleasure in scandal, using it both as a means of diversion and an instrument of government. In his eyes the monarchy had no better support than Catholicism; he believed that Josephinism in attacking religion was undermining the monarchy. In 1821 he addressed the president of the gymnasium at Laibach as follows: "Hold to that which is old, for that is good; if our ancestors were pleased with it to be so, why not we? New ideas are to-day being advanced of which I do not nor ever shall approve. Hold them in suspicion and keep to that which is approved. I have no need of learned men; I want faithful subjects. Be such! that is your duty; he who would serve me must do what I command. He who cannot do this, or who comes with new ideas, may leave us; if not, I shall send him." On another occasion he said to the French ambassador: "My peoples are strangers to one another; so much the better. They will not catch the same illness at the same time. In France when a fever comes, it takes you all on the same day. I send Hungarians to Italy and Italians to Hungary, and each one looks after his neighbor. They do not understand each other, they hate one another: but this very antipathy gives birth to order, and their mutual hatred secures the general peace."

With principles such as these the emperor did his utmost to make his empire secure against ideas of science and thought from abroad. The censorship of the press was ruthlessly applied, and literature was regarded as dangerous. Some remarkable men, it is true, had been taken into the Austrian service, as, for example, Gentz, Frederick Schlegel, and Adam Müller; but their works as publicists were intended for foreigners, and were almost unknown in Austria. Men of talent, and they were few, were regarded with suspicion; only one man, and he Metternich, succeeded in gaining the complete confidence of the emperor. The period of wars had come to an end, and Francis no longer had need of his generals; but the precarious state of Europe still assured a diplomat who had negotiated the treaties of Vienna a first place in the councils of his sovereign. It is true Metternich did not interfere with the internal administration of Austria, but his foreign policy reacted strongly on the home policy. A foreigner by birth, Metternich knew very little of the history of the states over which his sovereign ruled, and cared only indifferently about Austria's internal problems, so inherent in the history and ethnographic make-up of the empire. A man of the eighteenth century, he despised history, and had no inkling of the smoldering flames of revolution beneath the surface of the confused discontent and agitation about him. He owed his high position and the continuance of his good fortune less to his talent than to his tenacity of purpose and to a happy set of circumstances. He fell heir to the victories of Austria in 1813-1815. An obsequious flatterer, he was fortunate in having to deal with two monarchs who were too weak to do without him, and who therefore submitted foreign affairs entirely to his keeping. " Francis and Metternich," says the German historian Springer, " were the complements of each other. Metternich knew nothing about the details of government, and never interfered in them; while the emperor, on the contrary, attached the greatest importance to them. Francis had entered into an agreement to maintain order and had determined to carry out his engagement by maintaining a state of perfect tranquillity in his own empire. Metternich insisted on the passive obedience of all Austrian countries, in order to be able to employ the whole powers of the empire abroad. For the former absolutism was a matter of sentiment; for the latter of reason, and, thanks to their egotism, they confused the good of the state with their own personal interests. They believed the interests of the state satisfied if their own interests were, and in time regarded the political conspirator as no better than a parricide. Neither one had the slightest feeling of responsibility as stewards of the national resources."

Nor can it be said that Metternich's devotion was altogether disinterested. He was not above receiving subsidies from foreign princes, and managed the public funds in a manner that showed that he did not believe an account could ever be required of him. His gallantries on more than one occasion scandalized the good town of Vienna, that luxurious and corrupt city in which, according to the saying of a contemporary, the life of the inhabitants resembled that of hibernating animals. Indeed, in all of the Austrian states Metternich aimed to keep the people completely in a condition of tutelage, while abroad he sought to maintain the prestige and leadership which her military successes and her diplomacy had secured to her.

Metternich and his sovereign set about to act as the police of Europe. To their eyes revolutions, wherever they might occur, threatened Austria herself. Because of her German, Italian, and Polish possessions, Austria more than any other state was in danger of the contagion of liberalism. As early as 1815 the Italians began that secret war of conspiracies and secret societies which ended, after so many years of painful struggle, in the regeneration of their country. In Germany generous spirits, especially among the students and the more enlightened, demanded intellectual freedom and constitutional government. In 1819 the sovereigns of Austria and Prussia decided to put an end to all these dangerous demands and manifestations, and drew up the famous Carlsbad

Decrees for the suppression of liberalism. In 1820 the king of Naples, yielding to a military insurrection, granted a constitution to his subjects. A congress was called at Troppau, in 1820, and then at Laibach in 1821, to discuss methods for the suppression of the revolutionary spirit in Italy. This time Russia joined the two reactionary powers. Together they set up the claim to a right to regulate the affairs of the Italian states, despite the protests of England and France. The king of Naples appeared before the congress at

Laibach and renounced the concessions he had made. An Austrian army accompanied him back to Naples and restored him to all his absolute power. Some days later a similar movement was suppressed by an Austrian army in Piedmont, the armies of occupation remaining in both kingdoms. About the same time the gentle and lovable Silvio Pellico, guilty of patriotism, was thrown into the Spielberg dungeon. His book, "*I miei Prigioni*," ("My Prison Day"), translated a hundred times, and read throughout Europe, remains to this day as the most formidable indictment of Austrian rule in Italy.

Francis II. rewarded his minister by granting him for these ill-omened successes the title of chancellor of the empire. "Europe," said a contemporary, "praises, envies, or curses the power of Austria, but never thinks of the Austrian people. They think only of the prince and his minister." Metternich on his part was jubilant. "See what a revolution is when taken in time," he once exclaimed to the emperor of Russia. Thenceforth he thought all the affairs of Europe could be managed in congresses, in which Austria was naturally to take the leading part. The congress of Verona, in 1822, was called with the special purpose of considering the Spanish revolution, and this time the France of the Restoration became the instrument of the Austrian policy, and secured the discreditable honor of carrying out the decrees of the Holy Alliance against Spain. This congress also decided that Austria should evacuate Piedmont and maintain only a small garrison in Naples. In both states the reaction had been terrible, and Austria became an object of horror to the Italians. The cry, "Away with the Germans!" became the watchword of the patriots. These Germans were for the most part Magyars, Slavs, Slovenes, Servians, Poles, and Czechs, the unconscious instruments of a policy of oppression of which they were themselves also the victims.

The friendly relation between Austria and Russia, manifested in so many common undertakings during the Napoleonic period, was now to reveal itself again in connection with the Eastern Question, which has so long perplexed European diplomats. The prelude to the Greek revolution was beginning to attract general attention by 1820. The conflicts which the Austrian state had carried on against the Porte, her geographic position on the borders of the Turkish empire, and her ethnographic constitution, all seemed to point out Austria as the protectress of the Christians of Turkey and the possessor of those provinces which might revolt. The successor to the kings of Hungary might invoke claims to Bosnia and Bulgaria less hypothetical than those which had recently been made use of in regard to Galicia. Unfortunately, during the centuries which had preceded, Austria had been too much occupied in Germany to look after her affairs in the East, where her statesmen should have seen her paramount interests. Joseph II. had announced that he would curb the barbarians who had been the curse of Europe for so long, but he died before he could carry out his project, and while the Austrian state was absorbed in its struggles with the French Revolution, the influence of Russia steadily increased in the Balkan peninsula, where the people were not only one with her in race, but also in religion.

In the beginning of the nineteenth century the Servians had risen, driven out the Turks, and formed an independent principality on the frontier of Hungary (1804-1815). A little later the Greeks, concentrated in ancient Hellas or dispersed along the coast from the Ægean to the Danube, began to dream of freedom. Metternich and his master did not feel equal to carrying out the projects of Joseph II., and they were accustomed to regard as enemies all people who dared to think of their independence. At the congress of Laibach Metternich took great pains to convince the Tsar of the dangers of the revolutionary movements.

The official gazette of Vienna ostentatiously announced on March 29, 1821, that the Emperor Alexander did not in the slightest degree approve of the adventures of Prince Ypsilanti, that he had expelled this revolutionist from the Russian army, and had disavowed his enterprise at the court of Constantinople. Indeed, the court of Vienna showed in a much more direct way its sentiments regarding Turkey and the Greeks. When Ypsilanti crossed the frontier into Transylvania he was promptly seized and thrown into prison, while most of his accomplices were interned (1821). Metternich saw in the Greek revolution only a revolt of subjects against their legitimate sovereign, and gave a deaf ear to the advocates of the cause of the Greeks. Among these, many thought that Austria might, by taking part in the expulsion of the Turks, play the glorious rôle of liberator of the oppressed, and create for herself a strong marine on the Mediterranean. That Metternich's opposition to the Greeks was based partly, at least, on a fear of Russia must be admitted. He endeavored above all to bring about a cor-

dial understanding between Austria and England. In a journey
to Hanover in 1821 he had an interview with Castlereagh, and
assured himself of his coöperation. England was to use her influence at St. Petersburg, and Austria at Constantinople, to bring
about moderation and peace. Alexander at first yielded, and the
Greek envoys who appeared at the congress of Verona were not
granted an audience. In 1823 the two sovereigns met at Lemberg,
while Metternich had an extended interview with Nesselrode. The
continued success of the Greeks, however, greatly interfered
with the Austrian chancellor's plan for pacification. On the other
hand, Alexander, despite the overweening influence exercised over
him by Metternich, was unable to overcome either the interests of
Russia or his romantic humanitarian ideas. In 1824 a conference
was held at St. Petersburg for the purpose of pacifying Greece.
Austria participated in the deliberations, but her policy was directed toward delaying matters and preventing a definite solution.
The death of Alexander in December, 1825, brought no change
in the situation. Nicholas showed himself disposed to treat on
amicable terms with Turkey concerning the Danubian principalities and the rectification of the frontiers, while, thanks to Austrian
intervention, everything seemed to adjust itself once more. " The
hopes of a certain faction, enemies of public tranquillity, are shat-
tered," wrote the *Augsburg Gazette*. " The monarchs should unite
to crush revolution in whatsoever form it manifests itself, to
renounce momentary advantages and to hold firmly to the system
of the Holy Alliance. Any statesman who departs from this
course is an enemy to thrones and to peoples. The leading statesman of the continent, he whose wise councils have for so many
years secured the peace of Europe, who has always remained true
to himself, who despite the attacks of his enemies has never de-
parted from this straight road, this time again has defeated the
hopes of the Liberals!" But at the very moment when Metternich
was receiving, perhaps dictating, these praises, and believing himself
master of Europe, he was totally outwitted by Russia and England.
By a protocol signed in London, in April, 1826, the two powers
agreed to intervene in behalf of the Greeks. Austria in the meantime, by her ambiguous policy, suffered a well-merited decline in her
Eastern commerce. The Greek corsairs attacked her merchant vessels, capturing two hundred in 1826 alone. England recognized the
Greeks as belligerents, and the cabinet of Vienna, without going to

this length, was at least forced to admit that they had the right to seize Austrian vessels carrying contraband of war. In the month of July France gave her assent to the London protocol, and the three powers sent their Mediterranean fleets to Turkey.

In 1827 the battle of Navarino gave the final blow to the hopes of the Austrian chancellor. Europe had emphatically taken up the cause of the revolutionists. In 1828 war broke out between Russia and Turkey, and at Vienna confusion and fear prevailed. Austria was convinced, so Gentz wrote to Lord Stanhope, that the Tsar would push on to Constantinople. To prevent this she had not financial resources, an adequate army, or allies. Even France was hostile, Charles X. declaring that if the Emperor Nicholas attacked Austria he would await results, but if Austria attacked, he would immediately attack her. Fortunately Russia encountered greater difficulties on the Danube and in the Balkans than had been foreseen. The war ended in September, 1829, in the Treaty of Adrianople, in which the independence of Greece was recognized, and the Danubian principalities were left under Russian influence. much to the detriment of Austrian commerce.

The defeat of Turkey was regarded as a real catastrophe for Austria. The prestige of the cabinet of Vienna crumbled and a large part of its influence in Europe was lost; England and Russia had emphatically freed themselves from her tutelage. In diplomatic circles the narrowness of the Viennese statesmen was openly criticised. It was sufficient, in order to obtain the favor of Francis and his minister, Metternich, to be an avowed opponent of modern ideas. In 1821 a constitution had been proclaimed at Lisbon; the Austrian ambassador refused to illuminate his house. A constitution even upon the distant shores of the Atlantic was regarded as a menace by Francis II. It can be readily understood, therefore, with what fear the revolution of July, 1830, was regarded at Vienna. The events in Poland brought the danger more directly home to Austria. At the Congress of Vienna Metternich had protested against the cession of the grand duchy of Warsaw to Russia, and at this moment a secret grudge against Russia, arising out of the Turkish campaign, still rankled in the Austrian mind; Galicia was excited; the Hungarians, fearful of the aggrandizement of Russia, declared the future of their nation compromised by the growth of the Muscovite nation, and demanded intervention in favor of Poland; the Slavs were disturbed over the conflict between their kinsmen. Even the Germans—some because of their liberalism, others because of their religious convictions—favored Poland. At Vienna the policy of the cabinet on the Polish question was quite as ambiguous as in the Eastern Question. An army corps was stationed upon the Galician frontier to prevent the insurgents from entering Austrian territory, and to prohibit the importation of arms into Poland; but the Austrian minister remained at Warsaw, while Prussia, more correct from the standpoint of diplomatic etiquette, withdrew hers. Metternich did not announce his intention of intervening against the insurgents as he had done in Italy and Spain, and Gentz, in the *Augsburg Gazette,* even expressed the generally felt sympathy for them. There was even talk in the political circles of Vienna of an Austrian archduke for the throne of Poland. When the struggle had reached its climax Metternich offered his mediation, which was promptly declined, and Russia dealt with Poland as a conqueror with the conquered.

In the meantime disturbances again broke out in Italy. In February, 1831, the people of Parma and Modena revolted against their Austrian sovereign. Austria feared that the revolution would extend to Lombardy and Venetia, those fertile Italian provinces held by her since 1815, and from which revenues amounting annually to between fifty-seven and fifty-eight millions were derived. In view of this the Austrian troops entered Modena and Parma, and occupied the legations. But the latter were soon abandoned because of the protest by France. The following year, however, a new insurrection broke out, and Austria, on the request of the Pope, again entered the Papal territory. France replied by occupying Ancona. Thus Austria continued her mistaken policy, tightening her grasp on Italy, which rejected her, and turning her back on Poland, which would perhaps have accepted her with enthusiasm, if the heir of the Jagellons of Bohemia and of Hungary had wisely revived the traditions of the past, appealed to the sentiments of the Polish Catholics, and recalled the ancient alliance of the three kingdoms. In Germany the influence of Metternich, although dominant, was often paralyzed by the very multiplicity of states and sovereigns. More than once the Austrian minister had groaned over the weakness of governments which accepted laws imposed upon them by their people during revolts, and over the errors of peoples misguided by the example of the July revolution. The sovereigns, on their part, forced to make humiliating conces-

sions, gladly turned for assistance to the powerful chancellor, and
Metternich exercised over them a veritable tutelage.

Conferences analagous to the Congresses of Laibach and Troppau continued the alliance between the three courts of Russia,
Austria, and Prussia. In September, 1833, the three sovereigns
met at Münchengrätz and a treaty was signed which again confirmed
the alliance, or, perhaps better, the conspiracy of the three monarchs.
According to it no political refugee could find an asylum in any of
the three states, and all fugitives from justice were to be surrendered. Precautions were also taken against the spirit of liberty
which was again appearing in France. In case the French Government should be unable to suppress revolutionary plots against foreign states, the three emperors reserved to themselves the right to
intervene. But despite all this high-handed policy in international
matters, Austria was rapidly discovering the most deplorable state
of affairs within her own borders.

The financial situation was very grave, and despite the efforts
of Francis and his minister to stifle the new political ideas, the
most serious problems began to arise. Austria had paid dearly
for the glory of being the arbiter of Europe and the restorer of
legitimacy. The patent of 1811 was a frank avowal of bankruptcy.
An issue of forty-five million *Anticipatiouseheine* in 1813 had not
relieved the paper currency, and Stadion, who had been called to
reorganize the finances, found his task very difficult. The expenses of the expedition of 1815 had been covered by a loan of
fifty millions, out of which the government realized scarcely forty.
The imposts were increased till they overwhelmed the taxpayer.
Austria had received nearly fifty million florins indemnity from the
war. But England demanded the payment of the subsidies. From
1792 to 1814 the sum amounted to more than eleven million pounds
sterling. A new loan was necessary to balance this account, which
Austrian statesmen would fain have overlooked. Stadion elab-
orated a plan to remedy all these evils. No more paper money
was to be issued, and the National Bank of Austria was established,
which was to administer a sinking fund formed out of the war
indemnity. But the notes of this bank were refused, and fell into
the hands of the stock-jobbers. Other expedients had to be tried;
new loans were raised to pay old ones. It was at this time that
the famous banking houses of Vienna—the Barings, Labouchères,
Parishes, and, above all, the Rothschilds—took their rise and be-

gan to dictate to every European capital. As has been justly remarked, Vienna became the center of a financial aristocracy which administered the whole European public debt as if it were its private estate.

Hungary never agreed willingly to any national system of taxation, and down to the year 1827 custom houses were to be found along the frontiers of every province in the monarchy, and the prohibitive system paralyzed all industry. From an economical point of view the most important event of the reign of Francis II. was the establishment of the Austrian Lloyd, at Triest, which has become an important marine navigation company.

We have already said something of the system of repression which weighed upon everyone. An inquisitorial police watched over the lives of the citizens, and the censorship of the press interfered with every expression of opinion. Liberty of conscience was subject to most annoying restrictions; public education was placed entirely in the hands of the clergy; no one was allowed to study in a foreign university; and the central government persisted in refusing to recognize the rights of the diets. And yet, in spite of all this, public opinion was slowly working its way toward freedom with irresistible energy.

Chapter XXVI

HUNGARY AND THE SLAV COUNTRIES. 1790-1835

JOSEPH II. had left Hungary in a state of violent excite--
ment. The comitat of Pesth proclaimed the fall of the dynasty,
and others predicted it in case the new sovereign did not grant
the country her liberty. Everybody was agreed in demanding the
convocation of the diet, which was at last to give voice to the long-
suppressed wishes of the people. The revolutionary spirit which
was agitating France had passed to the Magyars, but between
France and Hungary there existed a remarkable difference: in
France the revolution occurred in the name of equality, while
among the Magyars the greater and lesser nobility alone represented the political element of the nation, and they demanded, in
the name of liberty, privileges which for the most part were absolutely contrary to the ideas of 1789. " Some of the comitats even
declared that it was not the peasants who had occasion to complain, but the lords; and that, instead of making regulations to
relieve serfdom, it was necessary to lend assistance to the nobles
in the enforcement of their privileges. Others, setting up this opinion as a doctrine, declared that Providence had planned that there
should be kings, nobles, and serfs." Among the recent reforms,
the only one regarded with favor by the Magyars was the toleration granted the Protestants, the lesser nobility being for the most
part of that faith.

Nevertheless a democratic party was gradually forming
which endeavored to excite the masses, and it was under these
circumstances that Leopold II. decided to convoke the diet. It held
its preliminary session in the castle of Buda. " O blessed day! day
of resurrection!" wrote the poet Baroti. " I hear the mother
tongue; the old costumes delight me." " We swear it, that as long
as the blood of Attila flows in our veins, as long as the name of
Magyar remains, this day will remain sacred in our memory!"
cried the poet Peozely. In the two chambers the nobles naturally

had the majority. From the opening session serious charges were made. Some accused the king of treason, others claimed for Hungary complete independence in regard to foreign affairs, and demanded a Magyar ambassador at Constantinople, and that Magyar regiments in time of peace should be stationed in Hungary, and be commanded by native officers only.

Leopold II., taking his stand on the Pragmatic Sanction, refused to recognize any other agreement with Hungary, and on November 15, 1790, caused himself to be crowned. He did more: he restored the palatine, the diet electing his son, the young Archduke Alexander, to the office. But it was little more than an empty title, since it was not at all likely that the young prince would show much energy in defending the rights of the kingdom against his father. Nevertheless these concessions, following immediately after the reign of Joseph II., called forth transports of joy among the Magyars. The measures adopted by the diet summed up the wishes of the people. The crown of St. Stephen was to remain at Buda; the king was to reside from time to time in Hungary; he was to consult, concerning Hungarian affairs, only with Magyar counselors, and not to apply the laws of the other states to Hungary. The diet was to be convoked at least every three years, and it alone possessed the legislative power and the right to spend money and to raise troops. These important decisions were completed by an act providing for liberty of conscience on a much more liberal basis than that established by Joseph II.

But a question more difficult of solution than all these was that of the amelioration of the lower classes—peasants, serfs, the Servians of the Banat, and the citizens of the free cities. The nobles were little disposed to surrender their privileges, and it was Leopold who advocated the cause of liberalism against them. The diet granted to the peasants the right of changing their abode, but refused to grant the abolition of corporal punishment. The bourgeoisie of the cities were for the most part of foreign origin. They now took up the principles of the French Revolution and demanded admission to public offices, and a real representation in the diet. The king did his best to conciliate their interests with those of the nobles; he likewise protected the Servians, and authorized them to assemble in congress to discuss the interests of their race. The Orthodox church was recognized, and a Servian chancery was created, despite the opposition of the Magyars. Death struck the emperor, Leopold II., down at the very beginning of his popularity, and at a time when the country had great need of him. When France declared war against Francis II. the Magyar aristocracy at once showed its readiness to support the sovereign. They were eager to be led against the revolutionists and democrats on the banks of the Seine. But gradually Francis, by his obscurantism, coupled with that of his minister, Thugut, lost the popularity which had greeted him on his accession. The censorship, and the persecution of Protestants, in which the Magyar Catholics themselves took a conspicuous part, created discontent. The adherents of the French Revolution increased throughout the kingdom and some even undertook to propagate the French doctrines in the form of a popular catechism. They were arrested, with many of their accomplices. Fifty citizens accused of high treason were shut up in the fortress of Buda. It was difficult to prove the plot, but the works of the accused showed tendencies hostile to royalty and to the nobility. One among them, Bascany, had translated the " Marseillaise." Five were sentenced to death on the scaffold, and in May, 1795, they were executed. Others, among whom was Bascany, were shut up in the Fortress Küfstein in the Tyrol, while many of their publications were burned by the hangman, notably the translation of the " Marseillaise." The author of this translation of the French Revolutionary hymn expiated his imprudence by nine years of imprisonment.

The Magyar nobles obtained important commands in the Austrian army, and the diet of 1796 voted the entire appropriation demanded of it. Hungary gave to Austria some of her best generals, as, for example, the well-known Alvinzy, while her poets encouraged their fellow-countrymen in the conflict. Up to the peace of Campo Formio Hungary had lost more than 100,000 men and 30,000,000 of florins. But the country, drained of its men and money, and badly cultivated, was reduced to the lowest depths of misery, foreign affairs having completely blinded the eyes of the Hungarians to the real interests of the kingdom. The diet of 1796 considered no other question but that of subsidies for the army.

The diet of 1802 had to deal with a very critical situation. It concerned the reform of the customs regulations, so unfavorable to the economic interests of the country. The Austrian Government, on the other hand, was occupied much more with another question, namely, the maintenance of the Hungarian army upon a war footing in the time of peace, which involved a supplementary subsidy of a million florins. The troops furnished by Hungary were twofold in character: the regular regiments and the insurrection, raised after a war had actually broken out. The government was anxious to strengthen the regular army at the expense of the insurrection. It wished that the assembly would give up its right of voting the contingent. On this point it failed, but it did succeed in obtaining 6000 recruits yearly in time of peace and 12,000 in time of war, who entered into obligations to serve for ten years. At the same time it obtained two millions for the war budget. In its turn the diet tried, though unsuccessfully, to secure the annexation of Dalmatia to Hungary. The debates concerning the privileges of the nobility revealed once again how stubbornly attached to its privileges was the Magyar aristocracy, and how utterly untouched by the ideas of equality by this time spread broadcast throughout Europe. This selfishness of the ruling classes was to stand royalty in good stead when, desiring to check the nobility finally, it found support in the people, especially the middle classes.

In the meantime the government continued its Germanizing policy. The German theater at Pesth was favored by a considerable subsidy. On the other hand the enthusiastic Hungarian poets, Csokonay, Verseghy, Berszenyi, and especially the immortal Kisfaludy, placed the Hungarian language on a firm basis by excellent productions, which rank with the very best poetry of western Europe. After the diet of 1802 the most important event of this period for Hungary was the creation of the official title of emperor of Austria, which deeply wounded the Hungarians, despite the assurances of the monarch that this would involve no change in the relations between the different states. The prestige of their kingdom of St. Stephen was henceforth to be subordinated to that of the empire. Nevertheless, the hereditary loyalty of the Magyars again triumphed, and when Napoleon, after the capitulation of Ulm, reached the gates of Vienna the diet would not sell its services. The Magyar aristocracy remained faithful to the hereditary dynasty. Nevertheless the diet would not consent to the levy *en masse* which the government asked. It demanded new concessions for the national language, notably the right of the comitats to correspond with the central government in the Magyar tongue. The frontiers of Hungary were soon exposed to the French arms. Napoleon was at Vienna, the army of Italy on the

Raab. But the Palatine Joseph did not wish to expose the kingdom to an invasion. He withdrew to Buda-Pesth, sent the sacred crown of St. Stephen to Munkacs, and left General Palffy at Presburg, with orders to obtain from Napoleon the neutrality of Hungary. Davoust readily consented to contenting himself with the occupation of Presburg without imposing either requisitions or contributions upon the inhabitants. At the same time Napoleon, as appears from his correspondence, gave orders that the grievances of the Hungarians against the Austrian government should be studied and use made of them.

The diet of 1807 devoted itself exclusively to internal questions, and the government made every effort to obtain supplies in view of future conflicts. It demanded levies, the number fixed once for all, and an extraordinary impost for military needs. The lower chamber refused the regular levy, claiming for Hungary the right to give or withhold its men as it wished. The chamber of magnates was more conciliatory, in form at least, and was more disposed to make the financial sacrifice. It granted a sixth of the revenue of the nobility, merchants, and bourgeoisie, and one per cent. of the value on all real property. Over the question of the regular levy the conflict was very bitter. The diet did not wish to surrender its right of determining the contingent, and even after it was voted the conflict was taken up by the comitats. It was at this diet that Paul Nagy, the great Magyar orator of Hungarian independence, first appeared. In spite of the protests of the court, the diet energetically maintained the autonomous position of Hungary within the Austrian monarchy.

In order to win for himself the sympathy of the Magyars, Francis II. decided to have the new empress-queen, his third wife, Marie Louise, crowned. This ceremony never fails to excite much enthusiasm among the Hungarians, and is always a source of profit to the monarchy. On the other hand Napoleon's war with Spain excited in the Hungarian nobility a lively indignation.

During the campaign of 1809 the diet added 20,000 conscripts to the 12,000 which they had voted previously, and decreed the insurrection. The poets, Verseghy and Kisfaludy, called the nation to arms. The great families made enormous sacrifices; Prince Esterhazy furnished two hundred horses, the archbishop of Kalocsa one hundred and twenty. The enthusiasm increased still more when, on May 1, 1809, the empress-queen and the heir-apparent, leaving Vienna, which was threatened by the enemy, came to seek an asylum in the imperial castle at Buda. Napoleon, who never properly estimated public sentiment in Hungary, thought the moment had come for striking a great blow at Austria by detaching from her the kingdom of St. Stephen. From his headquarters at Schönbrünn he addressed a proclamation to the Hungarians which was immediately scattered throughout the kingdom. This document had been translated by the poet Bacsanyi, who, thrown into the prison of Kufstein some time before, had there met Maret, ambassador of the French Republic, arrested by the Austrians. Maret, now duke of Bassano and minister of Napoleon, met again at Vienna his old companion in captivity, who undoubtedly aided him in drawing up the original and took upon himself the translation.

" Hungarians! " the proclamation said, " it is the emperor of Austria, and not the king of Hungary, who has declared war on me. Your consistent defensive system and the measures taken by your last diet have shown that you wished to maintain peace. The moment has come for you to recover your independence. I offer you peace, the integrity of your territory, of your liberty, and of your laws, either as they have existed, or modified by yourselves, if you think that the interests of the time and of your fellow-citizens demand it. I wish nothing of you and desire only to see you a free and independent nation. Your union with Austria has been your misfortune. Your blood has been shed for her in distant lands, and your dearest interests have been constantly sacrificed to those of the Hereditary States. You form the finest part of her empire, yet you are only a province, always enslaved to passions which are foreign to you.

" You have national customs and a national language; you are proud of your illustrious and ancient origin: resume then your existence as a nation. Have a king of your own choice, who may reign only for you, reside in your midst, and be surrounded only by your citizens and your soldiers. Hungarians! that is what all Europe, which is watching you, demands of you; that is what I, too, demand of you. A lasting peace, commercial relations, and assured independence, such is the reward that awaits you if you wish to be worthy of your ancestors and of yourselves. You will not reject such liberal and generous offers, you will not waste your blood for feeble princes, always enslaved to corrupt ministers and

sold to England. Assemble in a national diet on the field of
Rakos, in the manner of your ancestors, and make known to me
your resolutions."

This document, in spite of the incontestable ability with which
it had been drawn up, produced little impression in Hungary.
The insurrection took up arms and concentrated at Raab. Badly
equipped and poorly armed, it assembled in an entrenched camp
under the command of the Archduke John. But the formidable
French artillery and the inequalities of the marshy ground rendered unavailing the valor of the Hungarian cavalry, Raab was
taken, and the Austrians were not sparing in raillery to those fine
gentlemen who had allowed themselves to be beaten on their own
soil. After this reverse, the court still demanded 40,000 men of
Hungary. Soon furnished by voluntary enlistment, these went to
reinforce the army of the Archduke Charles. The kingdom suffered besides from requisitions and from military excesses
which have not rendered popular the memory of the French soldiers. The Treaty of Vienna detached from Hungary certain portions of Croatia, a wrong which the Magyars highly resented.

They had not hesitated to fight for Austria, but they refused
to lend themselves to the deplorable measures that the government of Vienna thought necessary in order to remedy the bad
state of its finances. The emperor, supported by his lieutenant,
the Palatine Joseph, had recourse to violent means. The recal-
citrant deputies were summoned *ad audiendum verbum regium,*
and one of them, Joseph Desseffvy, was excluded from the diet.
In the end they yielded to force. On the whole the Hungarians
were poorly repaid for their fidelity to Austria.

Nevertheless Hungary furnished a numerous and brave contingent for the campaign of 1813-1814, though it took part in
the struggle without enthusiasm. This time the poets and the
publicists celebrated neither the supreme conflict against the tyrant
of Europe nor the victories of the Austrian army. "We are
happy," said one address to Francis, "for the victories of your
majesty; they will permit you to think of the welfare of your subjects. The fear of the enemy has thus far prevented all your wishes
from being carried out." Hungary had fought more for the
dynasty than for her independence; she had postponed the discussion of questions touching her own especial interests; she hailed
the peace with joy, in the hope that the sovereign would at last

interest himself in his faithful Hungarians—an illusion that did not last long.

After 1815 Francis II. refused for some time to convoke the diet. While poets such as Kolczey, and Alexander and Charles Kisfaludy were attempting to revive the ancient glories of the nation, the Viennese government was endeavoring to stifle the development of public spirit by means of the censorship. But in the absence of the diet the people turned to the comitats. That of Bars, for instance, protested nobly. "We do not doubt," it said, "that this rigorous censorship imposed on our literature appears useful to his majesty's government. The ignorance of contemporary events that we owe to it makes easier, perhaps, the exercise of authority. We only ask if manly spirits will put up with such repression? What indeed are our sins? Why are the sources of civilization closed for us? Why are we cut off from human society?"

In the face of an adversary so tenacious as the Hungarian aristocracy the convocation of the diet could not be indefinitely postponed. The royal chancery at Pesth found itself powerless to govern without the legal concurrence of the country, the Archduke Joseph, who had been palatine for many years, had been somewhat influenced by the Magyar ideas of self-government, and Austria needed troops for the occupation of Italy. The king attempted to win over the Hungarians by flattery, and after a military review in 1820 made a speech in which he told them that, while the rest of the world was relinquishing old laws and seeking new forms of government, they had a constitution "which you love and I love and will preserve and transmit to our successors." This declaration had little effect upon the Magyars, however. The comitats refused to pay taxes or to furnish soldiers, and even after the sovereign had replaced the *foispan* by royal administrators, resisted still further, and all the officials resigned. The magistrates even refused to prosecute the cases for high treason sent them by the government at Vienna.

It now seemed that royal authority could be best strengthened through a national parliament, and the diet of 1825-1829, which met at Presburg, September 11, 1825, marks an important step in the constitutional history of Hungary. The king in his speech promised anew to observe the constitution and hand it down intact to his heirs, while he did not neglect a ceremony which has always had great prestige in Hungary, and his fourth wife, Charlotte of Bavaria, was crowned as queen. Among the deputies of the diet were Szechenyi in the upper chamber, known as the Great Magyar, and in the lower chamber Paul Nagy, whose fiery eloquence had signalized him in previous diets, and a young advocate of the comitat of Zala, Francis Deak. The deliberations were noisy and less docile perhaps than the court had hoped. There were recriminations against the violence of the government, the misdeeds of royal administrators, the violations of personal liberty, and the long adjournment of national representation —all with the verbiose eloquence and in the doubtful Latin which the assembled Magyars then employed. The dynasty had to hear some hard truths. Violent orators even proclaimed that the Hapsburgs were the hereditary enemies of Hungary, and the king was obliged to accord satisfaction and declare that he had not intended to violate the constitution. The Hungarians asked that there be added again to their kingdom those territories which had been a part of it by historic right, Dalmatia, for example, but they were not listened to. The financial measures of 1811 and of 1816 were stormily debated. One of the most important results of this diet was the development of the Magyar language and literature. Szechenyi used the national tongue in the tribune, and subscribed 60,000 florins to the founding of the Hungarian Academy, while a national theater arose at Pesth. A ready writer no less than an eloquent orator, Szechenyi undertook to reveal economic truths to his compatriots, and his book on " Credit " was epoch-making. The old world of magnates broke down under the force of modern ideas and the years which followed 1830 are marked by important works, such as the construction of the bridge at Pesth and the tunnel at Buda, and the regulation of the course of the Theiss.

In order to attach the Hungarians more closely to him, Francis II., during his lifetime, had his successor, the Archduke Ferdinand, crowned. After the July Revolution he needed to dispose of all the forces of Hungary, and convoked the diet in order to obtain new levies. Twenty thousand men were granted, but were only to be levied in case the monarchy should be directly attacked. The diet of 1833 had to determine some grave questions; this time it had to deal not only with the relations of the aristocracy with the sovereign, with taxes and with the constitution, but also with the emancipation of the agricultural classes and the economic development of the country. The Hungarian nobility, very zealous in the defense of its own interests, had always shown a deplorable egotism in its relations with the peasants. It had given good opportunity to the Austrian government to play a tutelary rôle toward the peasants. More than once terrible jacqueries had stained the provinces with blood, as for instance in 1831, at the time of the cholera, when the peasants of the comitat of Saros massacred some of their seigneurs accused of having poisoned the wells. The emperor now invited the diet to discuss a project of agrarian reform, the basis of which he himself laid down. The lower chamber agreed to this programme. Deak, Balogh, and Kolczey spoke eloquently of liberty and human dignity, while the chamber of magnates was rebellious at such liberal concessions, and not at all disposed to grant them. The discussions were prolonged for two years, when certain reforms were agreed upon. Hereafter the peasants were not to be at the mercy of the jurisdiction of the seigneur, who had been at the same time judge and party to the case; they could no longer be arrested by his order; they had the right of leaving their lands by selling their usufruct, and of acquiring property by an arrangement with the seigneur, without, however, breaking the feudal tie; and finally, they had no longer to bear the expenses of the diet, which, up to this time, they had had to pay alone. This was the first step toward equality of taxation, equality to which the old Magyar spirit was profoundly repugnant. It was regarded as a great event when Szechenyi obtained that on the new bridge at Pesth, all nobles and yeoman alike should pay toll. Cziraki, the supreme judge of the kingdom, declared with tears that he would never cross this bridge, which symbolized to him the ruin of the old national constitution.

It was the diet of 1833 that marked definitely the entrance of the Magyar language into parliamentary life. The lower chamber compelled the upper one to use this as the common medium of communication, while a young advocate, Louis Kossuth, edited in the Hungarian tongue a *Gazette* of the diet. This organ, distributed secretly in order to escape the censorship, interested the entire country in the parliamentary debates and carried to the most distant frontiers those political conflicts of which Presburg was the center. Some of these debates had dealt with the affairs of Poland. The Polish revolution had failed, but it had excited much sympathy in Hungary, and, when some of the Polish refugees in France tried to gain for their cause the intervention of the Hungarian assembly, a number of fiery speeches were delivered from the tribune, one orator even going so far as to reproach the government for having employed Hungarian soldiers in the oppression of Italian patriots. It required all the tact and popularity of the Palatine Joseph to prevent a diplomatic incident. The revolution of Warsaw, in 1830, prepared in a certain measure that of Pesth in 1848.

The other provinces of the empire are certainly not so interesting historically during the years from 1825 to 1835 as is Hungary, with its parliamentary and provincial institutions, its eloquent tribune, and its perpetual conflict between retrograde and liberal ideas. But the life of a people is not entirely in its official manifestations; it is at times concentrated in the development of that private opinion expressed by sudden explosions. For the Slavs of Austria the first thirty years of the nineteenth century were not less productive than for the Magyars. At the beginning of his reign Leopold II. had convoked the diet of Bohemia, whereupon it sent him a long memorandum of its grievances, demanded the repeal of all those measures passed in the two preceding reigns which struck at the rights of the kingdom or at ecclesiastical institutions, and asked for the right of taking part in the legislation which had been taken away from them in 1627 by the new constitution of Ferdinand II. Leopold made some concessions, but none that would enfeeble the authority of the central power. The diet regained only the right of levying and arranging for collecting taxes, and of discussing all laws proposed by the sovereign; the permanent committee was also reëstablished, but with very restricted powers. The crown of St. Vacslav was sent back to Prague, and the emperor rendered homage to the historical traditions by having himself crowned, an example which was followed by his successors, Francis I. and Ferdinand II. Indeed, the present sovereign is, with Joseph II., the only king who has broken with this time-honored custom.

The efforts of the diet to recover its prerogatives were only feeble symptoms of the intellectual movement which had begun toward the end of the eighteenth century. In 1774 one of the few remaining representatives of the native aristocracy, Count

Kinsky, had in a German pamphlet urged the maintenance and development of the national language. Some conscientious historians, Pelcel, Dobner, and Prochazka, began to study the early history of Bohemia, while the Royal Society of Sciences was founded in 1784. Interest in archæology led to philological researches, and it was no longer possible to disdain a language in which was found a curious genius of its own, a rich literature, and close connection with that wide group of Slav tongues that extends from the Adriatic to the Arctic. In 1793 a chair of the Czech language was established at the University of Prague, where Joseph II. had so shortly before ordered that all teaching should be in German. The great linguist, Dobrovsky (1753-1829), by his travels and his writings laid the basis for Slav comparative philology. His precursors had treated the Czech as a dead language. Now young poets gave life to it and made it the organ of their patriotic aspirations. Through the generosity of the Counts Sternberg the Czech Museum was founded at Prague in 1818, and its precious collections excited much sympathetic interest.

Archives and libraries were searched and the discovery of mediæval poems, such as the "Judgment of Libusa" and the "Manuscript of Kralove-Dvor," was received with veritable enthusiasm. The authenticity of these poems has been contested, but whether true or false it is certain that they exercised an irresistible influence and corresponded admirably to the public sentiments of the time. "It would be shameful for us to look to the Germans for justice," says the "Judgment of Libusa," "since it is determined for us by the laws which our fathers formerly carried into those countries." "The stranger has entered by force into our heritage and commands us in a foreign language, and that which he does from morning till night he forces our wives and our children to do," says the "Manuscript of Kralove-Dvor."

Bohemia recognized that alone she was too feeble to hold her own against both Austria and Germany at the same time, but to German solidarity she was able to oppose Slav solidarity; the Czech tongue was not only spoken by five or six millions of people, but those who spoke it could claim kinship with kindred tongues, Russian, Polish, Croatian, and Servian. This union of the Slavs became the watchword of the Czech patriots, and added much to their strength. It was celebrated by the poet Kollar in a famous pamphlet, and in the great poem which he consecrated to his race, under the name, "*Slava dcera,* the Daughter of the Slavs, or the Daughter of Glory (1824)." "After being born to a new life," sang Kollar, "we have entered into a great desert which heaven has not yet made productive; the Romance and Germanic peoples walk in a beaten path and we follow them with a slow step; but we are a young people, we know what others have done, while they are ignorant of what our rôle is to be in the annals of humanity. We do not wish for a victory which falls from heaven without sweat and without work." Elsewhere he evoked the memory of the tragic fate of the Slavs of the Elbe: "It is there! I see it through my tears, that broad land, formerly the cradle and now the tomb of a great nation. . . . From the sources of the Elbe to the Baltic there formerly resounded one great and generous tongue. Why does one hear it no longer? Shame to thee, jealous and covetous German. Thou hast caused torrents of our blood to be shed, and now thou dost continue to pour forth floods of calumny, hoping in these to drown our memories of the past. He alone who is worthy of liberty knows how to respect all liberties. He who puts slaves in irons is himself a slave."

Bohemia he shamed for having allowed herself to be invaded and colonized by the Germans. "Who, then, is that young and beautiful girl who runs in the fields? She must indeed be poor to wear a robe pieced from such diverse materials. It is our Bohemia dotted over with foreign colonists." Finally, he called upon all the Slavs to form a definite alliance: "Russians, Servians, Czechs, Poles, become united. . . . From Athos to Pomerania, from the fields of Silesia to the plain of Kosovo, from Constantinople to the Volga, wherever one hears the Slav language let us rejoice and embrace each other, happy in our immense fatherland, Slavia. Believe me, brothers, we have all that which assures continuance to a great people. Continents and seas stretch under our feet; gold and silver, strong and vigorous arms, a language rich and powerful—we possess everything, except concord and liberty." And following unremittingly this dream of unity he drew a vivid picture of the new Slavia: "I have said it a hundred times, I cry it again to you to-day, O dispersed Slavs, be united and not isolated groups, be united or nothing. Ah, have I said more than once when my spirit wavered, were our Slav people only of gold, of silver, or of copper, I would weld them into a single statue. Of Russia I would make the hands, of the Poles the bust, of the Czechs the arms and the head, and of the Servians the feet. The smaller nations, the Wends, Lusatians, Silesians, Croats, and Slovaks should be the vestments and the weapons. Europe should kneel before this image whose head should touch the clouds, and whose steps should reach across the world."

Around Kollar was grouped a school of patriot poets; Celakovsky, Hanka, and Vocel. The Slovak Safarik wrote a great work on Slav antiquities (1837), while the Moravian Palacky, appointed historiographer of the kingdom of Bohemia, commenced the history of his adopted country, which is one of the most remarkable works of our time and has taken more than half a century to complete. Thanks to such talents and patriotism Bohemia not only regained the consciousness of her own nationality, but put herself at the head of the Slav peoples of the empire, and the Slavs of the south were not slow to follow her example. Then it was that Croatia gave the signal for the awakening. That country had been profoundly stirred by the Servian revolution, and the works of the leading writers of the new principality, the Karadjitches and Obradnovitches, had found a sympathetic echo.

In 1826 a society of Servian literature had been founded by the Servians of Hungary, and in its turn the capital of Croatia became aroused. So far the diversity of provincial dialects had been an obstacle to the unity of the literature, but now an eminent publicist, Louis Gaj, undertook to unite into a harmonious whole the scattered forces of Illyria. He commenced by publishing two newspapers, one entitled the Croatian *Gazette,* the other the Croatian, Slavonian and Dalmatian *Aurora* (1835). He chose the following fiery motto: "A people without nationality is a body without bone." He then proposed to substitute for the local names of Servians, Croatians, Slovenes, and Dalmatians, the common one of Illyrians, which Napoleon had restored. The following year he gave to his two journals the titles of *Aurora,* and of the *Illyrian Gazette.* " Europe," said he, " rests on a three-cornered lyre. This lyre is Illyria. It extends from Villach to Varna and to Scutari; the strings of this lyre are Carinthia, Gorica, Istria, Carniola, Styria, Croatia, Slavonia, Dalmatia, Ragusa, Bosnia, Montenegro, Herzogovina, Servia, Bulgaria, and southern Hungary. They are not in accord with one another, but we wish to make them resound harmoniously." Illyrism, however, soon encountered violent opposition; at first from the Hungarians, who did not care to see the Slavs escaping from their hegemony, and then from the Servians, who feared that their traditions and hopes would be absorbed by the Croatians. So Illyrism lost ground little by little, until even its name has disappeared to-day, though there still remains to the southern Slavs a serious sentiment of their literary solidarity. The movement had indeed given a considerable impulse to mental development, and a poetical school appeared, less brilliant perhaps than that of Prague, but not less patriotic.

Thus, at the two extremities of the empire, the Slav peoples were awakening and ready to contend against the Magyars on the one hand, and against the Germans on the other. They were again claiming their place in the world. Separated by historical circumstances and geographical situation, they were acquiring a consciousness of their own solidarity and developing the moral force necessary for the approaching struggle.

Chapter XXVII

FERDINAND I—AUSTRIA ON THE EVE OF REVO-
LUTION. 1845-1848

FRANCIS II. died on March 2, 1835, much regretted by the Viennese, who were attached to him through his genial characteristics and the recollections of so many hard experiences. In the provinces the rumor was current that he had acquired a large fortune, and that he had left it to his subjects. The people awaited with impatience the opening of the will. But they were sadly disappointed, as the following lines from the document will indicate: "I avow my love to my people. I hope that I may be able to pray for them; I ask of them to show to my legitimate successor the fidelity and devotion which they have shown to me; I thank all the functionaries who have served me well." Louis XIV. could scarcely have spoken otherwise. The successor of Francis II., Ferdinand I., of a delicate constitution and subject to fits of epilepsy, was little fitted to take over the heavy heritage of the monarchy. Even when in good health his mind was never lucid nor was his will firm. The simple matter of affixing the royal signature was for him a real burden. Consequently, Metternich, whom Francis II. had recommended to his son as the best of ministers, retained all his influence. "Touch nothing at the base of the political edifice, change nothing. Have full confidence in Prince Metternich, my best friend and most faithful of servants. Undertake nothing without him." Nevertheless Metternich was not able to govern entirely in the place of the real sovereign, and a sort of regency was established, consisting of the following persons: Clam Martinitz, the emperor's adjutant-general and head of the military section of the council of state; Metternich, minister of foreign affairs; Kolovrat; and the Archdukes Louis and Francis Charles. Their meetings constituted the *Staatsconferenz,* which was the real organ of executive power. But its functions were never very well defined. Established in order to govern till the monarch should have regained his health, it always had more or less of a provisional character. This government has been justly reproached with entire lack of unity and an unusual insensibility to the real needs of the Austrian people.

A number of liberal measures, however, did mark the opening of the reign. An amnesty for political prisoners followed the accession, a consulship was established in Servia, notwithstanding the fact that the young principality owed its existence to an insurrection against the legitimate authority, a treaty of navigation was concluded with Greece, which was in the same position, and diplomatic relations were resumed with Portugal. At the same time the cabinet of Vienna extended its moral support to the Carlists in Spain and sent some meager subsidies. The alliance of the three northern powers continued, as the conduct of Austria in Polish affairs sufficiently attested.

The city of Cracow had been erected by the treaties of 1815 into an independent republic. It had become the center of plots and conspiracies, and was suspected by all the powers who had shared in the spoliation of Poland. In 1831 the Russians had occupied the territory of the republic in order to deprive the insurgents of one of their principal bases of operation and source of supplies. But they had to evacuate it because of the objections of Austria, and the city continued a hot-bed of agitation for the refugees of the Polish revolution. In 1836 the three powers demanded the expulsion of all persons who had taken part in the revolution of 1830 and decided to occupy Cracow. This time it was Austria who undertook to police the republic, notwithstanding the protestations of England and France. It was the first step toward definitive occupation.

On the other hand Galicia was gradually being invaded by the ideas of the patriotic revival and of a national revenge which were steadily propagated by the émigrés. It was a difficult matter to oppose this general movement, which enlisted in its cause the sympathies of liberal Europe, but Austria was able by a policy analagous to that which was often adopted in Hungary to find in Polish society itself the means of paralyzing the revolutionary elements. Harsher even than the Magyar aristocracy, the Polish *sznlachta* or nobility had aroused bitter hatred by their treatment of the ignorant peasantry. The government took pains to foment this class hatred; it opposed the agrarian reforms; it had imposed upon the nobles the rôle of acting as recruiting agents and collectors of imposts, while it gave to its own functionaries the tutelary rôle of redressing abuses. Nor should it be forgotten that in the greater part of Galicia the peasant is not Polish. In the eastern part of the province Ruthenians constitute the majority of the population, and they, even more than Polish peasants, had been made to suffer at the hands of the Galician magnates. Adherents of the Uniate Greek Church, they had on more than one occasion to groan under the fanatic persecution of their masters, who compelled them to pay for the privilege of worshiping in their churches or opened them to the Jews. The governor of Galicia, Stadion, knew of these grievances, and had taken careful note of them. The Polish nobility could not remain ignorant of the claims which were to be made against them. In the diet, in itself anything but liberal, which met from time to time at Lemberg, the demand had been made to take up the cause of the peasants in 1843, but the Austrian government cared little to regulate the conflicts out of which grew the conditions which gave it the opportunity to keep the different peoples divided and thus to rule them.

Nevertheless a Polish insurrection was preparing in Galicia and the duchy of Posen. On February 28, 1846, upon the announcement of a plot at Cracow, the Austrian General Collin occupied that city with about a thousand men and three cannon. For two days the city seemed tranquil, but on the third day under pressure of the revolutionary factions, the senate and the authorities of the republic resigned and the Austrian troops were attacked by the Poles and forced to beat a retreat. Colonel Benedek marched up from Lemberg and with the aid of the peasants defeated the revolutionary committee of Cracow and reoccupied the city on March 2. Benedek, the "falcon of the Vistula," then commenced a career which was to end in failure at Sadowa. The brief, ephemeral success of the revolutionists of Cracow had thrown Vienna into a state of terror; the police doubled the arrests throughout the empire, especially in Galicia. These measures suppressed an insurrection which would doubtless have spread rapidly into Russian Poland. The peasants not being in sympathy with their lords denounced them to the authorities or gave them up themselves. A veritable jacquerie broke out. Murder, pillage, and incendiarism raged, particularly in the circle of Tarnow, with the encouragement, it is said, of the Austrian government, its officers actually joining the bands. The peasants declared that they pillaged and massacred at the emperor's order. A personage of high rank, Ferdinand d'Este, replied to the wife of a Pole who had just been assassinated, that the death of her husband was a mistake, that it was her brother's which had been intended. It was at this time that the poet Ujejski composed the hymn " Z dymem pozarow," which is to-day a classic in Poland: " Amid the smoke of our burning homes, and the blood of our brothers, this song rises to Thee, O Lord. 'Tis a terrible cry of pity, a groan out of the infinite; prayers that cause the hair to grow white; the crown of thorns is piercing our heads. O Lord! O Lord! What has time brought us? The mother is killed by her son, brother has killed brother. Among us are many Cains, but, O Lord, they are innocent; other demons incite and urge them on. Punish, oh, punish, the execrable hand and not the unwitting sword."

The peasants were convinced that the emperor would free them from all obligations toward their lords as a reward for their devotion. The patent of April 13 granted only part of their expectations. It suppressed compulsory cartage and labor during harvest; and authorized the peasants to bring their complaints directly to the captains of the circles.

Meanwhile the city of Cracow remained in the hands of the Austrians. Its occupation was explained to the foreign powers as a temporary measure dictated by military necessity. The Austrian troops, it was urged, were sent only to insure the establishment of a regular government in the little republic. Soon, with the consent of Prussia and Russia, the occupation became definitive, and the officials of the districts where the outrages had been most violent were promoted. The protests of France and England were of no avail. This acquisition was the first which Austria had made since the Congress of Vienna. The new territory comprised about twenty-two square miles and 160,000 inhabitants.

The annexation of Cracow confirmed once again the solidarity of the three powers in respect to the partition of Poland. Nevertheless, in regard to the Eastern Question, during Ferdinand's reign, as in that of his predecessor, harmony between Russia and

Austria was maintained only with much difficulty. The Porte, weakened by the triumphs of its vassal, Mehemet-Ali of Egypt, got into serious difficulty with him and appealed to Europe. Metternich made the mistake of supporting the Sultan, and Vienna became the center of animated conferences in which he induced the representatives of the Tsar to agree to a collective note of the powers promising the support of Europe to the Porte. But Tsar Nicholas was deeply offended, disavowed the act of his ambassador, and treated directly with England without consulting Austria at all, in July, 1840. Austria, whose dealings with the Porte have been as a rule very clumsy, then found it necessary to follow the lead of the two contracting powers. Mehemet-Ali was asked to restore a large part of his conquests. He was deprived of Syria through the aid of the Austrian squadron, which now took its place for the first time among the maritime powers. In the month of July a treaty was concluded which forbade to all vessels of war entrance into the Straits of Dardanelles, except by the Sultan's permission.

But the chief interest of the reign of Ferdinand II. lies in the increasing spread of the ideas of liberty and of nationality among the different races of the Austrian monarchy, that secret fermentation in which appeared the forces which were to transform the old Austria. The various diets can be regarded only as the official expression of political ideas. Docile or subdued in Galicia, and silent in some of the provinces, as in Upper Austria, Moravia, Silesia and Carinthia, in Lower Austria, Bohemia, and especially in Hungary, even under the old feudal form in which they still continued, the estates began to show signs of liberal tendencies.

In the diet of Lower Austria the middle class was not even represented. They had no right other than that of being present and giving assent when the vote on the taxes was taken. But notwithstanding this, the new ideas which penetrated the capital had considerable influence upon the decisions of this assembly. It showed a certain independence in economic matters. It vigorously demanded the intervention of the estates in the government, and criticised Francis II. for having ruled without their help. In the Tyrol, on the contrary, clerical and ultramontane ideas were supreme. Public instruction was almost entirely in the hands of the clergy. Missions and miracles satisfied the

popular imagination. The introduction of railroads was stubbornly resisted, and in 1837 the diet had recalled the Jesuits into
this province, from which they had been excluded in the preceding
century.

In Bohemia the debates in the diet did not reveal any very
energetic intellectual activity. The first act of the reunited estates,
on April 13, 1835, was to vote a monument to Francis II. Nevertheless, little by little they reëstablished the ancient parliamentary
forms which had singularly fallen into disuse since Joseph II. The
diet drew up its privileges in the form of a code in order to determine what powers belonged to it and what to the permanent committee, which had become a simple organ of government. But even
these slight attempts at independence were reprimanded by the
monarch. Nevertheless when the permanent committee and the
government attempted to impose new imposts without the consent
of the diet a serious conflict broke out between Vienna and
Prague. Count Chotek, burggrave of the kingdom, resigned, and
the government in the hope of better restraining the turbulent
nobility placed the Archduke Stephen, son of the Palatine Joseph,
at the head of the Bohemian government. Lively protests were
raised against his rule, and the estates demanded a complete carrying out of the constitution of 1627, thus proclaiming the continuity
of their historic rights, so misapprehended since the end of
the preceding century. Unfortunately the Czech nobility was
inspired in these claims only by a narrow spirit of caste. It
manifested a spirit of selfish egotism, passionately defended its
feudal privileges, and showed little desire to admit the middle class
to its deliberations. Only four royal cities were represented in the
diet, which numbered fourteen bishops, one hundred and fifty-one
lords, forty-three knights, and seven representatives of the middle
class. But notwithstanding this the disputes with the monarch
showed the progress of public opinion. In 1847 the leaders of
the opposition in Bohemia had resolved to come to an understanding with the estates of the German provinces and with the diet
of Hungary concerning united action. When the year 1848 arrived all the *desiderata* of the diet were confined to demands for
the representation of the towns in the estates, and the use
of the Czech language in the schools. The assembly lacked that
strength which comes from the support of public opinion because
it was formed only of the privileged classes. But below this decrepit

institution were the people who for half a century had been making rapid progress and who before arriving at their political emancipation had started out on their intellectual and moral emancipation.

The literary renaissance in Bohemia during the first forty years of the century was purely of a poetical and archæological character, but in a state whose institutions are based upon historic rights, as is the case in Austria, it was impossible that the study of history would not have considerable influence upon the public mind. In re-reading the treaties concluded between the kingdom and the princes of the house of Hapsburg, Bohemian patriots were led to ask of themselves what had become of the terms of the agreements entered into. The episodes of the Thirty Years' War reawakened the recollection of rebellion prompted by generous motives and stifled in blood. The Hussite Wars recalled a great epoch of moral and intellectual development, of liberty of conscience maintained against religious intolerance, which during half a century made of a little people a great nation. Thus the study of its history, of its national language, and of its ancient literature led in Bohemia to an ominous reaction against Austrian Germanism.

The middle class now gloried in cultivating a language which they had previously despised. In the absence of a political life the intelligent now found a field for their patriotic desires. Certain of the nobility attached themselves to the movement, and the popular literary society, the *Matice Ceska,* soon became a center for the patriotic propaganda. Founded in 1831 with fifteen members, it numbered 1667 in 1846. But the real organ of political life is the press. Up to 1840 Bohemia's few journals devoted their attention solely to literature. In 1846 Charles Havlicek, a man of great talent and patriotism, with an ingenious spirit of sarcasm which at times recalls that of Voltaire and of Heine, founded the *Official Gazette.* Havlicek realized perfectly that it was necessary to overthrow the feudal régime and the privileged classes, and he addressed himself directly to the middle class and to the people. He pleaded the cause of his country, under the cloak of articles written on the sufferings and oppression of Ireland, whose struggle for autonomy he described in vivid, suggestive language. All Bohemia understood, and the word " Repeal " became, therefore, the watchword of the patriots. Havlicek played the same rôle at Prague as did Kossuth at Pesth and Louis Gaj at Agram.

The agitation for which Prague thus furnished the center extended as far as Moravia, and even to the Slovaks of Hungary. Nor was it purely political; it had an economic and a religious character as well. The patriots were interested less in the privileges of the nobility than in the miseries of the peasantry who had so faithfully guarded the national language and popular poetry; they were the natural apostles of all the measures destined to ameliorate this condition. Moreover, the mere recollection of the Thirty Years' War was sufficient to make them hostile to the spirit of intolerant devotion which reigned at Vienna in official circles.

In the history of modern Hungary, two tendencies are to be noted. On the one hand is the generous and truly patriotic spirit which animates the Magyars and leads them to the greatest sacrifices for the maintenance and recognition of their historic and national rights; on the other is a blind egotism which prevents the recognition of the rights of others living among them. This twofold aspect of their character explains both their success and their failures. After 1825 public opinion made remarkable progress in Hungary. From the time the national language was accorded the right of being employed from the tribune eloquent orators were numerous in the diet. The opposition adopted language toward the government very much bolder than that employed at Vienna or Prague. Her orators and statesmen ranked with the political orators of London and Paris. These eminent men added to a sincere love of country marked intelligence and an appreciation of the real needs of their country.

The session of the diet in 1836 was most remarkable. The orators of the opposition vigorously attacked the government, which, devoted to obscurantism, endeavored to shackle the movement for popular education. " The nation must rely upon itself alone," cried both Deak and Beszeredy; " we have the right and we have the power," added the latter, " to work for the salvation of our country." After the dissolution of the diet Kossuth undertook to educate public opinion by a periodical publication in which were brought together the deliberations of the various comitats. He was arrested and thrown into prison with several of his friends. But among the younger Hungarians liberal ideas spread with amazing rapidity. When the diet opened again in 1840 the government offered to the opposition the release of the prisoners in exchange for certain concessions. But Deak, who from this moment received the name of the sage of his country, refused in eloquent words: " Duty toward native land is greater and holier than sympathy for one's friends. They themselves would find a liberty acquired at this price more cruel than their sufferings." An amnesty reconciled for the moment the opposition and the authorities. The government obtained the soldiers it demanded, the Magyar language was permitted in communications with the court and in ecclesiastical affairs, and the diet completed the steps taken by the previous assembly in regard to the purchase of land by the peasants.

From 1840 onward democratic ideas continued to invade Hungary more and more. Kossuth founded the *Pesth Gazette,* which eloquently disseminated the doctrines of equality and political freedom. In some of the comitats the meetings took on the character of clubs. But social progress still came slowly. The equality of all citizens in regard to taxes, which was proposed to the diet in 1843, was not adopted. About the same time a young poet coming from the lower classes, Alexander Petöfi, published in the reviews passionate odes on the love of country and liberty. " Formerly Hungary was a sea in which all the fallen stars, stars of the north, of the east, and of the south, extinguished themselves. The glory of Hungary is like a comet which has disappeared, and after several centuries will return brilliant and terrible." Other poets excited the national patriotism in singing of the historic past of Hungary.

" The nation must be formed out of new elements," Kossuth wrote in his paper; a curious remark because one of the most serious grievances of the patriots against the government of Vienna was the progress of Slavism among the Croats and the Slovaks; and thus their egotism condemned among their neighbors those very aspirations of which they were so proud among themselves. Together with the Polish émigrés and the Pan-Germans, they conjured up the red specter of Panslavism, as a pretext for combating it and of persecuting their fellow-countrymen, the Servians, the Slovaks, and the Croatians. The Austrian government had no interest in creating a state of things from which Russia would profit; but in view of the possible struggle with the

Magyars it could not afford to aid them in crushing the people who claimed merely the right of existence. Nothing was less legitimate, however, than the efforts of the Viennese government to paralyze Hungarian liberty, commerce, and industry. At one time it thought it had arrived at a suppression of Hungarian obstinacy by attacking the very source of her national liberties, the institution of the comitat. The *foispan* of the comitat, or chief count, was often a great lord who, being frequently absent during a part of the year, was replaced by an *alispan* or administrator. The chancellor, Apponyi, filled the place of the *foispan* in the village districts by a royal administrator. This attack upon an ancient privilege excited the most lively irritation throughout all the country; the administrators were compared to the captains of the Austrian circles (*Kreishauptmänner*) and to the French prefects. They were possessed of unlimited powers and did not depend, as the prefects, upon responsible ministers. The stubborn patriotism and the judicial spirit of the Hungarians made the task of these new functionaries very difficult. Deak was one of the first to organize resistance. In conformity with the traditions of the country, he entered into correspondence with all the comitats of the kingdom, and secured a vote that the institution of the royal commissioners was illegal.

The diet of 1847 opened calmly enough, in spite of the fact that Kossuth had been elected at Pesth in opposition to the government. The monarch and his family appeared at the opening session and affected a sympathy for the Magyar language which touched the hearts of the patriots. The Archduke Stephen, son of the Palatine Joseph, who had recently died, enjoyed great popularity and was in his turn made palatine. The discussion of the speech from the throne gave rise to lively debates. The opposition insisted above all upon securing the autonomy of the comitats by depriving the crown of the right of appointing royal administrators. The Chamber of Magnates wished to treat the king with more respect. It was decided to leave the address to the throne without a reply, and while Kossuth excited the masses by his eloquence, Szechenyi exerted himself to keep his compatriots within the bounds of law and moderation. The programme of the opposition drawn up by Francis Deak set forth clearly the demands of the kingdom. "Hungary," says this remarkable document, "is a free country with a separate system of representation and legislation; it is sub-

FERDINAND I

ordinate to no other country. It is not our desire to put the interests of our country in opposition to those of the unity of the monarchy and the safety of its existence, but we regard it as contrary to law and justice that the interests of Hungary should be subordinated to any other power whatsoever. We will never consent to be sacrificed to the idea of unity in the system of government. . . . For us the constitutional life is a treasure which we are not permitted to sacrifice either to foreign interests or to material advantages, however great. Our first duty is to maintain and strengthen it. We are convinced that if the Hereditary States still enjoyed their ancient liberties, or if according to the needs of our century and of justice, they took their place among constitutional nations, our interests and theirs, which now are so often divided, sometimes even antagonistic, could easily be reconciled. . . . The monarchy, increasing in material and intellectual power, would be able to resist with greater assurance the storms which time and circumstances may some day bring."

The question of the official language added greatly to the excitement. A project for a law submitted for the royal sanction had in it the following provisions: Magyar is henceforth to be the official language of the kingdom. Laws published in any other language shall not be legal. . . . Croatia in its relations with the central government must make use only of Magyar, and this language shall be taught in all the schools of the kingdom. Hungarian writers meant to imitate the example of France in this attempt to secure the general use of Magyar, forgetting, however, that in France it was merely a question of local idiom, not of national language, which had to be overcome.

Croatia had been annexed to Hungary for many centuries, but it did not form an integral part of it. With Slavonia and Dalmatia it looked upon itself as constituting a triple kingdom with its capital city at Agram. In fact, Dalmatia, taken by the Austrians from the Venetians, formed a separate province which the government at Vienna refused to hand over to Hungary or to the Croats. At the head of the government of the two provinces there was a high official known as the ban, a sort of viceroy invested with civil and military powers and the right to call together the diet or general assembly. It consisted of the orders of the comitats of Croatia and the delegates from the three Slavonian comitats. This diet in its turn sent a deputy to the Hungarian Table of Magnates and two to the estates, while a certain number of Croatian and Slavonian magnates sat in their own right in the upper chamber. The diet of Agram reserved to itself the right of sanctioning the laws passed at Presburg. The ties which bound Croatia to Hungary were not clearly defined; the Hungarians looked upon Croatia as conquered territory, while the Croats claimed that their relations to Hungary grew out of a personal union only. They never forgot that the pragmatic sanction of Charles VI. had been voted by the Croats before it was voted by the Hungarians. So long as Latin had served as the common language between the two peoples no strong antagonism had arisen, but the struggle began as soon as the Magyars tried to impose their language. Out of the resistance to Magyar aggression there developed an independent literature in this province, to which reference was made above. This Illyrian or Yougo-Slav movement could not but be disagreeable to the Magyars, but they made the great mistake of attacking it and of seeing in it the hand of Russia; of denouncing it as the work of a Panslavist propaganda, which as a matter of fact did not exist.

The Servians complained of even more serious grievances. In 1792 the Magyars had brought about the suppression of the Illyrian chancery, and the Servians, looked upon with suspicion, were deprived of all political employment. Added to this was the fact that a part of their race which had been torn from the Ottoman yoke by Milosh Obrenovitch had been formed into a separate principality, a circumstance calculated to arouse their patriotism. In 1826 they had established at Pesth a literary society which served as a model for many similar institutions throughout the Slav countries. The military frontier was occupied largely by Slavs and Rumanians, subject, as we have already seen, to a separate administration. These were always ready to ally themselves to the cause of the dynasty either out of the instinct of military obedience or because it was also the cause of their Slav and Rumanian fellow-countrymen. In the northern comitats the Slovaks had long been treated as veritable helots. "A Slovak is not a man," says a Magyar proverb. Nevertheless the Slovaks could not remain indifferent to the movement which was then agitating Bohemia; two of its greatest writers, Safarik, the author of "Slav Antiquities," and Kollar, the poet of Panslavism, were Slovaks. They dreamed of creating a national literature apart and distinct from

FERDINAND I   357

that of Bohemia. Men of ability like Stur, Hodza, and Urban led the movement and demanded a place for their nation among civilized peoples. From 1843 onward they made energetic demands at the court of Vienna, but without effect. Their neighbors, the Ruthenians or Little Russians, also began to awake under the influence of the Slav movement.

The principality of Transylvania ever since its reannexation in 1699 had been governed directly from Vienna, although it had a diet of its own which sat at Klausenburg. A chancery of Transylvania was established at Vienna and a *gubernium regium* at Hermannstadt. In this province, as in the case of all the rest of the kingdom of St. Stephen, except in Croatia and in the purely Magyar lands, the majority was crushed by the ruling minority. The Hungarians, who numbered five hundred thousand, the one hundred and seventy thousand Szeklers, and the three hundred thousand Saxons alone were represented in the diet, while one million two hundred and fifty thousand Wallachians had not a single representative. But the time was near at hand when these Wallachians also were to claim political rights.

In Vienna, likewise, liberal ideas began to ferment. Official formality or red tape was unusually hated, and all the internal miseries of the empire were attributed to it. Metternich had grown old, and since the difficulties in the East his increasing weakness was apparent. The education of the people had progressed in spite of the shackles which the government had laid upon it. Up to 1830 Vienna had been a luxurious and indolent city, devoted to music and sensual pleasures—the Capua of the mind, as the Viennese poet, Grillparzer, called it. But gradually men's minds awakened, notwithstanding the detestable education which prevailed even in the higher schools, and the sole result of which was a very mediocre knowledge of Latin. The number of distinguished men produced by German Austria during this period was very small. In 1847 the Emperor Ferdinand founded the Academy of Sciences, to-day one of the most flourishing in Europe, and in order to gain literary credit for Austria abroad, the government supported the *Viennese Literary Review,* the only publication which had no cause of complaint against the censors, because it was in large part edited by them. Up to 1848 this censorship of the press was a veritable scourge to the country. Its powers and functions were not defined by any law, but the contraband sale of books which was carried on on a large scale—prohibition only exciting public curiosity and calling the attention of the public to the forbidden fruit—served in part at least to offset it. Pamphlets introduced by fraud made up for the silence of the press. To the close observer it was evident that the people so long kept down would rise at the first opportunity and, not being accustomed to enjoy liberty, would commit unfortunate errors when they first found themselves in possession of it.

PART VII

REVOLUTION AND REACTION. 1848-1867

Chapter XXVIII

THE REVOLUTIONARY MOVEMENT. 1848-1849

NO other country has so tempestuous a history as has Austria during the years 1848 and 1849. In united countries revolutions have one center only toward which the provincial movements gravitate; in Austria there were several. At Vienna, Venice, Pesth, Prague, Agram, and Lemberg popular uprisings occurred simultaneously. Three great races were suddenly aroused and hurried forward by different and even opposite paths to secure liberty. Their divergent interests and their old-time rivalry led to conflicts among themselves, which made their most generous efforts abortive and crushed their hopes for a long time to come.

If ever a sovereign was unfit to deal with popular outbreaks, it was Ferdinand I., surnamed the Beneficent. The news of the February revolution in Paris was a veritable thunderclap, both for him and for his councilors. Austria was no longer, as in 1830, isolated from France by a reactionary Germany. On all sides German princes, either won over or overwhelmed by the current of popular opinion, granted constitutions to their subjects. Indeed, Germany herself transmitted to Vienna the new ideas which had come from Paris. On March 13 petitions were laid before the diet of Lower Austria demanding the publication of the budget, the regular convocation of an assembly consisting not only of the privileged estates but of representatives from all classes of the population; liberty of the press; publicity of the public tribunals; and new municipal and communal institutions. The students of the university, united with the liberals, went in procession to present the petition to the estates. The troops tried in vain to disperse them. With cries of " Down with Metternich! " the crowd burned the villa of the minister who had for so many years controlled the destinies of the empire. His dismissal was demanded, and escaping from Vienna in a washerwoman's cart he fled to England.

"The last beam of the old system has given way," said the London *Times,* "or, to speak more respectfully of so experienced a statesman, Prince Metternich has been compelled to retire from a contest which he can no longer wage with the world, or even with the public opinion of the pacific inhabitants of Lower Austria. . . . The oldest minister of the oldest court has been driven from office. . . . After forty years of unlimited sway he leaves an empire by so much in arrear of the rest of Europe—

impoverished in its finances—divided in its provinces—and not obscurely threatened in its most important possessions. . . ."

The emperor was obliged to authorize the arming and formation of the students into an academic regiment, and the organization of a sort of national guard. He invited the estates to send delegates to a parliament at Vienna, and announced the abolition of the censorship and the publication of a liberal press law. Vienna believed in his promises and made holiday. Kolovrat was named president of the council and Ficquelmont minister of the interior and leader of the cabinet. This student of Metternich inspired little confidence; nevertheless he seemed to take seriously his rôle of reforming minister, and prepared the constitution which

THE OUTBREAK CF THE REVCLUTION OF 1848 IN VIENNA

The populace seizing the Octroi gates of the city
Drawing by W. Zweigle

was published on April 25 following. It was copied in large part from the Belgian charter, and took no account of the peculiar conditions of the Austrian state. Hungary and Lombardy were not included at all, and for the remainder of the empire it established two chambers: a senate composed of princes of the imperial family, members nominated for life by the monarch, and owners of large estates; and a chamber of deputies which was to consist of 383 elected members. The constitution also guaranteed the right of public meeting, liberty of conscience, and liberty of the press. It concerned itself with neither nationalities nor the promises so recently made by the sovereign to Bohemia. This charter granted by the monarch and proclaimed with great pomp did not satisfy the demands, and Ficquelmont was forced to resign as a result of a popular movement on May 4. His successor, Pillersdorf, drew up an electoral law which carefully excluded the laboring classes, and the excitement in Vienna redoubled. At first the monarch seemed to yield to the popular movement; on May 15 he granted the establishment of a single chamber elected by universal suffrage, but two days after he left Vienna and fled to Innsbruck. The populace of the capital, still too much imbued with the traditions of monarchy to think of usurping its power, was amazed and embarrassed. A few barricades were erected, it is true, and a few lives lost, but on the whole the government of the emperor remained unquestioned. The Archduke John was sent to Vienna and empowered to form a ministry which was slightly more liberal than the preceding one. Early in July the delegates to the parliament began to arrive, but from the events which had occurred in the provinces it could be readily seen that this assembly was not destined to play a very serious rôle, or to restore peace to the Austrian empire, now shaken to her very foundations by revolution.

In Bohemia the revolution had broken out even earlier than in Vienna. The signal had been given by a liberal club which bore the significant name of "Repeal." On March 11 a meeting held in the hall of the Baths of St. Vacslav drew up a petition which demanded the union of Moravia and Silesia with Bohemia under a common administration, the amelioration of the condition of the peasants, and provisions for public instruction. These demands were very moderate, but the news of the events in Vienna soon emboldened the Bohemian patriots. Czech students organized an academic legion, and the Committee of Petitions sat continually. The smoldering national life burst forth in all public activities with an unexpected vigor. Soon a second petition was drawn up demanding the reconstruction of the kingdom of Bohemia, with a central diet sitting at Prague, the establishment of a responsible ministry, and the recognition of equal rights for the two races, the Czechs and the Germans. A deputation carrying these demands went to Vienna, where it was favorably received. The government postponed the annexation of Moravia and Silesia till the meeting of the central parliament, but guaranteed equal rights to the two nations of Bohemia. It also promised to call a Bohemian diet, chosen on the basis of universal suffrage, and offered to Bohemia a considerable degree of local autonomy. A national committee was instructed to draw up the new reforms. But Bohemian autonomy, restricted though it was, was not looked upon with favor by the Germans of Vienna who wished to remain at the head of the empire, nor by the Hungarians in conflict with the Slavs, and always frightened by the specter of Panslavism. Still less did it please the Germans of Bohemia itself. They maintained that the kingdom belonged to them by the Treaty of Vienna and by ancient right, and looked forward to its being one of the parts of a Greater Germany. The Committee of Fifty, which met at Frankfort to prepare for the meeting of the German parliament, had invited Palacky, the great national historian of the Czechs, to take part in its deliberations. His famous reply clearly set forth the position of Bohemia and of Austria in regard to a new Germany.

"The aim proposed by your meeting," said he, " is to substitute a federation of peoples for the old federation of princes, to bring the German nation to a true unity, to strengthen the sentiment of German nationality, and to secure the greatness of Germany, both at home and abroad. I honor these efforts and the sentiments which inspire them, but that does not say that I can associate myself with them. I am not a German, or at least I do not feel as if I were one. And certainly you have not called me to join you that I might play the rôle of a supernumerary without opinion and wishes of my own. . . . I am a Czech, a Slav by descent, and the little that I may be worth is all at the service of my country. This country is doubtless small, but it has possessed since its origin an historic individuality. Its princes have acted in concert with German princes, but the people themselves have never looked upon themselves as German. . . . Moreover, you wish to enfeeble Austria forever and make it impossible for her to exist as an independent state. Now, the maintenance of the integrity and the development of Austria is of great importance, not only to my people, but to all Europe, to civilization, and to mankind."

But the German element was fully in sympathy with the ideas of the promoters of the Frankfort parliament, and orders were issued to elect deputies. This gave rise to serious disputes and disorders, which were still further increased by the publication of the Austrian constitution of April 25. It contained no reference to the engagements entered into by the government with Bohemia a few days before, and the popular indignation rose to its height. On the flight of the emperor to Innsbruck the Czechs declined to obey the ministry at Vienna, and set up a sort of provisional government. When Count Thun summoned the diet of the kingdom some of the most illustrious Czechs joined in a movement to convoke a Slav congress at Prague. It was the counterpart of the German parliament of Frankfort. For the first time the Slavs of all parts of the monarchy met together. The proclamation of the committee read as follows: "Brothers! Who does not look on the past of our race with sorrow? Who does not know that our sufferings have been the result of the ignorance in which we have remained in regard to one another, of our quarreling and of our scattered position? After so many centuries of misery we have become aware of our unity and solidarity." The congress was divided into three sections—the Czech section, including the representatives of Bohemia, Moravia, and the Slovak provinces; the Polish and Ruthenian section, and the Servo-Croat section. The relations of the Slavs of Austria among themselves, their relations with the Germans, the Magyars, and the Slavs under Turkish rule, their attitude toward other nations, especially toward the Germans now assembled in parliament at Frankfort, the conditions under which Austria could be made into a federal state, and the extent to which the decisions of the German parliament of Frankfort should be binding on the Slav countries of Austria, these were the questions which the congress set itself to consider.

It was also proposed to address a manifesto to the peoples of Europe in order to acquaint them with the conditions of a race too little known, or known abroad almost entirely through the calumnies of its enemies. Unfortunately, while the congress was pursuing its peaceful deliberations, a riot, the cause of which remains even to-day undetermined, broke out in Prague. On June 12 shots were exchanged between the students and the soldiers of the garrison. The wife of the military commander, Prince Windischgratz, was killed in her hotel. Barricades were raised, while the *commando,* securely established in the upper part of the town, bombarded the lower town for three days, till it surrendered unconditionally. The Slav congress was dissolved, a state of siege was proclaimed at Prague, and the plans for the convocation of the diet were abandoned.

A little later the elections to the assembly at Vienna took place. The Germans of the kingdom sent thither to represent them men whom they knew to be violently hostile to the Slavs. They were occupied more with the idea of a greater Germany than with Austria, and they seemed to regard the attempts of the Czechs to bring about their political emancipation as particularly directed against them. The Czechs, on their part, chose those of their compatriots who were most deeply compromised with the national movement. They went to Vienna with a programme demanding constitutional liberty, the preservation of the integrity of the empire, menaced by the Hungarians and the Germans, and the greatest possibly autonomy for the kingdom of Bohemia. The Germans of Bohemia on the contrary looked toward Frankfort, and would willingly have given up one-half of the kingdom to the Hungarians provided they could have secured a dominant position in the other.

In Galicia also the revolutionary movement of March had made itself felt. Quite early the Poles of Lemberg had made known their demands to the government. They did not ask for a separation from Austria, but demanded the dismissal of the unpopular officials, the suppression of the secret police, the administration of the country by the natives, and that Polish regiments should not be required to leave Galicia. But the Galician nobles dared do nothing, held in check by the fear of Russia on the one hand and of the peasants on the other. The people were excited by numerous political refugees who had returned to the country; a sort of provisional government was established at Cracow, and on April 26 an insurrection broke out which was promptly suppressed by a bombardment. A few days before, the governor, Stadion, in proclaiming the abolition of the corvée, deprived the nobles of the credit of a measure which they had themselves demanded. He also administered a clever check to the demands of the Poles by favoring the aspirations of the Ruthenians, who demanded the recognition of the equality of their nation with that of the Poles, and of the Uniate Greek with the Catholic clergy. He thus secured for the Austrian government the position of arbitrator, which greatly increased both its moral and material power in this ancient Polish province, and from this time Galicia gave Austria no further trouble.

Before passing to Hungary let us recall briefly the events which had taken place in Italy. On March 18 Milan had risen, and the Austrians had been forced to withdraw to the famous Quadrilateral, a strongly protected region guarded by fortresses, between Lombardy and Venetia. A little later they had been driven out of Venice, Modena, and Parma. Early in April, Charles Albert, king of Piedmont, had espoused the cause of the Italians and declared war on Austria. Before the end of the summer, however, he was defeated. Radetzky, the Austrian general, after an able campaign reoccupied Lombardy in August.

> *"In deinem Lager ist Oesterreich*
> *Wir andere sind einzelne Trümmer."*

"In your camp alone Austria is found, we others are but lonely ruins," wrote the Viennese poet Grillparzer. A long series of conflicts was needed to restore these isolated ruins to that fictitious unity in which absolutism maintained them for another half a century.

Chapter XXIX

THE HUNGARIAN REVOLUTION. 1848-1849

AS early as March 3 Kossuth had secured the adoption of an address by the chamber of deputies at Presburg demanding the appointment of a responsible ministry, and on the 15th a deputation took the address to the emperor. A whole series of radical measures was adopted providing for the reform of public education, religious equality, trial by jury, liberty of the press, the annual convocation of the diet, the union of Transylvania with Hungary, the participation of the nobles in the payment of the taxes, and the abolition of the corvées and other feudal dues upon payment of an indemnity to those who suffered losses. But while these measures were being passed at Presburg, the city of Pesth became the center of an agitation which proved to be the beginning of the Hungarian revolution. A number of young men, among them the well-known poet, Petöfi, the novelist, Jokai, and the fiery and popular orator, Vasvary, seized a printing press and in spite of the royal censorship printed the famous programme of March 15. This programme, divided into twelve sections, demanded most of the liberal measures recently voted at Presburg; but it asked, besides, that the diet be annually convoked at Pesth, that the ministry sit in that town, that a national guard and a Hungarian bank be established, and that an amnesty be declared for all political prisoners. The emperor-king acceded to the wishes of the diet, and the palatine called upon Count Batthyany to form the first Hungarian ministry. Kossuth was made minister of finance, Eötvös minister of public education, Szechenyi of public works, and Deak of justice. At the same time the diet worked out a new electoral law, based upon a limited suffrage, by which the number of electors was raised to one million two hundred thousand. Nothing up to this point showed any signs of a desire on the part of the Hungarians to break with the dynasty. On April 10, when Ferdinand came to close the sitting of the diet, he was enthusiastically received. But although the majority of the Magyars were satisfied with their position, the non-Magyar nations were not. The laws concerning the Hungarian language had greatly irritated the Croats and Servians. In an assembly held on May 13 at Karlowitz they voted the reëstablishment of the offices of patriarch and voïévode and the formation of the Servians into an independent nation under the Austrian crown.

On May 30 the diet of Transylvania met at Klausenburg and voted the union of that principality with Hungary. But here also an hitherto. unrecognized race was about to demand its rights. The Magyars, the Szeklers, and the Saxons had hitherto directed the affairs of the principality, but now the long-suppressed Rumanians raised their voices and in a large popular assembly held at Blasendorf they drew up a list of their demands, which involved a recognition of their nationality, religious equality, the suppression of all offensive expressions against the Rumanians contained in the Hungarian laws, and the postponement of the vote of union with Hungary until they should be represented in the diet. But the Magyars were too much infatuated with their own interests to listen to these just demands, and harshly rejected them.

A struggle between the Magyars and the other nationalities in the borders of Hungary was inevitable, and the Servians gave the signal for its beginning. After having come to an understanding with Jellacic, the new ban of Croatia, they seized the arsenal at Titel and established a camp near Karlowitz. They were commanded by an old lieutenant of hussars, Stratimirovic, who showed remarkable talent. In his manifesto he said: " We fight those who violate the constitution, who seek liberty only for themselves, and who will not pretend to do other than to employ for the benefit of the Magyar minority the treasure amassed by the labor of Slavs, Germans, and Rumanians." The soldiers of the military frontier made common cause with their compatriots, and numerous volunteers were sent from Servia. The court, which was established at Innsbruck, took good care not to suppress a movement which justified once again the old principle of the monarchy, " Divide et impera."

The Hungarian diet, which met at Pesth on July 5, assembled therefore under foreboding auspices. Kossuth, in a remarkable speech, pointed out the dangers to Hungary from the southern Slavs, and asked for a levy of men and a loan of forty-two million

florins.   Conferences between the Hungarians and Croats were
called at Vienna, but they settled nothing.   "We will soon meet
again on the banks of the Drave," said the president of the Hungarian ministry to the ban.   "No," replied Jellacic, "I will come
to find you on the Danube," and on September 11 he crossed the
Drave.

Stratimirovic had collected thirty thousand men and a hundred cannon.   In September the Magyars sent a deputation to
the parliament of Vienna, but that body, dominated by the Slavs
and irritated by the injustice of the Hungarians, refused to receive
it.   The palatine, divided between the duties of his official position
and those of his position as a prince of the imperial family, left
Pesth under the pretext of going to assume the leadership of the
national army.   Instead, he sought an interview with Jellacic, and
on being refused left Hungary to its fate and retired from office.
Louis Batthyany also resigned, and a committee of public defense,
presided over by Kossuth, was established by the diet on September 25.   The same day an imperial decree appointed General Count
Lamberg commissary-royal and commander of the military forces of
Hungary.   But soon after his arrival at Buda he was murdered
by an angry crowd.   To this act the emperor replied by appointing
Jellacic lieutenant of the king and commander of all the forces of
the kingdom, and the rupture between Hungary and the monarch
was complete.

The Magyars began to make preparations for the defense
of their country.   Kossuth issued a call for volunteers and recalled all the national troops doing garrison duty in Bohemia and
Galicia.   Jellacic was repulsed in his march upon Pesth and fell
back toward Vienna, whither the emperor had returned upon
August 12.   The diet, then in session in Vienna, espoused
the cause of the dynasty against the Magyars.   The populace of
the capital, on the contrary, out of hatred for the Slavs, and because of their own revolutionary sentiments, showed a passionate sympathy for the revolution at Pesth.   On October 17
they rose against the government to prevent reinforcements from
being sent to Jellacic, and appealed to the Hungarians for aid.
The Hungarians arrived too late and were forced to recross the
Leitha, while the Viennese had to open their gates to Windischgratz.   The events of this episode of the revolution will be
treated later.   In the meantime the Hungarians were still ham-

HUNGARIAN REVOLUTION 371

pered by the desire to remain loyal to the king of Hungary. The Hungarian ministers declared that they remained faithful "to the beloved king of Hungary," even though they were fighting the troops of the hated emperor.

But suddenly there was no longer any king. Ferdinand abdicated on December 2 in favor of his nephew, Francis Joseph. The Magyars would not recognize this abdication, and while revolting against the governing king maintained a platonic fidelity to the king who had abdicated. Kossuth put the kingdom in a state of defense, organized the famous battalions of the Honveds, or "defenders of their country," and formed foreign regiments, which were eagerly joined by the Poles. The struggle thus begun was terrible. Austria attacked Hungary by way of Moravia, Galicia, Styria, and the south, while the Rumanians in Transylvania energetically aided the imperial troops, less because of their love for the emperor than out of hatred for their old oppressors. In this unequal struggle Hungary was destined to be completely beaten. Windischgratz entered Presburg on the 18th and Raab on December 27. On January 1, 1849, the committee of defense was forced to quit Pesth, and to retire to Debreczen in a sandy and almost inaccessible region. A few days later the Hungarian troops also withdrew and the city was immediately occupied by Windischgratz. Batthyany was arrested, court-martials were established, and a reign of terror was inaugurated in the wretched capital.

On the other hand, Bem, a Pole, who had been one of the defenders of Vienna, carried on a marvelous campaign in Transylvania, in which the youthful poet Petöfi perished. For a long time his countrymen refused to believe in his death, and many years afterward Hungary was stirred up by the report that Petöfi was being held prisoner in Siberia by the Russians, and that after a captivity of thirty years he was about to return to his native land. In spite of the intervention of a Russian corps Hermannstadt fell into Bem's hands and the Austrians and Russians retreated into Wallachia. In the south Perczel reconquered a part of the Servian territory.

Fortune seemed again to smile upon the Hungarians. Windischgratz was dismissed and Kossuth believed himself strong enough to strike a decisive blow. On April 14 the diet at Debreczen voted the deposition of the house of Austria and the independence of Hungary. Kossuth was made governor-president and the decision as to the form of government reserved for the future. Hungary was far too aristocratic and too much imbued with monarchical traditions to proclaim a republic. In his new ministry Kossuth intrusted Count Batthyany with foreign affairs and Görgei was made minister of war. At last Hungary, which had seemed up to this time so attached to legal forms, definitely broke with its old traditions. But the only state of Europe which was willing to recognize her was the short-lived republic of Venice. A great success, however, followed the declaration of independence. On May 21 the fortress of Buda was captured from the Austrians.

But a new danger now threatened the Hungarian cause. Three weeks previous the *Official Gazette* of Vienna had announced that Tsar Nicholas had placed the Russian armies at the disposal of the Emperor Francis Joseph, in order that he might crush his revolted subjects. This meant the avowal of Austrian weakness, but it was at the same time, as has been remarked, a recognition of Russia as the natural protector of the oppressed Slavs against the Hungarians. In vain Vladislas Teleki at Paris, and Andrassy in Turkey, endeavored to bring about a counter-intervention in favor of the Magyars. The Russians crossed the Carpatians on June 4, while Haynau, who had already made himself notorious in Italy, defeated the Hungarian generals on the Danube and marched upon Pesth. One hundred thousand Russians under the command of Paskievitch entered Galicia, while fifty thousand pushed into Transylvania. During this time Görgei acted in the most suspicious fashion; while pretending to fight the enemy, he prepared to enter into negotiations with him, and to restore the monarchy. In dire straits, the diet at Debreczen proclaimed the equality of the races in Hungary. But it was too late. On August 11 Kossuth surrendered his dictatorship to Görgei, and two days later the latter capitulated at Vilagos to the Russians with twenty-three thousand men and one hundred and thirty cannon. This was the signal for flight. Bem, Kossuth, and those who could escape crossed over into Turkey, and Klapka was forced to surrender the almost impregnable fortress Komorn on September 27. "Hungary," wrote Paskievitch to the Tsar, "lies at the feet of your Majesty." With the fall of Komorn the last rampart of Hungary was gone.

It would have been wise and magnanimous to have honored by clemency a victory which, after all, had been gained only at the cost of foreign intervention. But other councils prevailed. The vengeance of the conqueror was pitiless. Louis Batthyany was shot at Pesth; the generals who had capitulated were either shot or hanged like malefactors, and the executions which followed recalled the bloody days of Eperies. Thousands of patriots, among them women of noble birth, were consigned to imprisonment. The property of the condemned was confiscated; Görgei escaped the death penalty, but was imprisoned in the fortress of Klagenfurt. Even those who had escaped into Turkey were persecuted, both Austria and Russia demanding their extradition. But the Sultan refused, and from this time may be dated the affection of the Magyars for the Turks, an affection which has been increased by their hatred of Russia and everything Slavic. The two powers did succeed, however, in their demand that certain of the refugees should not be allowed to leave Turkey. Many of them became Mohammedans, notably the Pole, Bem, who died shortly afterward at Aleppo. One of the refugees, Count Julius Andrassy, was one day to be called upon to direct the destinies of the Austro-Hungarian monarchy.

On the news of the capitulation of Vilagos Venice had surrendered, August 22, in Lombardy. Charles Albert, after a second attempt, had been defeated at Novara on March 23, 1849, and abdicated, leaving to his son, Victor Emmanuel, a kingdom harassed by difficulties. The Austrian rule was reimposed in northern Italy, and with Hungary also vanquished and pacified the reaction could have full play till the time when it should have worn itself out, or till events would permit the conquered people once again to assert themselves.

Chapter XXX

THE REVOLUTION IN VIENNA. 1849

WE have now to return to the attempts at constitutionalism in the Austrian countries outside of Hungary. The diet at Vienna was composed of 383 deputies, 53 for Upper and Lower Austria, 48 for Moravia, 91 for Bohemia, and 19 for Styria and other provinces. Among this number the rural deputies formed a considerable element. A great many of them, especially the Ruthenians and Galicians, did not understand German. The Austrian aristocracy had obtained no votes or had refused to become candidates, and the Germans were consequently in a minority. The radical papers, journals of the German party, fearful of this barbarian invasion, denounced it in unmeasured terms, some being printed with a black border. The Viennese in their anger went to such extremes in their hostility toward the Czech majority that only threats of a removal of the parliament to some other city could restore them to reason. On July 10 the deputies met in the imperial riding school to decide upon the rules of order. Representatives from eight different nationalities were present: Germans, Czechs, Servian-Croats from Dalmatia, Poles, Ruthenians, Italians from Istria, and Wallachians from Bukowina. The first difficulty arose over the language question. In what language should the deliberations be conducted? It was decided that interpreters should be furnished those who did not understand German; but no one dared declare German the official language. Schmidt, a lawyer of Vienna, was chosen president of the assembly; Strohbach, a Czech, and Smolka, a Pole, its vice-presidents. At first fixed parties did not appear; divisions followed rather lines of nationality; the Czechs with the Ruthenians occupied the right; the Tyrolese and the Austrian conservatives, the black-yellows, as they were called, the center, while the left was occupied more particularly by the Germans and the democrats. On July 22 the diet was opened, and the speech from the throne declared that it had been convoked " to finish the

374

great work of the revival of the Fatherland and to secure liberty." In the absence of the emperor the Archduke John occupied his place, but he was soon called away to Frankfort, where he had been proclaimed vicar of the empire. The assembly then besought the sovereign to return and he reëntered Vienna on August 12.

The chamber had appointed a committee to draw up a new constitution. The first question of importance with which it had to deal was the condition of the peasantry. The assembly was besieged with petitions which not infrequently partook of the nature of threats, and the discussions on this weighty question were all the more long and passionate because so many peasants were in the diet. By the end of the month of August the assembly voted to purchase at a reasonable price all the rights of the lords to dues and forced labor, and decided by a vote of 224 to 125 that a special indemnity fund should be created in each province. This was the first step toward federation.

While the parliament, a veritable Tower of Babel, deliberated with wise and often ludicrous slowness, the apostles of radicalism were at work in the capital. The laboring classes became excited, and the *Aula,* as the students' organization was called, exchanged fraternal greetings with the artisans. The ministry, after the example of the national workshops in France, had been paying the laborers at the rate of fifteen kreutzers per day, notwithstanding the fact that they did little or no work, and now the reduction of the wages led to riots that had to be put down by force.

The committee of safety which had been established in March was dissolved and with the great material distress troubles became frequent. The populace demanded the dismissal of the ministers, Latour, Schwarzer, and Bach. The assembly declared itself in continuous session, but it could not maintain order even within its own walls, for the radicals clamorously demanded the reëstablishment of the committee. A central committee of all radical associations was formed, and the popular excitement reached its height when the Hungarian deputies reached Vienna to plead the cause of their country before the diet. That body, under the influence of the Slavs, would not receive them. But the democrats of Vienna gave them an ovation and promised them brotherly assistance. They kept their word. Early in October they prevented the departure of the imperial troops against Hungary. A conflict occurred and the crowd destroyed the bridge over which the troops had to cross. Latour, the minister of war, was attacked in his house, brutally maltreated, and hanged. The diet, notwithstanding the heroic efforts of some of its members, was unable to prevent the excesses which disgraced these " October days." It formed a committee of safety which endeavored to act as a peacemaker between the government and the populace, and asked for a popular ministry and a change of policy toward Hungary. The emperor graciously received the deputation, but on the following day he fled to Olmütz in the midst of his Slav subjects, who alone seemed to furnish a shelter against the revolution. He left behind a manifesto in which he denounced the excesses of the preceding days in scathing terms, and announced that he would take measures for the deliverance of the people of Vienna and the maintenance of their freedom.

Three armies led by Generals Auersperg, Windischgratz, and Jellacic were soon brought against Vienna, and, left to itself, the capital could not long resist. Nevertheless it undertook to make a defense. The republicans of Frankfort, in order to encourage their political co-religionists, had sent a deputation at whose head was Robert Blum, a bookseller of Leipzig and one of the foremost of the German Liberals. After the departure of the emperor the conservatives of the diet, the Czechs leading, had quitted the assembly and retired to Prague, from which they issued a protest against the disturbances among their colleagues remaining at Vienna. The diet was thus reduced to impotence by its own dissensions, nor did the capital enjoy its triumph long. The attack was made by Windischgratz and Jellacic on October 28, and on the 31st the city capitulated. The Hungarians arrived too late to afford assistance to their allies, and defeated by Jellacic, they recrossed the Leitha in disorder. Windischgratz entered Vienna and at once proceeded to take terrible revenge, notwithstanding the fact that the German parliament protested vigorously. Messenhauser, the commandant of the national guard, and Robert Blum were shot, the latter's rank as a deputy of the parliament of Frankfort failing to save him. Others among his victims were Becker, the editor of the Radical, and his assistant Jellinek. The minister of the empire was forced to disavow Windischgratz, but the death of Latour was avenged.

But the emperor did not await the submission of the capital

to convoke the diet in a place where its deliberations would be assured of the necessary quiet and security. A rescript of October 22 suspended its sessions and invited it to resume its meetings on November 22 in the Moravian city of Kremsier. In this little town the diet might escape all demagogic influence. Here the Pole, Smolka, was elected president, and on the previous day a new cabinet came into office. The head of the new ministry was the "soldier-statesman," Prince Schwarzenberg, who had learned the art of suppressing revolutions by a long career in Italy. He had first served in St. Petersburg, subsequently at London, Turin, and Naples, where he had shown himself a passionate friend of absolutism, and later he had played an important rôle in the camp of Radetzky. The department of internal affairs was intrusted to Count Stadion, who had shown real talent for administration. The new ministry announced itself without reserve in favor of constitutional government, and declared that Austria would remain closely united to Germany, without, at the same time, sacrificing her own interests. This programme was made public on November 27, and on December 2 the diet was convoked in extraordinary session. To the great surprise of the assembly, the president announced that the Emperor Ferdinand had abdicated, that his brother, the Archduke Francis Charles, had renounced his rights, and that in consequence, the young son of that prince, the Archduke Francis Joseph, had succeeded to the imperial throne. The day before he had reached his eighteenth year and been declared of age. This grave decision had been made at a family meeting at which only the ministers, the privy council, Prince Windischgratz and Jellacic had been present. The very day of his abdication Ferdinand set out for Prague, where he continued to live in retirement till his death. His feeble health had for some time prevented him from performing the duties of his imperial office.

Chapter XXXI

EARLY YEARS OF THE REIGN OF FRANCIS JOSEPH— THE PERIOD OF REACTION. 1848-1860

FRANCIS JOSEPH began his reign by declaring his intention to rule as a constitutional monarch. In his first proclamation he said: "Firmly resolved to preserve without blemish the splendor of the crown, we hope with the aid of God and the coöperation of our people, with whom we are prepared to share our rights, to unite all the countries and all the races of the monarchy into one compact state." This programme seemed to indicate a firm resolve to make out of Austria-Hungary a centralized state. Since the constitution of the monarchy, or, to speak more correctly, of this polyglot polyarchy, had become the question of the day, three systems commanded the attention of statesmen—first, centralization, which grouped all the provinces, all the nationalities, and all the languages under a single government, either parliamentary or absolute, at Vienna; second, dualism, which left Hungary with her historic constitution and grouped all the other states about a factitious unity; and, third, federalism, which would satisfy both the national aspirations and the historic traditions of the different groups which composed the Austrian empire. Up to that moment no principle had been laid down for the solution of this grave problem. In point of fact, dualism already existed, for Hungary had not been invited to the deliberations of the diet at Vienna or at Kremsier. Federalism was demanded by the Slavs and some of the German groups, jealous of their traditions and of their autonomy, as, for example, the Tyrol. Palacky, the Czech historian, drew up a project which formulated the demands of the federalists. It provided for only four ministries for the whole empire, those of war, of marine, of finance, and of foreign affairs. Each province was to enjoy complete local independence, and the local diets were to choose a certain number of deputies who would constitute the central diet. Palacky's scheme recognized seven nationalities—Germans, Bohemians, Poles, Italians, Yougo-Slavs, Magyars, and Wallachians. Each of these was to be represented at Vienna by its own chancery. This project was naturally opposed by the German advocates of centralization, who wished to Germanize the empire. Besides, it was evident that there were many practical difficulties in the way. One of the most serious of these was that the deputies did not dare to dispose of Hungary without the concurrence of her representatives. It was hoped that the emperor would invite Hungarians to the diet, and that they might come. Three months passed in empty discussion without the government intervening or making known its intentions. Finally, on March 2, the work of constitution-making seemed to be finished.

It was hoped that after reaching an understanding with the government the constitution would be finally adopted, and that on March 15, the anniversary of the revolution of 1848, it should be solemnly proclaimed. But the deputies at Kremsier had overlooked the baneful influence of the German policy which had weighed so heavily on Austria for centuries. An Austrian archduke was chosen vicar of Germany, and the parliament at Frankfort looked upon Austria as an annex of Germany whose mission it was to Germanize the refractory elements and to carry out the motto, " *Drang nach Osten* " (Press on to the east). It voted the following articles in regard to Austria: No part of the German empire can be united into a single state with other non-German countries; if a German country has the same sovereign as a non-German country the relation between the two countries can only be regulated in accordance with the principles of a personal union." " When Austria and Germany, with renewed vigor shall each have decided on a new and definite form, then only can the nature of their political relations be settled," declared the manifesto of November 27.

The federalists, especially the Slavs, had accepted this declaration as a promise of emancipation from the yoke of Germany. The leaders of the German party had replied on January 14, 1849, by excluding Austria from the new German union. This gave very little concern to the Austrian cabinet, which persisted in looking upon Austria as the first of the great German states. A parliamentary *coup d'état* was decided upon, and on March 6 Stadion called together a number of deputies and informed them that in the absence of the Hungarians the assembly could not legally

adopt a constitution for the empire. In spite of the protests
of the deputies, the diet was dissolved, and the so-called constitution of March 4 was granted through an imperial decree.
It was little more than a copy of the Belgian and Berlin constitutions, and the *Gründrechte* of Germany. It declared the
Austrian empire to be independent, indivisible, and indissoluble;
and the equality of all the provinces, whose diets became purely
provincial councils. Two chambers were to assist the monarch,
who proclaimed his intention of being crowned emperor of Austria. The Hungarian constitution was to be maintained in so far
as it did not come into conflict with that of the empire. A special
statute was to regulate the status of Lombardy-Venetia. The
prohibitive censor was suppressed, and the free exercise of domestic
religion authorized; of the historic rights of the different provinces,
and of the equality of various nationalities not a word was said.

Two years later, in 1851, Schwarzenberg declared in a circular, " The constitution granted on March 4 was only the basis
on which it was expected to build up again the authority of
the throne. There was no time then to study the fundamental
provisions of a constitution, and so they were copied from foreign
models. Such an act could have no consequence and has had none."
In fact, the constitution of March 4 was never really put into practice. But although Austria was impotent at home, she nevertheless
played an important part in Germany. When the parliament of
Frankfort offered the imperial crown to the king of Prussia the
emperor of Austria broke with it, declaring that he was sovereign
of a single and united state, and that he would never admit
the intervention of a foreign monarch or assembly in any portion
of it.

The ten years which followed the pacification of Hungary and
of northern Italy mark a period of pitiless reaction. By the end
of 1849 order was reëstablished everywhere. Nothing stood in
the way of putting the constitution into practice. An imperial
decree of August 4 had declared: " It shall not remain a dead
letter. It will serve as a rampart of liberty, a guarantee of the
power, the glory and the unity of the monarchy." Stadion, who
had secured its adoption, was in honor bound to see it put into
practice, but he lost his mind and was replaced by a Viennese
lawyer, Alexander Bach, who a short time previous had been a
fiery radical. Having attained power, however, he became the

advocate of absolutism and reaction. Of all the gains of the revolution he preserved only the laws concerning the condition of the peasantry, and those which proclaimed civil equality for persons and property. The delusive constitution of March 4 was declared abrogated by imperial decree on December 31, 1851. The provinces of the monarchy were divided; the administrative head in each was appointed by the central government, and the functions of the diet were reduced to a minimum. Further, the centralizing bureaucracy became the instrument of a pitiless policy of Germanization, which weighed equally heavily on the Hungarians, who wished to dismember the empire, and the Slavs, who strove to maintain it. " A temporary arrangement "—such was the word which designated the system which was in vogue for ten entire years, and if such a thing were possible, said Springer, " one would have invented a temporary arrangement of temporary arrangements." " Distrust of the government became a state maxim," said another publicist, and the only remedy sought for this distrust was in material force.

Hungary was the first to suffer from the new absolutism. Everything was done to deprive her of her independence. A royal lieutenant was installed at Pesth, and the kingdom cut up into five divisions. Public offices were intrusted to Germans by preference, the German language was made the language of the administration, the courts, and the schools. A ruthless police watched over the citizens, and the state of siege was kept up till 1854, a general amnesty not being proclaimed until 1857. The annexed kingdoms, Transylvania, Croatia, and Servia, were again detached and given local independence. But the Slavs, thus freed from the Magyar yoke, fell under the rule of the Germans. The same policy was followed in Bohemia and Galicia, especially after the death of Schwarzenberg in 1852, when Bach became more powerful than ever. " Trial by jury and the right of public trial were suppressed," says Tomek, " the elections of the municipal bodies were suspended, and the equality of the Bohemian language with the German set aside in the schools; the police were arbitrary and harsh, interfering frequently with the ordinary courts. . . . The liberty of the press in everything which concerned public affairs was completely stifled; it was not even permissible to publish a journal in Czech. The Austrian government, solely occupied with establishing its influence in Germany, hoped to secure the sympathies of the Germans by securing to them a supremacy over the other nations of the empire."

The government, thus addicted to absolutism, readily saw that it could strengthen its position by an alliance with the church, for the Holy See and the bishops were its natural allies. In an assembly held at Vienna in 1849 the Austrian prelates had vigorously protested against the national movements. They had declared " nationality a relic of paganism and different languages a consequence of sin and the fall of man." It was decided that the last traces of Josephism, which provided for the supremacy of state over the church, should be abolished, and after extended negotiations the Concordat of 1855 was concluded. It declared Catholicism the privileged religion, placed both private and public instruction in the hands of the clergy, and authorized the publication of all pontifical documents without reference to the civil power, while the state bound itself not to permit the circulation of books censured by the clergy. The bishops were invested with the powers of imposing corporal punishment, as for example, imprisoning refractory priests, and the government pledges itself to aid them in executing their judgments. These measures gave an ecclesiastical bias to the centralized, absolutist system of the ten years from 1849 to 1859. All political life ceased, and intellectual torpor marks the period, while material conditions became steadily worse. The events of 1848-1849 had exhausted an already impoverished treasury, and the years immediately following brought no relief, so that in spite of constantly increasing taxes the annual deficit continued. In order to meet the exigencies of the situation the government was led to issue paper money subject to a discount, and banknotes down to the value of five cents were actually in circulation.

Abroad, Austria was able at the beginning of this period to make a fairly tolerable showing. In Germany, Schwarzenberg, whom public opinion was pleased to consider as a great minister, had succeeded in maintaining the federal compact which assured to Austria a dominant position among the German states. Prussia was checked by a coalition of princes cleverly grouped about Francis Joseph, and in November of 1850 she was forced to recede absolutely from her position in supporting the liberals of Hesse against their stupidly reactionary prince. At a conference at Olmütz the Prussian minister, Manteuffel, contributed still further to his country's humiliation. Most of the demands of Schwarzenberg were acceded to, and Prussia agreed to coöperate in reinstating the elector of Hesse, to act in Holstein only with the aid of Austria, and to take part in the conferences at Dresden to discuss the future organization of Germany. The conference at Dresden ended, as Austria advocated, in reëstablishing the old confederation with its diet at Frankfort. The only part of her programme that Austria was unable to carry through was her plan to secure the admission of all her Italian and Slav provinces into the empire. In 1854 Francis Joseph knit still closer the bonds with the south German princes by his marriage with Princess Elizabeth of Bavaria.

In the Eastern Question the Austrian policy during this period was entirely negative. All its positive force seems to have been directed toward Germany and Italy. In the Slav or Rumanian countries, subjected to the Turk, her intervention might at times have been favorably received, but it was impossible for her to espouse the cause of the Slavs in the Balkan peninsula when she was herself endeavoring to crush out Slavism in her own states. Hence a drifting, uncertain policy. Unable to wield a controlling influence in Turkey, she contented herself by counteracting that of Russia.

The Crimean War was a painful experience for Austria. She owed the Emperor Nicholas a definite obligation for the services rendered her during the Hungarian revolution. Yet Schwarzenberg was right when he said, " Austria will astonish the world by her ingratitude." When the dificulties in the East between Nicholas and the Porte first arose, the Austrian minister, Count Buol, proposed a conference. He guaranteed Austrian neutrality only on the condition that Russia promised to respect the integrity of the Ottoman empire. Some time later, in August, he demanded that the Danubian principalities be placed under the protection of the five great powers, that the navigation of the Danube should be free, that the treaty of 1841 be revised by the contracting powers, and that Russia renounce her claims to the protectorate over the Greek Christians subject to the Sultan.

When the campaigns of the Crimean War began the cabinet of Vienna allied itself with France and England to defend the Danubian principalities against Russia. The conferences held at Vienna were of no avail to maintain peace. Austria was not sorry to see Russia weakened without her armed intervention, and re-

mained satisfied with occupying the principalities with the consent
of the Porte. But an unexpected event caused serious anxiety to
Austrian statesmen. Piedmont, known to be be governed by an
ambitious and intelligent prince, joined the allies and sent an
army to the Crimea. Might this not be a portent of awakening
in Italy in spite of the rule of terror that prostrated her? In any
case, this new development was the signal for energetic measures
on the part of Austria to bring the war to a close. She renewed
her proposals of August 8, demanding Russia's withdrawal from
Bessarabia, and the neutralization of the Black Sea. She even
recalled her ambassador from St. Petersburg. Peace was thus
forced on Russia, and the terms of a final treaty drawn up at
the Congress of Paris were signed on March 30, 1856. The
Black Sea was neutralized, the navigation of the Danube made
free, the claim of Russia to a protectorate over the members of the
Orthodox Greek Church in Turkey renounced, and the other difficulties regarding the East referred to the powers.

But an incident occurred at the Congress of Paris which was
to have the most serious consequences for Austria. Piedmont was
represented by Cavour, and through him the Italian question was
brought up for discussion. Both Cavour and Walewski drew attention to the abnormal conditions in the peninsula, and the dangerous preponderance which Austria had acquired. Having crept
in under the shadow of the Eastern Question the Italian Question
was now to the front, and would not be long in finding the solution which had become inevitable.

Thus, on the whole, the results of the Crimean War were not
so favorable to Austria as at first appeared. She had secured the
free navigation of the Danube, but the principalities of Wallachia
and Moldavia had united to form the state of Rumania, thus
creating a center of attraction for the Rumanians in Austria.
The friendship of Russia had cooled and St. Petersburg even
accused Vienna of treason. But more significant still, Piedmont
had entered the European concert, and sure of the friendship of
Napoleon III., prepared for war. In the summer of 1858 Cavour
brought about an alliance with the French emperor by which the
latter promised to deliver the whole of Lombardy-Venetia as far
as the Adriatic in return for Savoy and Nice, and a marriage
alliance between the Princess Clotilde, daughter of Victor Emmanuel, and Prince Jerome.

Cavour also obtained the help of Lord Cowley, and through his good offices demanded of the Austrian government the creation of a national government for Lombardy-Venetia, the abandonment of the Romagna and the establishment of a constitutional system in Parma, Modena, and Tuscany. At this point England and Russia proposed a congress. But, fortunately for Italy, Buol, backed by the war party at Vienna, assumed the aggressive. In April he sent an ultimatum demanding the disarmament of Piedmont. This precipitated the war, and early in May official declarations of war were made by France and Sardinia against Austria. The minions of Austrian rule at once fled from the duchies, and her new general, Giulay, the veteran Radetzky having died the year before, showed none of his predecessor's ability. He did not understand how to invade Piedmont or to cut the road between Turin and Genoa, and was driven back toward Lombardy. After a number of defeats, notably at Magenta, the Austrians evacuated the whole of Lombardy and withdrew to the region of the "Quadrilateral." Here they were again severely defeated by the Italians and French at Solferino, June 23. But the fortified region of the "Quadrilateral" still protected Venetia, and Napoleon III. mistrusted his ability to carry out his entire programme. He had declared that he wished to free Italy "from the Alps to the Adriatic," but he now drew back from the execution of the project. He feared Germany, and he dared not take advantage of the desire of Hungary to rise, because that would be strengthening his cause by an alliance with revolution. On July 11 he had an interview at Villafranca with Francis Joseph. Peace was decided upon, without the consent of the Italians, and on November 10, 1859, Victor Emmanuel was obliged to agree to the Treaty of Zürich. By it the Austrian emperor surrendered to Napoleon, who was to give it to Sardinia, all of the province of Lombardy excepting the fortresses of Mantua and Peschiera. The grand dukes of Tuscany and Modena were to return to their states. Italy was to form a confederation in which Austria was to be a member by right of her possession of Venetia, fantastic dreams which the patient and wily policy of Cavour quickly annihilated.

Chapter XXXII

ATTEMPTS AT CONSTITUTIONAL GOVERNMENT—THE EXPULSION OF AUSTRIA FROM GERMANY. 1860-1867

THE absolute and centralized system had ended in the dismemberment of the empire, and in her defeat Austria could not even count upon the loyalty of her people. Some among them openly rejoiced at her disasters. Bohemian peasants declared: " If we are defeated we will have a constitution, if victorious, the inquisition." Francis Joseph at last realized that he had pursued a wrong policy, dismissed his reactionary minister Bach, and, after some hesitation, adopted a series of reforms looking toward the gradual introduction of a constitutional régime. On March 6, 1860, he extended his council by the addition of thirty-eight members, making of it a council of the empire in which the notables from the different countries were represented. But this council was, after all, merely a consultative body without any right of initiative, and was far from meeting the expectations and demands of the people. A Galician nobleman, Goluchowski, who did not share the rancors of the Germans and the Hungarians, was called to the ministry, and with his assistance the patent of October 20, 1860, was drawn up. It provided, among others, for the following reforms: The legislative power was to be vested in the hands of the emperor and the diet; the council of the empire, composed of 100 delegates from the diets, was to have charge of all matters concerning the common interests, such as finance, trade, ways of communication, and war. All other matters were left to the decision of the separate diets. Citizens were to be equal before the law in regard to religion, taxation, and military service. The common ministries of the interior, of justice, and of public worship were abolished. The diets retained the old organization based upon class distinctions.

The new minister, Schmerling, was intrusted with the task of developing and carrying into practice the principles of this patent, which he completed by the patent of February 26, 1861. Like

Bach and Metternich, his chief aim was to establish the ascendency of the German element. Besides, his attempt to apply to Austria the parliamentary theories which were suitable only to a homogeneous state could not but be unsuccessful. He established two chambers: the upper chamber, in which sat the princes, large land-owners, prelates, and some men of eminence chosen by the monarch; and the lower chamber, consisting of 343 members, elected by the provincial diets. The portfolios of the ministers of the interior, of public worship, and of justice were restored, and the authority of the central diet was increased at the expense of the provincial diets. The hopes raised by the patent of October among the federalists were destroyed. But it could scarcely be expected that the Hungarians would so readily consent to surrender their autonomy and willingly deliberate concerning the interests of their country in a diet with Czechs, Slovenes, and Poles. A conpromise was arranged by which their deputies took their seats only when the common interests of all the empire were being discussed. Their presence constituted the Reichsrath with full power, their absence changed the parliament into an assembly of limited powers in which the other groups busied themselves with questions beyond the competency of the separate diet. In this way the centralizing minister avoided dualism. At the same time, he organized all the provincial diets upon the same model, but with an elective system cleverly manipulated so as to stifle the Slav majority. Three classes were admitted to representation, large landholders, the middle class of the cities, and the peasants. Special privileges were granted to the large estates belonging to the aristocratic families whose owners were vassals of the sovereign, and to the towns in which there were numerous German colonists. The electoral divisions were made in the most arbitrary way. In Bohemia, for example, Slav towns had one deputy for 12,020 voters, while the German towns had one for every 10,315. In the rural districts the Slavs had one deputy for every 53,000 inhabitants, the Germans one for every 40,800. The German town of Reichenberg, with 19,000 inhabitants, had three deputies, while the Slav city of Prague with 153,000 inhabitants had only ten. Certain German towns were made into veritable rotten boroughs. The German hamlet of Parchen, with 500 inhabitants, had a deputy, while the Slav town of Kladno, with 8000 inhabitants, had none. In short this electoral system was a deception, and since its adoption the non-German people have never ceased to demand its repeal, but with certain modifications it continues in force to-day, and so long as it remains Austria cannot be regarded as having a truly representative government.

After the promulgation of the constitution of February the different peoples of the empire were divided as to whether they would accept it and send deputies to the new Reichsrath. The Italians in Venetia, the Magyars and the Croatians refused, and 140 deputies, more than one-third of the total 343, failed to appear. " We can wait," proudly remarked Schmerling. But all his diplomacy failed in the face of the judicial obstinacy of the Hungarians. " I know only the Hungarian constitution, and I can treat only with it as a basis," was the invariable reply of Deak to the propositions of the Viennese statesmen. The Hungarian diet convoked at Pesth in April, 1861, rejected all compromise, the rigorous legists even going so far as to refuse to recognize Francis Joseph as king, because he had never been crowned. For the coronation, said they, in a country whose rights are historical, is not merely a religious ceremony, but a bilateral contract. In it the sovereign takes an oath which recognizes the ancient rights of the kingdom. The legists wished to pass a resolution only, but Deak prevailed upon them to vote an address. In this document, remarkable for its lucidity and logic, he recalled the historical rights of the kingdom. " The fundamental condition of our political life and our national independence," said he, " is the legal independence and self-government of our land. Our first duty is to consecrate all our faculties to maintain Hungary as Hungary and to secure her constitutional rights. . . . We solemnly declare that we cannot sacrifice the rights based upon treaties, laws, royal letters, or coronation oaths, for any consideration or to any interests whatsoever." The address demanded that the law of 1848 and the engagements of the Pragmatic Sanction be put into effect. But the government of Vienna believed itself powerful enough to overcome the Hungarians by force, and dissolved the diet. Meetings of the comitats were forbidden, and royal commissioners were substituted for the refractory Foïspanak. But in spite of all this the resistance of the Magyars continued.

Bohemia was hardly more satisfied than Hungary. She justly complained of the electoral system granted by Schmerling, and sent deputies to the Reichsrath only after reserving all the rights of the kingdom. After 1863 her representatives ceased to take part in its deliberations. The only liberty granted by Schmerling to Bohemia was that of the press, but the Slavs profited little by this, for within the space of three years the owners and editors of fourteen Czech newspapers were condemned to sixty-one months of imprisonment, more or less severe, and an aggregate fine of 21,500 florins.

The Polish insurrection in 1863 caused great excitement in Galicia, and serious embarrassment to the cabinet of Vienna. Again a wavering policy was followed, while Prussia secured the friendship of Russia by concluding an agreement with that power against the insurgents. Austria, on the contrary, listened to the overtures of Napoleon, whose sympathies for the Poles were pronounced. He wanted to aid the cabinet of Vienna to regain Silesia, and to assure it of the Danubian principalities in exchange for Venetia, projects neither understood nor favored at Vienna. Austria contented herself by addressing diplomatic notes to St. Petersburg and by declaring a state of siege in Galicia. This double policy irritated not only the Poles, but also the Czechs of Bohemia and Moravia, who were more inclined to sympathize with the Polish revolutionists than with the Muscovite autocrats.

The work of Schmerling was becoming increasingly impracticable. In 1865 the emperor journeyed to Pesth in order to come to an understanding with the Hungarians. He gave them a new chancellor, and Schmerling resigned. The doctrinaire advocates of Germanism groaned, but in the provinces the joy was great, and the cities of Prague, Pesth, and Lemberg illuminated. Francis Joseph declared the February constitution suspended, and adjourned the Reichsrath until the diets of Hungary and of Croatia should have expressed themselves as to their relations to the empire. Belcredi, a Moravian, was given Schmerling's place. The diets of the larger Slav provinces, Bohemia and Galicia, showed their gratitude for the change of ministry, and hastened to undo the Germanizing measures of the previous cabinet. In Galicia, for example, the Polish language was introduced into all the schools. In the Hungarian diet, which was opened on September 14, 1865, the extreme left demanded the unequivocal execution of the laws of 1848, but the liberal party, under the direction of Deak, drew up a programme which endeavored to reconcile the practical needs with the maintenance of Hungary's historical rights. To do this it was necessary to put the laws of 1848 into force and to nominate a responsible ministry, which alone would have the right to impose the necessary modifications. The debates dragged on for a long time and were finally interrupted by the war with Prussia and Italy in 1866.

Prussia had not forgotten her humiliation at Olmütz. She was not only longing for revenge, but ready to assert her leadership in Germany. For this rôle it must be admitted she was much better suited than her rival, for except in the duchy of Posen and some parts of Silesia, the Prussian state was entirely German. William I., who was crowned in 1861, had found in Bismarck the minister whose policy enabled Prussia not only to crush Austria, but to raise herself to a position of undisputed leadership among the German states. The mistaken policy of Austria in Germany at the Congress of Vienna, and thenceforward under the guidance of Metternich; her steady support of reaction against the growing sentiment in favor of liberalism, of the independence of the small states as against the yearning for a strongly united Fatherland; her hostility to Prussia and the Zollverein; and, as we have just seen, her triumph in again saddling upon Germany the effete system of the Confederation after the movement of 1848, had plainly allied her with a doomed cause. Prussia, on the other hand, particularly during the decade following Olmütz, gained rapidly in strength and prestige. Her customs union was a constant source of material strength and its success a practical guarantee of her fitness for leadership. By 1860 the union had practically closed its doors to Austria by the adoption of such low duties that the old protective system to which that country clung tenaciously made her membership impossible.

But the final solution of the question of the place of Austria in Germany was to come about through an entirely different matter. Already during the troublesome years of 1848 and 1849 the Schleswig-Holstein question had led to serious difficulties. The two duchies of Schleswig and Holstein were united to Denmark by a personal union, although the populations were largely German. Geographically, too, they were closely connected with Prussia, and it was only natural that the attempts of Denmark in 1848 to incorporate them should have met with protests, and even armed intervention. In 1852 the London Conference, to which Austria and Prussia were parties, established the semi-independence of the duchies under Denmark. In violation of this arrangement the king of Denmark tried, in 1863, to incorporate them. The dispute which followed led to the joint intervention of Austria and Prussia in January of 1864. The Danes, deceived in their hopes of foreign assistance, were easily defeated, and by the Treaty of Vienna, October 30, 1864, Christian IX. ceded all his rights to Schleswig, Holstein, and Lauenberg to the victors.

The two powers were thus left with the spoils, and difficulties over the disposition of them soon arose. Austria was naturally at a disadvantage because of her geographic separation from the conquered territory. Finally, after much negotiating, the Treaty of Gastein was signed on August 14, 1865, by which Austria retained Holstein, and Prussia, Schleswig and Lauenberg, with certain guarantees concerning the right of transit through Holstein.

Trouble soon arose over the administration of the duchies. Prussia vigorously suppressed all liberalism and all movements looking toward the establishment of the duchies as independent states of the Germanic Confederation, while Austria on her side encouraged these movements in Holstein. Bismarck protested, and when Austria submitted the difficulties to the diet at Frankfort he refused absolutely to be bound by its decisions and accused Austria of having violated the agreement of Gastein.

Both powers prepared for war. For Prussia this meant the first steps toward mobilization only. Her army and her alliances had been prepared long before the crisis came. The former under the direction of Moltke and Roon had been developed into the most perfect military machine the world had seen. The latter had been readily effected by Bismarck's able diplomacy. The friendship of Russia had been won, as we have seen, by his policy toward the Polish insurrection in 1863, and with Italy a definitive offensive alliance was made, by which the latter power was to obtain Venetia. Poor distracted Austria, on the other hand, was far from ready from the military standpoint. Even to the last moment Francis Joseph seemed to regard war with Prussia as well-nigh impossible. Nevertheless Austria had apparently important allies. With a few minor exceptions the princes of Germany, jealous of Prussia, were on her side. Napoleon III., too, seemed favorably disposed.

Immediately on the outbreak of the war the detached forces of the smaller German states were promptly crushed by the Prussians and the respective capitals occupied. The three south German states alone held out, and that rather because of the fact that they were so far removed from the base of Prussian military operations than by virtue of any special military prowess. Italy sent her fleet into the Adriatic and her armies against the " Quadrilateral," and although defeated on land by Archduke Albert at Custozza, and on sea by Rear Admiral Tegethoff at Lissa, she was nevertheless instrumental in keeping a large and formidable Austrian force occupied in the south, while Prussia was pushing her lightning campaign in the north. Here was fought what proved to be the decisive battle of the war, and indeed one of the decisive battles of the world. The Prussian forces entered Hannover, Hesse-Cassel, and Saxony, and on June 18 occupied Dresden, the Austrian commander, Benedek, having made the mistake of not supporting the Saxons, but of waiting for the Prussians in Bohemia. Thither the Prussian forces in three main divisions proceeded to find him, and after two minor successes drove him back in some confusion upon Königgratz and the village of Sadowa. Here he decided to make a stand, and it soon became evident that the crisis of the campaign had been reached. King William, Moltke, and Bismarck joined the Prussian army, and on July 3 the great battle of Sadowa was fought. The Austrians were completely defeated and the road to Vienna lay open to the enemy. He promptly took advantage of it, marching southward by way of Moravia. Austria lay helpless before the march of the victorious Prussian army, and Francis Joseph was not slow to accept the overtures of peace proffered him by Bismarck, who was particularly anxious to come to a settlement before the French emperor should have an opportunity to intervene. Preliminaries were signed at Nikolsburg on July 26, and on August 23 a definitive treaty was agreed to at Prague. By the terms of this treaty Austria agreed to the dissolution of the German Confederation and her own exclusion from the affairs of Germany, the enlargement and consolidation of Prussia by extensive annexations in north Germany, the foundation of a North German Confederation under Prussian leadership, the payment of a war indemnity, and the surrender of Venetia through Napoleon III. to Italy, the relations with the latter state being arranged by a separate treaty signed on October 3.

Thus in a short campaign of six weeks the proud Hapsburgs had again been sorely humiliated by their old rival, and Prussia took the place of Austria, not only in Germany, but in Europe. To contemporaries it seemed as if the loosely knit Austrian empire could scarcely survive the catastrophe. After half a century of constant effort to maintain her supremacy in Italy and Germany she found herself excluded from both, with her army demoralized, her finances ruined, and face to face with a discontented Slav and Magyar people, not to mention the sorrow and humiliation of the sad fate at this very time of her most popular prince, the Archduke Maximilian, a younger brother of the emperor, who fell a victim to the ambition and wiles of Napoleon III. in Mexico.

PART VIII

AUSTRIA-HUNGARY. 1867-1906

Chapter XXXIII

THE ESTABLISHMENT OF DUALISM. 1867-1871

THE task of reëstablishing the shaken edifice of the Austrian empire was perilous and difficult. Hungary and Bohemia were in a state of profound irritation. The Magyars had all but been driven into the camp of Prussia. During the war they had held proudly aloof, and now, after Austria's defeat they would accept no settlement which did not recognize their national independence and the equality of Hungary with Austria. The Czechs likewise had taken little part in the conflict, the government having actually refused their request for arms to defend their country, because it had so little faith in their loyalty. With these two discontented elements the government had now to deal face to face. Austria could no longer look for her center of gravity in Germany or in Italy, nor hope to dominate the Slav and Magyar races by the theory of the greater interests of the German empire. To aid him in the solution of the problem Francis Joseph called the Saxon statesman and opponent of Bismarck, Baron von Beust, from Dresden, and with his assistance what is known as the *Ausgleich,* or dual agreement with Hungary, was arranged. Realizing that Hungary had too highly developed a national existence to enter into a centralized monarchy, he agreed to her separation that he might have her for an ally, by whose help the demands of the other nationalities for a federal state could then be resisted. Negotiations were accordingly opened with the committee of the Hungarian diet, at whost head was the great patriot and legist, Francis Deak, the Franklin of Hungary.

Early in 1867 the political individuality of Hungary was agreed upon by the creation of a separate ministry under Count Julius Andrassy, one of the exiles of 1849, and the emperor guaranteed the nation's historic rights by being crowned at Buda on June 8. Thus was instituted the system which is to-day the basic principle of the government of Austria-Hungary, and which established a dual government in the dominions of the Hapsburgs by dividing them into two states with strictly equal rights, each with its separate government, but subject to the same sovereign and with the same flag. Officially the state was to be known as Austria-Hungary. Hungary was to consist of those provinces which had in times past been a part of the dominions of the crown of St. Stephen, namely, Hungary proper, Croatia, Slavonia, Transylvania, Servia, and the military frontier. Austria comprised the rest—seventeen provinces in all. The Hungarian group is known as Transleithania and the Austrian as Cisleithania, names derived from the river Leitha, which marks the boundary between Austria and Hungary.

In its details, the agreement with Hungary provides for the general rights of the Magyar kingdom as they appear in the act of inauguration and the coronation oath; the king excuses himself for not having, "owing to circumstances," been crowned earlier, and renews the engagements of his predecessors in all that concerns the constitution, independence, privileges, and territorial integrity of Hungary. He promises to exercise the executive power himself and to abolish the office of the palatine; that if the diet be dissolved before voting the budget, a new diet is to be convoked within a year. The defense of the country is declared the common business of Hungary and all the other states, just as foreign affairs are common to all. But the Hungarian diet alone must vote the Hungarian contingent. The finances, the army, and foreign affairs are declared common to both parts of the monarchy. The financial liabilities of each are left to be arranged by special negotiations. Hungary can enter into union with constitutional governments only, and it is therefore necessary that the other nationalities shall be legally represented in a legislative assembly. A special ministry is to be created to deal with affairs common to the whole empire. A delegation from her two chambers is to arrange all common affairs with the delegations from the parliament " of the other countries." These two delegations are to have the same number of members and meet alternately at Pesth and Vienna. They shall discuss public affairs in writing and in the language best suited to their convenience. The common ministry is subject to the two delegations, whose special function is the discussion of the common budget. The delegations exercise the right of initiative, and if either of the two parliaments is dissolved its delegation is *ipso facto* dissolved also. Hungary is not to be

THE CORONATION OF THE EMPEROR FRANCIS JOSEPH I. AND THE EMPRESS ELIZABETH AS KING AND QUEEN OF HUNGARY AT BUDA, JUNE 8, 1867

responsible for debts contracted without the consent of her diet, but she is ready to accept a fair share (thirty per cent.) of the common debt. Hungary accepts the Austrian customs system, the revenues of which are applied to the common defense of the empire. The coinage is to be uniform, but Hungary reserves the right to use her own language on her coins.

Such, in the main, was the compromise which the wise pertinacity of Deak had forced upon both parties. This upright citizen, whose name is thus indelibly associated with one of the most important acts of his nation's history, would accept neither honors nor dignities; he even refused a portfolio in the new Hungarian ministry, resting content with being the leader of the moderate party in the diet, which maintained the privileges of Hungary, the dignity of the dynasty, and the integrity of the monarchy. His great compatriot, Louis Kossuth, remained a voluntary exile, refusing to profit by the general amnesty and protesting to the last against a compromise which lost sight of Hungarian independence. But liberal Europe applauded the work of Deak, little dreaming of the policy of repression and Magyarization soon to be inaugurated in Hungary. With their habitual egotism the Magyars thought only of themselves, having little regard for the other races. Indeed, the Austro-Hungarian monarchy organized by the compromise left a ruling race in each division, the Germans in Cisleithania, the Magyars in Transleithania. In order to reduce the refractory elements within their boundary to obedience, the Magyars had recourse to measures far from legitimate; they took advantage of their victory to impose severe and harsh laws upon the Rumanians, Servians, and Slovaks, whose grievances have frequently reached western Europe through the press. With the exception of the Croats, who, thanks to the strength of their historic claims, have succeeded in obtaining a fair share of local self-government and a special ministry at Pesth, the non-Magyar people have been kept in a kind of serfdom, and to keep them there the Hungarians are under the necessity of supporting the German Austrians, for they know that the emancipation of the Slavs of Bohemia, Carinthia, and Carniola would give a moral force to the Servians and Slovaks in Hungary which could not be resisted.

In both parts of the monarchy the compromise was marked by the reëstablishment of constitutional government. The constitution of 1848, modified so as to allow the right of selecting the ministers to the king, was restored in Hungary. The executive power was vested in the ministry, responsible to the diet, which consisted of two houses, a chamber of magnates and a chamber of deputies. The former, composed mainly of hereditary nobles and having in 1867 over 800 members, remained aristocratic, while the latter was democratic, being elected by popular vote on an extended suffrage. In Austria the constitution of 1861 was so modified by the " fundamental laws " of 1867 as to make it really liberal. They proclaimed equality before the law, recognized personal, religious, and political liberty, and reassured the non-German peoples by proclaiming equality of race and language. " All races in the state enjoy equal rights, and each has an inviolable right to its own nationality and tongue. The equal rights (*Gleichberechtigung*) of all the languages in use is recognized by the state in school, office, and public life. In countries where different nationalities existed public education was to be so arranged that every citizen might acquire all the necessary instruction without having to learn a second language. This provision, which would have no point in a unified country, such as France or Italy, is the expression of a necessary right in a polyglot state such as Cisleithania, but it has never been honestly carried out. The Czechs in Bohemia, the Slovenes in Carinthia, Carniola, and Istria, complain ·that their primary and secondary schools are in the hands of German or Italian masters.

The Reichsrath consisted of two houses, and the ministry was responsible to it, but possessed the right of initiative. The lower house was elected by the diets of the seventeen provinces. Between the Reichsrath and the provincial diets powers were carefully distributed so as to give control very largely into the hands of the central government, securing to it even the regulation of the press, public meetings, association, " confessional relations," education, criminal justice, civil and commercial rights, and organization of the courts and the administration. The exercise of the franchise was, as we have seen, based upon class and property qualifications. Four classes of electors had been established, based on economic status; great landholders, chambers of commerce, cities and rural districts. Each class elected its own deputies. A change in the constitution could be effected only by a two-thirds vote. Thus, as M. Seignobos says, " Austria became a liberal constitutional monarchy, almost parliamentary, with a

DUALISM 401

representative system in three stages: in each of the seventeen provinces a diet (*Landtag*) voting the laws and the budget of the province; for Austria, the Reichsrath; for the whole Austro-Hungarian monarchy, the Delegations."

But this system was far from satisfying the non-German peoples of Austria, nor should it be supposed that because the work of reconciliation was accomplished with so little difficulty between Hungary and the sovereign, that matters were as readily adjusted in " the other countries of his Majesty." The diets of these provinces had been convoked at the same time as that of Pesth, but they were not consulted concerning their relations with the sovereign and the others countries of the monarchy. They were simply invited to send deputies to the Reichsrath at Vienna. This was deciding the question in advance. The Magyars had refused to allow themselves to be absorbed in a centralized monarchy; the Slavs had the same right to protest against this closely centralized government which was presented to them under the form of dualism. The Germans naturally supported a system which favored their pretensions, and which, thanks to Schmerling's electoral system, would assure their domination in a great part of the empire. Of the others only the Poles, who, not possessing any historic rights, and seeing the harsh treatment of their compatriots in Prussia and Russia, hoped for better treatment if they assented to the programme of Baron von Beust, sent deputies to Vienna. But the Czechs of Bohemia and Moravia and the Slovenes of Carniola insisted upon affirming their separate existence and refused to go to the new parliament.

In the Bohemian diet, Rieger pointed out with much ability and energy the dangers of dualism and the Germanizing policy. On the other hand, the adherence of the Galicians to the policy of Beust materially cooled the sympathy which the events of 1863 had aroused in Bohemia for the Poles. Some of the most eminent men of Bohemia and of the other Slav countries, dreading the triumph of the German policy, drew toward Russia, the one state in whom they saw a possible protector against German greed. The journey of a number of Slavs to Moscow on the occasion of an ethnographic exhibition caused much talk both in Bohemia and in the west of Europe. In regard to the Reichsrath the Slavs of Bohemia and Moravia adopted a policy of passive resistance, and stubbornly refused to send deputies to the Austrian parliament.

In the meantime the ministry, under the presidency of Baron von Beust, although ignoring the claims of the Slavs, proceeded, nevertheless, to inaugurate a series of liberal measures which won the good opinion of the whole of Europe. Foreigners only heard of the liberal measures; they did not appreciate the conditions arising from their execution, nor did they even know of the existence of such different people. The " fundamental laws " of December 21, 1867, were often cited as a model of liberal legislation.

In December, 1867, the first parliamentary ministry of Cisleithania was formed under the presidency of Prince Auersperg. It consisted of eight Germans and one Pole, Count Potocki. Its first work was to free Austria from the clerical and ultramontane yoke under which she had suffered since 1855. The Concordat was modified, a new marriage law decreed that marriages could be contracted before the civil authorities in case of refusal of a priest to solemnize them, and that all disputes concerning matrimony must be tried before the ordinary courts. Later came an important law concerning schools, which freed education from the tutelage of the church. But as this law encroached upon the autonomy of the provincial diets, it was passed only with difficulty, the Poles, Slovenes, and Tyrolese withdrawing from the Reichsrath. But thanks to Schmerling's electoral system, the German deputies were still sufficiently numerous to enable the assembly to continue its deliberations. Another law, designed to regulate the relations arising from mixed marriages, was also adopted. The court of Rome and several members of the higher Austrian clergy protested against these measures, but the government persisted and even summoned some of the bishops, whose pastoral letters had urged their flocks to disobey the laws, before the civil tribunal. These energetic measures in ecclesiastical matters were accompanied by reforms in justice, finance, and the army. Trial by jury was reëstablished, even in cases in which the press was concerned, though cleverly nullified among the nationalities opposed to dualism. A financial measure introduced by Brestel unified the national debt and increased the tax on coupons 20 per cent., a measure which seriously impaired the credit of Austria abroad. A new military law reorganized the army according to the Prussian system, and provided an army in time of peace of 255,000 and of 800,000 in time of war. A force of volunteers, serving one year, was introduced, and the efficiency of the army increased by the intro-

DUALISM

duction of the breech-loading rifle. A little later, in 1870 and 1871, the general staff and the war office were completely reorganized.

But these useful reforms must not make us overlook the long struggle of the non-German races to secure their rights and their autonomy against the encroachments of the new administration centralized at Vienna. In 1867 the Czechs, as we have seen above, refused to send deputies to Vienna. As soon as the right of public meeting was proclaimed they organized monster mass meetings in which they formulated and demanded their rights. In 1868 the Emperor Francis Joseph visited Prague, but his interviews with the chiefs of the national party, Palacky, Rieger, and Clam Martinitz, did not result in a solution of the difficulties. The ministry continued pitiless in its persecution of the Bohemian press. Because of the law providing trial by jury a curious state of affairs arose. As juries in the Czech towns never failed to acquit their fellow-countrymen, the government sent the journalists before juries in German towns, where the incriminating articles could not even be read in the original. When the provincial diets were convoked, the Czechs, who were still kept in a factitious minority through the electoral system of Schmerling, refused to attend, and published a manifesto, known as the "Declaration," which remains to this day the best expression of their claims.

This declaration by the Czech deputies, which was dated August 22, 1868, consisted of eight articles, which may be summarized as follows: Article I. There exists between Bohemia and the sovereign mutual rights and treaties which are equally binding on both. Article II. Austria is not one undivided state; the kingdom of Bohemia is attached to the rest of the empire by a personal union only. Article III. No modifications of this relationship can be made except by a new contract between the kingdom and the dynasty. Article IV. No assembly, Reichsrath, or chamber of deputies foreign to Bohemia can impose upon the kingdom the debt of the empire or any other public burdens. Article V. The Hungarians have a right to treat with the sovereign concerning their own interests, but not those of Bohemia. Article VI. Cisleithania is a division of the country which has no historical foundation, and Bohemia is not bound to send deputies to the Cisleithanian assembly. Article VII. The constitutional questions now pending are to be regulated by common agreement between the sovereign and the Bohemian nation "represented upon the basis of a just electoral law and an honest election."

A short time after the Slav deputies of the Moravian diet published a similar declaration. They declared that the Reichsrath had no power to decide what were the rights of the various nations, nor the relations which, according to these rights, exist between them. "Dualism," said they, "is founded neither on historical nor political rights; no deputy of Moravia has had the right to treat in the name of his country in the Reichsrath"—the German deputies are plainly implied—"nor to cede the legislative power and the political rights of the Moravian diet to the representatives of another state. The constituent power of the Reichsrath is based on a manifest violation of ancient laws, and its decisions are null and void. No arrangement can endure except one founded on our historic rights, and entered into by the sovereign in agreement with our lawfully constituted and elected diet." In accordance with this declaration the Czech deputies of Moravia refused to sit in the diet of Brünn, which they did not consider a "lawfully constituted and elected diet."

The fifth centenary of the birth of John Huss, in July, 1868, was made the occasion for a great national demonstration, and the opposition reached such a point that the government proclaimed a state of siege at Prague, which was not raised till April 29, 1869. In the elections for the diet of this year those who had signed the "Declaration" were reëlected, both in Bohemia and Moravia, and both states refused to send deputies to the Reichsrath at Vienna. This led the government to devise the plan of having deputies for the Reichsrath elected by the electors directly and not by the diets, but even this measure, though not tried till some time later, proved ineffective. The offers of successive cabinets at Vienna to the leaders of the national party for an arrangement based upon the existing constitution were consistently rejected, because it was precisely this constitution which the Czechs would not accept. They insisted on the terms of the "Declaration," and the situation remained unchanged till the Franco-German War.

In Galicia, the Poles and Ruthenians, possessing no historic rights in the monarchy, and not having a contract with the dynasty, were more conciliatory. Under the leadership of Goluchowski, the diet at Lemberg had voted to send deputies to the

DUALISM

Reichsrath, notwithstanding the opposition of the party led by Smolka, who demanded a close alliance with the Czechs. By this act they recognized the new constitution. But most of the Poles looked upon themselves as only temporary guests in the Austrian monarchy and troubled themselves very little with the interests of the other provinces or races. Awaiting better times, they endeavored to obtain the best terms possible for themselves, and aimed at making Galicia the cornerstone for the restored Poland of their dreams. There was, however, a federalist, democratic party among them, which in September of 1868 propagated its views in a resolution similar to the Czech declaration. It declared that the diet of the country alone could choose the deputies for the Reichsrath, that the central government had no right to order direct election, that Galician deputies could take part in the deliberations of the Reichsrath only when matters common to Galicia and the other Cisleithanian countries were concerned, that commerce, finance, rights of citizenship, status of foreigners, education, justice, and administration were matters over which the diet alone had power. It demanded a supreme court for Galicia and a separate administration responsible to her diet. Needless to say, these demands were rejected in the Reichsrath. When they were submitted to this assembly in 1869 they were laid on the table. They were even opposed by the Ruthenian deputies, who, fearful of the dominance of the Poles, wished the support of a strong central power. In the southwestern portion of the monarchy the Slovenes also, in numerous meetings, demanded the formation of a separate kingdom to be known either as Slovenia or Illyria, which should include Trieste, Istria, Gorica, Gradisca, Carniola, southern Carinthia, and southern Styria. The opposition in Dalmatia was not less vigorous. In the diet at Zara a strong conflict arose between the Italian minority, supported by the government and always hostile to the Slavs, and the representatives of the Servo-Croats. Toward the end of 1869 an insurrection broke out in the Bocche de Cattaro, though this insurrection was due rather to the opposition aroused by the attempt to introduce the new law concerning the *landwehr* among the warlike Servians of this district. They were willing, they said, to defend their own mountains, but would not enroll themselves in the regular army and be turned into *Kaiserliks*. The revolt was suppressed with great difficulty, and that more by persuasion and a general amnesty than by force.

But if this dissatisfaction prevailed in the Austrian or Cis-leithanian part of the dual monarchy, the situation in the Trans-leithanian portion was little better. When the dual agreement had been finally arranged, Count von Beust is reported to have said to Deak: " Now take care of your barbarians, and we will take care of ours." By barbarians were meant, of course, the non-German and non-Magyar races. The difficulties of carrying out this pro-gramme in Cisleithania have been indicated, and it will appear later how the Germans have failed almost entirely in their efforts to Germanize and restrain the other races. The Hungarians, on their part, for reasons that will appear, have been much more suc-cessful. At the time the agreement between the German and the Magyar elements was made, the Magyars were by no means the largest race numerically in Hungary. Of a total population of six-teen millions in 1867, they numbered only a little more than six millions. But the Magyars possessed the advantage of being a com-pact group, strongly aristocratic in its tastes and accustomed to rul-ing, while the other races, apart from the scattered Germans and Jews, were composed mainly of masses of peasants without strong political aspirations. One group, however, the Croats, in the king-dom of Croatia-Slavonia in the southwest, had a national organiza-tion. The Croats had always been dissatisfied with conditions imposed upon them by the Magyars, and in 1866 their diet declared that Croatia would not give up her right to self-government, that she would no longer send deputies to the Hungarian diet, and that she would treat directly with the sovereign. As a consequence, the Magyars twice dissolved the diet at Agram. Bishop Strossmayer, later distinguished by his part in the Vatican council, and the soul of the national opposition in Croatia, was exiled, and a man of very doubtful reputation appointed *locum tenens banalis* of Croatia. The port of Fiume was annexed by Hungary, notwithstanding the protests of the Croatians. Finally the Hungarian government had recourse to an expedient similar to the measures employed by Schmerling. The electoral law was altered, and a subservient as-sembly secured which readily lent itself to the designs of the larger kingdom. By this diet many of the ancient rights of Croatia were surrendered. But the Magyars did not feel strong enough to disre-gard the claims of the kingdom entirely, and a ˜compromise was made in 1868 which left to the kingdom of Croatia-Slavonia its ban and its diet, and its own system of justice, education, religion, official national language, and coat-of-arms. Common affairs, such as foreign relations, finance, commerce, and communication were under the control of the Hungarian diet and ministry in which Croatia was represented by forty deputies and a Croatian minister, while the financial arrangement allowed Croatia forty-five per cent. of her taxes.

But if the Croats complained of their treatment, the other races of Hungary fared much worse. The Servians of the southeast received no recognition and the Rumanians in Transylvania found themselves completely incorporated in the kingdom of Hungary, deprived of their diet and independent administration, and their kingdom divided into districts represented in the diet at Pesth. But even in this modicum of representation they had little share, because of the property qualification in the electoral law, which secured even the rural seats to the Magyars and their Saxon allies, a little group of Germans in Transylvania of about two hundred thousand souls, which has always retained its solidarity.

Chapter XXXIV

PARLIAMENTARY STRUGGLE FOR FEDERALISM
1871-1878

IN view of the conditions just described, it is scarcely to be expected that the *Ausgleich* would satisfy any of the peoples of Austria except the Magyars and the Germans. The Poles of Galicia accepted it, it is true, but did all in their power to make it subservient to their own plans for the future, while the other races made no secret of their discontent. The situation of the cabinet in the Austrian part of the monarchy was difficult indeed. Ministries succeeded each other in rapid succession. Violent disputes marked all the sessions of the *Reichsrath*, and the deputies from the Tyrol, Galicia, and Slavonia in turn withdrew from the assembly. The Potocki cabinet attempted to work out a plan which would preserve the constitution of 1867 and still make some concessions to the demands of the federalists. According to this, the upper chamber was to consist of members elected by the diets of the provinces, the Reichsrath of members chosen by direct election. But their good intentions came to nothing, the situation being complicated still further by the Franco-German War. Austria, from the military standpoint, was not in a condition to aid France or to take revenge on Prussia for Sadowa. Its government, moreover, was in the hands of the Germans, who applauded the success of their kinsmen and celebrated the glory of the new Germany in newspapers inspired from Berlin. The Magyars also, for the most part, rejoiced in the victories of Prussia, for they believed that if Cisleithania were once absorbed by the greater Germany their hands would be free for the realization of their ambitions for the complete independence of their own country.

Things were in this condition when the emperor considered it his duty to appoint, in February, 1871, a cabinet which would carry out the federalist policy. Its leader, Charles Hohenwart, governor of Upper Austria, offered two positions in the cabinet to Czechs, a fact in itself indicative of the attitude of the new ministry. But its task was a difficult one; to be successful it was necessary to deprive the German element of that supremacy which the actual organization of the electoral system secured it by legal right, and in doing this, the opposition of the Germans both at home and abroad would have to be overcome. One of the leaders of the German party declared in the Reichsrath: " To concede to Bohemia what might be granted to Galicia would be to reduce two million Germans to the position of the Ruthenians. It must not be forgotten that these Germans are the kindred of a great neighboring people." Another speaker said: " We have not conquered at Sedan in order to become the helots of the Czechs "; while certain newspapers compared the condition of Bohemia with that of Schleswig, plainly insinuating the rôle to be played by Prussia as liberator.

Nevertheless, the minister set heroically to work. He entered into negotiations with the Bohemian leaders, Rieger and Palacky, and laid before the Reichsrath a new law, which increased the functions of the provincial diets and granted them initiative in matters of legislation, but his proposal was naturally defeated. A little later he introduced a special project in regard to Galicia, granting the principal points of the Galician " Resolution." On an interpolation as to whether he proposed to introduce similar measures regulating the rights of the other provinces, he frankly declared his programme. If, he said, Bohemia would be satisfied with the concessions which he was preparing for Galicia, he would not hesitate to make the offer. This was the signal for a general outbreak, and the Germans of the Reichsrath passed a motion of lack of confidence in the ministry. The Reichsrath was dissolved, and the provincial diets convoked for September. In the meantime negotiations were carried on between Vienna and Prague. Rieger, who occupied much the same place in Bohemia as did Deak in Hungary, drew up in collaboration with Clam Martinitz a plan on which was to be based the final reconciliation of Bohemia with the constitutional government. Both sovereign and minister showed their readiness to make important concessions. On September 12 the Bohemian diet was opened. This time the Czech deputies, who had so long absented themselves, reappeared, and, thanks to the new election in which for the first time the government had not falsified the returns, they had a majority, notwithstanding Schmerling's electoral law. The king's speech promised to recognize the rights of the kingdom of Bohemia. The diet was asked to make known by what means cordial relations could be

established between the kingdom and the rest of the monarchy.
" Recognizing the political importance of the crown of Bohemia,"
said the emperor, " and recollecting the renown and glory which the
crown has conferred upon our predecessors, and grateful for the
loyalty with which the Bohemian nation has supported our throne,
we are ready to recognize the rights of the kingdom and to renew
this recognition by the coronation oath." This declaration was received with enthusiastic joy by Bohemia, Moravia, and Carniola,
but excited great anger among the Germans. A project for a new
election law, and another concerning the nationalities, was laid
before the diet at Prague. The German deputies immediately protested and withdrew. A commission was, however, appointed to
draw up the definite plan called for in the emperor's speech, upon
which the relations of Bohemia to the rest of the Austro-Hungarian
states should be based. This plan was drawn up and voted by
the Slav deputies of the diet, and has become known as the " Fundamental Articles." It was sent to Vienna and the diet adjourned
to await the reply of the sovereign.

According to these " Fundamental Articles," Bohemia, like
Hungary, was to be represented in all matters common to the empire by a delegation named by the diet at Prague and not by the
Reichsrath. She was to treat with the other Cisleithanian states
only through these deputies. Her self-government was to be assured, and only matters relating to war, diplomacy, and commerce
were to be considered the common affairs of the monarchy. A
senate, composed of members nominated by the emperor, was to
arrange all differences which might arise between the different kingdoms or provinces. Finally, the representation of the towns and
rural communities was to be considerably increased, a measure
which would assure that preponderance of the Czech nation which it
was claimed belonged to it both by virtue of its numbers and its
historic rights. The diet of Moravia accepted the " Fundamental
Articles," and at the same time demanded the reëstablishment of
a special chancery for the countries of St. Vacslav. The Slavs of
the monarchy ardently longed for the success of a policy which,
in leading Austria toward federalism, would put an end to the
German and Magyar supremacy.

It was not surprising, therefore, that these projects of the Slavs,
so ably formulated by Rieger and Clam Martinitz, aroused the
hostility of the Germans and the Hungarians to the highest pitch.

We have already shown why the Magyars dreaded Slavism. As for the Austrian Germans, there were very few who held in practice to the well-known saying of Francis II.: *" Justitia erga omnes nationes est fundamentum Austriæ."* Besides many of them longed for a greater Germany and were anxious for the destruction of the Czech nation, which so obstinately interjected itself between Vienna and Berlin and which is, as has so often been said, a thorn in the side of Germany (*ein Pfeil im deutschen Fleisch*).

Unfortunately for the aspirations of the Czechs, these enemies of federalism were too powerful, and their plans were again defeated. If, according to the Treaty of Prague, Austria was to abstain from interfering in the internal affairs of Germany, the same rule has by no means been observed by Germany in regard to Austria. Statesmen of Berlin have continued to bestow upon their kinsmen on the Upper Elbe and the Danube the same jealous attention that they formerly showed toward their brethren in Schleswig and Alsace. They carried on a constant agitation in a part of the Viennese press. Numerous interviews between Emperors William I. and Francis Joseph, for which the baths of Gastein afforded the excuse, presented opportunities for the interchange of views in which German interests were generally less frequently sacrificed than the Austrian. In the summer of 1871 these interviews were particularly frequent, the two emperors being sometimes joined by Bismarck, Beust, and Andrassy. All the German and Magyar influences united to checkmate the Bohemians, and to this coalition the Emperor Francis Joseph believed himself obliged to yield. The first signs of retreat appeared when the ministry declared that the " Fundamental Articles " would be submitted to the approaching Reichsrath. To all who knew the character of this assembly, the result of such a step could not be doubtful. Rieger, in a visit to Vienna, made a final effort to induce the sovereign to fulfill his engagements, but, less fortunate than Deak, he failed in his attempt. On his return to Prague, however, he was made the object of an enthusiastic ovation. Then followed several curious developments. Hohenwart resigned on October 30, 1871; Baron von Beust was shortly afterward relieved of his duties as chancellor, and transferred to the embassy at London, while Count Andrassy, the head of the Hungarian cabinet, was placed in charge of foreign affairs, thus securing the preponderance of the Magyar influence in the monarchy.

The new Austrian ministry, consisting entirely of Germans and presided over by Auersperg, blandly invited the diet of Prague to send deputies to the Reichsrath. Persecutions against the Slav press were resumed, and a spectacle, never before witnessed in any other country, occurred when the police publicly destroyed the copies of the imperial manifesto. When the Bohemian diet refused to treat with anyone but the legitimate king, it was dissolved, as were the diets of the other provinces in November. A new Reichsrath was called, and in spite of the absence of the federalists, a large enough number favorable to the constitution obeyed the summons, to enable a legal sitting to take place. Dualism was reconfirmed in full force, and the hopes of Bohemia indefinitely postponed.

The next six years, from 1872 to 1878, are marked by ministries ardently supporting the constitution. In 1873 an important electoral law was brought forward and passed which increased the number of deputies in the Reichsrath and established the principle of election by direct vote instead of by the diets. The number of deputies was set at 353: 85 to landowners, 139 to cities and chambers of commerce, and 129 to rural districts. The results of the new law continued much of the inequality of representation and still gave the Germans a majority in the chamber, there being up to 1878 about 220 Germans as against 115 Czechs and 15 Italians. The anti-clerical policy was continued, and in 1874 the system of the Concordat was abolished by the "May Laws." Non-Catholic societies were granted the right to found religious societies and bishops were ordered to report all vacancies and all nominations in the church to the civil authorities.

In the Hungarian part of the monarchy the years between the Compromise and the annexation of Bosnia and Herzegovina were marked by a political calm. The place assigned the non-Magyar races in the monarchy has been noted; the Magyars were in undisputed control, the secondary peoples having only insignificant representation at Pesth. Questions of policy, therefore, and not race and national disputes, mark the party divisions. Deak's party became the liberal ministerial party, and was opposed by the party of the left, democrats and followers of Kossuth, the irreconcilable enemies of Austria. The reform of the army, the administration and the financial system occupied the government. The *honved*, or militia, was reorganized into a purely Hungarian force, while the active army remained common to the entire monarchy and retained German as the language of command. In the reform of the administrative system, the ancient comitats remained self-governing under the direction of delegates, one-half of whom were elected, the other half appointed, by the heaviest taxpayers. In the matter of the relations between the state and the church, the government, fearful of losing the support of the Catholics, introduced no radical measures. Nor was this fear of loss of support imaginary, for in 1875 the government was saved from overwhelming defeat only by the complete change in front of a large part of the left under the leadership of Tisza, who renounced the policy of a personal union and rallied to the support of Deak. In August of this year Tisza became head of the liberal ministry, a position he continued to occupy for fifteen years.

But if this period failed to secure for the Slavs the recognition of their rights which they demanded with so much persistency, and the painful and irritating causes for disputes and conflicts remained, because the greater part of the peoples of the Austro-Hungarian state did not succeed in realizing the political ideals to which they aspired, it nevertheless witnessed the accomplishment, besides the establishment of dualism and electoral reform, of great social and economic reform and progress. Numerous lines of railroad were constructed; Vienna, Pesth, and Prague were brought into touch with the most distant points of the monarchy and with the great capitals of foreign countries, including Constantinople. Treaties of commerce were concluded with France, England, and Russia. Industrial development in the various provinces made rapid progress, as was evidenced by the great international exposition held in Vienna in 1873, which was one of the most interesting of the international expositions of this epoch. Unfortunately, it coincided with a calamitous financial crash in the monarchy, and its beneficent results were greatly lessened. This disaster in the financial world which destroyed the public credit for many years was due largely to the bad policy of the ministry of finance and to overspeculation. Vienna had become after 1815 a center of banking and of speculation. The institution of the lottery had developed among the population a taste for speculation and stock-jobbing. Unbridled speculation ended in the now famous *Krach* or financial disaster of 1873. Of 147 joint-stock banks, 96 failed in three years, and hundreds of families were ruined.

But notwithstanding the unfortunate results of the *Krach*, this period of the reign of Francis Joseph was an era of restoration, rebuilding, expansion, and artistic embellishment for the large cities. Vienna set the example, and by a transformation as thorough and wise as it was necessary, inspired the other cities to improvements that have made of Pesth, Prague, and other capitals well-appointed

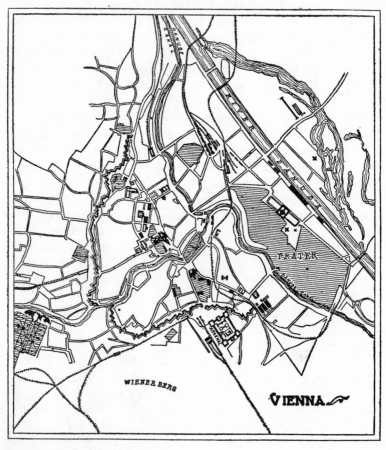

modern cities. And in each of these cases the rebuilding and embellishment of the city became an object for the exercise of the national pride and patriotism of the particular race it represented. The German Austrians made a new Vienna, which rivals even Paris in its fine streets, magnificent buildings, and in the excellence of its municipal appointments.

Till the middle of the last century Vienna was in many respects one of the worst cities of Europe. Thoroughly mediæval in character and shut up behind its thick walls which had served it against the Turks, the population was fearfully congested in a tangle of narrow, crooked, and filthy streets. Beyond the fortifications encircling the city were grouped a series of miserable villages from which transit to and from the town was doubly difficult because of the bad roads and the congestion of traffic at barriers. In 1857, after careful deliberation, an order was issued by the imperial government for the demolition of the fortifications. Fortunately these were unusually extensive; besides the usual wall and moat, there was a broad open space beyond called the glacis, so that altogether the available open space regained included an area larger than the inner city itself. All of this was now cleared in accordance with a systematic plan, in the carrying out of which the city, the diet of Lower Austria, and above all, the imperial government, coöperated most unselfishly. The main feature of the plan was a fine octagonal street (*Ringstrasse*) about sixty yards wide, following the line of the fortifications. Flanking this broad and well-constructed thoroughfare a series of parks, gardens, open spaces, and large public buildings was laid out and erected. Only about one-fifth of the entire area was sold to private purchasers, who were naturally restricted in the use to be made of the land and manner and style of buildings erected. After the *Ring* came the renovation of the inner city. Private enterprise was stimulated by the city through laws exempting new and improved buildings from taxation, the exemption usually ranging from twelve to thirty years, a considerable inducement in a city like Vienna, where the taxes are very high. The details of the progress made by the other cities cannot be introduced here; the significance of the transformation of Pesth in the national revival of Hungary will be readily appreciated. The courses of the Danube and the Theiss have been regulated and confined within narrower limits, thus giving a much more rapid current and better facilities for commerce.

Side by side with the modernizing of the cities, architecture and painting naturally flourished. Vienna, Pesth, Prague, and Cracow, each produced its masters, not a few of whom deserve to be remembered by posterity. The leader of the Viennese school of painting was Hans Makart, who excelled in decorative work. In Galicia the grandiose works of Matejko reproduced the more glorious episodes of Polish history. Bohemia produced Czermak, the painter of the southern Slavs, and Brozik, who devotes himself to the Middle Ages and the Renaissance; Hungary, Munkaczy, Benczur, and Zichy. In sculpture there was a similar renaissance, and numerous societies were organized to encourage the liberal arts and to organize annual exhibitions.

But architecture, especially, had a most extraordinary development, thanks to the extensive public works which were undertaken in the different capitals. Vienna was, as we have seen,

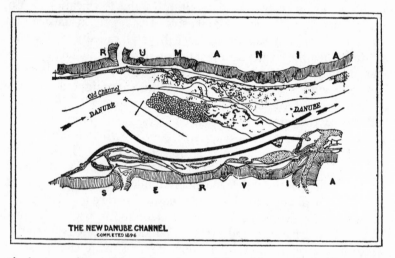

THE NEW DANUBE CHANNEL
COMPLETED 1896

entirely transformed and in place of its old poorly built quarters there was erected a city of spacious streets and squares and magnificent edifices, adorned with monuments and works of art. Among the many remarkable buildings of this period are especially to be noted the new Opera House by Van der Nult and Riccardsburg, the Academy of Fine Arts, the new Reichsrath building, the Exchange, the Conservatory of Music by Schmidt, the beautiful Votive Church, with its graceful Gothic towers by Ferstel, the Rathhaus, one of the best adaptations of the Gothic architecture to secular uses, and the chaste Palace of Justice in the German Renaissance. By virtue of the coöperation of the authorities with these artists the *Ring* became a street of rare magnificence, and all Vienna shows the signs of this commendable partnership of authority with taste and technical skill.

In music this period did not produce in Austria such rare and gifted geniuses as Haydn, Mozart, or Beethoven. But there flourishes at Vienna, Prague, Pesth, and Florence interesting schools of music of which certain productions bid fair to live. All the world knows Liszt's Hungarian fantasies and the exhilarating waltz music of Strauss. The works of the Bohemian school are less known, though they are quite as good, and the names of Dvorak and Smetana are likely to pass down to posterity.

The intellectual development, particularly public instruction, shared in the general prosperity and progress. The schools were withdrawn from clerical control and education placed on a more liberal basis. Two new universities were founded, one at Agram in 1874, destined to become the intellectual heart of the Slavs of the north, and that of Czernowitz, in 1876, upon the jubilee of the annexation of Bukowina. Croatia was allowed to furnish advanced instruction in the sciences in its own language, but Bukowina was less fortunate; her university is German and serves as the last landmark of German civilization on the Russian frontier. Two academies were also founded, one at Agram, which is rapidly becoming the Athens of the Yougo-Slavs, the other at Cracow in 1871. The latter owes its existence to the liberal efforts of the minister Jirecek; it has become the great literary and scientific center of the Poles. At Vienna the faculty of Protestant theology, the academy of fine arts and the polytechnic institute were reorganized, while at Pesth the national university of the Magyars was remodeled and improved. Copyright agreements for the protection of authors and their publishers were made with other nations.

If Austria were made up of one people who spoke one language we might speak here of her literature. But as the history of the state shows that there is no unity, so there is not, and cannot be, an Austrian literature. The various languages have made unequal progress, and manifiested their genius in widely different ways. The German literature which flourished at Vienna, at Prague, or even at Pesth, is simply an offshoot of that of Germany. The Hungarian literature, on the other hand, which has its home at Pesth, is an indigenous production in the Magyar soil and the Magyar mind, as the work of the well-known novelist, Jokai, readily illustrates. The Slav literatures, however, in spite of their common origin, are far from following the same tendencies; they have but few points of contact, and, as a rule, follow different paths.

The Poles and Ruthenians in Galicia derive their inspiration from divergent and often even opposite traditions. The Czechs, whose intellectual superiority among the Slavs is incontestable, have not been able to impose their language upon the Slovaks, who, in their turn, have great difficulty in maintaining themselves against the Magyars. The Croats find themselves separated by religious differences from the Catholic Slovenes and the Orthodox Servians. Nevertheless, in all the provincial centers the most active intellectual life prevails, and the development of the national literatures is doing much to keep alive the spirit of local independence.

In foreign affairs the military and financial weakness of Austria after 1866 completely lost her the position of predominance she had previously held. In 1870 the startling successes of the Prussians prevented her, even if she had desired, from avenging herself on Prussia, and reasserting her leadership in Germany, by an alliance with France. Recognizing the predominance of Prussia on the Rhine, she thenceforward directed her efforts toward the Danube and the Orient. The old causes of dispute with Prussia were removed, and in 1871 the friendly relations between Austria and Germany were consolidated by frequent meetings of the emperors and diplomats, and the establishment in 1872 of the so-called "alliance of the three emperors" by association of the tsar with them. Gradually Italy, alarmed at the activity of the Catholic party and the aggressive policy of France in Tunis, attached herself to them, and central and eastern Europe seemed closely united in the interests of a peaceful policy. But troubles among the peoples of Turkey were soon to reveal that Austrian and Russian interests in those regions at least were far from identical.

In 1875 an insurrection broke out among the Slavs of Herzegovina, caused by the excesses and abuses of Turkish rule. Instead of boldly taking the part of the Christians and assuming the rôle of champion and deliverer of the oppressed, Austria was rendered helpless by her own internal disorders and the opposition of Russia against a strong Austrian policy on the Lower Danube.

From its very beginning, therefore, the insurrection in Bosnia and Herzegovina caused serious difficulty to Austria. She had not only to contend with the ill-will of the Magyars, but also with the restless jealousy of her ally. The Hungarians had no wish to see the Slav element of the dual monarchy, which was already too large, increased by the addition of new territory which might be instrumental in aiding some day in submerging them under a Slav majority. It was also to the interests of Russia and Prussia not to allow their ally to enlarge her frontiers and to augment her army by the warlike populations of the two provinces. The result was that after 1875 Austria pursued a policy often at variance with itself; at one time the Turks were allowed to violate her territory with impunity, and even ravage the frontiers of Croatia; at another she would forbid them to disembark arms on their own territory at Klek. At Constantinople her ambassador, in concert with General Ignatiev, obtained the promise of the Porte to carry out those famous reforms which it is always promising and never doing, and which the diplomats who recommended them knew perfectly well could never be accomplished. In December, 1875, Count Andrassy's note formulated the wishes of civilized Europe on this point. "Christianity should be put on the same footing with Islamism, in theory and practice, . . . tax-farming should be abolished once and for all . . . and the execution of the reforms left to a controlling board of Christians and Mussulmans." But the conference at Constantinople in December of the next year resulted only in revealing once again the powerlessness of diplomacy, and the incorrigible obstinacy of the Porte. Servia and Montenegro had meanwhile espoused the cause of their oppressed kinsmen in Bosnia and Herzegovina and declared war against Turkey. This still further increased the difficulties of Austria. The Slavs of the monarchy called upon the government to take part in the conflict, and followed the various phases of the heroic but fatally unequal struggle with feverish interest. The Hungarians, on their part, neglected no opportunity to show their hatred for the Servians and their sympathy for Turkey. When Abdul-Kerim Pasha won the battle of Djunis over the Servians a subscription was raised to present him with a sword. A Magyar deputation went to Constantinople to express the enthusiastic friendship of Hungary to the softas, or Mussulman students. The Hungarian general, Klapka, the old defender of Komorn, who had once offered his sword to Prussia against Austria, now offered the service of his military experience to the Porte. Some time later the softas visited Pesth to return the visit of their Magyar brethren, and the Sultan, in order to express his gratitude to the Hungarians, sent the emperor-king some remains of the library established by Matthias Corvinus, but pillaged by the Turks. These manifestations, puerile enough

in themselves, were directed especially against Russia, whose policy
in 1849 the Hungarians had never forgiven. But they deeply
offended the Slavs, who looked upon the cause of the Servians
and Bulgarians as their own. Counter manifestations took place
in Prague in honor of the Russian general Tcherniaiev, but these
were vigorously suppressed by the Austrian police.

At Pesth Andrassy endeavored in vain to restrain his violent
countrymen, and to make them understand that street demonstrations would not influence the policy of the government. On
the other hand he caused the arrest of the Servian Stratimirovic,
one of the heroes of 1848, who had offered his sword to Prince
Milan Obrenovic. He had the journalist-deputy Miletic thrown
into prison on the charge of having wished success for his countrymen and negotiated a loan for their cause. To justify these extraordinary measures, laws of former days were invoked which
pronounced all those who furnished arms to the Turks or to other
infidels guilty of treason.

Thus the monarchy, divided against itself, painfully followed
the lead of its two powerful allies, and in spite of the enthusiasm
of the Slavs and the indignation of the Magyars was compelled
to remain a placid observer of the victories of the Russians, who,
after the fall of Plevna, pushed their victorious troops forward
to the very gates of Constantinople. Nor could she have forced
a modification of the Treaty of San Stefano, which Russia imposed upon Turkey in 1878. Fortunately for her the terms exacted by the tsar so nearly destroyed the power of Turkey in
the interests of Russia that the European powers united in demanding a revision of the treaty and the submission of the entire Eastern
Question to a European congress. At the Congress of Berlin
the three Christian states of Rumania, Servia, and Montenegro
were enlarged and declared independent, while Bulgaria was
greatly reduced. To Austria-Hungary the congress granted the
occupation of the provinces of Bosnia and Herzegovina for an indefinite period.

Chapter XXXV

ACQUISITION AND INCORPORATION OF BOSNIA AND HERZEGOVINA. 1878-1894

ACCORDING to the secret agreement made with Russia before the war, Austria was to receive some compensation in exchange for her benevolent neutrality. This compensation, as we have seen, was secured in the occupation of the provinces of Bosnia and Herzegovina. It was from these provinces that the signal for the insurrection had gone out which brought on the war in the Balkan peninsula and provoked the victorious intervention of Russia. They might well have hoped, now that the Turk had been vanquished, to be made into an independent principality like Bulgaria, or allowed to form a part of the neighboring Slav states of Servia or Montenegro, with which they were closely allied in race and religion. The preliminary Treaty of San Stefano declared merely that "the ameliorations proposed by the conference of Constantinople with such modifications as should be agreed upon by the Porte, Russia, and Austria-Hungary should be applied to them." The Treaty of Berlin, signed on the following July 13, by the representatives of all the great powers assembled in congress, decided: "The provinces of Bosnia and Herzegovina shall be occupied and governed by Austria-Hungary. The government of Austria-Hungary not wishing to undertake the administration of the government of the sandjak of Novibazar, which extends between Servia and Montenegro on the southeast as far as Mitrovitza, the administration shall there remain in the hands of the Turkish government. Nevertheless, in order that the new political situation may be maintained and that the means of communication may be free and safe, Austria-Hungary reserves the right of keeping garrisons and of having military and commercial roads in all this portion of the old vilayet of Bosnia."

The last clause was of great importance. The sandjak of Novibazar is that portion of Bosnia which separates Servia from Montenegro. By virtue of its actual military control the govern-

ment of Vienna isolated the two Servian principalities and could
at any time prevent their united action either against Turkey or
against itself. Austria-Hungary still further dominated these
two principalities, Montenegro by her command of the Gulf of
Cattaro, and Servia by her position on the Danube. Her occupation
of Bosnia and Herzegovina, therefore, completely destroyed the
hopes of the Servian and Montenegrian patriots, who had dreamed
of reëstablishing the ancient empire of the tsar douchan as a center
for a larger Slav state. By crushing at the outset the hopes of
the Servian patriots, Austria averted a serious danger. But a
feeling of profound disappointment was felt at Belgrade and Cet-
tinje. Many of the patriots went so far as to express themselves
willing to sacrifice all the advantages secured to the two principalities by the Treaty of Berlin, if only the conditions that existed before
the war could be reëstablished. So long as Bosnia and Herzegovina belonged to Turkey pretexts would never have been wanting to the other Slav states to intervene. But all these opportunities
passed away with the advent of Austrian rule in the provinces, and
the introduction of the principles of religious tolerance, equality
of race, and European administration.

Apart from the interests of Servia and Montenegro, and perhaps even of the inhabitants of Bosnia and Herzegovina themselves, this clause of the Treaty of Berlin might have the most
serious consequences for the future of the Balkan peninsula and
the peace of Europe. Up to 1878 no European power had secured
much share in the spoliation of Turkey. Only the Servians, Greeks,
Rumanians, and Bulgarians had profited by the revolutions in
their respective provinces. Even Russia, after having reached the
very gate of Constantinople, had withdrawn with nothing but a few
remote and unimportant advantages in exchange for her sacrifices.
But a new principle seemed now set up by the Congress of Berlin, to
the effect that the provinces of the Ottoman empire might at any
moment become the spoil of the various European powers. If
Austria established herself in Bosnia and Herzegovina, why should
not Italy seek to do the same in Dalmatia, Russia at the base of
the Balkans, and England in Constantinople? This is a very grave
question, by no means solved as yet. Some day it will certainly
force itself again into recognition, with serious risks to the cause
of justice and peace. The only equitable solution of the Eastern
Question is that which assures to each of the people under the Otto-

man yoke the peaceful and complete possession of that soil which is theirs by right of history and of race.

Moreover, Article 29 of the Treaty of Berlin raises further apprehensions. In establishing Austria in the sandjak of Novibazar at the head of the railway and of the military road running from Mitrovitza to Salonica by the valley of the Vardar, a ready means is afforded the statesmen of Vienna of some day seizing this commercial and military line and assuring themselves of this most excellent outlet into the Ægean Sea and the East.

As soon as Austria received the mandate confided to her by the Congress of Berlin she began to carry it into effect. In the summer of 1878 her troops crossed the Save and entered the newly acquired provinces. The occupation was not expected to cause any serious difficulties, but altogether unlooked-for obstacles arose. The Bosnian Mussulmans, who formed the upper class of the country, could not calmly witness the separation from their coreligionists at Constantinople, or the overthrow of a state of things which had profited them for centuries. The Orthodox Greek, in his turn, mourned the loss of hopes for union with Servian countries. The Catholics alone welcomed the occupation. And although the Turkish government did not officially decline to obey the commands of Europe, it nevertheless secretly conveyed arms and ammunition to the two provinces. A revolution broke out at Serajevo and a provisional government was organized to resist the foreign occupation, the brave and fanatical General Hadji Loja at its head with the title of First Patriot of the Land. The first successful resistance occurred in the mountain defiles. The Austrians were also repulsed at Maglaj and at Gradac, and found themselves opposed not merely by a few hastily improvised bands of militia, but by well-organized battalions of the Turkish army provided with artillery. The Austrian position became critical. The inhabitants, as a rule, quitted the towns and found shelter behind the natural defenses of the country, whence they inflicted serious losses on the army of occupation. Serajevo, the capital of Bosnia, was reached only on August 19, but even then hostilities did not cease. Herzegovina was not completely occupied before September and Bosnia not till a month later; the task of occupying the principalities' had required three entire army corps and cost the enormous sum of sixty-two million florins.

The occupation of Bosnia and Herzegovina, notwithstanding

its apparently temporary character, is evidently regarded as a definite conquest by Austria-Hungary, although the Sultan remains nominally sovereign. Austria-Hungary alone has charge of the administration, and she certainly has no intention of abandoning it. These possessions open to her, as has been indicated, the route to Salonica, and afford large outlets to her commerce, while securing safe and easy communication between Hungary and Dalmatia. In short, they form a very ample compensation for the loss of Venice. The area of the two provinces is 23,262 square miles, and they had in 1895 a population of 1,568,092, all speaking the Servian or Croat dialect, although divided, as to religion, into three principle groups, of 548,632 Mohammedans, 334,142 Orthodox Greeks, and 673,246 Catholics. These groups maintain a tolerably even balance of power, thus giving Austria an excellent opportunity to act again on her favorite maxim, " Divide in order to govern."

The provinces are governed in the name of the emperor-king by a special bureau under the minister of finance common to the whole monarchy, and most of the privileges of the Mohammedans were left undisturbed. From the material point of view the country has made rapid progress. Railways have been constructed between Brod and Serajevo, Gabela and Cattaro, and Mitrovitza and Serajevo. The last mentioned town has become more and more European and its economic condition has been greatly improved. In 1881 compulsory military service was introduced into the two provinces, and a number of insurrections occurred, which were, however, promptly suppressed, notwithstanding the official remonstrance of the Porte.

The political consequences of the absorption by Austria-Hungary of these two provinces have been numerous. For a time it brought about a close dependence upon Russia in Servia and Montenegro. But the prompt recognition of King Milan in 1882, and the gradual domination of the kingdom's financial and economic interests, by Austria, brought Servia into close relationship with her. Montenegro remained faithful to her Russian protector for a much longer period, and more recently through marriage alliance with the royal house of Italy has drawn very close to that country, thus introducing Italy as a much interested party in the relations of Austria to the Balkan states.

The latter power very naturally, although adopting a peaceful policy in regard to the Balkan peninsula, sought to reap every benefit the acquisition of the two provinces promised, by increasing her influence with the Christians of the Balkans and by opening for herself a trade route to Salonica. This brought increased rivalry with Russia, and fearful of a disturbance of the existing

conditions, Austria concluded a secret treaty with Germany in 1879, which was published in 1888, at a time when Russia seemed to be assuming a threatening attitude. This treaty, called " an alliance for peace and mutual defense," pledged the two states to maintain the state of things established at Berlin, especially against Russia.

This understanding between Austria-Hungary and Germany, brought about by the divergence of Russian and Austrian inter-

ests in the Balkan peninsula, was the first step in what has since
become the well-known Triple Alliance. Angered and alarmed
at the action of France in occupying Tunis, Italy joined the two
powers of central Europe. In 1881 King Humbert visited Vienna
and prepared the way for the formal alliance two years later. The
object of this alliance was the maintenance of the peace of Europe
by a coalition of the three central powers. In order to live up
to the engagements imposed by the Triple Alliance, Austria-
Hungary was forced to augment the efficiency of her armies, and
in 1886 the two parts of the monarchy passed a new law for the
organization of the *Landsturm*. It is doubtful whether this force
will ever be directed against Prussia. Austria has completely forgotten Custozza and Sadowa, and she has behaved toward the new
German empire with a friendliness that has at times astonished the
world. Notwithstanding the official alliance, however, relations
between Vienna and Rome have not been so cordial. The claims
of the Italians on Trentem and Istria, and the agitations of the
Irridenta, occasionally give rise to painful incidents. The Italians
of Istria invariably make violent protests whenever the government tries to do justice to the Slavs of the province, and this the
patriots of Italy applaud enthusiastically. In short, the Emperor
Francis Joseph has been compelled to rest for support at home on
the Magyars, who revolted in 1848, and abroad on Prussia and
Italy, who fought him in 1866.

Within the monarchy the annexation of Bosnia and Herzegovina entailed, as we have seen, heavy expenditures for the army
of occupation, and a further complication of the inter-racial strife
brought about a crisis. The parliaments in both parts of the
monarchy were displeased with the government for having undertaken the occupation. The Treaty of Berlin ought, they claimed,
in the points affecting Austria-Hungary, to have been submitted to
them. Finally the Hungarian diet voted the appropriations, but in
the Reichsrath at Vienna the German constitutionalist party was
staunch in its opposition. Like the Magyars, they feared further
increase of the Slav populations of the monarchy. At last the
emperor appealed to the Czechs, aristocratic federalists and ultra-
montanes. Count Taaffe, the representative of the federalists,
supplanted Auersperg. He announced his intention of treating all
nationalities with impartiality. His appointment was, in fact, a
defeat of the factions whose aim was the maintenance of German

influence throughout Cisleithania. Count Taaffe succeeded in persuading the Czechs to again take part in the Austrian *Reichsrath*. They declared that they did not, by so doing, give up their principles in regard to the rights of Bohemia, but that they took part without hesitation in the work of the new cabinet. Prazak, a deputy from Moravia and a friend of the political leaders of Bohemia, was appointed to a place as minister without portfolio and later became minister of justice. Two Poles of Galicia were made members of the cabinet. This alliance with the Czechs, Poles, extreme German Catholics, and the aristocracy assured a compact majority to the new ministry, the elections of 1879 having returned 145 constitutionalists (94 liberals and 51 progressists); 168 federalists in three groups (54 Czechs, 57 Poles, and 57 German federalists, Slovenes, Dalmatians, and Croatians); and 40 unclassified deputies, whom Taaffe skillfully used to hold the balance of power. The Taaffe ministry, thus organized and pledged to a moderate federalist policy, lasted for fourteen years, to 1893. It maintained the constitution but constantly tended toward concessions to the Slavs and to the Catholic clergy at the expense of the Germans and the lay power.

The Czechs in particular, using their support of the government as a lever, gained concession after concession. In 1882 they secured a national university by the division of the University of Prague into two universities, one German, the other Czech. Four years later they made a great gain in the language strife by a decree of the minister of justice obliging all officeholders to answer questions in the language, Czech or German, in which it was made, a measure plainly aimed at the Germans who would not speak Czech. A large national theater was built at Prague by private subscription and a school fund or *matice skolska* created to enable the Czech schools to compete with the German schools and to further education in remote districts. The property qualification for the exercise of the franchise was reduced, and a new division of the electoral districts made, which enabled the Czechs to secure a majority in the parliament of Prague, a majority which would have been still more increased if certain electoral fictions in regard to a number of Czech deputies had been removed. The Germans demanded that the kingdom of Bohemia be divided into two administrative divisions, one German, the other Czech, and finally refused to take part in the deliberations of the diet at Prague.

On the whole the Slavs of Bohemia owe a debt of gratitude to Taaffe; he endeavored, as far as possible and often under the most difficult circumstances, to put in practice the old motto: *Justitia erga omnes nationes est fundamentum Austriæ.* The Czechs have every interest in being patient, and concentrating their energies upon gaining what is practicable, securing from time to time such concessions as they can in favor of their language and their nationality. They have been divided into two well-defined factions since 1887; that of the Young Czechs, who are radical, demanding universal suffrage, liberty of the press and of public meeting and lay schools, and that of the Old Czechs, who are more moderate in their wishes and more inclined to compromise with the government, and represent the interests of the nobles and the clergy. The former carried on an active campaign of mass-meetings, demonstrations, and protestations in support of their principles, and bitterly attacked Rieger, the leader of the Old Czechs. This soon gave them the support of the country, and the Old Czechs in alarm turned to the Germans. These agreed to resume their seats in the diet, and a compact was agreed upon in January, 1890. A compromise diet was held in May, and an agreement reached according to which the kingdom was to be divided into districts in which one language only should be recognized, the regulation requiring officials to speak both languages was to be repealed, and the diet was to be divided into a German and a Czech section, as were also the principal bodies of the administration, as, for example, the courts and educational council, The scheme met with violent opposition on the part of the Young Czechs, who saw in it the defeat of all their hopes for the future autonomy of their country, and it failed completely. Taaffe now asked the emperor to dissolve the Reichsrath. His policy did not receive the support of the electors, especially in Bohemia, where the Young Czechs carried more than three-fourths of the seats. When the Reichsrath assembled Taaffe was forced to admit that he did not have a majority, but asked for a postponement of the race questions till commercial treaties were arranged with Italy, Germany, and Switzerland in 1892, while negotiations for similar agreements were carried on with Russia and Rumania. Measures were passed regulating taxation and currency, and other bills were pending when the agitation of the Czechs in Bohemia again forced the government to direct its attention to their demands. Following stormy scenes in the diet came rioting and demonstrations in the streets of Prague, till the government was obliged to place the city in a state of minor siege, suppressing nationalist and socialistic newspapers and dissolving Czech societies, especally the National Liberal Club, to which the Young Czech deputies belonged.

Count Taaffe determined, nevertheless, to make concessions, and proposed a measure for a reform of the electoral law which would practically have established universal suffrage and increased the number of voters from 1,500,000 to 4,500,000. This greatly alarmed the conservative parties, and, supported by the emperor, who was opposed to the Young Czechs and the socialists alike, they combined against Taaffe and forced him to resign. With the resignation of the minister ended, for the time at least, the federalist policy pursued by him since his advent to office in 1879. In November, 1893, a new ministry was formed by Windischgratz, which was to last for two years and serve as a temporary stop-gap.

In the meantime the Transleithanian or Hungarian part of the monarchy had been developing rapidly since 1878. The occupation of Bosnia and Herzegovina, although causing a crisis in the affairs of the monarchy, brought no serious change in the policy of the government at Pesth. The liberal ministerial party retained its majority, and Tisza continued in the direction of affairs. He was opposed to concessions for the minor races in Austria or Hungary. Nevertheless, the newly acquired provinces gave fresh hopes to the Croats, who now began to dream of a greater Croatia, independent of Hungary and united to the monarchy by a personal union only. They demanded and were granted the incorporation of the military frontier by Croatia, but Dalmatia and Fiume they failed to obtain. In 1883 their stolid opposition to the Magyars broke out into open acts of violence; a new coat-of-arms placed by the minister of finance over his door was torn down by a mob, and in 1885 the forcible removal of the Agram archives to Pesth produced such tumultuous scenes in the diet that several radical deputies were arrested and imprisoned. But the agitation against Magyarization and in favor of a greater Croatia continued, and on the occasions of the king's visit in 1895 a Magyar flag was openly burned by the students. The smaller nationalities, having no political organization, were in no position to make their grievances felt. But although deprived of all adequate means of agitation, their protests were frequently heard. The Slovaks in the north tried to make common cause with their kinsmen, the Czechs, only to find themselves the subject of attack by both the government and the Lutheran clergy. All pastors and teachers in a Slovak country were forbidden to join in the Slav propaganda. The Rumanians, among whom a party looking for an ultimate union with Rumania had arisen, found the leaders of their deputation to "the emperor" with a memorandum asking for a separate government for Transylvania arrested and imprisoned. Of the other races, the Saxons, favored by the electoral law, objected occasionally to the policy of the government, but in the main they made common cause with the Magyars, and the agitations of the Servians in 1884, to regain the privilege of electing their metropolitan and of managing the affairs of their school and church, were not of sufficient importance to cause the government much anxiety.

In economic and social matters the period is marked by a policy far-reaching in its effects. The acquisition by the state of the Hungarian railways was effected with energy and credit, and in 1889 Barossa, minister of public works, introduced the zone system of fares. The fares were greatly reduced and the passenger traffic in Hungary trebled in one year. This increased intercommunication was likewise of great advantage to the new industries, which the government did its utmost to encourage. With the rising importance of industry and commerce came the decline of the influence of the old landed aristocracy, and the increase of that of the Jews. An attempt to place the latter on a footing of equality with other races was accordingly met by bitter race prejudice. Tisza's measure to allow mixed marriages between Jews and Christians passed the lower house, but was thrown out by the house of magnates. This led to a reform of the upper chamber, which greatly reduced the number of magnates. At the same time the mandate of the deputies was increased from three to five years.

In 1890 Tisza, after having ruled in Hungary like a dictator for fourteen years, resigned. He had been losing ground even with his own party, and the last years of his dominance were marked by flagrant political corruption. In 1889 the opposition in the diet became tumultuous, and the next year, finding himself deserted by his colleagues on his measure to abrogate the law expatriating Kossuth, he handed in his resignation. He was succeeded by Szapary, who was, however, unable to weather the storm aroused by an attempted reform of the administration of the comitats and by the disputes over the relations between church and state, especially on the question of mixed marriages. Before the end of the year the able financier, Dr. Wekerle, was appointed in his stead. Wekerle's entry upon office is significant because he was the first minister-president to come from the ranks of the middle class, and also because it marks the serious inauguration of the conflict between church and state in Hungary.

He entered at once upon the work of reform, and notwithstanding the frenzied attacks of the clergy and the conservative aristocracy, secured the adoption of his project by the lower house. The plan involved five points: first, the freedom of worship to all religious bodies in Hungary; second, the civil registration of births, marriages, and deaths; third, the recognition of the Jewish religion; fourth, the permission of mixed marriages; and fifth, and most important, compulsory civil marriage. The magnates rejected the measure regarding civil marriages and the greatest excitement prevailed. Encouraged by the popular support, Wekerle submitted his project to the lower house a second time, by whom it was again passed by an enormous majority. But again the peers rejected it, and the king, who all along was suspected of fearing the effect of the example of such a law on Austria, and therefore secretly opposing it, refused to create a sufficient number of new peers to carry the measure, and the minister resigned. The resignation came at the very moment when Hungary was cast into deep mourning by the death, in exile, of her renowned patriot, Kossuth, in 1894.

Chapter XXXVI

RECENT HISTORY. 1894-1906

THE history of Austria-Hungary during the last twelve years is marked by a continuance, often in violent form, of the race rivalry, and by the perplexing conditions of a parliamentary deadlock in both parts of the monarchy, side by side with much that is significant in the field of intellectual and national development. No material change has been made in the political relations of the two parts of the monarchy, and yet it has been impossible for nearly a decade to obtain a parliamentary sanction to the *Ausgleich* or *modus vivendi* upon which .the continuance of the dual agreement must ultimately depend. The attitude of the minor races has changed but little; they are, if anything, more insistent in their demands, and better organized than in previous years. In economic matters great progress has been made, but in these, as in foreign affairs, the absence of political harmony and a strong central government has had an unfortunate influence. The old prestige of the monarchy and the loyalty to Francis Joseph has done considerable to counteract the evils of the political situation, but conditions in the dual monarchy are discouraging in the extreme.

Taaffe's resignation had been the result of the opposition aroused by his liberal plans for electoral reform. His successor, Count Windischgratz, whose appointment was regarded as a makeshift, found that the opposition to the reform measure had by no means abated with the withdrawal of its author. On the other hand, the Social Democrats, who were rapidly increasing in numbers, the Czechs, and the German Liberals carried on the agitation for universal suffrage. The premier decided on a compromise. He proposed the creation of a fifth electoral group to be added to the four already existing. This group was to consist of the artisans of the towns and all Austrians who had paid direct taxes for two years. The proposal satisfied none of the liberal parties, while the Socialists were bitter in their attack upon it. About this time

RECENT HISTORY 433

the race conflict between Slavs and Germans broke out anew because of the government's proposal to give instruction in the Slovene language in the high school at Cilli in Steiermark, and the German parties withdrew their support from the ministry. Windischgratz was forced to resign without having passed his electoral bill. After a brief space of provisional rule under Count Kiellmansegg the remarkable opportunist government of Badeni was inaugurated in September, 1895.

A Pole from Galicia, Badeni, had served a thorough apprenticeship in the art of manipulating political parties. He now organized a ministry including representatives of the most diverse views, declaring that it was the intention of the government to direct, not to follow, the chambers. Sure of the support of the Poles, Clericals, Conservatives, and the court, he announced a programme which would, it was hoped, secure the support of the Germans as a whole. He would, he said, stand by the Germans, though giving at the same time due regard to the just demands of all nationalities. He would renew the *Ausgleich* and introduce electoral reform. All parties were asked to give their support to this programme, which, he ominously hinted, embodied the last effort of the king at constitutional government. If it failed Austria would return to absolutism.

Early in 1896 the new electoral bill was presented to the Reichsrath. It fell far short of the reforms proposed by Taaffe. Indeed, it was less a reform than a makeshift compromise. Like the proposals of Windischgratz, it created a fifth group of electors. It was to consist of all Austrians over twenty-four years of age, not included in the other four groups, who had had a residence of six months in the district. To this group, which would include the great mass of the voters, over 5,500,000, was allotted 72 seats in the Reichsrath, while the other four groups, which counted only 1,700,000 voters, still retained their 353 seats, or 83 per cent. of the total representation. To the great mass of workingmen and peasants, therefore, the bill gave 72 deputies, whom they might, in conjunction with the other four classes, elect; to the large landed proprietors, 85; to the chambers of commerce and industry, 21; to the towns, 118, and to the rural communes, 129. It was manifestly the best that could be secured, and with the support of the German Liberals and the Young Czechs the measure was passed in June, 1896.

The elections held under the new law in March, 1897, were
very tumultuous, and proved a grievous disappointment to the government. No less than twenty-eight parties and twelve national
groups were represented in the new Reichsrath. A consistent
working majority could not be got together, and Badeni tendered
his resignation. But the emperor refused to accept it, declaring
that " the general interests of the state " were superior to parties.
The premier remained in office and in April issued the now famous
" language decrees," putting the Czech language on an equal footing with the German in Bohemia and Moravia. By 1907 all
officials were to know both languages, and in the courts of justice
either language should be used according to the wish of the parties
in the case.

The promulgation of these decrees was the signal for violent
outbursts of anger among the Germans, and the inauguration of
that notorious policy of obstruction which has since been copied
by the opposition parties in both Austria and Hungary, and which
has made a by-word of parliamentary government in the dual
monarchy. Indeed, Badeni's " language decrees " may be said to
mark the inauguration of a decade of unconstitutional government in Austria. *La constitution ne fonctionne plus,* as the French
aptly express it.

The Germans objected to the unconstitutionality of the decrees. A matter so vital to the interests of the state was clearly
a subject for legislation and could not be disposed of by imperial
ordinance. They urged the inexpediency and unfairness of the
measures. It was both easy and profitable for the Czechs to learn
German, a language spoken by the great mass of the people of
central Europe. For the German official to learn Czech was not
only extremely difficult, but unprofitable, since a knowledge of the
language, they claimed, had little or no commercial value. To
the Czech argument that Bohemia was a united and indivisible kingdom they replied that there were three distinct divisions, one in
which Czech alone was used, a second in which both Czech and
German were in use, and a third in which German was used exclusively. The most unseemly tactics were resorted to in order
to force the government to reconsider the decrees. Prolonged
speeches, Dr. Lecher talking for twelve hours at a stretch, inter-
ruptions, stamping and slamming of desks, and even assaults upon
opposition members marked the sessions. Nor was the obstruction

confined to the Reichsrath. Wherever possible, in town and village councils, and in provincial diets a vigorous campaign of obstruction was carried on to hamper the administration. Motion after motion was introduced for the impeachment of Badeni, and the house refused to vote the Delegations. Personal recriminations le.* to a duel between a pan-German member, Herr Wolf, and the premier, in which the latter was wounded. Finally, after the deputies had engaged in more than one pitched battle, the ministry resorted to a police measure, the " lex Fallenheyn." This led to hostile demonstrations against the ministry in the streets of Vienna, and the emperor at last agreed to Badeni's resignation, in December, 1897.

Baron Gautsch succeeded to the ministry, but notwithstanding the fact that he chose his cabinet entirely from the Germans, they declared that they would continue their obstruction till the "language decrees" were modified, and the renewal of the *Ausgleich,* which was a matter of deep concern to the government, and which had been agreed to by the parliament at Pesth, could not be effected. On the basis of article fourteen of the constitution it was continued provisionally by royal decree. The ministry's compromise measure in regard to the language question in Bohemia was likewise rejected, and in March, 1898, Gautsch was replaced by Count Thun.

Thun fell heir to an extremely difficult situation. The language controversy continued, the obstructionist tactics of the Reichsrath had passed to the provincial diets, the commercial arrangement with Hungary remained unconfirmed, and the dynastic sentiment was losing ground. In outlining his policy the new premier adopted a decidedly conciliatory tone, appealing in the name of Austria to all parties to aid the government in securing justice to all nationalities, and in effecting the necessary social and economic reforms. But in spite of this appeal the obstruction continued, and no business was done. Again recourse was had to the powers conferred on the government by article fourteen of the constitution. The term of the *Ausgleich* was again extended, and certain taxes, as, for instance, the duty on spirits and the sugar tax and bounty, prolonged indefinitely. An imperial message was issued thanking the provincial diets for the expressions of loyalty during the celebration of the emperor's jubilee, and promising an extension of the functions of the diets. This greatly enraged the Germans, who saw in it mere truckling to the Slavs. The extremists determined to continue the obstruction, and during the whole of 1899 they carried out their programme. To the government's request to legislate on measures necessary to the existence of the state, as, for example, the bill for raising the annual contingent of recruits, they replied, "there is no greater necessity of state than the withdrawal of the language decrees." Scenes of violence again marked the sessions, and the Reichsrath was prorogued. But the extensive application of article fourteen to ordinary matters of legislation aroused a storm of opposition throughout the country. Meetings and demonstrations were organized, scores of municipalities, chambers of commerce, and other public bodies joined in the agitation, and Thun was forced to resign in September, 1899.

The selection of Clary Aldingen revealed a tendency on the part of the emperor to revert to a policy more favorable to the Germans. One of his first acts was to withdraw the "language decrees." The Germans had triumphed at last. But the withdrawal of the decrees by no means restored order into Austrian politics. The Czechs now took the place of the Germans in blocking legislation, and before long it became again necessary to appeal to the power conferred on the emperor by article fourteen. This the premier refused to do, and resigned.

In January, 1900, Dr. Körber formed a new ministry. He secured the election of the Delegations, but failing to carry any other measures, he asked the emperor to dissolve the Reichsrath. Soon afterward the sovereign declared that this would be positively the last attempt at constitutional effort to end the crisis. He lauded the Poles as the only one of the nationalities that refrained from obstruction and worked in the interests of the state. The elections were conducted amid gloomy forebodings, the Viennese press adopting a particularly despondent tone. The result of the elections did not promise much improvement. The old supporters of the government, the Clericals, sustained severe defeats; likewise did the anti-Semites, while the gains went to the extremists who had been responsible for the deadlock. Owing largely, however, to the increasing injury to the material interests of the country, and to the premier's skillful policy, a stop, temporary it is true, was at last put to the paralysis of legislation which had lasted for four years.

The Czechs and radical parties agreed to suspend the strife over language and national rights, and take up measures of vital importance to the welfare of the country. Night and day sessions were held and much important legislation was carried. Bills for the amalgamation of the railroads, the building of new lines, the construction of an extensive system of internal canals connecting the Danube, the Elbe, and the Moldau, the improvement of industrial conditions, and the abolition of some of the most irksome customs duties were passed. But only a provisional budget was adopted, and the rivalry between Czechs and Germans again became so violent that the work of the Reichsrath came to a standstill, and the second session of 1901 had to be adjourned without a vote on the budget. In the meantime a decided feeling against the demands of Hungary in the matter of the *Ausgleich* was beginning to manifest itself in the Austrian part of the monarchy. The provisional arrangement of 1896 was denounced, and Dr. Körber formally declared that the government was resolved to secure better terms for Austria, or put an end to all the existing economic arrangements with Hungary.

But the dissatisfaction with Hungary in no way relieved the difficulties between the races in the Austrian Reichsrath. The Czech deputies continued to obstruct legislation, and in November, 1903, they issued a manifesto setting forth a complete statement of the demands. It asked for the federalization of the monarchy, the application of the principle of equality to the Czech and German languages in the lands of the Bohemian crown, the foundation of Czech technical, secondary, and primary schools in Silesia, and of Czech public schools in Lower Austria, especially in Vienna for the Czech population, the protection of national minorities, electoral reform, and the same rights for the use of the Czech language in the army as those to be accorded the Magyars. Till an effort was made to grant these demands they threatened to block the work of the house. The budget and other urgent measures could not pass, and at the end of the year matters of immediate importance were again regulated by imperial decree.

The next year brought no improvement. Indeed, the situation seemed, if anything, rather worse, for in most of the provincial diets, excepting that of Galicia, the disgraceful proceedings of the Reichsrath were reënacted during 1904. At Prague the sittings assumed such a violent turn that the session had to be suspended after the second day. Throughout the country the racial antagonism grew steadily worse. Cities, towns, and villages were divided. Germans were mobbed in Prague, while Czechs were maltreated in Vienna and other places. At the same time difficulties with the Italians of Austria developed. In November a conflict occurred at Innsbrück between German and Italian students over the establishment of a faculty of law for the Italians. The action of the government was severely criticised even by the Germans, and the affair finally led to the resignation of the Körber ministry.

Baron Gautcsh succeeded to the premiership, but during the year 1905 the conflict of nationalities and the strained relations with Hungary paralyzed all effective parliamentary action. A sharp rebuke was administered to Hungary in a long statement by the premier in which he declared that Hungary must fulfill her engagements and accept the commercial treaties, in regard to which Austria would make no concessions. If these arrangements were not satisfactorily concluded by March 1, 1906, Austria would act independently. In May the Austrian parliament passed the *Ausgleich*, upon which, as a basis, commercial treaties with Germany, Italy, Russia, Belgium, and Switzerland were pending, but the Hungarian parliament would not pass the measure. Much bitterness of feeling against Hungary developed, Pan-German members of the Reichsrath boldly demanding a severance of the economic relationship with Hungary for one with the German empire.

But of equal or even greater import than the race conflict and the strained relations with Hungary during these years was the increasing strength of socialism. In 1895 Herr Bebel of the German Reichstag had brought the Austrian socialists into closer touch with those of other countries, and had by his active propaganda effected a more thorough organization among them. This work manifested itself in the steady growth of the party, and by 1905 it had assumed proportions truly alarming to the supporters of the old electoral system. Meetings and demonstrations demanding equal suffrage occurred in all the principal Austrian towns. In November a monster demonstration of from 200,000 to 300,000 workingmen and women carrying red flags took place in front of the parliament buildings in Vienna while the Reichsrath was in session, and the government promised to lay before parlia-

RECENT HISTORY 439

ment not later than February a measure for the reform of the franchise, based on the principle of universal suffrage. On February 23, 1906, this important measure was presented to the Reichsrath. It made a clean sweep of the old electoral system with its divisions into groups or classes, placing all electors on an equal footing, except where racial considerations made a special arrangement necessary. Every male citizen who had completed his twenty-fourth year and had resided in the electoral district for one year, unless under legal disabilities, was to have a right to vote. The bill abolished plural voting and further provided for a division of the electoral districts, which gave to the Germans 205 representatives, the Slavs, comprising Czechs, Poles, Slovenes, and others, 229, the Italians 17, and the Rumanians 4. Considerable opposition to the measure developed among some of the German parties, who feared for the majorities in the Reichsrath and the provincial diets. On March 23 the bill passed its first reading in the Reichsrath.

The political development in Hungary during the years from 1894, when Dr. Wekerle resigned from his first premiership, to the summer of 1906, when he was called to office to form a cabinet from the coalition opposition, presents many features found in the story of the Austrian part of the monarchy for this period. There are the same difficulties over parliamentary procedure, the same obstructionist tactics, the same difficulties over the *Ausgleich,* the same, though in a markedly less degree, antagonism between races and the same progress toward electoral reform. Added to this is a growing demand for separation from Austria in all matters except the sovereign, a movement which has in recent years become so powerful that it is represented by the majority in parliament.

Finding it impossible to secure a compromise ministry after the withdrawal of Wekerle, the emperor, in 1895, asked Count Banffy to continue the work and policy of the former premier. The Liberals were jubilant and in their enthusiam succeeded in passing the most important measures advocated by their former leader. Among these, it will be remembered, the laws establishing obligatory civil marriage and liberty of education for children of mixed marriages were the most important. But the opposition of the Clericals, and of the Separatists, or party of Independence, led by young Kossuth, increased, notwithstanding a conciliatory visit of the emperor-king to Hungary. A measure to provide for the continuance of the *Ausgleich* for one year on the understanding that if no permanent agreement had been arrived at between the two parliaments by May, 1898, the ministry would present proposals for a settlement based more exclusively on the interests of Hungary, was not allowed to pass. Other government bills met with the same fate, neither the budget nor the provisions for the customs, the bank, or the levy of recruits being approved. Only one measure of importance passed the houses in 1897, a law providing for the rigid control of agricultural labor. During the following year the obstruction continued, and the government was forced to adopt the English rules of order and to carry out the enactments necessary for the budget, the *Ausgleich,* and other indispensable measures without reference to parliament. This drastic policy alienated many of the Liberals, but Banffy remained firm. By 1898, therefore, it was necessary to sanction by the royal prerogative measures approved by the majority in parliament both at Vienna and Pesth, but which could not be regularly passed.

Finally the minority was successful in forcing Banffy to resign. Count Apponyi, a Magyar of the Magyars, had withdrawn his support, and in February, 1899, Szell, a follower of Deak, became premier. Szell pledged the government to rule constitutionally, and the Liberals, who had seceded because of Banffy's drastic measures, returned to the support of the ministry. Obstruction ceased, and the *Ausgleich,* with a slight modification in regard to the bank, which had been continued provisionally, was finally adopted for the decade ending in 1907. But the parliament at Vienna would not do its part and refused to ratify the agreement. In the ensuing year Premier Szell uttered some very ominous words, asserting that in case Austria proved unable to fulfill her engagements he was fully prepared to " assert the rights of Hungary and its independence." . . . " Meanwhile let us husband our strength and keep our powder dry." These remarkable words were the more ominous because of the recognized conservatism of the speaker.

Late in 1900 the jealousy between the two states reached a crisis on the question of the extension of the Bosnian railways, in the settlement of which Austrian interests were shamefully sacrificed in favor of the continuance of Hungary's monopoly of the traffic to that province. In the summer of 1901 scandalous corruption was disclosed in the matter of government contracts, many members of parliament being associated with industries and commercial enterprises which held large contracts from the state. To prevent collusion and corruption for the future an incompatibility bill was introduced and passed, in which it was clearly specified what occupation or other circumstances are incompatible with a seat in parliament.

In the elections of this year the returns showed a distinct gain for the party of Independence, and during the following year Kossuth and his followers lost no opportunity of asserting the claims of Magyarism and demanding total independence, going to such extremes that even the veteran novelist and patriot Jokai published an indignant appeal to the people against them. Premier Szell continued his policy of maintaining the dual agreement, replying to Kossuth that the political features of the dual agreement, as, for example, the dynasty, the succession to the throne, the common army and navy, the diplomatic service and the Delegations were irrevocable and not subject to revision. On the questions of the quota, the customs tariff, and other commercial and economic matters he hoped soon to reach a satisfactory arrangement. That such a settlement was infinitely more difficult than had previously been the case was evident.

On the occasion of the first renewal of the *Ausgleich* considerble difficulty had been experienced in arriving at a satisfactory arrangement. The Hungarians demanded the establishment of an Hungarian national bank and a revision of the tariff and commercial relations. After more than two years of negotiations an agreement had finally been concluded in June, 1878. A national bank on a dualist basis was created, and Hungary retained 31.4 per cent. of the quota, or common expense of the monarchy, as against 68.6 per cent. for Austria, a modification of the original arrangement made on the occasion of the addition of the military frontiers to Hungary. As no difficulty arose over the renewal ten years later, this arrangement remained in force for two decades. Fully two years before the date of its expiration in 1897 the statesmen in both halves of the monarchy took steps to prepare the way for its renewal. Preliminary conferences were held and special commissions appointed. At first difficulties arose over the quota, Austria demanding that Hungary pay a larger share, while Hungary, although she at first agreed to the old arrangement, later demanded a radical modification of its provisions. Her economic interests being so largely agricultural, the protective system in favor of Austrian industries was naturally disadvantageous to her. The lack of success attending the efforts of the governments, both at Vienna and Pesth, in arriving at an adjustment has been seen. The possibilities were still further decreased by the growth of the Independence party, which demanded the abolition of the compromise entirely.

After 1897 the compromise, so far as Hungary was concerned, was maintained under a provisional arrangement known as the " Szell formula," by which it was agreed that if no definite arrangement could be reached by the end of 1902, both parties were free to dissolve the customs union in 1904. Owing largely to the personal intervention of the emperor and the successful policy of Premier Szell, the arrangements, despite the hostile action of the Reichsrath, were renewed. Both governments submitted the details of the project simultaneously to both parliaments in January, 1903. But again the obstructionists blocked the way, and the bills giving effect to the agreement did not come to a vote.

This was the more unfortunate because new problems were arising which made its adoption more difficult than ever. The first of these appeared in connection with a bill providing for an increase in the number of recruits for the army from 103,100 to 125,000 men. The increase was nothing more than an adjustment of the size of the army to the increased population, and under normal conditions ought not to have called forth serious objections, but the Magyars, especially the Independence party, made it the occasion for an attack on the common army system, and on the dual agreement as a whole.

Premier Szell was unable to overcome the opposition and resigned in June, 1903, being succeeded by Count Hedervary, a former ban of Croatia. Hedervary was as much a man of the government as Szell had been, and the Kossuthites continued to obstruct business in parliament. They asked that Hungarian words of command should be adopted for the Hungarian regiments of the army, that all Hungarian officers be transferred to these regiments, with other demands looking toward the ultimate establishment of an independent Hungarian army. A majority of the parties in the lower house supported these demands, and the government was at a loss how to proceed. To yield was impossible, the emperor declared, for the common army was one of the bulwarks of the monarchy. Besides, the Austrian Germans strongly opposed the proposed changes. If Hungary obtained control of her contingent of the army, then Austria, whose proportion of recruits was only 56 per cent., should no longer pay 65 per cent. of the cost of maintenance, according to the arrangement of 1899. They also urged that to yield to the Hungarian demand in regard to the words of command would lead to similar demands by the Czechs, Poles, and other nationalities, not only in the Austrian division of the army, but in the Hungarian itself. To bring the obstruction of its policy directly home to the people and at the same time to make up the deficiency caused by the Hungarians in refusing to vote the recruit bill, the government issued a decree detaining the time expired men, who would normally be allowed to return to citizen life, with the colors for an indefinite period.

Late in the summer, during the military maneuvers in Galicia, the emperor announced in strong terms his determination to uphold the unity of the army and its existing organization. The Austrian premier declared that in matters affecting the imperial army the Austrian half of the monarchy had a legal right to interfere. The effect of this firm language was largely destroyed by the emperor's explanatory communication some time later, which had much the air of an embarrassed apology. And when Hedervary defended the view of the Austrian premier before the Hungarian house he raised such a storm of protest that he was forced to resign.

Count Tisza, the son of Hungary's veteran premier, succeeded Hedervary in October, 1903. An agreement satisfactory to the majority had been reached with the king regarding the proposed army changes and the royal prerogatives. It involved the use of Hungarian standards and military emblems by the side of the Austrian ones on all military buildings in Hungary, the use of Magyar among Hungarian officers, greater facilities for the education of Hungarian cadets to insure an adequate number of Hungarian officers, the reduction of the period of service from three to two years, the transfer of all Hungarian officers to Hungarian regiments, and the retention of the common language of command and of service. But the opposition would not accept the agreement, Apponyi claiming that it did not go far enough in the matter of education of Hungarian officers. Two sessions a day were resorted to in order to overcome the obstruction. This gave rise to disgraceful scenes, it is true, but it finally brought about a compromise, by which the Independents agreed to refrain from further obstruction on condition that double sittings should be abolished and that parliament should declare that " in Hungary the source of every right and in the army the source of rights appertaining to the language of service and command is the will of the nation expressed through the legislature."

Early in the next year the premier proposed a new set of standing rules of order of extreme severity, and in order to force the hands of the opposition withdrew all other bills. The threat proved effective. The recruit bill, an indemnity bill, and a provisional agreement with Croatia were allowed to pass. This parliamentary victory was marked by another against the strike of the employees of the state railroad, incited, it was believed, by the opposition. But this merely embittered the conflict in the house. Kossuth and Count Apponyi led a large majority in a vote against Tisza's proposed revision of the rules of order, and the premier's hold on the situation seemed to weaken. He was able, however, to rally his supporters about him and replied to the obstructionists by a revival of the " guillotine " or the closure, now called the " lex Daniel," because the bill was introduced by Baron Daniel. The passage of this measure raised the opposition to fever heat. They appealed to the crown, and to the people; public meetings and demonstrations were organized, and all the proposals of the premier for moderation scouted. At the opening of the session in December they entered the house early, assaulted the police, broke up the furniture, and finally had themselves photographed amid the débris, Kossuth glorifying the action as "a symbol of the political maturity of the Magyars, who, after asserting their rights, refrain from violence."

Tisza finally resolved to appeal to the country and announced the elections for February, 1905, asking the house to vote the supplies for the year. This the opposition refused to permit unless the " lex Daniel " were annulled. They declared at the same time that unless the supplies were voted the laws of 1848 made the dissolution illegal, the elections void. Tisza replied that the laws of 1867 gave the crown the right to dissolve parliament at any time provided the ministry convoked the new parliament in time to vote the estimates. The issues were clearly drawn, and finally all the parties of the opposition took their stand with Kossuth in favor of the laws of 1848, which was a virtual declaration that the dual agreement did not exist.

The appeal to the people was conducted with great feeling and passion, and the elections resulted in an overwhelming defeat of the government, which elected only 152 deputies, while the Kossuthites elected 163, the Clerical Socialists, 23, Banffy's party, 11, Andrassy's, 23, and the non-Magyar nationalities, 8. The country had spoken in no uncertain terms, and Tisza at once sent in his resignation. For the first time in the history of Hungary since the establishment of the dual monarchy the opposition possessed a majority, and the king sent for Kossuth.

But the latter's views were entirely incompatible with the continuance of the existing political relations between the two parts of the monarchy, and no arrangement could be made with him. It was therefore necessary to make the attempt with a ministry from the minority, and in June Baron Fejervary was appointed premier. In the meantime the chamber had, by a large majority, passed an address to the crown in which it demanded the appointment of a responsible government supported by the majority; the reform of the parliamentary and electoral system; the commercial and financial independence of Hungary, and the nationalizing of the Hungarian army by the introduction of the Magyar language and emblems. A formal vote of censure on Tisza was passed, and on July 18 a manifesto was issued declaring the Fejervary ministry unconstitutional and urging everyone to withhold all public services from it. Officials were given to understand that they might refuse to coöperate in the collection of taxes and the enrollment of recruits, indemnification being promised in case of dismissal. This threatened to carry the deadlock hitherto confined to the legislative department of the government into the administrative also.

But the threat was of no avail, and in September the king informed the leaders of the opposition coalition that he would submit the government of the country to them on the following conditions only: First, the elimination of their demands in regard to the language of command and of service for the army; second, the continuance, untouched, of the Pragmatic union of the two states

with respect to the army and foreign affairs; third, the revision
of the economic relations only through negotiations with the Austrian part of the monarchy and subject to the approval of the
crown; fourth, an agreement to pass the measures necessary for the
conduct of the government as laid down by the constitution, as, for
example, the recruit bill, the commercial treaties, and the election
of the Delegations; and fifth, an obligation to vote the supplies
necessary for the military and naval reforms voted by the last
Delegations. Nothing could be more diametrically counter to
the April address, and the Magyar leaders refused to accept the
conditions. The deadlock thus created seemed likely to last for
some time, when a new factor which had hitherto been of minor
importance arose.

In Hungary, as in Austria, during these years the political
ideas of the masses were slowly undergoing an evolution in the
direction of universal suffrage. In September a socialist agitation began at Pesth and spread rapidly over the country, till
the demands of the masses for admission to the franchise bade
fare to eclipse the interest in the conflict over the relations with
Austria and the crown. The new development was one of extreme importance to the government, which saw in these demands
a new factor which might be effectively used against the opposition. For, bent at all hazards on a continuance of Magyar dominance, which in the words of Bebel meant the rule of the nobles,
the large landholders, the clergy, and the bourgeoisie, the Hungarian leaders were naturally opposed to an extension of the suffrage which would enfranchise the great agricultural and artisan
proletariate, and secure to the non-Magyar elements of the population a proportionate share in the representation. Realizing this,
Fejervary made universal suffrage, " with due provision for safe-
guarding state and national interests," the main feature of his
political programme. The programme contained many other progressive proposals, but they were all completely overshadowed by
this tremendously important issue. In his letter to the Hungarian
Socialists Herr Bebel vehemently supported the government's proposal. He inveighed against the dominant class which holds up
its hands in pharisaical horror at the violation of the letter of the
parliamentary law while it keeps the majority of the nation from
its natural right of representation. " I subscribe word for word,"
he declared, " to the judgment pronounced by Premier Fejervary

concerning the sterility and total insufficiency of Hungarian parliamentarism hitherto. I only wish that he might be able to carry out his programme, which would make of Hungary what it has not hitherto been, a modern state."

Whether the socialist leader is right or not, there is no question of the fact that the opposition felt the force of the argument, and the danger to its majority in the house unless it identified itself with the movement. After considerable hesitation Kossuth in a public letter accepted universal suffrage as a part of his party's policy. At the same time the passive resistance to the government was continued. The Delegations could not be elected and the county administrations could not " levy taxes or enroll recruits for an unconstitutional government." The financial disorder increased, and with it the difficulties of the ministry. Fejervary resigned, but the king declined to accept his resignation, and ordered the dissolution of the diet. On February 19 the royal message reached the house, and on a resolution by that body not to accept the rescript, a military officer entered the chamber and read the order. After entering a verbal protest the deputies submitted to the clearing of the hall, the forced dissolution being, contrary to expectation, orderly and without violence.

The order declared that "whereas, the majority constituted by the allied parties of the chamber have, in spite of our repeated summons, refused persistently to take over the government on an acceptable basis without violating our royal rights as by law guaranteed, we, to the sorrow of our hearts, are not able to expect from this parliament an activity conducive to the interest of the country, and, therefore, on the proposal of our Hungarian ministry, declare the parliament convoked on February 15, 1905, to be dissolved, and reserve to ourselves the convocation of a new parliament as soon as may be." The political deadlock seemed to have reached a crisis, but early in April the opposition, fearing a period of absolutism, at last agreed to a compromise on the basis of which they accepted office under the leadership of Dr. Wekerle. Associated with him were the leaders of the different groups of the opposition, Kossuth, Apponyi, Andrassy, and Zichy. They were pledged to pass the budget, the new commercial treaties, and a bill for general, equal, and direct suffrage, while the king agreed to carry out the elections under the old law and assemble parliament in May.

The foreign affairs of Austria-Hungary, which, with the army and navy, and finances connected with the general expenses, are common to both parts of the monarchy, have been during this period under the direction of Count Goluchowski, one of the ablest diplomats of recent years. He was appointed in May, 1895, and has throughout been in entire accord with the emperor-king, giving to the Austrian policy its essentially dynastic character. Its basic features have been the maintenance of the Triple Alliance in central Europe, the peaceful solution of the difficulties in the Balkan peninsula without any change in the existing state system, and the promotion of the monarchy's commercial interests.

The evidence of the policy in the Near East appeared as early as 1879 in the alliance with Germany against Russia, and its extension by the admission of Italy. In 1896 it made itself still more apparent in Goluchowski's declaration that the integrity and liberty of Turkey must be preserved, warning the Greeks against sending aid to the Cretans, and by the unexpected agreement with Russia against England in opposing the proposed intervention in behalf of the Armenians. During the visit of the tsar to Vienna an understanding was reached by which it was agreed that nothing happening in the Balkans should disturb the friendly relations between Austria-Hungary and Russia. "The repeated meetings," said Francis Joseph in 1897, "which I have had with the emperor of Russia have convinced me of the agreement of our views, and upon them has been founded a relation of mutual confidence between our countries, the consolidation of which cannot but promise well for the future." In elaborating upon the new policy the foreign minister explained that the differences between Austria-Hungary, and Great Britain over matters in the Near East had afforded the opportunity for the *rapprochement* with Russia. A programme of action in regard to what he described as "the hot ground of Eastern Europe," was drawn up, which he later declared had as its foremost advantage the principle of non-intervention in the internal affairs of the Balkan states, and the further existence of Turkey in its present undiminished limits.

The understanding between the two eastern powers seemed for a time in some danger of breaking up owing to the active propaganda by Russian agents in Bulgaria and Rumania, the reawakening of the Panslavist movement, and the present of arms by the tsar to the king of Montenegro, but it passed off without seriously affecting the relations of the two powers. Indeed, the lines were soon drawn closer through the joint action of the two powers in Macedonia. A plan since known as the Austro-Russian plan of reform was intrusted for its execution by the powers to Austria-Hungary and Russia, and these two states have since been jointly supervising the reorganization of the gendarmerie and the development of the new communal authority in the affected regions. In 1903 Goluchowski warned Turkey that she " must change if she wishes to live," and that resistance to the Austro-Russian reforms would not be tolerated. The next year he declared that the two powers would not rest till the reforms had been carried into effect, and in his review of the monarchy's foreign relations in the summer of 1906 he added that to the policy of the firm maintenance of the Dreibund is " effectually attached an understanding with Russia in regard to the treatment of questions affecting the Near East."

The maintenance of the alliance between the three central powers of Europe has, however, in recent years met with much criticism and considerable opposition in Austria-Hungary. Owing largely to Germany's high tariff and the dislike of the non-German races for the pan-German propaganda, the Triple Alliance has become unpopular. The renewal of the alliance in 1902 was received with considerable dissatisfaction. "Our monarchy and Italy," declared a leading Hungarian paper, "have nothing to show for this alliance but enormous material sacrifices and no profit." The partnership with Italy the opposition criticised as unnatural. The close relationship between the royal families of Italy and Montenegro has raised Italian interests in Albania which are distinctly antagonistic to those of Austria. Italian-speaking subjects of Austria in the southern Tyrol and along the shores of the Adriatic, and the demands of the " Irredentists " for the annexation of these regions to Italy, stand in the way of a cordial understanding between the peoples of the two countries. The latter have on a number of occasions threatened to cause serious trouble, especially in 1902 during the agitations in Albania and the disorders in Triest. Austria was also further piqued by the slight in being omitted from the round of visits made by Victor Emmanuel in this year.

But the government adhered to its policy, Goluchowski, in his statement to the Delegations, laying great stress on the value

of the Triple Alliance as affording a real guarantee of peace, and
an opportunity for its members to enjoy adequate freedom in
looking after their own interests without the fear of danger from
abroad. " The Irredentist demonstrations," he said, " were due
to the wild antics of certain political jobbers and fanatical agi-
tators," designed to embarrass the Italian government. And as
late as June, 1906, in commenting on the cordial reply of the king
of Italy to the joint message by Francis Joseph and William II.
in regard to the Triple Alliance, Goluchowski declared the alliance
to be as strong as ever; " the keystone of that political system
which has existed for more than a quarter of a century, and whose
continuance constitutes an eminent pledge of the peace of the
whole European continent."

The close relations with the Vatican were considerably disturbed during the early part of this period. Difficulties arose over
the question of the civil marriage law in Hungary and the campaign in Austria for the overthrow of clerical influence—the " Los
von Rom " movement. The Vatican took an active part in both
cases. But no serious development occurred, unless it be the
gradual weakening of the close bonds which have heretofore united
Vienna and the Vatican.

Goluchowski's suggestions for regulating the increasing
stream of emigration and urging upon the government to do all
it its power to correct the conditions responsible for this loss of
productive force, were moderate and wise. His policy has also
been marked by an earnest effort to promote foreign commerce.
In his programme for the expansion of Austro-Hungarian trade he
frankly admitted the inability of the monarchy to acquire or govern
colonies, but laid down excellent projects for the improvement of
trans-oceanic trade. The merchants and manufacturers were urged
to found commercial houses in countries beyond the sea, to organize large syndicates and found an institution for the education of capable commercial travelers. The navy should be increased. And the disgraceful strife of nationalities which " sapped
the vitality of the whole country, delayed the most urgent business
of the state," and had a most " unfavorable influence on the foreign relations of the monarchy," should cease.

Indeed, the question of Austria-Hungary's commercial relations with the other powers of Europe was of particular importance because negotiations for new commercial treaties were

RECENT HISTORY 451

being carried on with many of the European states at this time. In fact, it seemed for some time as if all possibility of adopting a tariff conformable to the proposed treaties was out of the question. By the spring of 1906 conditions in this respect, because of the Hungarian deadlock, appeared worse than ever. But before March 1, the date on which the new treaties negotiated with Germany, Italy, Russia, Belguim, and Switzerland were to go into operation, the government overcame the difficulties and put the new tariff into effect. These treaties were drawn for twelve years and provide for a conventional tariff for products exchanged with the treaty powers, the general tariff, regulated in certain cases by the most favored nation clause, holding in all other cases. Negotiations were also under way looking toward the establishment of reciprocity rates with Servia, Bulgaria, and Rumania. Considerable friction existed between Austria-Hungary and the first of these states and it was hoped that a reduction in the dual monarchy's duties on live stock and agricultural products would largely remove the difficulties.

But if strong reasons existed for the cessation of the political warfare in Austria-Hungary because of its evil effects on the country's foreign relations, more, and stronger ones, are to be found during this period in its influence upon her economic development at home. At one of its meetings in 1900 the Vienna Chamber of Commerce resolved that the political and parliamentary condition of affairs in Austria, through the development it had undergone during the last three years, had had the most prejudicial influence on interior political affairs, as well as on the economic situation of the monarchy. It had become impossible to establish constitutional and stable relations with Hungary. Government measures for promoting native commerce, industry, and trade could not be carried out. The Chamber of Commerce realized that to put order into the affairs of state and to remedy the prevailing economic evils, it was necessary that the nationality questions in Austria should be definitely solved in a sense which would secure the state against illegitimate opposition and aspirations, and that a definite and energetic economic policy should be inaugurated. In the previous year a number of the leading Vienna silk and Bohemian textile industries transferred their factories to Hungary, and there was for a few years a distinct falling off in the amount of Austrian production.

Indeed, there has been during recent years a remarkable addition to the economic interests of Hungary. From being entirely an agricultural state it has gradually become, to a considerable degree at least, industrial also. In 1897, when the agricultural bill was introduced, it was found that two-thirds of the members of the lower house and all the members of the upper house were landowners. To-day many represent industrial and commercial interests. Legislation on economic matters, if we except the Agricultural Employers' and Workmen's Act, which, as originally passed in 1897, has probably no parallel in point of severity upon the laborer, has been generally enlightened and progressive. No better comment on the social and economic progress in Hungary in recent years can be made than appears in the third section of the government's programme of October, 1905. It announced that the agrarian and industrial policy of the past years must be enlarged and intensified, and public works, particularly canals and other waterways, vigorously developed. Children and workmen must be legally protected; better provisions must be made against sickness, accident, and old age; workmen's dwellings must be erected in the large cities, and hospitals and sanitary institutions for the working classes; the administration of justice must be modernized, the penal code revised, and the commercial code amended so as to protect the consuming public by insuring the purity of food; the laws in distraint and usury must be revised and taxation reformed by the introduction of a progressive income tax, by the regulation of oppressive ecclesiastical dues, and by the diminution of the duties on staple articles of food; primary education must be universal, compulsory, and free; in the primary schools the Magyar state language must be taught and the economic position of the teacher improved; proper provision must be made for the maintenance of Catholic priests; the salaries of officials must be increased, and the power of the central authorities over the local administration must be extended. These ideas are thoroughly in accord with the most influential public thought of the state.

The remarkable improvement and modernizing of the capitals of Vienna and Buda-Pesth has been alluded to in the previous chapter. The municipal administration is good, though still laboring under the difficulties of an electoral system based upon groups or classes. Vienna has made extensive experiments in municipal ownership. Besides its municipal gas and electric plants, Vienna has owned and operated since 1903 the largest municipal street railway system in the world. The extensive municipalization of public monopolies has been effected largely as the result of a political movement which has as yet figured only to a minor degree in the national issues. It is known as Christian socialism, and in Vienna has found a leader of remarkable organizing ability in Karl Lueger. It is clerical, socialist, and intensely anti-Semitic. Since 1897 Lueger has controlled the city, his success in the elections being based on the antagonism to the increasing influence and success of the Jews, and the opposition of the small trader and shopkeeper to the large industries and capitalists.

The never-ending and all-important race strife in Austria-Hungary has entered so persistently into the history of the monarchy, and underlies so many of its problems, that some of its more important phases require special attention. The incessant conflict over language and nationality, is, of course, merely the outward expression of the struggle for power on the part of some of the races, and for existence on the part of others. In the Austrian half of the monarchy the practical outcome of the struggle has been greater confusion than ever, if by confusion we mean an increased vitality of the non-German tongues. Less fortunate than their Magyar allies, the Germans have failed utterly to Germanize the various races of Austria. Indeed, they have been forced to yield ground, and to-day accord a place to the other languages which even the most ardent Slavophile would not have predicted in 1867.

The temporary success of the Czechs in making Czech along with German the official language of Bohemia in 1897, reveals the extent of the tendency, while the presence of twelve clearly defined national groups in the Reichsrath scarcely indicates a successful policy of amalgamation on the part of the hitherto dominant race.

In Hungary the development has been strikingly different. Ever since the establishment of the dual monarchy the Magyars have bent all their energies to bring about national unity by Magyarizing their country. And owing to their superior organization and civilization, and to their intense patriotism, they have secured remarkable results in attracting large numbers of the non-Magyar races into their own ranks, and crushing their national aspirations. These, if we except the Jews, are represented by the Saxons, Croats and other Slavs, and the Rumanians. The Croatians alone possessed a certain degree of national organization before 1867, and, as a consequence, they have also been the only ones able to resist the Magyarizing influences.

But the concessions to Croatia left the Magyars free to deal with renewed vigor with the other races. A rigorous propaganda was inaugurated, and the government adopted drastic measures to establish the Magyar language, not only as the language of the government and the university, but of secondary education, the administration, courts, and fiscal offices. Railroad employees had to learn Magyar; Hungarian geographical names were Magyarized. Non-Magyar elements are practically excluded from participating in the government by the carefully devised franchise laws, and political preferment in the municipalities is for the Magyars only. German is ostracized from the theaters and the café-chantants, and at the Millennium Exhibition at Pesth in 1896 the exclusive use of Magyar labels was prescribed by the government, notwithstanding the fact that they were unintelligible to most of the visitors. Non-Magyar schools have been a special object of attack, and every effort is made to suppress the teaching in other than the Magyar tongue. Of the large number of German schools in 1867, only a few remained in 1906.

Every inducement is held out to the other nationalities to abandon their nationality and language and become Magyars. Special laws facilitating this process have been enacted; a Magyar name may be had for a mere pittance, " fifty kreutzer," and the result is that thousands of Jews, Slavs, and Germans, either from necessity or interest, are exchanging their old names for Magyar ones. The historian Mommsen's experience is well known. To his remark that he had seen on his journey to Pesth three persons of the true Magyar type, Erdy, Matraï, and Toldy, he received the surprising reply that the original names of his three Magyars were Lutzenbacher, Rothcrebs, and Schaedel. " The famous artist Munkacsy was of German parentage." But despite the success of Magyarization, it is difficult to accept the claim of Kossuth that in Hungary the race question does not exist. After nearly forty years of dualism, both parts of the monarchy are still terribly polyglot. Even Hungary has her Croatia guarding its national idiom and its national privileges with jealous anxiety, and in the recent elections a national Rumanian party had as the first point in its programme the demand for "the recognition of Rumanian citizens of Hungary as a state-supporting entity."

The results of these conditions in the political and industrial life of the state have been made apparent in the history of this phase of the country's development, but the worst feature of the race problem lies deeper and is less apparent. The races of Austria-Hungary are often not massed, but intermingled. The territory of each is dotted with ethnographical islands. Hundreds of towns and villages are made up of two or three such rival elements, more or less exclusive of each other. And herein lies the serious difficulty.

The loss of time and of productive energy through this lack of mutual good-will and confidence, the inability, and often unwillingness, to understand each other, and the absence of a common medium of communication, is very serious. Confusion and distrust result from the use of different languages in the scores of social and economic relationships of a community. In many sections of the monarchy a judge may be quite unable to understand the witness, one or more of the jurors to understand the judge, while one of the parties in the case is likely to speak a dialect which tests the linguistic powers of the opposition lawyer to their full capacity. The official interpreter is everywhere in demand. Austria is the most polyglot country in the world, and yet nowhere has the claim to public and official use of a given idiom been more zealously, more fanatically, urged. Everywhere throughout the monarchy, where rival races live side by side, the racial antagonism manifests itself, in the provinces as well as in the capitals and other centers of the national life.

That this confusion and strife has gradually undermined the loyalty to the dynasty is doubtless true, even though the love for the kindly old emperor is still strong. Born in August, 1830, Francis Joseph is now in his seventy-eighth year. As a young man of eighteen he succeeded to the Austrian throne in 1848, in consequence of the abdication of his uncle and the suppression of the widespread revolutions of that year in the Austrian dominions. His long reign has been marked by a series of overwhelming disasters in the history of Austria, and deep sorrow and disappointment in his domestic life. As if the inglorious loss of the Italian provinces, the crushing defeat at the hands of Prussia, and the subsequent necessity to yield to the Magyars, were not enough, the life of Francis Joseph has been saddened by the bereavement of the three persons nearest to him and his hopes.

The unfortunate fate of his favorite brother, the Archduke Maximilian, in Mexico is well known. In 1899 the emperor's only son and heir, the Crown Prince Rudolf, was found dead with the Baroness Marie Vetsera at the hunting-lodge of Myerling, near Vienna. The mysterious circumstances of the tragedy excited universal comment, and in Austria-Hungary the untimely death of the popular young prince was deeply mourned. It was a heavy blow to the emperor. " There is nothing more left to me," he said to Count Tisza, " excepting my duty to my people." About the same time in addressing the president of the Reichsrath he said, " How much I owe to my dear wife; how much I have to thank her for the great support she has given me during this terrible trying time, I cannot describe or express in language sufficiently grateful."

The beautiful Empress Elizabeth, a Bavarian princess, was worthy of these words. She was especially popular in Hungary, and general sorrow was expressed at her tragic death by the hand of an assassin in Geneva, Switzerland, a few years later. Since then the life of the old emperor-king has been very lonely. He is popular and universally beloved by his people, and the loyalty to Francis Joseph is to-day one of the strong bonds against the disintegrating tendencies in Austria-Hungary.

The succession at the death of the crown prince passed to the Archduke Karl Ludwig, the brother of the emperor, who passed it on to his eldest son, Francis Ferdinand, the present heir. But even he seems to value the ancient scepter of the house of Hapsburg lightly. In 1900 he married, morganatically, the Countess Sophia Chotek, and by virtue of this union he formally renounced the claims of his future children to the thrones of Austria and Hungary. He is not popular, being suspected of clerical and Czech sympathies.

Looking back over this recent period of Austro-Hungarian history, there are a few features that stand out conspicuously. In both Cisleithania and Transleithania there have been the same disturbances and conflicts over the rights and claims of rival nationalities, with this difference, however, that in Hungary the development has been steadily toward Magyar dominance and a national language, while in Austria, German has to a large degree lost its dominant place as the other languages, particularly the Czech, have asserted themselves. Both at Vienna and at Pesth there have been the same difficulties over parliamentary procedure, resulting, except on rare occasions, in the complete paralysis of all parliamentary machinery; dualism during most of this time has existed only in name. In Hungary the Independence party increased in strength at each election, until it secured a controlling majority in 1905.

Likewise common to both parts of the monarchy has been the influence of the church in politics. Besides the old clerical groups, a new party, the Christian Socialist, entered the political arena, hoping, by allying itself with the rights of the people and the hostility toward the Jews, to turn back the tide which threatened the long-established influence and power of the church in the realm of the Hapsburgs. But by far the most important development common to every part of Austria-Hungary during this period has been the rapid and consistent progress of socialism. Its demands for the abolition of the effete electoral system, with its division into groups or classes, have at last forced recognition. In both parliaments legislation for free, equal, and universal suffrage is not only promised, but being enacted.

Amid all these racial, political, ecclesiastical, and social struggles, with their countless cross-currents of rival interests, what is to be the outcome? Is the present dualism to continue or is dissolution inevitable? And if disintegration, what of the different parts of the monarchy? Are the expectations of the pan-Germans to be realized, and is all of German Austria to form a part of a greater Germany, stretching from the North Sea to the Adriatic? Are Hungary and Bohemia to become independent, but satellites of the larger Germany, reaching out for new fields of influence in the Near East and Asia Minor? Or is the Magyar to lead in the organization of an empire of the middle and lower Danube? Or is there still another possibility, one dreamed of by many a Slavophile, the union of all the Slavic peoples of these regions into a great Slav kingdom? More likely, at least for the near future, and more in accord with the historic forces operating in recent years in Austria-Hungary, is the transformation of the present dual monarchy into a federal state in which the local autonomy of the different national groups will be respected and recognized. But whatever the outcome, one thing is plain, that before these perplexing problems are solved, the voice of a new Austria-Hungary will be heard. The establishment of universal suffrage and a consequent parliamentary representation in both parts of the monarchy of such a character that there will be no further questioning its authority, will contribute much toward an amelioration of the political anarchy, and the establishment of a new *modus vivendi* between the different races.

APPENDIX

APPENDIX

HOUSE OF BABENBERG, (973-1246)

Leopold I (Margrave) . .	973-994	Leopold IV	1136-1141
Henry I	994-1018	Henry Iasomirgott (Duke) .	1141-1177
Adalbert the Victorious . .	1018-1056	Leopold (V) the Pious . .	1177-1194
Ernest the Valiant . . .	1056-1075	Frederick I	1194-1198
Leopold II	1075-1096	Leopold (VI) the Proud . .	1198-1230
Leopold III the Saint . .	1096-1136	Frederick (II) the Fighter .	1230-1246

HOUSE OF HAPSBURG

Rudolf I, Emperor of Germany	1273-1291	Frederick, King of the Romans from 1314, with Louis of Bavaria	
Albert I, Duke of Austria (Emperor in 1298) . .	1282-1308	Albert the Wise	1330-1358
Leopold, Duke of Austria .	1308-1326	Rudolf the Founder . . .	1358-1365
and Frederick the Handsome, Duke of Austria .	1308-1330		

ALBERTINE BRANCH	LEOPOLDINE BRANCH	
Austria, properly so called	Styria, Carinthia, Carniola, Tyrol, Outer Austria	
Albert (III), with the Plaited Hair . . 1365-1395	Leopold III 1365-1406	
Albert IV 1395-1404	William 1386-1406	
Albert V (in 1438	Leopold IV 1386-1411	
King of Bohemia	Styria, Carinthia, Carniola, Trieste, (Capital at Gratz)	Tyrol, Outer Austria, (Capital at Innsbruck)
and Hungary, and		
Emperor of Ger-		
many as Albert II) 1404-1439	Ernest 1411-1424	Frederick IV
Ladislav the Posthu-	Albert VI . . . 1424-1463	(Empty
mous, King of Bo-	Federick V (Em-	Purse) . 1411-1439
hemia and Hungary 1439-1457	peror) . . . 1440-1493	Sigismund 1439-1496
	Maximilian I . . 1493-1519	

HOUSE OF HAPSBURG

Spanish Branch	Austrian Branch		
Charles V . 1517-1556 Philip II . 1555-1598 Philip III . 1598-1621 Philip IV . 1621-1665 Charles II . 1665-1700	Ferdinand I (King of Bohemia and Hungary in 1526, Emperor in 1558) 1519-1564		
	Bohemia, Hungary, Austria	Styria, Carinthia, Carniola, Gorica	Tyrol and Outer Austria
	Maximilian II (Emperor) 1564-1576 Rudolf II 1576-1612 Mathias 1612-1619	Charles II 1564-1590 Ferdinand II (Emperor in 1619) 1590-1637	Ferdinand 1564-1595

Tuscany	Austrian Branch	
Leopold I (II) (Emperor in 1790) . . . . . 1765-1790 Ferdinand III. 1790 and 1814-1824 Leopold II . . . . 1824-1859 Ferdinand IV . . . 1859	Bohemia, Austria, Hungary	Tyrol
	Ferdinand III 1637-1657 Leopold I . . 1657-1705	Leopold V 1623-1632 Ferdinand Charles 1632-1662
House of Hapsburgeste at Modena Ferdinand . . . 1803-1806 Francis IV . . . 1814-1846 Francis V . . . 1846-1859	Joseph I . . . . 1705-1711 Charles VI 1711-1740	
	Hapsburg–Lorraine	
	Maria Theresa and Francis I . . 1740-1780 Joseph II (Emperor in 1765) . . 1780-1790 Leopold II . . . . 1790-1792 Francis II (Emperor of Austria in 1806). . . . . 1792-1835 Ferdinand IV . . . . . . 1835-1848 Francis Joseph 1848-1916	

BIBLIOGRAPHY

BIBLIOGRAPHY

The history of Austria-Hungary has not been a popular subject with English historians. In the foreign languages, on the other hand, especially in German, the number of good works is considerable, though here also there are few general histories of first-rate importance. The best guides to the literature of the subject are:

Dahlmann-Waitz.—"*Quellenkunde der Deutschen Geschichte.*" 7th edition, Leipzig, 1906.

Krones, M.—"*Grundriss der Oesterreichischen Geschichte.*" 2d edition. Vienna, 1882.

This gives a careful and detailed bibliography of the works published before 1881.

Mühlbrecht.—"*Wegweiser durch die neuere Literatur der Rechts- und Staatswissenschaften.*" 2 vols. Berlin, 1893.

Deutsche Zeitschrift für Geschichtswissenschaft.

In the appendix to this periodical a current bibliography of books on Austrian history will be found, while reviews and notices of works on the subject are numerous.

Historisches Jahrbuch.

This periodical, published under the auspices of the Görres-Gesellschaft, also gives an excellent current bibliography on Austria under the divisions of *Deutsches Reich und Oesterreich,* and *Ungarn und Balkan Staaten.*

Among the general histories, the following are the best:

Coxe, W.—"History of the House of Austria from Rudolph of Hapsburg to the Death of Leopold II." 3 vols. London.

There have been several editions and a continuation to 1852.

Whitman, S.—"The Realm of the Hapsburgs." London, 1893.

A short survey of the main features of the history of the Hapsburg lands.

——"Austria." London, 1899.

In "The Story of the Nations" Series.

Leger, L.—"*Histoire de l'Autriche-Hongrie.*" 4th edition. 1895.

This work, on which the present history is based, has been partly discussed in the preface. It is strongly Slavophil and federalist. It contains a select bibliography, pp. 641-659.

Leger-Hill.—"The Austro-Hungarian Monarchy."

A faithful translation of Leger's third edition (1893), without any attempt at correction or revision. It is without the bibliography of the original, but has a long introduction of considerable interest by Professor Freeman.

Mayer.—"*Geschichte Oesterreichs.*" 2 vols. 1874.

Written with special reference to the history of civilization.

"*Oesterreichische Geschichte für das Volk.*" Vienna, 1864 ff.

This collection is the result of the collaboration of a group of historians, some of whom, notably Jirecek, Zeissberg, Krones, and Gindeley, have written excellent volumes.

Huber, A.—"*Geschichte Oesterreichs.*" 4 vols. Gotha, 1885-1892.

Wurzbach, C. v.—"Biographisches Lexikon des Kaiserthums Oesterreich." 60 vols. Vienna, 1856-1891.
"Die Oesterreich-Ungarische Monarchie in Wort und Bild." 1-397, Vienna, 1886-1902.
This interesting work was begun under the auspices of the Archduke Rudolph.
"Archiv für Kunde der Geschichtsquellen Oesterreichs." Vienna, 1848—.
This publication is scholarly in character and is published by the Academy of Sciences, Vienna. The historical section of the Academy also publishes:
"Fontes rerum Austriacarum." Vienna, 1855—.
"Fontes rerum Bohemicarum." Prague, 1871—.
"Historiae Hungaricae fontes domestici." Budapest, 1881—.

For the study of the geography and races the following works are the best:
Himly.—"Histoire de la formation territoriale des États de l'Europe centrale." 2 vols. Paris, 1876. An excellent work, frequently cited by historians.
Sprüner, K. v.—"Historisch-geographischer Atlas des Oesterreichischen Staats." Gotha, 1866.
Réclus, E.—"Nouvelle Géographie Universelle." Vol. iii. 3d edition. Paris, 1878.
Auerbach.—"Les Races et les Nationalités en Autriche-Hongrie."

Much local history for Austria has been written. Separate histories of nearly every division of the monarchy exist, but only a few of the more important can be mentioned here.
Vambery.—"Hungary." London, 1889.
Sajous, E.—"Histoire Générale des Hongrois." 2 vols. Paris, 1876.
The 2d edition, Paris, 1900, was crowned by the Academy, and is much the best general history of Hungary for the foreigner who does not understand the Magyar. It has a good historical bibliography.

For Bohemia and Moravia, especially for the Middle Ages.
Denis.—"Huss et la Guerre des Hussites." Paris, 1878.
The work has an excellent bibliographical guide.
Palacky, F.—"Geschichte von Böhmen." 5 vols. Prague, 1836-1867.
Also in the Czech language.
Tomek.—"History of the Kingdom of Bohemia" (in the Czech). 3d edition. 1876.
Lützow, Count.—"Bohemia, an Historical Sketch." London, 1896.
Maurice, C. E.—"Bohemia from the Earliest Times to 1620." London, 1896.
In the "Story of the Nations" Series.

The history of Austria during the eighteenth century, owing to the acquisition of lands outside the limits of Austria, and to such remarkable rulers as Maria Theresa and Joseph II, was peculiarly European in its character, and for this reason no doubt the period has been a favorite subject with historical writers. The following are of the more important works:
Wolf, A.—"Oesterreich unter Maria Theresia, Joseph II, und Leopold II." Berlin, 1882.
Continued by Zwiedineck-Südenhorst, 1884. (In Oncken's "Allg. Gesch. in Einzeldarstellung.)
Arneth, A. v.—"Geschichte Maria Theresias." 10 vols. Vienna, 1863-1879.
The standard work on the famous Austrian queen.

"Correspondance de Marie-Thérèse avec le Comte de Merci-Argenteau."
Edited by Arneth and Geoffroy. 3 vols. Paris, 1874.
"Mémories du Cardinal Bernis." 2 vols. Paris, 1878.

Austrian affairs during the troublesome period of the revolutionary and Napoleonic eras are so intimately connected with those of Germany, France, and Italy that the best accounts are still to be found in the German and French histories of the period, as for example in:

Häusser.—*"Geschichte Deutschlands seit dem Tode Friederichs des Grossen bis zur Gründung des Deutschen Bunds."* 4 vols. 1854.
Sybel, H. von.—*"Geschichte der Revolutionszeit von 1789-1800."* 5 vols. Stuttgart, 1882. Continuation: *"Oesterreich und Deutschland in Revolutionskriege."* Düsseldorf, 1868.
Oncken, W.—*"Das Zeitalter der Revolution, des Kaiserreichs und der Befreiungs-Kriege."* 2 vols. Berlin, 1884-1887.
Sajous.—*"Histoire des Hongrois et de leur litterature politique de 1790 à 1815."* Paris, 1872.
Metternich-Winneberg.—*"Oesterreichs Theilnahme an den Befreiungskriegen."* 1867. The work is based on Austrian documents.

Sorel.—*"L'Europe et la Revolution Française."* 8 vols. Paris, 1885-1905.
For the years from 1815 to 1867:
Krones, A.—*"Geschichte der Neuzeit Oesterreichs vom 18. Jahrh. bis auf die Gegenwart."* Berlin, 1879.
Accurate and painstaking, but quite uninteresting.
Springer, A.—*"Geschichte Oesterreichs seit dem Wiener Frieden, 1809."* 2 vols. Leipsig, 1863-1865.
This is the best and most complete history for this period. It was published in the series of *"Staatengeschichte der Neuesten Zeit,"* and is written from the standpoint of a German Liberal.
Bulle, C.—*"Geschichte der Neuesten Zeit."* 2d edition. 1886-1887.
Reliable and more entertaining than Krones.
Rogge, W.—*"Oesterreich von Vilagos bis zur Gegenwart."* 3 vols. Vienna, 1872-1873.
Anti-clerical and partial to the Germans.

For the Congress of Vienna, there is:
Kluber, J. L.—*"Akten des Wiener Kongresses."* 8 vols. Erlangen, 1815-1819.
Supplementary volume in 1835.
"Dispatches of Wellington." 8 vols. London, 1844-1847. Also "Supplementary Dispatches and Memoranda." 15 vols. London, 1858-1872.
These afford a remarkable view of the Congress from the English standpoint, and, like the correspondence of Prince Talleyrand, and the records of Münster, Stein, Di Borgo and others, must be regarded as strongly partisan and personal. The same is true of Prince Metternich's "Mémoires."

For Austro-Hungarian history since the establishment of the dual monarchy no single work of adequate proportions and scholarship exists.

Baron de Worms.—"The Austro-Hungarian Empire. A Political Sketch of Men and Events." London, 1876. 2d edition. 1877.
Good but quite inadequate.

Pressig, E.—" Short Outline of the History of Austria-Hungary." Brooklyn. 1905.

Umlauft, F.—" *Die Oesterreich-Ungarische Monarchie.*" 3d edition. Vienna, 1896.

Bertha, A. de.—" *La Hongrie Moderne, 1849-1901.*" Paris, 1901.

Patterson, A. J.—" The Magyars; their Country and its Institutions." 2 vols. London, 1870.

Much good work has been done in the line of biography, as for example, " Life of Deak," by Forster, and " Count Beust," by De Worms. Articles of more or less historical value are found in the historical and political reviews, but they are as a rule partisan in character and of little historical value. Besides the articles in the *Fortnightly, Westminster* and other English periodicals, the *Preussische Jahrbücher*, the *Deutsche Rundschau* and the *Revue Politique et Parlementaire* frequently have excellent expositions of different phases of the contemporary history of the dual monarchy.

The record of facts and events with the more important documents are found in the official publications of the government, and in such annuals as Schulthess " *Europäischer Geschichts Kalendar*," 1860 (the section on Austria is very good, though German in its attitude), the " *Annual Register*," and " *L'Année Politique*." As a convenient statistical survey, the section on Austria-Hungary in the " Statesman's Year Book" for 1905 will be found very useful.

INDEX

INDEX

A

Abdul-Kerim Pasha: wins battle of Djunis, 419

Achmet II, Sultan of Turkey: recognizes Bocskai as voïévode of Transylvania, 224

Acre: siege of (1191), 92

Adalbert, St., Bishop of Prague: his work in Hungary, 46; career of, 63

Adalbert, Margrave of Babenberg: reign of, 89

Adam of Sternberg: see Sternberg, Adam of

Adrian II, Pope: honors Saints Cyril and Methodius, 32

Adrianople, Treaty of (1829), 326

Afensberg: battle of (1809), 298

Agram: popular uprising in (1848), 361

Agron, King of the Illyrians: pays tribute to Rome, 11

Aix: battle of (102 B.C.), 11

Aix-la-Chapelle, Treaty of (1748), 242

Ala, Samuel, King of Hungary: reign of, 50

Albert I, Holy Roman emperor: reign, 101

Albert II, Holy Roman emperor, I, King of Hungary, V, Duke of Austria: his reign as Duke of Austria, 105; his reign as King of Bohemia, 142; reign of, as King of Hungary, 157

Albert (II) the Wise, Duke of Austria: reign of, 101

Albert (III) with the Plaited Hair, Duke of Austria: reign of, 105

Albert IV, Duke of Austria: reign of, 105

Albert V, Duke of Austria: see Albert II, Holy Roman Emperor

Albert, Archduke of Austria: at battle of Custozza, 392

Albert VI, Duke of Styria: disputes the possession of Austrian domains, 108

Albert of Saxony: marries Maria Christina of Austria, 245

Alboin, King of the Lombards: defeats the Gepidæ, 17

Alemanni: repulsed by the Romans (356 A.D.), 15

Alexander V, Pope: chosen Pontiff, 122

Alexander VI, Pope: refuses to sanction the Kuttenberg Agreement and the *Compactata,* 148

Alexander the Great, King of Macedonia: receives Celtic deputies, 10

Alexander I, Emperor of Russia: his relations with the Eastern Question, 324; death of, 325

Alexander, Archduke of Austria: made count palatine, 331

Almos, King of Croatia: accession of, 51; dethroned, 52; blinded, 53

Alvinzy (Alvinczi), Joseph, Baron von Barberck: defeated at Arcola and Rivoli, 282; sketch of, 332

Ambrones: location of, 11

Ancona: occupied by the French, 327

Andrassy: in Dr. Wekerle's ministry, 447

Andrassy, Count Julius: attempts to obtain foreign aid for the Magyars, 372; made premier of Hungary, 397; made minister of foreign affairs, 411

Andrassy Note, The (1875), 419

Andrew I, King of Hungary: reign of, 50

Andrew II, King of Hungary: reign of, 55

Andrew III, King of Hungary: reign of, 60

Andrew, son of Charles Robert of Anjou: marries Joan of Naples, 151

471

I, J